To the Rainbow and Beyond

To the Rainbow and Beyond

Costas E. Pappas with Thetis H. Pappas

VANTAGE PRESS
New York

Published by Vantage Press, Inc.
516 West 34th Street, New York, New York 10001

Manufactured in the United States of America
ISBN: 0-533-10226-X

Library of Congress Catalog Card No.: 92-93305

0 9 8 7 6 5 4 3 2 1

To our children, Alceste and Conrad, who have followed the teachings and emulations of their grandparents and parents to excel in their endeavors and, above all, to adjust their innate potential commensurate with the ever-changing environment

Contents

Preface

My goal as an aerospace engineer was to contribute to the design of vehicles that could fly to the rainbow and beyond to outer space. As a youngster, I marveled at those barnstorming pilots who would take off from the makeshift dusty runways in the flimsy aircraft of the 1920s. These pilots were an inspiration to me. As a result, I sought an education that would prepare me for designing aircraft that would lead to the progress of aviation. My aircraft experience led me through a spectrum of designs, eventually leading to my concept of the aerospace plane.

Even the experiences of our lives bring to mind the rainbow. Our aim is to find that elusive quantity the rainbow projects. The changes in our lives are comparable to the multilayered structure of the rainbow. We proceeded from the primary to the secondary to the supernumerary rainbows, attaining ever-higher goals and aspirations. With each ascending layer, we paused and took our bearings to determine our next ascendency. Our goal was to attain the elusive and evanescent ultimate. Our attainments, like the resolution of light into an array of colors ranging from red to violet, were composed of activities in the aircraft industry, raising a family, involvement in community affairs, counseling the unemployed professional, and contributing to the solution of community problems.

The physical properties of the rainbow are analogous to many of the principles of life Thetis and I have endeavored to pursue. When we look at the rainbow after a thunderstorm, we are impressed by its beauty, the wonders of nature, and the portrayal of peace and tranquillity. Its presence is a manifestation of hope and the will to go on in spite of great odds. The rainbow is a crown of hope for all mankind as it spans the sky.

The resolution of the sun's rays into various colors is representative of the way nature resolves its complex phenomena into simpler components. It sets an example for us as to how we might analyze our problems into factors that are more amenable to solution. It teaches us that only under certain conditions will one's dreams be realized. To see the rainbow in its full glory and splendor, certain conditions must be met. Time of day, size of raindrops, location of the sun with respect to the rain cloud, and the precise elevation angle of the rainbow with respect to the ground are all factors that must be met before an observer can see the rainbow. For events to occur, certain prescribed conditions must prevail. As humans we, too, must follow certain conditions if we are to succeed in our endeavors.

Our parents indoctrinated us into the inviolable, fundamental principles of life. We were guided by the principles that sweat comes before achievement in one's endeavors. To excel and be above all others in whatever business, profession, or activities one chooses requires perseverance and commitment. We were taught to adhere to morals and to respect the dignity and honor of mankind. One of our responsibilities was to make whatever contributions we could to society that would improve the general welfare of all. Above all, it was our duty to leave a better world for our children to inherit.

Acknowledgments

Our thanks to Madge Rutherford Minton and the P-47 Thunderbolt Pilots Association, Ltd., for permission to quote part of her poem "A Pilot's Prayer," which was published in the pilot's publication *Looking Back 1941–1991,* copyright 1991, P-47 Thunderbolt Pilots Association, Ltd.

Our thanks also to the Seversky Aircraft Corporation for the use of photos 1 to 3; to Republic Aviation Corporation for photos 4 to 8 and 10 to 14; and to NYU College of Engineering, University Heights, for photo 9.

Introduction

Since the days of the Wright brothers, we have witnessed gargantuan progress in the aeronautical and aerospace fields in a relatively short period of time. Aeronautics can be characterized as that field of endeavor that was and is attracted by people who are driven by the desire and passion to extend man's ability to migrate from one point to another in less time. The unknowns involved are ever so intriguing and challenging that engineers and scientists are driven by the desire to contribute to the betterment of man's future. They are dedicated people who are willing to take great risks and abide by uncertainties and lack of funding to see their dreams and concepts come to realization.

Aeronautics is like a queen bee that attracts others to her hive. Only those with innovative, daring ideas are attracted. They are primarily motivated by the challenge confronting them. With such a group of personnel, it is no wonder that great progress was and is being made. Man is desirous of reaching the rainbow in his aspirations to explore the many exciting layers of possibilities that exist.

Aeronautics has been a predominant leader in progress and has shown the way to accomplish this by fostering improvement in transportation. It was realized by the pioneers of aviation that a key element to progress and the economic welfare of the nation is ultimately linked with the attainment of better, quicker, and more efficient transportation over long distances.

Aeronautics made the great strides it did because of those who dared to introduce new concepts. No sooner is a breakthrough achieved than it is time to ascend to greater heights of progress. Network analyses were introduced such as PERT (Program Evaluation and Review Technique) and CPM (Critical Path Method) during World War II to monitor complex projects. These techniques were introduced to forecast bottlenecks that might occur in production schedules. This was accomplished by monitoring each step of progress in the production process. In addition, there was the introduction and implementation of systems technology, computer graphics in design work, application of supercomputers to simulate complex aerodynamic problems in the hypersonic flow region and conduct sophisticated flight simulation tests on space craft, and materials research leading to structures that can withstand high temperatures. Finally, aeronautics has transcended to space, with all the ramifications and extensions that it entails.

For an established system or project, improvement in the product is an ongoing thing. If one is to be above the competition, one constantly strives for superiority. To assume parity with competition is to allow oneself to fall behind the leader. One must always strive for the ultimate. For me, the ultimate was attained in 1960 with the concept of the aerospace plane. At the present time, the design is progressing on a global scale. Eventually we are led to the concept of limit of extensionalism, with its attendant limits imposed by cost, time, and complexity.

Aeronautics has progressed from low velocities to velocities many times the speed of sound. The early aeronautical engineer received an education as a mechanical engineer with a smattering of subsonic theory in aerodynamics, conventional civil-engineering-type structures, and engineering mechanics. As time progressed, interdisciplinarity came into focus. The aeronautical engineer became, by necessity, involved in quantum chemistry, physical chemistry, astrophysics, control theory, electronics, computer science, relativity theory, biochemistry, psychology, and physiology, to mention but a few of the disciplines now required to cope with aerospace.

In 1921, Dr. Alexander Klemin, director of the Daniel Guggenheim School of Aeronautics of New York University, wrote:

> The growing importance of aviation in military, naval and commercial applications led to an investigation of its possibilities by the Department of Mechanical Engineering of New York University in 1921. Subsequently, a course of lectures was given . . . to senior students in mechanical engineering during the academic year of 1921–1922. Later, the Council of the University authorized the aeronautical option for an experimental period of three years on a modest budget. This budget was underwritten by over a hundred men prominent in the

aeronautical world, in banking and business. The courage and generosity of these men in standing behind this pioneer effort is commemorated by a tablet in the new building of the Daniel Guggenhcim School of Aeronautics ("Technical Notes of the Daniel Guggenheim School of Aeronautics, No. 1." New York: *Aviation Engineering*, Jan. 1931.)

This was the establishment of the first Daniel Guggenheim School of Aeronautics in this country. Through his enthusiasm of faith, belief, and the great potentialities inherent in the future of aeronautics, Dr. Klemin was instrumental in having Daniel Guggenheim endow the school with a gift of $500,000.

An advisory committee, with pioneer Orville Wright as chairman, was established, and construction of a building and wind tunnel at University Heights was completed around 1927. As a design tool, the wind tunnel attracted commercial and military researchers. In addition to airplane and zeppelin model testing, streamlined trains and automobiles (including Chrysler's "airflow" model) were tested there. Even the famous Perisphere and Trylon of the 1939 World's Fair were tested for aerodynamic loading at the Heights. These required structural analysis because of their size. The Perisphere, which was 180 feet in diameter, represented the earth. The Trylon was a triangular structure, tapering to a point 728 feet in height.

I shall always be grateful to Daniel Guggenheim for his vision and faith in aviation. It provided me with the education I needed to become an aeronautical engineer and to witness and be part of all the miraculous aeronautical and aerospace events that have occurred since my graduation.

To the Rainbow and Beyond

1. Childhood Memories of Connecticut

Providence, Rhode Island, was my birthplace. I have no remembrances of Providence since my parents moved to Ansonia, Connecticut, when I was a year old. My formative years were spent in Ansonia.

When my father first came to this country at the turn of the nineteenth century, he first surveyed the area around Lowell, Massachusetts. He was especially interested in Lowell since it was one of the principal shoe-manufacturing centers at the time. Dad was a shoemaker, specializing in the design of shoes for people afflicted with foot disorders. He took great delight in designing shoes that would alleviate the suffering of those whose legs were of unequal length, those who needed custom-made shoes to conform with their deformed feet, and those who were afflicted with an enlargement of the foot from chronic inflammation. In short, Dad was a podiatrist at heart whose approach was not medical but mechanical.

Dad made a thorough search of business opportunities in the areas of Lowell and in areas around New Haven, Connecticut. As he related his findings to me, he observed that since Lowell was the Mecca of the shoe industry, there were far too many seeking employment there. Since Dad was a very independent person, he decided to become an entrepreneur and to establish his own business. His survey of the environs of New Haven eventually led him to the town of Ansonia. There he found there was no one offering services in his trade. He recognized Ansonia as a place favorable for exercising his skill and providing an opportunity to offer unique services to those afflicted with foot problems. Of all the places he investigated, Ansonia offered the best alternative course of action to take.

Dad recognized that he could not survive solely on revenues derived from isolated cases in the fabrication of custom-made shoes. He supplemented his income by repairing shoes. Instead of relying on old techniques of resoling by hand stitching, he was the first in town to install machinery. In so doing, he demonstrated that he was

1

innovative and was willing to take the corresponding risks. He recognized that if all went well he could handle a much larger volume of business. He told me he had some trepidation in making the decision to go mechanical since he was not fully convinced he could rely on the equipment, but he was willing to take the gamble. As was his good fortune, he witnessed and survived the debugging period. In the long term, his business flourished and the machinery worked satisfactorily. Ansonia at long last had its first shoemaker!

Ansonia was a grand place for a boy to grow up. The four seasons provided the change necessary for the fulfillment of a boy's changing moods. In addition, the wooded areas of the town were a paradise, providing freedom to explore the wonders of Nature. Winters were inclement but provided fun for the youngsters since they could don their ice skates, go sleigh riding and tobogganing. I well remember the fun we had whenever we had a severe snowfall followed by a freezing rain. The latter provided a crust of ice on top of the snow. When this occurred a group of us boys would select the highest point of the terrain from which we could begin our steepest descent on our ice skates. Since the wooded area was made up of a series of descending hills, we could skate continuously from one level to the next lower level until we reached the river. The river in turn was frozen, which permitted us to cross it. By this time we had reached the lowest point in our journey.

We would hold contests among us to see who would reach the riverbed in the minimum time. I didn't realize at the time that this kind of problem arises in the calculus of variations known as the brachistochrone problem. The problem is to determine the path that a particle situated at a given height acting under the action of gravity will reach a given lower level in the minimum time.

The winners were those who were daring enough to reach speeds of thirty to forty miles per hour. We knew we were going fast by the tearing of our eyes. The faster we went, the more we could feel the wind resistance. We soon learned to attain more speed by bending forward to minimize the body area exposed to the air.

It was a real experience to ride on the homemade sleighs that accommodated ten or twelve people. The sleigh was made of a four-by-twelve inch plank, ten to fifteen feet in length. The plank was mounted on two sleighs. The rear sleigh was fixed, and the front sleigh could be rotated by the driver. Steering was performed by the driver, who could apply pressure through his feet on a crossbar mounted on the sleigh. The driver was the most important individual, since he had to steer properly on the turns to prevent overturning. The plank was attached to the sleighs by vertical posts.

Shinning trees was a great pastime for the group. In the area surrounding the park, which housed a bandstand structure, were trees with moderate diameters with no branches up to a height of some fifteen to twenty feet. The bark was fairly smooth, thereby preventing injury to the groin and the calves. We had contests to see who would be the first to reach the lower branch. Our shinning resulted in torn stockings and badly frayed trousers. Our principal concern was facing Mother when we got home.

We even found that school could be fun. Elementary school consisted of grades one through eight. Upon completion of grade eight, we were ready to enter high school. We were given courses on physiology, geography, proper manners and conduct, how to show respect for our elders when passing them on the street, how the man would tip his hat to a passing lady, how when escorting a lady the gentleman would always take the side of the street facing the road. Great emphasis was laid on hygienics and morals. During the morning, time was taken out to exercise. Prior to exercising, those who were selected as monitors would open the windows of the classroom to allow fresh air into the room. This was rather chilling in winter, but with the increase in blood circulation due to exercising, we were able to endure the cooler temperatures.

Great fun and a keen sense of challenge was developed when the teacher would call a spelling-bee contest. Half the class would be asked to stand at one side of the room and the other half on the other side. The teacher would then give us words to spell. The side that won would receive a gold star on its record.

My experiences in arithmetic were interesting. When we came to the study of fractions, a number of my fellow students had difficulty. At first, I didn't comprehend the technique essential to solving fractions. It wasn't long until I discovered the trick. I realized that one had to arrive at a common denominator before proceeding further in the solution. This common denominator could be arrived at by multiplying each number in the denominator of the various fractions. Each numerator now had to be multiplied by the product of the denominators of the other remaining fractions, exclusive of the fraction under consideration. The answer would then be the sum of all numerators divided by the common denominator. The final answer was arrived at by canceling out common multipliers in the numerator and denominator. This was accomplished by starting with the number 2 and dividing it into both the numerator and denominator. Having done this, the number 3 was next applied in similar fashion. This process was continued until no further reduction could be had. I was more than delighted to explain my technique to those students who needed help. It was a great sense of accomplishment and pride to have helped someone.

Upon graduation from the elementary school, I entered as a freshman in Ansonia High School. The school was located on the summit of a hill, and to get to it, we had to climb many steps. By the time we reached the last step, we were exhausted, especially when we had to double up on the steps when we were late for class. I chose math and Latin as my major subjects. I pursued these subjects throughout my high school year. My stay at this high school lasted for one year because my dad sold his business and decided to move to New York. I was somewhat disappointed, since it was my desire to matriculate at Yale University.

Even though I was unhappy to leave Ansonia, I soon became reconciled to the fact that I was entering one of the finest high schools on Long Island. Newtown High School provided me with the training I needed to become an engineer. The math courses were outstanding, and in my senior year, we were introduced to the underlying philosophy of calculus.

In addition, I pursued Latin for four years and in my senior year, I had an outstanding teacher who was the head of the Latin Department. He also taught Ancient Greek and Latin at Columbia University. Our principal study covered Virgil's *Aeneid*. In addition, he introduced us to other Latin poets, such as Ovid and Catullus. One quote made a lasting impression on me when we read certain passages of the *Metamorphoses* of Ovid: "Who would ever believe that man would take possession of the aerial highways."

My thoughts were always on aeronautical engineering. This was instilled in me when I witnessed several biplane demonstrations and aerial acrobatics in town. In the early twenties, there was a frenzy of excitement in flying. There were daring aerial acrobats who would perform various maneuvers, such as Immelmann turns, inside and

4

outside loops, flying close to the ground, stunts performed by men walking out on the wing, the barrel roll, the tailspin, steep dives followed by steep climbs approaching a vertical climb, during which the pilot would execute several rolls until he stalled out, and other daring feats that were developed by American, British, German, French, and Canadian pilots during World War I. These maneuvers were developed during World War I to outfox the other pilot or as an evasive maneuver in case the machine gun(s) were jammed.

The Immelmann turn was conceived by this German pilot during World War I. The maneuver effectively accomplished a reverse turn. The turn is initiated by executing a half-loop, at the top of which the airplane is then rolled half of a complete turn. During World War I, Lieutenant Immelmann would fly over Paris, dropping bombs. It was said that on one of these flights he also dropped a bag of sand, which contained a note. The note read: "People of Paris! Surrender! The Germans are at your gate. You will soon be ours! signed, Lieutenant Immelmann—Air Scout."

As a youngster I was very much impressed by the spectacular sight that took place along Main Street in Ansonia every Saturday morning. A retinue of sports cars filled with spectators would be headed for the Yale football games. The men wore full-length raccoon coats with their Daniel Boone caps. To get to New Haven, people coming from the north found it convenient to travel through Ansonia. New Haven is situated approximately fifteen miles southeast of Ansonia. What surprised me most was the make and type of car the people drove. Most of the cars were sportsters and were apparently of foreign make, since I did not recognize any of them. Upon inspecting some of the cars that were temporarily parked, I remember the names Stutz, Rolls Royce, and the Italian IF (Isotta-Fraschini)

There were several other events that left an indelible impression on me while growing up in Ansonia. On Friday evenings the band would play in the park, which was beautifully landscaped and impeccably maintained. There were indigenous plants interspersed with many different kinds of flowers in localized areas throughout the park. The park was essentially circular, with a circular path around the bandstand. I was one of a group of boys of the neighborhood who practiced the instructions of our teachers in hygienics. We made it a routine practice to run several times around the circular path that enclosed the bandstand. The bandstand was cylindrical in design, with a roof to protect the players in the event of rain. The players performed on a platform some five to six feet above the ground so that the people could see and hear them as they walked around the path.

Not only did the band music have a fascination for me, but I looked forward to munching on a hot dog that a vendor would serve. His apparatus was mounted on a portable vehicle, which made for flexibility and freedom of movement. The frankfurter was heated in boiling water and placed in a split roll. For embellishment I would specify the gamut of condiments—ketchup, mustard, with a smattering of sauerkraut. While devouring the frankfurter, I would utter interjectionally "hot dog"—my psychic approval of a gastronomical delight.

Policemen actually patrolled the streets. I stood in awe when the policeman would twirl his two- to three-foot-long club in the most fascinating ways. The motion of the stick resembled Lissajous figures. Most of the policemen were of Irish descent. They were tall and especially selected for their assignments. What made them appear even taller were the high helmets they wore. They were very compassionate, yet they instilled the fear of the Lord in one. As a child, I always considered them as guardian angels. It was reassuring to me to see them patrolling the streets.

Shopping for groceries at the corner country store was fun in a way. Mother would give me a list of the items she wanted me to purchase. When purchasing sugar I went to the barrel that was located in one corner of the store, and with the scooper in the barrel and bag in the other hand, I would scoop out what I thought was an approximation of the amount Mother wanted. The sugar available was brown. White sugar was much more expensive and not as nutritious. Butter came in a five gallon tub, at which the proprietor would hack away with a large spatula. After several weighings the correct amount was arrived at. Fresh vegetables were on display throughout the store, and the proprietor would weigh them in after I specified what I wanted. Milk came in large cans and was meted out according to the wants of the customer. Various assortments of candies were stored in large jars that were mounted on a shelf. This procedure took considerable time, and one had to exercise extreme patience. It is no wonder that the concept of the supermarket eventually came into existence.

One of greatest thrills was derived from the incorporation of the electric trolley car in Ansonia. Since Dad was not one of the daring people to own a car, I had to walk to my destination, whether it be to the corner grocery store, downtown to Dad's business, the school, etc. Dad was skeptical about purchasing a car since he had heard so many neighbors breaking their wrists while cranking the engine by hand. To start the engine, one had to use a hand crank. The starter, as we know it today, had not been invented as yet. The engine would frequently backfire, and if the hand crank was not held properly, one could end up with a broken wrist. The advent of the trolley car was a real blessing, for it eliminated some of the peripatetics. This was especially the case in Ansonia because no matter where one went, one had to surmount an excessive number of wooden stairs to go from one level to a higher or lower level of the hills of the town.

The electric cars ran down Main Street and eventually ended up in the residential areas. Electricity was provided by an overhead wire to which a grooved wheel was carried at the end of a trolley pole, the wheel making rolling contact with the trolley wire. As I recall the trolley would travel the length of Main Street and would eventually encircle most of the residential area in the northwest and southwest portions of the town, ending up at Wakelee Avenue.

I couldn't wait for the summer to arrive to ride the "open-air breezer." This trolley was entirely open, and one could feel the breeze when it would attain speeds of thirty-to-forty miles per hour. To get to Lighthouse Point, Savin Rock, or to the East/West Rock Park, we would ride the trolley. Since the tracks were not in proper alignment, the trolley would sway laterally rather violently. At times, I thought we had surely jumped the tracks. At this point in time, the grooved wheel carried at the end of the trolley pole would disengage from the trolley wire and the electrical supply to the motors would be cut off. Consequently, the motorman had to get out and reengage the wheel to the overhead electric wire. This would occur several times during our trip. This was aggravating to the motorman, to say the least.

In retrospect, there were many happenings and experiences that I could not explain satisfactorily at the time, but upon further reflection, the effects of what were observed had their causes. The most perplexing observation was the color of the river that ran through the town. The river referred to is the Naugatuck River, which runs

7

through the town and eventually joins in with the Housatonic River south of Ansonia in the Shelton area. The rear of Dad's business faced the river. Main Street and the Naugatuck River ran parallel and were within two- to three-hundred feet of each other.

Access to the river could be had by exiting from the cellar of Dad's business. To get to the river, one had to cross the railroad tracks. From the southernmost bridge, which spanned the river and which connected the west side of the town with the east side, I wondered why the color of the river would change from time to time. As a curious boy, I would wander over to the bank of the river to see what I might discover. I knew water was clear in texture and that one could see the bottom. I expected to see some sort of marine life.

I could not understand why at times the river water was a murky yellow color and at times a brownish color. I was aware that several factories bordered the river. I do remember two factories in town, Anaconda Copper and Farrell Foundry and Machine Company. It was fun to watch operations going on in Anaconda Copper from the bridge. This bridge was the second one to span the Naugatuck and was situated north of the previously mentioned one. The bridge was constructed of concrete and was a much more rigid structure than the first-mentioned bridge. When crossing the latter bridge on foot, one could feel a swaying motion of the bridge when a vehicle was on the roadway. At times I wondered about the safety of the bridge, the deflections were so prominent.

The operations going on in Anaconda Copper were most fascinating to me. The bridge offered an excellent view of the processes going on in the factory. Glowing copper ingots would come out of the furnaces, to be eventually transformed into copper wire. The process of wire-drawing was intriguing. The massive ingot, which was an elongated rod, was forced through various rollers and dies, to form copper sheets and wire of various gauges. The length of wire would be several feet long curled on the floor.

The Farrell Foundry and Machine Company specialized in machining huge pieces of metal. The street ran alongside the huge building, and during summer months, when the windows were open on the street side, I was amazed at the huge pieces of metal that were being machined on a slowly rotating platform.

The Naugatuck was "Ol' Man River" to me. The river originates in the northwest part of Connecticut and has many tributaries. For most of the time, the river was fairly low and tranquil. Normally I could walk out a short distance into the river by spanning rocks that were exposed because of the low volume passing a given cross-section. This tranquil and serene river could turn into a torrential monster when springtime would arrive. Depending upon the rain accumulation and the thawing of snow this time of the year, the river could inflict destruction and cause floods of great damage.

Connecticut is a network of riverlets, eventually finding their way into major watersheds, such as the Naugatuck, the Housatonic, and Connecticut rivers. I remember several occurrences of flooding when the Naugatuck would overflow its bank on the side of the railroad tracks. The unusual swelling can be explained when one takes into account the excessive discharge of the tributaries into the Naugatuck. By the time all the tributaries north of Ansonia empty their share of water into the Naugatuck, it is no wonder the river reaches flood conditions.

In the vicinity of Dad's business, the west side of the bank was fortified by retaining walls substantially higher than the normal level of the river. Businesses on this side were generally protected from flooding. The east side of the river had neither retaining walls nor levee and would become a flood plain when the level of the river exceeded the height of the bank.

I remember the time when Dad's basement was inundated with flood water. The railroad was inoperative until such time that the waters receded. On one occasion during the swelling of the river, I had a close-up view of the river from its west bank. I was literally frightened to watch the velocity of the river, with its accompanying increase in volume. I was frightened because I could see several ice floes, uprooted trees, dead animals that were entrapped in the raging waters, debris of all descriptions—boxes and other articles that were drawn into the river when its banks swelled beyond its confinements. My fear was primarily for the bridge that spanned the river. Huge ice floes could easily have impaired the foundations of the bridge. The bridge was an old and rickety structure at that. Men were constantly repairing the bridge by replacing girders and rivets.

In June of 1990, I had occasion to visit New Haven, Connecticut. While there, I decided to visit Ansonia and pay my respects to some of the people I had known. The section of town that I knew had changed materially. Where I expected to see some of the buildings

9

along the west bank of the Naugatuck in the vicinity of the bridge, I saw empty lots. Upon further inspection of the grounds. I read an inscription on a plaque commemorating what had happened.

The Naugatuck had overflowed its banks on the west side and wiped out a section of the buildings in the area of the bridge. I was chagrined to read this because the store of the one man whom I revered while a child had been completely wiped out during a cataclysmic flooding. I was not surprised at what had happened because I had seen the river rise to unprecedented heights in the past and often wondered what might happen if the west side embankment was not sufficient in height to contain the river. When all forces of Nature conspire to act in conjunction—excessive precipitation concurrent with the thawing of winter snows and ice, and a myriad of contributaries to boot—there isn't much man can do but to respect a superior power and hope there will be no loss of human lives.

Horse-drawn vehicles were another source of pollution during the 1920s. The problem was severe enough to necessitate the employment of a street cleaner, whose prime responsibility was to clean the streets of the droppings left by the horses. He was equipped with a large container mounted on wheels and a broom and shovel.

As a youngster growing up in Connecticut, I experienced and witnessed many changes in our life-style. We transitioned from gas lights in our home and streets to electric lamps, improvement of indoor sanitary water systems, changes in the transportation system, as evidenced by the percentage yearly increase in number of automobiles appearing on the highways.

It was interesting to witness the keen competition among automobile inventors who introduced different concepts and designs. The early 1920s ushered in several different engine-design features, the internal-combustion engine, the Franklin air-cooled engine, the electric, and the steam engine. This was a period of experimentation, and the ultimate winner, as we now know, was the internal-combustion engine. In terms of efficiency and reliability, the internal-combustion engine would be the winner. This flourish of activity was a manifestation of man's desire to improve transportation. The design and development of the automobile was not the result of the efforts of any one person but the conglomerate effort of many daring and innovative individuals the world over—Germany, France, Britain, Italy, Austria, the U.S.A., Spain.

The introduction of so many model and engine versions caused a great deal of uncertainty in the minds of would-be purchasers. I well remember some of the hotly debated conversations and arguments my Dad had with our neighbors. Of all the vehicles available with radically different engines, the question was which one should a person select? Considerations of initial expense, cost of maintenance, reliability, and style came under discussion.

People who owned cars and had some experience in driving them were complaining about the tires and the malfunctioning of the carburetor. Tires had to be changed frequently. The introduction of carbon black in the manufacture of the tire was not known in the early 1920s. Tires wore out quickly because of the poor abrasive- and wear-resistance qualities of rubber. As a result, blowouts would occur frequently. This put a severe limitation on the desirability of owning a car. In addition, most cars were open. On the East Coast, with its attendant inclement weather, the automobile could not be driven in cold weather. The only protection from inclement weather was provided by canvas and isinglass side curtains.

The Franklin air-cooled engine relied on the utilization of air for cooling. Severe problems were encountered, especially during the summer months. Various duct schemes were tried to augment the supply of cooling air to the engine but to no avail. After a few years of testing various combinations of ducting to the individual cylinders, the engine was finally abandoned. It was difficult to accurately regulate the temperature of the cylinders to the degree possible when water cooling was utilized. It is interesting to note that radial aircraft engines are air-cooled. This was accomplished by the utilization of metal fins attached to the individual cylinders in conjunction with cowling/ducting. The thin metal fins provide additional surfaces to increase the rate of heat transfer.

Unlike the internal-combustion engine, which derives its energy from the combustion of gasoline, the electric car was driven by electric motors, the electricity being supplied by a bank of storage batteries. This system required an inordinate number of batteries, which made it impractical, inefficient, and expensive. The range, when compared with the internal-combustion engine, was extremely low. Even though the first electric car in this country was built and tested around 1885, we have progressed very little. To this very day, the electric car is restricted in range and very expensive because of the limitation imposed by the batteries. Consequently, the main obstacle in the further development of the electric car is the storage battery. Much research is going on at the present time in improving the efficiency, weight, and size of the storage battery. It is worth noting that by the mid-1990s, General Motors hopes to introduce an electric car whose range will be 125 miles, a speed of 110 miles per hour, and its batteries would be rechargeable in two hours.

The Stanley Steamer incorporated a steam engine in combination with a boiler for converting water into steam under pressure. The Stanley was first introduced in 1911. It was still in production in the early 1920s, and several could be seen in town. Energy was derived from the high-pressure steam by allowing it to expand, thereby producing the required motive power. The system proved to be inefficient, cumbersome, and unreliable.

2. Compassion and Inspiration Derived from My Parents

I was very fortunate to have been raised during the early years of this century. As a newcomer, my dad had as his main goal the raising of a family that the community and his newly adopted country would be proud of. His aim was to give his children the finest and best-equipped education he could afford. He felt he had been deprived of such an opportunity in his country, and as a result, he wanted to make up for this deficiency through his children. He often told his children that it was up to them to exhibit the desire and love for knowledge and he would invest his last penny for education. For him, learning was "a possession forever," as Thucidydes said in his account of the Peloponnesian Wars.

Father was the disciplinarian of the family. As part of my training, he encouraged me to play the violin at eight years of age. Accordingly, I trained myself to practice each day from six to eight hours. This was good training, from several points of view. First of all, I came to appreciate fine music and the pleasure one derives from it. Second, it accustomed me to the stringent ardors of engineering later on. Furthermore, it taught me that any serious undertaking is never-ending, that one has to pursue and update whatever is undertaken initially. This applies to any profession if one is to excel and remain abreast of events.

Dad was motivated and determined to make his finest investment in the education of his children. In addition, his desire was to see them attain excellence in their endeavors as set forth in Homer's *Iliad*: "To forever excel and be above all others."

Even though Dad was a disciplinarian, he never used force, but rather he relied on persuasion. He would advise us accordingly, would relate his experiences to us, and then have us as individuals make our own decisions. After we made our decisions, he never questioned their sagacity. His children are greatly indebted to him

13

for his unfailing yet stern help and advice rendered in the establishment of our future careers.

Mother, on the other hand, was a more liberal type in the sense that whatever "will be, will be." She was not a disciplinarian, and if a situation became a problem, she would relax and walk away from it. However, she gave unstintingly of her love and devotion in time of illness or distress on our part and was a consoling spirit.

Mother was a lot more socially oriented than Dad. I well remember the times when I would dance the polka or mazurka with her. Mother was a stout woman of about 210 pounds at the time and stood barely five feet tall. Yet when it came to the rapid gyrations of the dance, she was as light as a feather and would literally twirl me around. My masculine ego was injured when I realized who was doing the commandeering. I must admit I was dizzy from the incessant gyrations I was subjected to. I have been in many airplane spins with rapid turns per minute, but never have I ever witnessed anything as wild as those of my mother's. God rest her soul.

I am proud and privileged to have been nurtured among the immigrant population of the early 1900s. These people came to this country to flee from the injustices, lack of economic opportunities and education, and excessive governmental interference in their personal lives. They represented the highest of aspirations, hope, and faith. They were so proud to see sons and daughters of their fellow newcomers receive an education and excel in their endeavors. It didn't matter what their nationality was; they were all of one "melting pot" and were proud of it. Their top priority was to master the English language, and they insisted their children speak only English at home.

They were grateful to the U.S. government for allowing them to come to this country. Consequently, they made a commitment to do their best in proving they were worthy of the honor.

It was beautiful and inspiring to see the newcomers setting the groundwork for their future in America through their untiring, determined efforts to achieve their goals and through their children. We can see the results of their sweat and toil today in their offspring. Family ties were of cardinal importance, and a helping hand was not only extended to members of their family and relatives but also to fellow newcomers.

As a further manifestation of his insatiable zeal and love for his newly adopted country, Father set out to obtain his citizenship papers. It was a tremendous challenge for him, since he had to learn an additional language to the two he already knew. I say it was a challenge for him because the languages he knew were not Romance languages, and as a result, they did not contain many cognates that he could fall back on. As I recall, he would consult me in regard to learning the alphabet. At the time I was only in elementary school, but I helped as much as I could.

I was eager to help because his enthusiasm rubbed off on me. I learned from him the desire and ability to ask questions without being embarrassed. Explanations had to be perfectly clear and reasonable before he would proceed further. He would make constant use of the analogy of a building structure in relation to its foundation. Without a solid foundation, the building at best is on shaky ground. He would say that it was essential that he learn the English language to avoid muttering words and the using of hands to indicate what he wanted when shopping and communicating with people.

Not only did he seek explanations from his children, but he would talk to his fellow newcomers as to what they were doing in obtaining their citizenship papers. The group would meet regularly to determine the progress each had made and the tactics pursued. In this way exchanges were made and after a while, it became a matter of who would be the first to obtain his papers. The competition was not only keen but invigorating and challenging.

Discussions bordering on frenzy went on in their attempts to learn all they could about the history of the United States. Parallels were drawn between their native histories and that of the United States.

The names of past presidents of the United States were memorized, and each participant was able to spew out the list at machine-gun rate. It was amazing to see and hear them exhibit such zeal and desire to learn. Their next task was what each president represented in terms of his goals, policies, and issues. The fun really began when an analysis was made as to the merits and wisdom that a specific president had introduced as legislation during his administration. Each participant spoke his mind and voiced his candid opinion, and from what Dad said, pandemonium ensued. At this point I had to remind him that he had better use discretion in what he had to say before he appeared before the judge in New Haven, Connecticut. Being too forthright could result in being misjudged.

In retrospect, their conversations, from what I was told, must have been inspirational. They were willing to accept the existing government but they were already discussing how things might be improved. They were striving for perfection, and nothing but the best was acceptable. This was the caliber of men who came to this country in the early 1900s. They were men who were willing to take risks, hardships, and sacrifices to make things and the quality of life better. These principles made them founders and pioneers in many respects.

They realized that their zeal and enthusiasm could only be carried so far. After all, they reasoned, they were somewhat hamstrung insofar as English was concerned. One can now appreciate the motivation behind these people when they were hell-bent in providing education for their children. Their fervent hope and eternal faith was in their children. For one day as engineers, doctors, lawyers, administrators, politicians, etc., they would carry forward the Olympic torch of perfection and epistemology. Knowledge to them was of paramount importance. How well their dreams and aspirations have succeeded is manifest throughout the United States.

It is gratifying to see that some of the modern generation are emulating these old-timers and are carrying the torch to ever increasing heights of attainment. One of the most prominent movements at the present time is the quest for world peace and stability. This movement is gaining momentum not only in this country but on a global scale.

3. Achieving a Career in Aeronautics

To achieve my goal of becoming an aeronautical engineer, I commuted every day to New York University via the elevated trains and subway system from Flushing, Long Island, to University Heights in the Bronx. In the early thirties, there was no graffiti on the trains and the service was very reliable. The trip took over an hour. Since I was achieving my goal, I did not mind the inconvenience. The first three years were devoted primarily to basic engineering courses, with additional courses in economics, political science, technical report writing, and public speaking. All of these minor courses were very helpful in later years. However, I felt that they prevented me from spending more time on my engineering subjects.

As I progressed through college and industry, I became aware of the importance of having a broad perspective. In my interviews with various prospective employers, I realized how fortunate I was to have listened to my curriculum advisers. My engineering courses were but a part of my overall educational training. In the real world, I had to be prepared to deal with the humanistic side of the equation to achieve an overall balance.

In my senior year, I decided to put into practice some of the public-oriented courses I had taken. I became associated with the Society of Automotive Engineers. In addition, I became the first chairman of the newly organized chapter of the Student Branch of the Institute of Aeronautical Sciences. I believe I was the first student in our country to acquire such an office since the IAS was founded in 1931. The experience gained was of inestimable value. In later life I took on the role of Planning Commissioner and became the founder of the San Francisco Tau Beta Pi Alumni Association. I have served on a Redwood City Mayoral Board, the Growth Policy Advisory Council of the San Mateo County Economic Development Association, and am a member of several committees of San Mateo County/Redwood City Chamber of Commerce.

Upon graduation from NYU in 1933, it was very difficult to find a position in industry. As a result, my father advised me that, as far as he was concerned, he could not make a better investment than educating his children.

Dr. Klemin, the school's director, on the other hand, was somewhat perturbed, since he felt I had all the necessary education for becoming a full-fledged aeronautical engineer at that time. Nevertheless, I followed my father's advice and returned to the Heights for my master's degree, majoring in physics. This proved to be a blessing in later years when I became involved in the design of high-speed airplanes and spacecraft. There is no limit to the knowledge that is required as the speed spectrum increases from subsonic to transonic to supersonic to hypersonic to space flight. Knowledge is still lacking in many areas of high speed and space flight. Physics is the cornerstone of the applications that the engineer makes in his analyses. Fundamental considerations find their basis in physics and chemistry.

Even with a master's degree, finding a position in aeronautical engineering was difficult during the depression era. At this point Dad suggested I go back to school for my doctorate. I had followed his advice when it came to the master's degree. However, I felt that relying upon my father to assist me through a doctorate degree was too much. Enough was enough! It was not my intention to become a perennial student.

I persisted in knocking on corporate doors and left no stone unturned. Prof. Alexander Klemin arranged an interview for me at Chrysler Corporation, where they were applying aerodynamic principles to automotive design. Their work culminated in the design and production of the "Airflow Car." Like all other organizations, Chrysler was hit by the economic crunch of the 1930s. Even though they showed interest in what I had to offer in aerodynamic design ideas, they were unable to hire anyone at the time. This was a familiar response from all prior interviews. I was not discouraged. Professor Klemin had forewarned his students about the uncertainties and vicissitudes of the aircraft industry. Undaunted and determined to attain my goal in obtaining employment, I carried on!

Imagine my delight when I received a telegram from Dick Bowman, also a graduate of the Daniel Guggenheim School of Aeronautics at NYU, to come for an interview at Seversky Aircraft.

18

I wasted no time in going to Farmingdale where I was interviewed by Alexander Kartveli, the chief engineer. Kartveli was a Georgian from the USSR. He took great delight in telling people he was from Georgia without saying any more. People would look at him quizzically and wonder where on earth he acquired such a unique U.S. Georgian accent. After much consternation on the part of the inquiring person, he would say that he was not from the U.S.A. but from the USSR. His accent was a mixture of Russian, French, and Armenian. If one can imagine such a conglomeration of languages, one can readily understand the confusion people had when they tried to unfathom the accent mystery. Alexander (Sasha) Kartveli had joined Seversky Aircraft in 1931 as assistant chief engineer. Sasha had graduated from L'Ecole Superieure Aeronautique and L'Ecole Superieure Electricité in Paris, France. Consequently, the French accent was quite predominant.

What a surprise! Kartveli hired me on the spot. He assigned me immediately to work on stress-analyzing the horizontal tail surface of the BT-8 basic trainer. At the time the stress department was comprised of five or six people. The entire engineering department consisted of some twenty individuals of various disciplines—primarily draftsmen, stress analysts, and weight engineers. Whenever aerodynamic calculations had to be performed, I changed hats and performed the necessary analysis. The same applied to power plant calculations. This type of operation kept me on my toes all the time, not knowing where the next crisis might arise. We were jacks-of-all-trades. This made us universalists in aviation with no fear of becoming specialists. This was to occur later when we expanded our force overnight during World War II.

In the early 30s, Alexander (Sasha) Seversky determined his own airplane specifications and rules as to what the air force needed. In order to get things moving, he would get the necessary financing, and if this was not available, he would go into hock in order to build an experimental plane to demonstrate its flying characteristics to the Air Corps. There was essentially no team effort; it was practically a one-man decision as to what was needed. He had all the answers. In many respects he was right. At a very early stage, for example, he advocated wing-tip tanks to increase the range of fighters. In this connection, he went a step further and suggested refueling in flight. All these innovative suggestions apparently fell on deaf ears at the time.

There was one lesson I learned from this: One must expect, unfortunately, to be turned down when innovative ideas are out of sync with the demand. Eventually, as we all know now, these concepts were inaugurated during World War II. As a matter of fact, they became a requirement for fighter aircraft when ferrying them to Europe and other long-distance destinations.

During Seversky's time, it was difficult to land contracts in the aviation field. The effects of the depression were still lingering over our heads, and monies available from any source were scarcer than a hen's tooth. Seversky was a real go-getter. He was a salesman par excellence, but so enthusiastic that at times he would lose his patience and fly off the handle. Nevertheless, he was able to land a contract with the Air Corps for an order of eight basic trainers. This order was the real beginning of Seversky Aircraft. The preparation of technical data for submission to the Air Corps was a hair-raising event. We were allotted about a month's time to prepare the proposal. This was sufficient time, but one could count on Seversky to change the performance calculations at zero hour. One glance at the high-speed figures and no matter how optimistic the calculations were, he would raise them to loftier heights. When it was shown that the changes he proposed were overly optimistic, his response was that it was worth the gamble to fudge in order to get the contract. We did get the P-35 contract for thirty-five aircraft. This was a boon for Seversky, for it established him on firmer ground for future business. The P-35 achieved speed records when flown by such notables as Jacqueline Cochran, Frank Fuller, and Jimmy Doolittle. Seversky was jubilant!

Seversky had begun his flying career during World War I in Czarist Russia. He had served on fifty-seven combat missions and shot down thirteen enemy planes. Arriving in America in 1918, he became a test pilot and aeronautical engineer for the U.S. Government. He founded Seversky Aircraft Corporation in Farmingdale, Long Island, New York, which in 1938 became Republic Aviation Corporation.

Seversky invented many flying devices and designed the first cantilever, all-metal, high-speed fighter. In World War II, he was a consultant to the War Department and later represented the Secretary of War at the Bikini A-bomb tests. His *Victory through Air Power* and *Air Power: Key to Survival* were texts used in most military colleges. He lectured extensively at Air War, Air Command, and

Staff Colleges of the U.S. Air University.

In 1954 Seversky challenged Charles A. Lindbergh's statement that there was "no defense" in atomic war. Seversky took the stand that Lindbergh was dead wrong on basic concepts of national security. Seversky's patriotism and military knowledge prompted him to come to the forefront and openly refute Lindbergh's contention that there was no defense in atomic war. Seversky acknowledged "Lindbergh's skill as an airman was as far beyond question as his patriotism and integrity. But aviation skill, no matter how great, does not in itself guarantee a grasp of military facts. It is no comfortable thing for a fellow airman to take issue with his opinions and judgments. I venture to do so, as I did back in 1941, reluctantly, and only out of a deep concern and survival of our country."

This is a typical example of Sasha's candid remarks. He would not compromise his sincere beliefs, but would respond with a bombastic approach. His comments were pungent, and he did not mince any words. He came out forthright in a polemic fashion. This trait, noble and patriotic as it was, offended many people in the military and eventually it boomeranged back at him when he was president of Seversky Aircraft.

There were many charming incidents that were told about Seversky. I would like to recount one that I experienced. Seversky was very anxious to be accommodating to a fellow pilot, who was assigned by the French government to assess the P-35 for possible purchase. The pilot was of short stature, and when he sat in the cockpit, he could not reach the rudder pedals. Try as hard as he could, he was not able to reach the pedals. The seat adjustment had reached its gamut! Recognizing the dilemma his fellow pilot was in, Seversky came to the rescue by climbing up to the side of the cockpit. Seversky, with the spirit of a Sir Walter Raleigh, suggested that a cushion could be used behind his back to prop him forward.

Unfortunately, the pilot knew very little English and did not comprehend the meaning of the word *cushion*. Try as hard as he could, Seversky could not get across to him. Finally, in desperation, after trying all combinations of the letters in cushion, Seversky concocted, "Would you like a *cochon, cochon, cochon!*" The Frenchman was literally dumbfounded, and his reaction was to leave the cockpit and declare a revolution. (Incidentally, *cochon* in French means pig.)

The day was saved, however, when word got to the crowd assembled around the plane that what was needed was someone who could speak French. The interpreter's first chore was to explain as diplomatically as possible that a faux pas had been committed and what was intended was a cushion that could be used to prop the pilot forward. After the explanation was delivered by the interpreter, serenity prevailed and a great big smile of understanding emerged on the pilot's face.

4. Systems Approach—a Team Effort

When Seversky Aircraft became Republic Aviation Corporation around 1938, its management and operation became more organized. No longer would we tell the Air Corps what they needed from a tactical viewpoint. When a request for a proposal with specifications was received, we assembled in the chief engineer's office for discussion and plan of action.

By we, I mean the assemblage of various engineering department chiefs whose input would lead to the conceptual design of the vehicle. This group consisted of the chiefs of aerodynamics, thermodynamics, weights and structures. The chief engineer acted as the monitor of the group and eventually made the final decisions. It was recognized at the outset that the design was a conglomeration of many components. There was a delicate balance among all groups involved as to what compromises had to be made. In the design of aircraft, weight is of paramount importance, since the overall flight performance can be adversely affected. Here again, weight cannot be minimized, for example, at the sacrifice of maintenance problems that can ensue in service. A vehicle is of little value if it is plagued with maintenance problems. This results in its being nonoperational for an inordinate period of time.

When the first approximation of weight is made, aerodynamic analyses must be made to determine if the spec requirements can be met subject to the availability of the power required. As a rule, it is difficult to attain the desired performance requirements as specified in the RFP (Request for Proposal) and accordingly, one must turn to the thermodynamicists or power-plant personnel. They in turn can determine the feasibility of attaining the power needed to obtain the required performance figures. In addition to our own personnel, we could turn to the engine manufacturers for the power plant required. In some designs of an advanced type, the aircraft and engine manufacturers pooled their technical efforts to produce the type of power plant required. Kartveli would call in Dr. William J. O'Donnell for assistance.

Once the aerodynamics and power-plant groups made their rounds of preliminary calculations, the structures group would be called in to estimate the type of structure that would be required to sustain the required aerodynamic loadings. Several alternatives would be analyzed to arrive at the one alternative that would result in the minimum weight. With their additional input, it was inevitable that the original optimistic estimated weight was too low. This being the case, aerodynamics would recalculate their estimates to determine the degree of loss of performance. When this occurred, the chief engineer had to reevaluate the impacts this change would have on the various affected groups. This resulted in making further compromises. This iterative process would continue after many trials and alterations were made. We eventually reached a limit in the process when it was realized that very little could be achieved, for example, in performance.

An explanation of the systems concept is in order since we will be making reference to it throughout. What constitutes a system? First of all, a system is made up of many component parts, each of which partially defines the makeup of the overall system. In the preceding discussion, we outlined a few of the many components that determine the overall design of an airplane (in more generic terms, the airplane constitutes a "system").

Each component has associated with it certain limits or range of values that must be complied with (imposed constraints). Each component, in addition, can influence (interact with) other components when a change is made in a specific item of a given component. These interactions can be very important, since the nature of the decision rendered can be materially affected.

In order to arrive at a near-optimal solution, the chief engineer would consider several alternatives to determine the one alternative that in his estimation would best meet the requirements as specified in the RFP. There were times when the assembled group would get into a heated discussion with Sasha. We would try to convince him that he should not compromise to the extent that he did on the maintenance of the vehicle. He was gung-ho on the aerodynamic sleekness of the design. If the aerodynamic outline was not pleasing to his eye, he would call it a *"pomme de terre"* (a potato).

24

The systems concept is quite universal and can be applied to all types of problems involving decision-making, whether one is serving as a director of engineering, a planning commissioner, council member, administrator, business executive, supervisor, mayor, state legislator, or president of the United States. As an example, on the presidential level the members of his cabinet are there to input the various components that constitute the system under discussion. We shall give examples of this principle as applied to our personal lives.

Our experiences at Seversky Aircraft are memorable. In the initial years of its existence, the company was small. As a result, a closely knit family atmosphere prevailed. We were invited by Sasha Kartveli to attend a party at his home to meet and become acquainted with some of his cosmopolitan friends. As the evening progressed, we were introduced to Prince so-and-so; later on, Prince so-and-so, and so it went on for quite some time. Thetis and I were both intrigued and honored that we were in the presence of so much royalty. Upon querying Sasha as to why there were so many princes in USSR Georgia, he smiled and told us that was a title that was given to those who were affluent in Georgia. We then surmised by Sasha's implication that these so-called princes were quite wealthy. Sasha responded, "No, that's not quite correct. They are people who were the proud owners of five or more sheep." To this very day, we don't know whether there is any credence to that story, but sooner or later, we intend to find out.

Sasha filled us in a bit on the Georgian language, their customs, literary efforts, and religion. Their alphabet is most intriguing, apparently a composite derived from Aramaic, Armenian, and Greek. When one realizes the proximity of Georgia to Armenia, it is not surprising that this is so. Their writing resembles a mathematical equation from generalized relativity, equally incomprehensible and complicated. Sasha illustrated his point by selecting a few letters of the Georgian alphabet. Their letter pronounced "*tseel*" is represented by an inverted triangle covered over by a canopy of inverted wave forms. The grammar is similar to Latin, but more complicated in that there are seven cases to decline, no articles, and no gender. The latter characteristic can lead to utter confusion and embarrassment.

The Georgian is very warm and friendly. They are basically mountainous people and love their bucolic background and the joy of living. At parties they have their lamb roasting on a spit outdoors and balalaikas filling the air with their native music. It is truly living it up in the epicurean way.

These Georgians had traveled through many countries before making their home in the United States. Consequently, they were fluent in many languages. It was fascinating to listen to them converse in Turkish, Armenian, Georgian, French, Russian, and German. Our high school French and German wasn't of much help in keeping up with them.

Sasha led the pace by quoting Pushkin, Lermontov in Russian, Georgian poetry, Victor Hugo's *Les Miserables* in French, Cicero and Catullus in Latin. We soon realized that Americans tend to be content with knowing only one language, which leaves us at a disadvantage. This is especially the case now that we have to face international competition.

The Georgians were fantastic story-tellers. When one of them finished with their recital, another would start his story. They could go on for hours, emulating Scheherazade, the fictitious queen who narrated Arabian tales in *A Thousand and One Nights*. Like Scheherazade they continued to tell their stories as if their lives depended upon it. If one wanted to be the life of the party, story-telling was a must. Everyone would listen attentively, laugh at the punch lines, and exhibit emotion and sorrow when the occasion arose during the story-telling.

Silence and melancholia would not reign for long at their parties. The balalaikas would flare up. Singing and dancing would transcend the group.

My association with Sasha Kartveli involved more than engineering. He was a Latin scholar par excellence. He would keep me on my toes when, after quoting passages from Cicero, he wanted to know what oration or philosophical work it came from. For a Georgian, Sasha had the most beautiful and well-pronounced Latin I have ever heard. When he would ramble on and on, I felt Cicero reincarnated speaking in the Roman Senate. It was a rare privilege for me. He was especially fond of the Cataline Orations and Pro Lege Manilia.

Cataline was a profligate Roman aristocrat who conspired to overthrow the existing government of Rome in 63 B.C. He raised so much havoc among the populace of Rome that Cicero felt it his duty to defend the republic. Cicero felt it was time to put an end to the nefarious and sinister actions of Cataline, who was planning to overthrow the republic. Accordingly, Cicero appeared before the Roman Senate to strip him of his powers.

The Manilian law dealt with the appointment of Pompey as commander-in-chief of all forces in the Mediterranean area to wipe out Mithradates, king of Pontus, who was inflicting destruction upon the Roman mercantile fleet. Piracy, which had been growing worse ever since the fall of Carthage and the subsequent decline of the Roman navy, had become so dangerous that the economic welfare and prosperity of the entire republic were seriously threatened. As a result, a bill was introduced in the Roman Senate to remedy the situation. Cicero rose to the occasion and recommended Pompey as the commander-in-chief. Thus, through Sasha, I learned something about Pompey.

One of my most memorable sojourns with Sasha Kartveli was our stay at the Mark Hopkins Hotel in San Francisco in 1959. We had visited the University of California at Berkeley and were en route to see Dr. Clark Millikan of the California Institute of Technology, Pasadena. Clark was the son of Robert Millikan, the Nobel Laureate in physics who had measured the charge of the electron. Clark was the director of the California Technical School of Aeronautics and director of the Cooperative Wind Tunnel, composed of the consortium of various companies: Douglas Aircraft, Lockheed Aircraft, McDonnell Aircraft, etc.

We wanted to obtain Clark's advice and counsel about the types of personnel we should consider in meeting the requirements of the future in aeronautics and what the future of space technology might require of industrial management. Clark admitted he was as much in a quandary as we were at this stage of the game and didn't know what was in store for us in industry. In a sense, I couldn't blame him for answering the way he did. We were interested in establishing a space laboratory involving millions of dollars and should his advice in proceeding along his suggested course of implementation not pan out, we would be committed to non-utilizable, expensive equipment.

During one evening in San Francisco, Sasha and I decided to dine at Alexis's Tangier restaurant, which was two blocks west of the Mark Hopkins Hotel on California Avenue. When we walked into the place, Sasha turned to me and said, "Do you see that *narghile* on the shelf in the far corner of the room, that *ibrik* on our immediate left, etc.?" Indeed I could. The scene brought back many memories to me, for as a child in Ansonia, Connecticut, I well remember some of the elder folk puffing away on their *narghile* and sipping on what I thought was water, but as I was told later, it was ouzo, the water of fire transported by Prometheus from Mount Olympus.

For the record, the *narghile* is an apparatus used in the Near East that cools the tobacco smoke by passing it through a reservoir of water in a bottle shaped like a large teardrop. Several long, flexible tubes draw the smoke through the water by a sucking action on the part of the smoker. The *narghile* looks very much like an octopus whose large head is equivalent to the reservoir of water, with the various flexible tubes resembling the arms of the octopus. It was quite a scene to see the smokers arranged peripherally around the *narghile*, each in turn drawing smoke through the reservoir. I must admit that I don't know whether a sequential action was required or not on the part of the smokers. I say this because in the event all participants were to draw at the same time, it is conceivable that the apparatus would malfunction.

The *narghile* is a Persian word for the coconut tree, *nargil*, because the pipe was originally made from a coconut shell. The *ibrik* (with accent on the ultimate) is a brass, coffee-making pot, coated with tin on the interior. The pot is equipped with a long handle and has a wide base and narrow neck.

After we were seated, Sasha and I were very curious as to what kind of a restaurant we were in. Our curiosity built up to such a crescendo that I told Sasha we had to launch an expeditionary party of one, namely me, to talk to the proprietor.

After much interrogation and suspicion among the waiters as to our real motive for desiring to talk to the proprietor, we were finally introduced to him. With great tact and diplomacy, I, first of all, complimented Alexis on the beautiful *narghile* and the various *ibriks* of all sizes, ranging from small, which served two demi-tasse portions to large, serving a party of six to eight, which were on display all around the room. Furthermore, the vases that were on display were also very beautiful and of exotic origin (this will be clarified in a moment). Upon hearing my exclamations and complimentary remarks, he immediately responded by asking, "Are you Georgian?" I said, "No, but I am with someone who is." At this point Alexis thought I was being a wise guy and I could see his disposition rising to a boiling point. However, I assured him I was not being frivolous and if he would have the kindness to follow me to the table, I would be more than happy to introduce him.

Upon introducing Sasha to Alexis, all the heavens opened up to their full regalia of radiance and resplendency, and the waters of the Nile parted when Sasha answered him in Georgian. Alexis immediately embraced Sasha. From that moment on, we were treated with the highest of hospitality and congeniality. Alexis couldn't do enough for us. He transferred us from our table d'hote to an intimate inner sanctum sanctorum reserved exclusively for the boss himself. In the meantime, we were invited to sit at the bar and imbibe whatever we desired. His hospitality and cordiality were out of this world, and I was left an orphan when the two conversed in Georgian for long periods of time.

Occasionally, Alexis and Sasha would turn to me and ask, "You don't mind if we converse in Georgian, do you?"

I responded by saying, "On the contrary, I am really intrigued and fascinated by the sounds of the Georgian language when spoken by the two of you. The sounds are unlike anything I have heard in Russian, Armenian, and Turkish. What really intrigues me is, I thought I heard some French in your conversation."

Sasha responded, "Yes, you are quite correct. The reason for this is that I couldn't remember the word I wanted to use in Georgian, so I used the equivalent one in French. When one doesn't use Georgian frequently, one is apt to forget its usage."

Georgian is apparently a language all unto its own. Alexis explained to me later that the language has no cognates with other languages, since the country is virtually isolated from its neighboring countries. This is the case since the country is very mountainous and all external influences are practically nonexistent.

Alexis made us an aperitif, which he called the "cobra." Quite an appropriate name! It was an exotic concoction and rivals that of some of the drinks one orders at Trader Vic's and Don the Beachcomber. It was made with a jigger of Slivovitz (this was not Hungarian but Yugoslavian plum brandy) with a dash of vodka, rum, cointreau, and fresh lemon juice. For hors d'oeuvres, we had the most delicious *dolmades* (little rolls made from tender grape leaves stuffed with a mixture of rice and chopped meat and steamed until cooked). Alexis told us that this tidbit originated at the time of Alexander the Great.

For our main course, Alexis served us shish kebab, pilaf, and other trimmings, with the most exquisite Bordeaux imaginable. After our meal, he had us sit in a special alcove where we could hear recordings of Georgian folklore and songs—the music and intonations were reminiscent of the Greek and Turkish. In this time interval, we were served baklava (it is of Byzantine origin and is the aristocrat of pastry desserts). It is made of layers of nut filling—pistachios, walnuts, and hazelnuts. Each layer is separated by a thin membrane of philo dough. The pastry is made up of a multitude of layers and the full-fledged baklava is an inch and a half to two inches in height and is then doused in honey.

We were served Georgian coffee, which resembled the Arabian powdered coffee. When first served, this coffee should be allowed to stand for a sufficient time so that the fine particulates can settle to the bottom of the demi-tasse cup. If not, one would be drinking a very muddy liquid, with a recalcitrant tongue rebelling against the hotness and muddy texture. While we were sipping the coffee ever so gently, liqueurs were being served.

I was truly amazed at the Georgian hospitality and cordiality that was extended to us during the evening. Parting was such "sweet sorrow," and many blessings and good tidings were exchanged.

5. Systems Approach Applied to Our Personal Lives

Now that we have outlined the fundamentals of what constitutes a systems approach, it was time for me to apply it to my personal life. After working at Seversky Aircraft for a few years, I felt somewhat secure financially. There was a small nest egg in the bank, which meant I could consider marriage. This would correspond to adding an additional vital component to my personal system.

Designing airplanes was relatively easy, since I would be dealing with an inanimate system. In the case of adding an animate component to my personal system, I would be dealing with a much more complex component. This component could contain many subcomponents, which in turn could be subdivided into further subcomponents, ad infinitum. Some of the major subcomponents I am referring to would pertain to emotional, psychological, and behavior factors, which can not be evaluated quantitatively. One can not design a wife to specifications subject to constraints without incurring severe interactions among already existing components. These considerations took some doing.

One day as I was having coffee with some friends, one of their acquaintances dropped by. I was promptly introduced to him as an engineer. During our ensuing discussion, I was asked a number of questions regarding the type of work I was engaged in. By this time the acquaintance and I were getting along on a more intimate basis. He asked me to drop the formalities and call him Tom.

Tom asked me whether or not I was familiar with calculus. I responded by saying that was our mainstay in engineering. Without it, we couldn't very well do our work. After giving a number of examples of how it was applied, I thought the subject was closed. As time went by, however, the subject was raised again and again. Needless to say, I became a bit suspicious as to why Tom was so interested in calculus. Could it be that he was a frustrated engineer who didn't make the grade? Or was it that he was studying the subject on his own?

Finally, Tom admitted he knew someone who needed tutoring in calculus. I was in no mood to tutor anyone at this time, as I was knee-deep in overtime work. Accordingly, I told Tom that it would not be possible for me to undertake this assignment at the time. I could see Tom was disappointed in my response. Finally, I asked him who this person was. When he replied it was his daughter, that drastically changed the complexion of things. In addition, there were facial expressions of anxiety and concern by my hosts that I should reconsider my decision. The only civil thing to do was to reconsider the situation. Upon further querying Tom, I was told that she was having difficulty in her course in calculus and was quite concerned about passing the course. I could well understand her plight when Tom said it was near the end of the semester and finals would be close by. Time was of the essence. What to do? What was her difficulty? There was only one thing to do. My curiosity got the best of me, and I had to find out for myself.

An appointment was made. This appointment was two-pronged. On the one hand, I was curious about her difficulties in calculus and on the other hand, I was intrigued as to her interests in studying the subject. What kind of a person might she be? The plot thickened. Her dad had told me she was a sophomore at Hofstra College and had always been an excellent student in high school math. As an eligible bachelor, I was becoming more and more interested beyond the realms of math.

When I arrived at Tom's home, I was introduced to his wife. She bid me the fondest of welcomes and felicitations and was most gracious. I could readily see she was a highly educated person from the way she spoke. She immediately made me feel at home. After many exchanges of protocol, their daughter was introduced to me. So far, so good! We were following proper protocol. No slip-ups! Thetis's mother suggested we use the large, oak, dining-room table. This suggestion was made so that we could have plenty of room to spread out our books and papers.

During my initial discussions with Thetis, I found out what her difficulty was. As an instructor she had a young graduate of Harvard who was imbued with the theory of limits to such an extent that he was confounding the entire class. It was all pure theory, with no apparent applications.

I then went on to say that calculus is basically a quantitative philosophy of arriving at change. Sir Isaac Newton, one of the founders of calculus, called it the theory of "fluxions." All phenomena of Nature are subject to unrelenting, inexorable change. Then one is confronted with the concept of change of change; that is, change in itself can change. The degree of change can go on as long as there is the existence of further change, there being a limit to change when change no longer occurs. This constitutes a static condition. So far, so good! Thetis was making headway with my pedagogical endeavors.

With change, one has to consider limiting processes. To illustrate a limiting process, I took the perimeter of a circle as an illustration. The perimeter of a circle can be approximated by inscribing a polygon. As the number of sides of the polygon is increased, the better the approximation to the length of the perimeter becomes. At this point I could see Thetis was beginning to ask some poignant questions. "But how far does this increase in the sides of the polygon proceed?" she asked. I then responded by saying that the answer to the question depended on the degree of accuracy required. This concept was foreign to her; she had difficulty comprehending this remark.

I reminded her of high school geometry when studying the circle. The ratio of the perimeter to the diameter of the circle came out an irrational number, pi, which never had a numerical end. The more one would calculate the value of pi, the more additional numbers would appear. If one is content, as an engineer for example, with four decimal places, then that is the degree of accuracy required. On the other hand, an astrophysicist might require four hundred places.

At this point Thetis was beginning to see the light at the end of the tunnel. In a burst of excitement, she, out of amazement, made the remark, "Is this what my teacher meant by the 'epsilonic value'?" I was very gratified to see that I was making progress.

The crowning point of the lesson occurred when she asked me about the osculating circle. Thetis inquired about this with some trepidation, for she wondered how "kissing" was related to calculus. The answer to this question posed a delicate situation for me: Should I illustrate the concept physically or should I proceed along scholarly lines and make use of the concepts we had already discussed in limiting processes? At this stage of the game, I chose the latter. This was no time for upsetting the apple cart.

When I was asked this question, I could readily understand her plight. As preliminary background, it was necessary to outline what it was we were trying to define and explain. As a first approximation, a point on a plane curve can be represented by its tangent, and by the osculating circle or circle of curvature as a second approximation. The osculating circle represented a higher degree of accuracy than the tangent line. Like the tangent line, the circle of curvature is the limiting position of a secant circle to the curve under investigation.

To illustrate this in more detail, I took the standard approach of a circle passing through three points. By allowing two of the points to approach the third point, one obtains the so-called osculating circle at the third point. Thetis could readily understand the limiting process that occurred in this case, since we allowed two of the three points to approach ever so closely to the third point. "Ever so closely" was apparently the key phrase that impressed Thetis. I proceeded to define the reciprocal of the radius of the osculating circle as the measure of the rotation of the tangent per unit length of arc of the curve. This reciprocal, in turn, was called the curvature at the point under investigation. With the aid of several diagrams, Thetis had a much better concept of the osculating circle while I iterated again and again, that limiting processes will terminate only upon the accuracy required of the investigator.

After two meetings she had a much better understanding of calculus. I was delighted to learn that she passed the course. When she took her second semester of calculus, she received an A. Her faith and confidence in mathematics was restored again. This was crucial in her pursuit of chemistry, since mathematics is used quite extensively in physical chemistry.

I was impressed with the rapidity at which she comprehended the geometrical meaning of the osculating circle. This concept is not an easy one to grasp. Needless to say, I had become quite interested in her and wanted to carry on with our relationship. I felt she would be the ideal component of my personal system I was looking for. She had the same qualities of love for science, music, and philosophy as I had.

I had a ponderous decision to make. If I were to ask Thetis directly, the chances were great that I would be turned down. During our discussions she implied that she wanted to become a neurosurgeon. She was a sophomore in college and was determined to proceed with her courses. I had the feeling that nothing would change her mind about attaining her goal. For this I admired her all the more, for she demonstrated to me that she was a person of principle and determination. The other alternative was to let her father know of my intentions. I chose the latter.

Tom called me a few days later to say that he talked to Thetis and that she wanted three days to think about my proposal for marriage. As far as I was concerned, it was love at first sight. I was convinced she was the girl for me. The question that had to be resolved was: would she have me? Did she have many doubts about me that would render her decision unfavorable? In the jargon of systems analysis, were there many constraints that might be imposed by her that would render a negative decision? The more constraints one imposes, the less likelihood of a favorable decision.

To complicate the matter further, it never occurred to her that I was personally interested in her in spite of the seeming innuendos made during the discussions on the osculating circle. She was so imbued in passing calculus and going on to med school that she was totally oblivious and unsuspecting of my marital interests. What concerned me the most was the fact that I was not man enough to approach her directly but took a roundabout approach by seeking the help of her father.

After three days of anxious waiting on my part, Tom called and invited me to dinner. He also said her answer was "Yes." What delight and jubilation on my part! The heavens opened up for me at that point. What a propitious and letitious (unrestrained joyfulness) moment! My searching for the marital component of my life had come to an end.

Thetis's uncle, Gigi, was somewhat concerned about her getting married at her stage of life. To him it meant she would have to terminate her graduating from college and bringing to an abrupt end her goal of becoming an MD. I respected Uncle Gigi, for he was one who would discuss overtly what was on his mind. On the other hand, he was tactful not to make mincemeat of me. He was very fond, and rightfully so, of his niece and wanted to make sure she would be happy.

On the other hand, Uncle Nick admonished his brother that "She was too young to get married" and that the engineer was robbing the cradle. I owe a great deal of thanks to Thetis's father and mother for allowing the marriage to go forward.

I assured everyone that I had no intention of disrupting Thetis's education—at least at the undergraduate level. I well remembered my father's remark when I went back to school for my M.S. degree at the time, when I couldn't find a position in engineering. What better investment could I have made than to make sure Thetis would obtain her degree in chemistry? This was security for the future. With this explanation, everyone was quite content that the future son-in-law was on the right track and indeed had the best interests of the family at heart. Peace and tranquillity reigned.

It was a whirlwind courtship over a calculus textbook! I tutored her in January. We were engaged a few days after Valentine's Day and were married on June ninth.

When we were on our honeymoon, enjoying the grandeur and psychedelic environment of Maine, everything was quiet and serene. There were no phones or radio to disturb us in our log cabin on Moosehead Lake. We were roughing it in a very civilized manner. One day we drove down to the general store for some bread and groceries. While buying our groceries, we learned that Paris had fallen to the Nazis. The Maginot Line was destroyed.

The crumbling of the Maginot Line is an illustrative example of what can happen when one clings to old ideas and concepts and is not flexible enough to incorporate changes that have occurred. In the design of the Maginot Line, French thought was centered around the lessons learned in World War I. The concept of fixed, immobile defenses was the way to defend the country against future attacks by the Germans. The Nazis, on the other hand, introduced new military concepts and tactics into warfare by the introduction of mobility and surprise attack (blitzkrieg). With the Nazis having flanked the line with the help of their highly mobilized tank corps, aircraft, and motorized infantry, the Maginot Line was totally ineffective under the onslaught. The French were, literally speaking, sitting ducks in their immobile abode. Constant pounding of the line by tanks and attack bombers made mincemeat of the massive line of inert, rein-forced concrete.

The usual inhabitants of the Maine hamlet were gathered around in a state of shock. How could this have ever happened? The Maginot line was supposed to be impregnable—solid and impenetrable. We decided it was best not to commiserate any further with the bewildered New England folk.

We then proceeded to put our groceries in our newly bought trusty, second-hand, but otherwise solid Packard. The car was equipped with beautiful white-walled tires, with two externally mounted spare tires on either side of the car on the running board. We then headed back to our cabin. We, too, were in a state of shock. One could feel an ominous, intuitive feeling of the beginning of World War II. Everyone hoped and prayed that somehow the war would end quickly. We were an ocean away, which gave some people a sense of security.

The time had come for us to end our honeymoon and drive back to Long Island to our first home. Thetis left Long Island as a happy teenage bride, to return as a young woman with additional responsibilities to assume. This increased the number of subcomponents of our personal systems concept. Our lives were destined to change, not only for us but for everyone. There were many decisions to be made in the years that followed. Our systems philosophy helped us in making prudent decisions in the years that followed.

Thetis attended a branch of New York University located in Hempstead, Long Island, New York. Later it was to become Hofstra University, when ties with NYU were broken. I wanted to make sure that she acquired a career she could count on in the event anything were to happen. I assured her that we could make no finer and wiser investment than vesting in education.

When she registered for the fall classes, she realized that it was unrealistic to pursue her M.D. since time was of the essence. Fortunately, with her math and science background, it was easy to carry on as a major in chemistry. In retrospect, that decision was a propitious one. It enabled her to help me when it came to high-speed flight, since air molecules dissociate into ions and atoms due to the high temperatures created behind a shock wave. She was helpful in applying quantum chemistry to the formulation of the problem.

We applied strategic planning in deciding to postpone having a family during the war. We reasoned that it would be a wise and sagacious move. We looked forward to the day when peace would be restored so that we could proceed with our plans in building our first home and having children.

It was quite an experience for both of us when December 7,

1941 came. As chief of aerodynamics and flight test, I would spend most of my time at the plant. From then on we were pursuing separate lives. I was spending eighteen hours of the day, seven days a week, for practically the duration of the war, away from home. I would leave at daybreak and return late at night. I was like an overworked resident doctor nursing his critically ill patient, the P-47.

The only thing for Thetis to do, outside of the never-ending house chores and cleaning, was to keep busy, studying physical chemistry, math, and engaging in chemical research. These were the kind of courses that had her studying at night and spending Saturdays in the chem lab. After a while she found that beakers had other functional uses. They were appropriate and convenient for heating soup and stews. Not very luxurious but a very practical way to eat in the labs.

At night when she finally got into bed, she was alone. She knew when I arrived at home. Not that I made any noises as I meandered through our home (for I was moving about at a very low Mach number, emitting no sound waves), but the bed would creak on my side, thereby emitting sound pulses. Her ears were tuned to the wave patterns emitted, otherwise she would have screamed for help. Even though I was very quiet, that one avionic bed board that was attuned to squeak at a prescribed IFF frequency would announce my happy presence to Thetis. This assured her of my identification: friend.

6. Debut of the P-47 Thunderbolt

The designer of aircraft must face the day of reckoning, for that is the day when the first flight and subsequent flights of the aircraft occur. This determines how well the flight performance of the aircraft agrees with the theoretical predictions made. Theoretical predictions and actuality must coincide to make the project successful.

The P-47 was designed in 1940 and flown in 1941. At that time I was newly married, not only to my wife, but primarily to the P-47. Because of the war, I spent seven days a week and sixteen to eighteen hours daily at the factory, working on stepped-up flight schedules. After all, Gen. Hap Arnold was coming to Republic to inspect the progress being made in flight-testing and the degree of success being attained. All of us at Republic could understand the urgency of expediting the tests on the P-47 because the battle for the skies over Europe was going badly for the Allies in 1940. An increase in fighter-escort protection was badly needed by the bomber squadrons. The Nazis had introduced their new jet fighters that could easily penetrate and attack our bomber formations. Accordingly, the P-47 was badly needed in the war zone to stem the onslaught of the Nazi Luftwaffe. Republic built over sixteen thousand in the four-year period during World War II.

It is interesting to note that the P-47 was designed in nine months and the first test flight took place on May 6, 1941. The first impression of the aircraft by pilots was not very favorable. It was bulky and built to withstand severe punishment when shot at by flak and machine-gun fire. However, regardless of how badly the P-47 was shot up, she would bring the pilot back to terra firma. A number of pilots who had flown her in combat would say that they had entered the portals of Saint Peter only to find, miraculously, that they were back safe on the ground. Once out of the cockpit, they kneeled on the ground, kissed it, and made their supplication to God. At that particular moment, the P-47 was their house of consecration.

The P-47 has been called bulky by some, bratwurst with aeronautical appendages by the English pilots, and Sasha Kartveli on occasions has referred to it as the *"pomme de terre."* The fuselage very definitely gave the physical appearance that it was pregnant. That was an illusion.

The bottom portion of the fuselage housed the air inlet that led to the supercharger. The P-47 was designed to fly at altitudes above 25,000 feet. Ironically, as it turned out, most of its flying was performed at altitudes of 10,000-15,000 feet and several ground-strafing missions were made. The depth of the inlet, as I recall, was from twelve to sixteen inches. Aerodynamically, this does not add materially to the drag other than skin-friction drag. As long as air flows through the inlet, no substantial increase in drag is incurred.

Our supersonic aircraft appear bulky as well because of the huge amounts of air that the jet engine requires. Physical appearances once again are deceiving to the eye. If the aircraft were as bulky aerodynamically as it appears physically, rest assured, supersonic speeds would be very difficult, if not impossible, to attain.

The initial flight tests were conducted by Lowery Brabham, Republic's chief test pilot. I was privileged to have worked closely with Brab, for he was an engineering test pilot who possessed good judgment in time of distress. This is an attribute that is vital in experimental test-flying. I well remember on one flight, the engine had blown a piston head and the entire aircraft was smeared with oil. After he landed the plane, I asked him how he was able to see through the oil-covered windshield. His calm and collected reply was that he didn't, but by exerting every muscle in his body, especially his neck, he was barely able to see out from the side of the cockpit. He felt as though he were dangling near the edge of a tree branch. After this harrowing experience, he could understand how it must feel when one lays his head on the executioner's block. Brab contributed substantially to the war effort through his work with the P-47 program. His activities constituted a major advancement, not only for the company, but for the air force as well.

At the end of the war, many pilots changed their original opinions about the plane. Though shot up badly with half an aileron missing, or part of the horizontal or vertical tail shot away, the Jug, as the P-47 was affectionately called, was able to limp back to an airfield. As it turned out effectively, the plane could fly in various other configurations and still return safely to ground. This suggests that in any given design alternative, configurations be studied to determine the feasibility of flight from a safety point of view. This should apply especially to commercial flight.

Cognizant of the love and an inanimate consanguinity for the plane by the pilots who had flown her in combat, Bob Johnson, a P-47 ace credited with twenty-eight planes, suggested to Republic officials in the public relations department that a ceremony marking the twentieth anniversary of the first test flight of the P-47 be held. The ceremony was held on May 6, 1961. Any Air Force pilot who had flown her was invited to attend. To everyone's surprise some one thousand pilots responded. This was indeed a clear manifestation of the adoration they had for the Jug.

Her experiences in flight led to the Götterdämmerung of propellers and conventional wings when attempting to fly close to the speed of sound. A new era of design had to be ushered in if we were to fly faster than the P-47.

The P-47 encountered, for the first time, compressibility effects. The phenomenon reared its ugly head through the performance of the propeller. By increasing engine power, it was observed that a proportionately lower increment in high speed resulted. Republic went from a three-bladed propeller to four blades. That alleviated the situation somewhat. We went further and experimented with counter-rotating propellers.

Herb Fisher conducted a number of additional tests on the Jug at the Curtiss Wright Corporation, Propeller Division. He made over a hundred dives, ranging from 550 to 700 miles per hour in a vertical dive. As a propeller manufacturer, it was imperative to demonstrate its value and performance as the speed of sound was approached. Starting at thirty-eight thousand feet, Herb conducted an evaluation of experimental transonic and swept-back propellers.

As one can surmise by this time, no matter what propeller configurations one could conceive of, we had reached the end of the rope. We had verily reached a limiting point as to the capability of the propeller. It became obvious that as we asymptotically increased the high speed, we were compelled to input a disproportionate increase in engine power. We had reached the point of diminishing returns. No doubt, there was a limit to what we could do in terms of the propeller. The results of these tests sounded the death knell of propellers for flight approaching Mach 1. The airplane design itself had also reached a limiting point, as we shall describe in detail.

At the risk of becoming too technical, a few details will be illustrated to indicate the detailed care that is required in design to mitigate compressibility effects.

Since the P-47 had attained a Mach number of 0.85—0.90 in dives, it was not surprising that difficulties were encountered. It is unfortunate that Nature has decreed that the type of flow pattern changes as we approach the speed of sound. With the establishment of shock waves, the flow over the wing changes in such a way as to induce flow separation.

This results in material increase in the wing wake (flow shed behind the wing) of such a magnitude as to envelop the horizontal tail surface. The wing wake is a region of very turbulent airflow and because of this turbulence, the tail is subjected to buffeting (shaking). At about 0.8 times the speed of sound (known technically as the Mach number), the pilots would experience sudden changes in the control of the airplane. The problem was quite serious, and the air force wanted steps taken to at least alleviate the uncontrollability some pilots encountered in their dives.

The P-47 had a fairly thick airfoil section and a straight leading-edge wing. At about 0.8 Mach number, there developed local regions of sonic and supersonic flows over the wing. This condition may seem paradoxical at first, but, due to the curvature of the upper surface of the wing, the air accelerates, thereby producing local flows of much greater velocity than the forward speed of the airplane. Our flight-test pilots would report that under certain atmospheric conditions, they could see normal shock waves standing off the upper surface of the wing.

The NACA had been researching into the aeronautical unknown, looking ahead into the not-yet-existing future of high-speed flight, testing for solutions to not-yet-existing practical problems. The NACA, true to form, did indeed come up with devices that were installed on the wing, which ameliorated the handling of the aircraft.

We at Republic Aviation were aware of the work of the Flying Qualities Group at Langley Memorial. Bob Gilruth and Hartley Soule had done considerable work on the handling qualities of new military airplanes. Furthermore, Gilruth was in charge of the Pilotless Aircraft Research Station at Wallops Island, Virginia, and had obtained considerable transonic data from rocket-launched models. Accordingly, we consulted with Gilruth on the problems we had encountered in flight on the P-47.

I was especially impressed by the services and assistance extended to us in the mitigation of compressibility problems on the P-47. The foresight in providing such services was truly amazing. Gilruth and his staff went so far as to predetermine from wind-tunnel tests the flying qualities of an airplane. This resulted from correlating flight-test results of the full-scale airplane with wind-tunnel results. This situation constituted prognostication in the highest. As a member of the aeronautical industry, it was very gratifying for me to know that advanced technical data was available to help us in time of need.

Gilruth suggested some of the items that were finally incorporated in the P-47: the wing-dive flap, modifications in detail design of the control surfaces, and the incorporation of bob-weights in the control system that would alleviate control stick forces under "g" conditions.

We shall enumerate briefly some of the experiences encountered with the Jug in high-speed dives and a few of the steps taken in flight tests to mitigate the difficulties.

During high-speed dives, compressibility had manifested itself through buffeting of the elevator, increased stick forces, and a decrease in elevator effectiveness. We learned that special care had to be exercised by the designer with regard to the slot and aerodynamic balance. The leading edge of the elevator balance should not protrude beyond the normal contour of the stabilizer-elevator combination. If it does, high localized velocities will result. At this point, shock waves appear, followed by separation of flow. Flow separation, in turn, produced buffeting. This was experienced by the pilot as a slight shake of the control stick.

From the high-speed aspect, larger horizontal tail surfaces might be used, or an adjustable stabilizer required. All of these suggestions were incorporated on later models. Internally sealed balances were also incorporated. The observations applicable to the elevators also applied to the rudder.

The Frise type aileron caused some difficulty at high speeds where the aileron's nose was deflected downward approximately four degrees. At this point, the nose protruded into the free stream, thereby producing a flow breakdown, causing the ailerons to buffet. The distribution of forces on the ailerons changed in character so suddenly and to such a degree that the pilot was unable to hold the control stick at a given point. The control stick would move violently from one side of the cockpit to the other. This characteristic is referred to as "aileron snatch."

Several modifications were tried. The best results were obtained by moving the hinge line and the incorporation of a blunt-nosed aileron with a variable mechanical advantage in the control system to reduce stick forces. The blunt-nosed aileron with the differential control eliminated aileron snatch at speeds up to five hundred miles per hour and produced greater rolling velocities at all speeds.

With flow conditions altered over the wing, corresponding changes occurred over the horizontal tail, thereby rendering the control of the aircraft difficult. In dives at Mach numbers above 0.80, the greatest increase in diving moment occurred as a result of compressibility effects. The plane tended to nose down and control became difficult until an altitude of approximately twelve thousand feet was reached. Neither elevator nor full-tab motion was very effective, although the full-tab deflection raised the altitude at which pullout was possible, by a few thousand feet. The pullout, when it occurred at approximately twelve thousand feet, was relatively sudden and abrupt. Excessive loads could be developed because of dynamic effects that made this situation unsafe.

The difficulties that we experienced at Republic were also encountered at other aircraft manufacturers throughout the country. Some aircraft would pitch up during dives and others pitch down. This depended on the geometrical layout of the wing with respect to the horizontal tail.

The solution to this condition was the installation of a wing dive-flap. With this flap, a controlled pullout was achieved at any altitude and Mach number.

There is a reason for the alleviation of air flows over a swept, leading-edge wing in contrast to a straight wing. The flow over a straight, leading-edge wing is constrained to flow in a two-dimensional direction. The swept, leading-edge wing allows the flow to relieve itself, so to speak, by allowing a lateral flow in addition to the two-dimensional flow. This feature represents a three-dimensional flow.

In addition to the help we received from the NACA, we were at liberty to talk to our competitors as to the nature of their problems during compressibility dives and what alleviating devices they resorted to. It took a war to establish such a camaraderie, but it was most helpful in solving our problems encountered in high-speed dives.

As an illustration of this camaraderie, I remember Harrison Storms of North American Aviation being assigned by the air force to help Republic solve a problem that manifested itself in high-speed dives when tip tanks were employed on the wing tips. In that case, wing divergence could occur because of the unstable moments induced by the tip tanks. Divergence did occur, since with incremental increases in speed, the wing would twist more and more to a point where the wing would twist off (the speed at which this occurs is called the divergence speed) because of the continuous increase in air loads being built up on the wing.

To fly faster than 0.80 Mach number, a radical change in the design of the wing had to be made. It was necessary to utilize a thinner airfoil section and leading-edge sweep. This was to occur on our next series of aircraft, the F-84.

Nature gave us many clues as to how to proceed when designing aircraft for high speed. Had we been more observant of the physiognomy of the shark, we should have guessed without resorting to elaborate mathematics what might have been done. The shark is one of the fastest marine fishes and its tail and fins are highly swept, a number of the latter being triangular in shape. When one realizes that water is about a thousand times denser than air, it follows that the sweep-back endowed by Nature to the shark is tantamount to high speed in air.

The foregoing examples suffice to illustrate the care that must be considered in the design of high-speed aircraft. Each design will exhibit peculiarities of its own, and extreme care must be exercised not to permit protuberances that will cause the onset of shock waves, the coalescence of shock waves, and the prevention of flow separation due to compressibility effects.

The plane was initially designed for high-altitude flight to serve as an escort for the medium and heavy bombers. Altitude of flight of up to 40-42,000 feet was attainable with the turbo-supercharger. Because of the limited range of the P-47s, the P-51s eventually took their place. The Jug was relegated to the task of ground-strafing. The pilots were especially impressed by the fire power of the eight .50-caliber machine guns mounted in the wing. Whatever could be appended to the airplane, was. The Jug served in various capacities: in fighter sweeps, attacking airfields, dive-bombing, attacking armored vehicles and supply trains. Other missions were strafing, marshalling yards, bridges, antiaircraft emplacements, and reconnaissance. Pilots recounted how they performed level bombing from above overcasts, guided by ground-controlled radar.

The ultimate high speed that was attained on the P-47 series of aircraft was the P-47J model, which flew for the first time on November 26, 1943. On August 4, 1944, the plane attained a speed of 521 miles per hour in level flight, gaining the distinction of becoming the first propeller-driven fighter to exceed 500 miles per hour. This corresponded to a Mach number of 0.78. With all the modifications that we could muster together, this speed was the maximum we could attain.

At this point I should like to relate my experience when handling the P-47 in flight. I had occasion to fly with our pilots in the P-47 on a two-seat version of the aircraft. On one flight I was asked to take over the control stick. At an indicated speed of around 250 miles per hour, I moved the stick to the right as I was accustomed to do on the Taylor Cub, which I learned to fly and solo in. The cruise speed of the Cub was around 50-55 miles per hour. Not compensating for the difference in airspeeds, I literally scared myself to death. I was in the most embarrassing position imaginable. I was dangling upside down, with my head close to the canopy, being held in place by my seat belt. Fortunately, the pilot was able to right the plane and everything was under control. I was indeed impressed by how small a movement of the stick is required to perform turns in a fighter craft and how rapid the response of the aircraft can become with increase in air speed.

On this basis one can appreciate the situation that prevails at supersonic speeds and the response time associated with high speeds. The pilot must rely more and more on guidance and control devices built into the plane. The response time becomes of such short duration that the pilot can easily overcontrol and miss his target.

7. Cooperation between Industry and NACA

In my relationship with the National Advisory Committee for Aeronautics (NACA), several outstanding qualities characterized the scientific and managerial characteristics of the organization. Its cooperation with industry, dedication to serving and advancing the aeronautical sciences, commitment to producing the highest level of research, and the promulgation of advanced scientific information to the aircraft industry, civil and military, have made this country the leader of the aeronautical world. These outstanding features left an indelible impression on me. Not only was there scientific output of the highest quality but administratively as well.

As a result, the assistance Republic Aviation received during the years of my association with the NACA in 1935-1958 were of inestimable help in improving the performance and reliability of our airplanes. Personnel at Langley Memorial Aeronautical Laboratory (LMAL), Virginia, and Ames Aeronautical Laboratory (AML), California, were dedicated, eager to help in time of need when problems would appear after the airplane entered service. In spite of the modest support of the government in aeronautical research, the quality of work produced was outstanding. Quality of output was the last item to be compromised in times of a budgetary crunch.

There were characteristics of NACA that made it an outstanding organization. As a governmental agency, it ranked first among all other agencies in terms of efficiency, dedication, and willingness to help without undue bureaucratic delay. Conferences were held periodically with industry to update the industrial complex of the latest advanced research results. This enabled industry to design advanced aircraft with more confidence and certainty. The new data was used by manufacturers to conceive of new, more advanced designs.

An eagerness existed on the part of NACA to work synergistically with industry. The NACA was eager to see the results of their research transformed into practical designs as soon as possible. There existed a coalition or partnership with industry, which resulted in a product of ever higher quality. NACA always looked ahead to anticipate what the next step might be in designing new aircraft. By correlating wind-tunnel tests with flight tests, they were in the unique position of helping industry and the military when problems reared their head in service. In this way, NACA was Johnny on the spot. Immediate suggestions were available, which minimized the time delay in finding a solution or mitigation to a particular problem. This was especially important in the case of military aircraft.

LMAL was the oldest center of the three centers under the aegis of NACA. Langley supplied the core of scientists and engineers who later staffed the other centers throughout the United States. Smitty de France was sent to head up the Ames Research Center in Mountain View, California, and Abe Silverstein the Engine Research Laboratory at Cleveland, Ohio.

I remember de France in charge of the largest wind tunnel at LMAL, the thirty-by-sixty-foot tunnel. This tunnel could accommodate full-scale aircraft. He was responsible for the design and construction of most of the major wind tunnels. As a result of his experience, he was the ideal person to head up Ames Research Center.

Abe Silverstein was engaged in the design of high-speed tunnels, and it was he who introduced the concept of the sliding-block, which could vary the throat area of the tunnel, thus increasing the speed of the test section. This permitted great flexibility, and of the various schemes that were proposed for varying the throat area, this arrangement was the most practical.

Abe was not only an outstanding research man but a lover of classical music. On many occasions he would invite me to his home to play recordings of the Beethoven String Quartets. After the playing, we would discuss what Beethoven was trying to portray in his music. The discussion would usually focus on Beethoven's passion for changing the character of music as composed in his day to a more mature, philosophic mode. Existing music was generally written in a style pleasing to the ear rather than conveying a message to the listener.

Langley was the fountain head from which all other laboratories would derive their management expertise. Langley had achieved worldwide recognition for its research work and contributions it made and was making to the aeronautical profession.

In the resolution of our problems with personnel of LMAL, the following names were preeminent: Ira Abbott, Harvey Allen, Al Eggers, John Stack, Bob Gilruth, Hartley Soule, Paul Purser, and Richard Whitcomb. These men were dedicated and knowledgeable in their respective fields of endeavor.

Eastman Jacobs of LMAL was invited to deliver a paper in Rome, Italy, in 1935. Jacobs was engaged primarily in airfoil research and in 1941 was in the process of building a two-dimensional tunnel for the specific purpose of testing the characteristics of airfoil sections. The object of his research was to minimize drag by designing the section in such a way that the flow of air over it would remain laminar over as much of the chord of the airfoil as was feasible. The reasoning behind this centered around the concept of attaining an accelerating flow as long as possible. Turbulent flow sets in when the flow is no longer accelerating. John Stack, Harvey Allen, and Ira Abbott were also engaged in airfoil research.

Stack discovered a similarity between preservation of laminar flow and an airfoil designed for high speed. Maintaining an accelerating flow for the maintenance of laminar flow precipitated the onset of a shock wave. It would appear, then, that an airfoil designed for high speed would also be good as a laminar flow airfoil. This meant pushing the maximum thickness of the section as far to the rear as possible.

It was primarily on the basis of this type of research that Eastman delivered a paper on compressibility effects at an international congress of scientists in Rome, Italy. Italy was represented by its foremost scientists of the day: E. Pistolesi, Giacomelli, Luigi Crocco, and Ferrari. Arturo Crocco, the father of Luigi Crocco, was appointed by Mussolini to be the director of research for Italy.

It was Eastman's judgment that the greatest Italian aerodynamicist was Ferrari. It's of historical interest to note that Pistolesi was the one outside of Germany to call attention to Prandtl's airfoil theory. In his lecture before the Italian Aerotechnical Association in 1921, he expounded Prandtl's theory under the title "The Theory of Vortices in Aerodynamics."

After the lecture in Rome, Eastman went on to Germany where he met and conversed with Ludwig Prandtl, Betz, and others. Prandtl was considered by many the greatest aerodynamicist of the world. Prandtl, at the time, was about seventy years of age and quite spry. From there, Eastman went to England. He visited Cambridge University and went to Trinity College. Trinity was Sir Isaac Newton's alma mater. Eastman visited the class rooms at Trinity and saw the apparatus and lecture rooms that Newton had used and taught in.

During one of the evenings that Eastman stayed at Cambridge, he was invited to attend a meeting of the Trinity College alumni— truly a rare occasion and honor. Needless to say, Eastman was elated. Those present at the meeting were Lord Rutherford, a Nobel physicist who demonstrated that the atom had a core, the nucleus, and who did extensive research in radioactivity; Sir J.J. Thomson, a Nobel physicist who discovered the electron and performed research in the conduction of electricity through gases; Sir James Jeans, physicist and astronomer; Sir Arthur Eddington, physicist and astronomer; Prof. G. I. Taylor, one of the world's outstanding physicists and aerodynamicists, and several other prominent men.

With Eastman was Theodore von Karman who, incidentally, accompanied him on the same ship to Rome. One can well appreciate the pomp and circumstance of the occasion, especially in the presence of the sedate and proper J. J. Thomson.

The story as related by Eastman about the jovial behavior of Rutherford at the meeting bordered on hilarity and defiance of the rigors of protocol. Rutherford was the life of the party. His enthusiasm and joviality permeated the entire group, with one exception. The most sedate and proper J. J. Thomson frowned upon the unseemly behavior of the whippersnapper Rutherford. Eastman said that Rutherford acted more like an American than an Englishman. His behavior probably stemmed from his being part-Canadian. At any rate, Rutherford continued with his antics, much to the chagrin of J.J. It was, after all, undignified to act in an irreverent manner in such an august body and especially in the spirit and memory of Sir Isaac Newton.

Ira Abbott was an experimentalist who conducted extensive research in airfoil design. The results of his many investigations have been published in the "Theory of Wing Sections," in conjunction with von Doenhoff. Abbott, along with others, advocated the concept of designing an airfoil such that the flow over it would be continually accelerating. This would result in less drag, since the flow would be laminar. The problem was to determine the optimum thickness distribution along the chord. It is of interest to note that the design of such airfoil sections in the low-speed range were later found to have desirable properties in the high-speed range. Abbott eventually became the director of the Office of Advanced Research Programs for the NACA.

Harvey Allen was a theoretical aerodynamicist and is best known for his work on reducing heating of a reentry vehicle by the use of a blunt-nosed shape. This was especially useful for the intercontinental ballistics missiles (IBM's). Harvey reasoned that heat transfer to the nose of the vehicle could be attenuated by pressure drag due to the formation of a compression shock wave. He was not content to stop with his contributions in theoretical aerodynamics. He vigorously pushed for applications of his investigations. Harvey, along with Al Eggers, did much of the basic work in hypersonic flows that led to the design and development of the space shuttle.

Al Eggers did extensive work in hypersonic flows and is the author of "Hypersonic Flow." At the time I consulted with Al at AML, he was chief of the new Vehicle Environment Division. He was an ebullient person and full of advanced ideas. His enthusiasm and cooperativeness made for a most informative and instructive meeting. He was instrumental in promulgating this air of ebullience throughout the entire laboratory. Al was most helpful in connection with our work on the aerospace plane. The design involved hypersonic flows and as a result, many factors, for example, such as dissociation of the boundary layer gas and chemical reactions, had to be considered. As a result of these phenomena, enormous heat-transfer rates to the body were encountered. I was aware of the advanced research work Al had been doing in reentry physics and his involvement with the boost-glide missile.

John Stack led the work on the attainment of transonic wind-tunnel data. Transonic flow fields are defined as flows when the local speed equals or exceeds the speed of sound. The problems that we encountered in high-speed dives on the P-47 involved such flows. Pilots would report "dancing shock waves" over the upper surface of the wing, uncontrollable stick motions, buffeting, ineffectiveness, and in some cases the phenomenon of "reversal" which involved motions of the stick opposite to what the pilot expected. It is unfortunate that transonic flow does not lend itself readily to theoretical analysis, since it is a hodgepodge of a mixture of nonstationary flows and a conglomeration of subsonic, sonic, and supersonic velocities. In view of this situation, it was necessary to resort to experimentation. As a result of the problems encountered by military aircraft in high-speed dives, the transonic tunnel became an indispensable tool.

It was known that when the test section of the tunnel reached a Mach number 1, no further increase in Mach number could be attained. This condition was dubbed "choking." The solution to this problem was the incorporation of elliptical slots in the walls of the test section, which permitted an expansion in air flow. This mitigated the choking and the reflection of shock waves from the walls of the tunnel. It was most fortunate that a solution to the "choking" problem was found.

Bob Gilruth along with Hartley Soule were instrumental in developing criteria for acceptable flying attributes of aircraft. The military adopted their recommendations, and as a result, a request for proposal by the military incorporated what was expected of the flying qualities of the aircraft. This led to a diminution of future problems that might be encountered on aircraft once in production. This resulted in great savings of time and money to the military.

Technical competence and a firm commitment to provide data that would produce a military plane second to none was illustrated by Paul Purser and Dick Whitcomb of LMAL. Paul Purser and Dick Whitcomb at LMAL were involved in the design of Republic's F-105. Paul Purser suggested various changes in design based on wind-tunnel tests. Accordingly, many configurations were tested in the tunnel before the final design was selected.

Richard Whitcomb was also instrumental in the design of the F-105 when Republic applied his theory of the "Area Rule." He did much of his experimental research in the transonic tunnel, which led him to enunciate his concept of the "Area Rule." This will be explained in more detail when we discuss the design of the F-105.

When President Kennedy announced that the U.S. would proceed with plans to send a man to the moon, it was natural that Bob would be a prime candidate. This was the case in view of his experience in flight qualities and his extensive experience and innovativeness exercised as head of the High Speed Flight Section at Wallops Island, Virginia. By means of rocket-launched models, he was able to acquire experimental data in the transonic and supersonic ranges. This was accomplished by means of multi-channeling telemetry.

When it came to manned space flight to the moon, it was natural for Bob Gilruth to be named director of the Space Task Group at Langley Field. I say natural, because he had launched a successful campaign against those who maintained that man was an unnecessary addition to an already overly complex design and would be subjected to many unknown hazards in flight. Man would unnecessarily add weight and complication to the design; larger rocket boosters would be required with its attendant increase in cost.

Bob, on the other hand, maintained that no instruments or computers could make on-spot decisions as quickly as man. Instruments could be designed to meet certain requirements, but since the flight to the moon would be fraught with unknowns, man could make last-minute corrections or modifications in the flight plan if necessary. This could not be realized if the vehicle were unmanned. This was proven time and again on subsequent flights of Mercury, Gemini, and Apollo.

In 1961, the Space Agency revised its set-up to speed up the manned lunar project. Bob was then appointed the director of the Manned Spacecraft Center at Houston, Texas.

At LMAL, Bob had been in charge of the Mercury space-capsule flights. These flights were earth-orbiting, precursors of the Apollos, which would take the astronauts to the moon.

Following the Mercury flights, the Gemini two-man flights were scheduled next. These flights were crucial, since extended orbital operations, rendezvous and docking techniques and procedures in space had to be demonstrated. These tests were essential in view of the forthcoming Apollo flights. Takeoff of the lunar module from the lunar surface would entail rendezvous and docking in lunar orbit with the command and service modules.

When it appeared that the booster rockets would be available, a three-man space ship, the Apollo, would be ready to fly around the moon in late 1965. In 1967, the same type ship should be able to land its crew on the moon and bring them back safely. This schedule would beat President Kennedy's "end of the decade" deadline. This was optimistic. It was not until December 1968 that Apollo went into orbit around the moon. This was the beginning of a long series of

Apollo flights that would eventually land the astronauts on the surface of the moon.

It was planned initially that about thirty Apollo craft would be needed. A few years later, the number was cut back to twenty. Some of these would be used for manned and unmanned flight tests on earth and for prolonged manned orbitings of the earth.

The success of landing a man on the moon was due to the leadership of Bob Gilruth and his staff at the Johnson Space Center. The manner in which plans were formulated and implemented constitute an accomplishment and a paradigm of meticulous planning and feasibility of the highest caliber in engineering. The overall program was organized in three phases. Bob realized that the experiments would be fraught with many unknowns and that debugging would be an inevitable outcome of the many flight tests that were scheduled to take place. Flight tests were to proceed methodically, step by step, starting with the Mercury capsule tests. Having determined that sufficient tests had been obtained in phase one, tests proceeded on the Gemini series, the second phase of the program. Finally, the third phase got under way with the Apollo series.

8. Fulfillment of Dreams and Aspirations

During the war years, Thetis and I traveled mostly by train. These were the days of the Twentieth Century Limited; the New York Central; Penn Central; Union Pacific; Southern Pacific; the Atchison, Topeka and Santa Fe, to mention a few. It was slow traveling, but somehow you managed to arrive at your destination, rain or shine. Snowstorms were something to reckon with, especially through the mountain passes.

The trains were especially convenient for overnight trips. The Pullman cars, especially the compartments, were comfortable, but noisy and bumpy. You could feel the unevenness of the rails and the centripetal force when the train was rounding a curve. As you walked from car to car, you could feel the sway of the train from side to side. To maintain one's equilibrium required some acrobatics and a skill in balance. Notwithstanding all the discomforts, the probability of arriving at our destination, especially in wintertime, was greater than travel by the airlines. In those days there were no commercial jets.

Then there was the problem of getting some sleep. When you were finally able to succumb to the rhythm of the train, you could snatch some sleep. When this blissful, soporific moment arrived, the train would inevitably round a curve and you would be rudely awakened by being slammed against the window or the door of the compartment. Or one would find oneself folded at the foot of the berth when the train stopped suddenly. These abrupt movements could not be avoided, whether on ground or in the air. In an airplane, especially in turbulent air, one is subjected to these gyrations.

Then you would straighten yourself out from the coiled position of a cobra, pick up the blankets, and try to fall asleep again as the cobra finds appeasement to the music emerging from the clarinet. The music in our situation was cacophonous, since it was coming from the clanking of the car and the rail. It was quite an adventure, but somehow experienced travelers managed to cope with these small inconveniences. Or was it that one became so fatigued that, no matter what, one could sleep standing up? One consolation was that one could look forward the following morning to a delicious breakfast in the Pullman dining car.

On one of our many train trips, we were scheduled to go to Detroit. This was a special trip for us because I was to present a paper before the Society of Automotive Engineers, War Engineering Production Meeting, on January 13, 1943. The meeting was held at the Book-Cadillac Hotel in Detroit, Michigan, from January 11th to the 15th, 1943.

This was especially exciting for me, since this was the first serious, technical paper I was to present. We arrived in Detroit at 10:30 A.M. on January 13th. Somehow we had managed to get some sleep periodically on the train. The berths were OK, but the clanking of the train's wheels were still reverberating in our ears.

I delivered my paper, "The Determination of Fuselage Moments." After the presentation Thetis was complimentary in the way I delivered the paper and the manner in which I answered the questions. I welcomed the opportunity of being able to answer on the spot. As I told Thetis later, the ability to answer impromptu is an indication of how thoroughly one has prepared his material. If there are too many unanswered questions, then one has not presented the material in a lucid way, thereby leading to many unanswered questions in the minds of the audience. Or the author has presented material that is not crystal clear in his own mind and as a result, he muddles through an explanation not satisfactory to the audience. In any event, Thetis and I were quite pleased with the presentation.

It is of interest to note that the data presented was used years later to solve a problem that occurred on the F-84s. The aircraft ran into difficulties when wing-tip tanks were installed. The tanks were used to house additional fuel to increase the range of the F-84. The tanks were symmetrical, streamlined bodies. Such forms incur unstable moments if not stabilized by a tail surface. This unstable moment was transferred to the wing structure. In high-speed dives, the effect of the unstable moment was most pronounced and of such magnitude that the wing was subjected to additional loads due to wing-twisting. The wing could twist to such a degree that it was in danger of shearing off.

A few cases did occur in flight, and the air force mandated

Republic to solve the problem. The solution to the problem was found by the incorporation of a horizontal tail located at the outboard portion of the tank. The tail surface was quite effective, since it was acting in an augmented flow field due to the wing-tip vortex. As a result, the surface was quite small.

That evening we had a lovely dinner with some of my friends. In particular, there was George Brady, chief engineer of the Curtiss-Wright Propeller Division, with us. I had worked very closely with George on the P-47s. There was much reminiscing. We spoke of the nomadic character of the industry and the necessity of coping with the accelerative changes that constantly took place. To insure one's livelihood, engineers had to migrate often to companies where the contracts had been awarded.

The search for jobs in the aeronautical industry raised havoc with their family life. Wives were tired of packing and unpacking periodically. In some cases there was a prolonged period of time before a new job opportunity would appear on the scene. This created financial problems and would often lead to loss of homes when mortgage payments could not be met. The children of these employees were unhappy to leave their school friends behind. Starting over again in new neighborhoods was, on the one hand, a chore, and on the other, an opportunity to make new friends. Change constitutes challenge and opens up new vistas of challenges and possibilities. It was unusual for engineers to remain at one aircraft company for a number of years. I was with Republic for well-nigh thirty years. This was remarkable. Or was it that Republic had the engineering talent to keep the designs flowing for that long a period?

Having discussed the plight of the aeronautical engineer, George was concerned with his propeller performance on the P-47. He could foresee limitations in its efficiency as forward speeds were increased. As a result, he established a propeller flight-test department under Herb Fisher to investigate all possible configurations. The outcome of such tests has been discussed previously.

A happy day was ushered in on March 8, 1944 when we received a letter from Peter Altman, chairman of the SAE committee for the Wright Brothers award.

The Wright Brothers medal is awarded to the author of the best paper on aerodynamics, structural theory, aeroplane design, or research that is an original contribution. This coveted award originated in 1924 to honor Wilbur and Orville Wright. I was happy but couldn't understand why the paper deserved such merit. To hit the jackpot on my first technical paper was most gratifying. I was grateful for this acknowledgment. The award was the fulfillment of dreams and aspirations of every young aircraft designer. This was my first paper to be published in a professional journal. As the nineteenth recipient of this honor, I received a gold metal, a bronze medal, and a certificate of recognition.

This was a very meaningful award to me, since it was my second recognition from the SAE. The first had come when I was chairman of the Student Branch of the Society of Automotive Engineers at the NYU Daniel Guggenheim School of Aeronautics during my graduate year in 1933 and 1934. In appreciation of my effort at that time, I was presented with a pair of chrome-plated automobile horns that could be mounted externally on a car. This was an accepted procedure in those days for flashy sports cars. At that time I did not have the car for the installation of the horns. However, I still treasure those horns.

The presentation of the Wright Brothers medal was made at the National Aeronautic meeting of the Society of Automotive Engineers at the Hotel New Yorker, New York City. The meeting was held from April 5 to 7, 1944. The actual presentation of the medal was at the gala dinner on April 6th. Peter Altman made the presentation. Thetis was elated when John "Pop" Warner, the venerable statesman of SAE, presented her with a beautiful lavender orchid. She wore it proudly. To this very day, that orchid still maintains its lavender hue of a momentous, unforgettable evening.

I knew John Warner from my student days at NYU. When I graduated in 1933, job opportunities were scarcer than a hen's tooth. Even menial jobs were not to be had because of the lingering depression of the 30s. As a last recourse, I went to Warner for assistance in finding a job. As it turned out, Warner had gone to school with the director of the Langley Memorial Aeronautical Laboratory. He put me in touch with the director of the laboratory. Warner was most compassionate and cooperative. Had it not been for him, I would have given up the aeronautical profession.

The visit to Langley was in vain, because of cutbacks in employment and the budgetary crunch imposed by Congress. Research in times of a financial squeeze is the first to succumb to dire cuts in employment and curtailment and elimination of programs. All was not in vain, however. My father encouraged me to go back to graduate school to pursue my studies. When Thetis complimented my father for making such a prudent decision in later years, his remark was, "What better investment could I have made? I want my children to receive all the education they are capable of absorbing. This is the least I can do to better secure their future."

We were delighted to see my name added to the SAE roll of distinguished engineers who had previously received the award. I was complimented on the progress I had made in the aircraft industry in so short a period of time. I was a student in 1934 and the recipient of the award in 1943. This was a momentous event for me.

The award started a cascade of events. In turn, the Board of Directors of Republic Aviation Corporation presented me with a beautiful, hand-engraved scroll for my outstanding contribution to the field of aeronautical engineering in July 1944. Invitations to lecture before various societies, high schools, and colleges followed. These lectures afforded me the opportunity to counsel the students of the portent of things to come in the future and how best to meet challenges of an incessantly changing environment.

Encouraged by these happenings, I decided to continue writing technical papers. Publishing provides an opportunity to make oneself known to a larger group of people outside one's inner circle of acquaintances. This involves a certain amount of risk to one's reputation, which can be favorable or unfavorable. The degree of success one attains is proportional to the amount the individual is willing to speculate. Speculation can be tempered somewhat by resorting to prologue. When taking quantum jumps in design, however, there is danger of exceeding demand, thereby resulting in lack of funds to pursue the necessary research.

In view of our high-speed flight experiences on the P-47, I published a paper entitled "Analyzing the Aspects of Future Flight" in *Aviation* magazine, November 1945. I shall recount some of the highlights given therein. It was stated that every indication pointed to the need for high-altitude flight, since the tendency for flying at higher and higher speeds in a dense atmosphere results in excessive surface heating, flow instability, and for supersonic flight, a tremendous increase in energy. Problems associated with extremely high-speed flight in an atmosphere would be almost insurmountable. It would appear logical to fly at extremely high altitudes where the density of the atmosphere tends toward zero. It was also conceded that with high-altitude flight, extreme high-altitude operation would usher in new and knotty problems of a rarefied atmosphere and the entrance into a new realm of unknowns when flying at hypersonic and orbital speeds.

Prognostication poses a real challenge and kindles the spirit of innovativeness and imagination. The many technological changes that were occurring in the aeronautical industry in the 1940s led me to believe that we were at the threshold of unusual and significant developments in design of future aircraft and spacecraft. New vistas were being explored, and the future held great promise for those who were pioneers at heart.

As a result of my intuitive feeling for the future, the concept of the aerospace plane was conceived. I realized I was out meandering in the blue yonder, but I was willing to speculate. Curiosity, desire to extend the frontiers of knowledge, challenge and inquisitiveness constitute components of the drive for exploring the unknown.

9. Planning Our Family

When it appeared that the Allies had the upper hand during World War II, we decided to put into action our long-delayed strategic plan. Thetis wanted four children—a pair of kings and two queens. I must confess that's not a bad poker hand, but was that asking for too much?

This was a serious time for planning our family. We did not want to leave this to chance. Through our knowledge of the principles and practice of systems technology, we concluded that by the time our children grew up and were ready for college, we could probably afford only two. We calculated what our future value would be based on savings that we could put aside on a monthly basis. For the record our calculations worked out according to plan.

Our planning and timing were perfect. Our darling, curly-top daughter was born just a few days before "V-E Day" (Victory in Europe Day, May 8,1945). On that day pandemonium broke out in the hospital among the staff, nurses, doctors, patients, and visitors. Everyone was laughing through their tears. What joy! Now we hoped for "V-J Day." Hopefully, this war would end all wars and all mankind would be one in promoting peace, hope, and brotherhood throughout the world. Maybe Beethoven's wish as expounded so aptly in his Ninth Symphony would, at last, bear fruition.

Actually, we should have named our daughter Irene, since she was our "Peace Child" or "Laetitia" (a day of ultimate joy), but we decided against it. Finally, we chose Alceste. Why? We are fond of opera and especially enjoy listening to Gluck's opera *Alcestis*, based on a play by Euripides. When we were expecting our first-born and pondering over what name we should select in the event the baby was a girl, we happened to hear a recording of the opera on the radio. In addition, the story of Alceste centers around a devoted wife who begs the gods to let her die in order that her husband may live. In his dramas, Euripides could make the heartstrings vibrate with passion and emotion.

I also insisted that she should have a second name. Thetis was moved. In addition, her godfather, Sasha Kartveli, gave her a third name—Nina, in honor of Nino, the woman saint who brought Christianity to Georgia in Russia. We were told that she made a cross with two small branches from a tree and bound them with strands cut from her long hair. With this cross she preached Christianity to the Georgians. As a result, she became the Patron Saint of Georgia.

Being pregnant during the war presented some difficulties. There was food- and gas-rationing. This meant that pregnant women were able to apply for some extra food stamps and gas stamps to visit the doctor. Thetis's parents were more than generous. They fed the two of us over the weekend at their home or should I say two plus one anticipated? They also shared some of their food stamps with us. After all, this was to be their first grandchild and everything had to be perfect. It turned out to be that way, believe me! Thetis gained forty-six pounds, and when Alceste was born, she weighed only seven pounds four ounces. Fortunately, by fussing over Alceste, Thetis was able to come back to her normal 110 pounds in one month.

Alceste's birth was quite an experience for me. There I was, sleeping soundly in the middle of the night, when I felt a pat on my shoulder; then I heard Thetis say, "It's time to go." I replied, "Go where?"

When she said to the hospital, then I became excited and started to dress. My first thought was to put Thetis in our trusty old Packard and get her to the hospital fast. Since she was in the capable hands of the nursing staff, my assistance was not needed. Hence I dashed off like a bunny to her parents' home. I needed someone to share my concerns with. The problem was: what strategy should I use to make my presence known? To ring the front doorbell would frighten them at 3:30 A.M. I knew the location of their bedroom.

To wake them up, I resorted to my boyhood days of throwing small pebbles at the window. Mother was the heroic one who came to the window. When she saw me, she immediately surmised what was happening. After alerting them that their grandchild was on its way, I departed. However, Alceste was not to be rushed. She kept us in suspense for some twelve hours. As an aerodynamicist, I was most pleased with the test results. Alceste was indeed a curly-top, fulfilling my expectations of a well-streamlined body, petite though she was (fineness ratio on the high side!).

When our daughter, Alceste, was born, we lived in a small, two-bedroom home. Long Island had a serious housing shortage. This shortage was the result of World War II when one could not build during the war. Even after the cessation of the hostilities, it was difficult to find materials for construction for several years. The demand was great, and there was a slow buildup of inventories.

In addition, it was difficult to find a rental. At least we were able to find a home in a good neighborhood. The house was small for the simple reason that we both loved books and still do. We kept every college textbook we had and invariably bought additional books for reference each semester. Both of us would be unhappy to be without our favorite books. I contributed my share by keeping abreast of new developments in the aeronautical field. Thetis had her share of books on chemistry, biology, psychology, and philosophy. The whole house was filled with books, and no room was left unscathed. Even the bathrooms had their share, for great moments of creative outbursts have no spatial limitations.

Our friends would tell us that we did not live in a home but in a library. They were exaggerating, as friends do, of course. Our second bedroom was really a miniature library on its own merit. We managed to convert the center of the room to a makeshift nursery. Consequently, our first-born was surrounded peripherally with books. This environment probably explains why she also became a bibliophile.

Shortly thereafter, the real estate agent informed us that the house was for sale. Since the house was not large enough for us and our books, we declined his special offer. The other compelling reason was our discovery of termite infestation. One morning, as we stepped into the living room, it appeared that the two-tone beige pattern on the carpet was moving. At first we thought our eyes were playing tricks. Then upon closer observation, we noticed that the carpet was covered with wings and swarming with termites. At first we couldn't understand what had invited them into our home. After a little research on our part, we surmised that this was the season when termites sought new headquarters.

Unfortunately, the basement of the house was partially ex-cavated near the coal-fired furnace. Half of the basement area was left in its natural state of exposed dirt. The basement floor was covered with more wings and swarming termites than the living room. With that much termite activity, the structural integrity of the floor beams was under question. We immediately notified our agent who called his termite exterminator. Now, we were fully convinced that this house was not for us, much to the chagrin of the real estate agent. We started out on our house hunt. Problem number one we encountered was "NO CHILDREN" signs wherever we saw a rare vacancy. This was most discouraging.

In the meantime, the real estate agent continued to knock on our door unannounced to show our home to prospective clients. One day he knocked on our door as Thetis was bathing our baby. For this reason she was unable to respond to his knock. Shortly thereafter, she received a very nasty telephone call from the agent, accusing her of ignoring him and threatening us with legal action. At this point we were at our rope's end and desperate. Thetis would set out each day with our baby in her auto bed in search of property for a house.

Fortunately, Thetis's Dad was a builder, and he allayed our fears by alerting us to landowners who had property for sale. One of these landowners was a descendant of the Gould railroad fame. He was in the process of dividing a large tract of land into parcels of six or more acres. Dad took us over to see these parcels. There were only two left. The hilly land was covered with venerable oaks, tall pines, laurel, and wild flowers. It was a beautiful parcel. At last, our dream had come true.

At first we wondered what we would do with eight-plus acres. However, since we were desperate, we decided to dig into our piggy bank and bought it. As it turned out, it was the finest investment we made. Carrying the property financially was not burdensome, since the realty taxes were nominal. This was because the property was located in a wooded area outside of the town.

Building our home would be no problem for us. Dad and Uncle Gigi were anxious to help. With her trusty old twelve-inch ruler, Thetis started designing our home-to-be. At this point she was grateful to her high school art teacher for showing her how to draw a straight line. When she showed Dad the plans, he said they were feasible and the layout would be functional. He then helped her prepare the second set of plans, which showed the plumbing and electrical connections. Then she proceeded to draw those plans which showed the elevations. Believe it or not! We did not need an architect. The first cost-saving feature was accomplished.

The plans were submitted to the building department, and they were approved. There were no requirements for an environmental report at that time. The area was zoned for housing on one-acre parcels. All that was required was a permit from the building department with certain specifications, such as the size of the house and the lot lines. Life was much simpler in those days. Thetis was complimented on being a budding architect. Henceforth, she was a chemist turned architect. This architectural talent she undoubtedly acquired by osmosis from her dad. When you are desperate, you can surmount almost anything. This flexibility was the result of having a broad background in math, science, and logic.

We feel that there are lessons to be derived from the experiences we encountered in building our home. From the initial stage of felling trees to clearing the land, architectural design, construction, interior layouts, landscaping, and provisions for contingencies are decisive elements that contribute to the attainment of the ultimate goal. It illustrates what can be done with a minimum of cost in conjunction with innovativeness and sweat labor.

At each step of construction, we considered alternatives. The question was usually raised: what if this or that is done? Change is inevitable. How would we take change into account? In this connection, we were guided by the principle that in the event of a necessary change, the cost would be a minimum and the utilization factor a maximum. We knew we would be confronted with changes in our family. With each stage of maturity, the children as well as we would be confronted with new self-imposed conditions. Our aim was to strive for perfection. This we were taught by our parents, and it has always been our goal.

Together with Dad, we drove to our property to decide where to place the house on the hillside. We found the perfect spot in a grove of tall oaks. Our next step was to proceed with the execution of the plans. This was important if we were to avoid any serious delays or conflicts in the scheduling of our work. Weather was also a factor to be considered.

The next day the surveyor came to lay out his stakes. Clearing the area of oak trees was the next big job. Uncle Gigi and I accomplished this by the use of a two-man saw, wedges, and a woodsman's axe. We felt like pioneers in this process. It was hard work, but we enjoyed the exercise. After the trees were felled, the two-man saw and wedges were used to cut the trunk of the trees into six-to-eight-foot lengths. These were in turn split by using the wedges and sledgehammer. These sections of timber were later used to terrace the hill to avoid soil erosion. After a working schedule like this, we could always look forward to a nourishing meal that Thetis had prepared.

When our work was completed, the bulldozer came into action to remove the huge stumps and to excavate the basement. When the cavity was completed, it measured seventy feet by forty feet. The excavator's remark when he had finished was, "What in the world are you going to build? A bowling alley?" He was amazed. Our tremendous basement turned out to be a blessing.

Later on we would put this basement to good use. Our aim was to allow for expansion in the future. In starting from the beginning, it cost us a little more, but it would save on future costs. When the need arose, we compartmentalized the basement into four sections: a huge rumpus room, a work shop, a storage area, and a water pump area.

Since we were located in rural country, there were no city water or sewer lines. As a result we had to supply our own facilities, including telephone poles for our electric power. Areas had to be set aside for well water and waste disposal. Watching the well-driller was an experience in itself. In time we became experts in hydrostatics. Samples that were taken at various depths were of significance, and from these samples, the driller knew when he was about to strike water.

It was also important to go beyond the first strike of water to allow for drought periods when the water table would fall. This would cost more at the beginning to be sure, but it was again a case of minimizing the overall cost in the future. Going deeper in the initial drilling would be less costly than having to drill later on when conditions changed.

Every time the drilling extended a foot, the cash register rang $4.50 for the well-driller. That was an expensive item at the time. Since we were on a hill and a few hundred feet above sea level, it meant we had more drilling to do than our neighbors.

Watching the drilling was expensively painful, We kept waiting anxiously to hear him say "Water! Water!" First there was sand, then clay, then rock, then sand again, etc. One day as Thetis parked our trusty old Packard at the site, the driller yelled out, "Good news! We've struck gravel." Thetis wondered what was so great about gravel. You can't drink it. He assured her that it was a positive indication that water would be forthcoming. It was almost like digging for oil. At any moment, we would be witnessing a gusher, hopefully!

Sure enough! His prognostication turned out to be favorable. A short time later, he did strike water. It was clear, cool, and delicious. To us, this was champagne from the earth. We were grateful that Mother Nature was so obliging. This made us environmentalists, to be sure, and made us respect this beautiful tract of land we had. Our well was over two hundred feet deep. It was a great success, and we were fortunate to have made allowances for contingencies. In the future we were grateful that we always had a good supply of water even during the drought years. Nevertheless, while we were in the process of well-drilling, many of our townspeople would wonder if we were drilling for oil. It was a long period of drilling, and we had everyone intrigued.

The next job was to put in the driveway so that materials could be delivered to the site. With a four-hundred-foot frontage, we had several choices to make as to the design of the driveway. Our designs were then narrowed to two. A decision was to be made as to whether it should be horseshoe shape, spanning the entire frontage, or a direct drive from the road to the garage, with only one access.

In the event of a winter snowstorm or emergency, it could be to our advantage to have two exits to the road. Hence, we concluded that the driveway should be of horseshoe shape. The driveway turned out to be over four hundred feet long, allowing for the curvature and slope. Most of the driveway on the upper section was somewhat level. It was the north and south ends that were on an incline. To prevent soil erosion, these sections required asphalt. One of our concerned workmen remarked, "You're sure gonna have a lot of snow to shovel." Truer words were never spoken! We could count on snowstorms. Long Island is situated on the Atlantic Ocean, just south of Connecticut. This makes it a prime target for snowstorms in the winter and seasonal hurricanes. When the weather is fine, it is a wonderful place to live.

Now with the driveway in place, we could proceed with the foundation. Dad sent over his crew and before we knew it, the foundation was completed. We recognized that the foundation required special consideration, since the loads of the superstructure would be transmitted to very sandy soil.

Furthermore, a solid foundation would prevent differential settlement and cracking of the walls. The basement walls were constructed of cement blocks, and the walls of the house were of cinder-block construction. This meant a heavier load would be transmitted to the foundation than if the house had a frame superstructure.

When the basement was completed, the workers commented that it would make a great dance hall. We had become used to these remarks and even began to enjoy them. At this point, the crew left us, and I was relegated the job of applying tar to the exterior walls of the basement. Thetis maintained this was another way to save some money and get some exercise. I must confess that I wished the basement was smaller. The walls seemed endless. Tarring was sticky, gunky, smelly—you name it and it would qualify for the description of the task.

While the house was under construction, our neighbors and men from the engineering department would drop by. They were interested in the progress we were making and encouraged us with their customary pep talks. Our most frequent visitor was Frank Mullholland. Frank and Uncle Gigi got along well. I must have presented quite a contrast from my three-piece-suit attire at the office to my soiled workman's overalls at the job. This was especially the case when I was tarring or painting. When I was finished with the tarring, the crew returned to put up the cinder-block walls. Again we heard some more comments from our neighbors and well-wishers: "What solid construction!!! Are you building for posterity?"

This remark was not unusual for Dad. With my engineering background and Dad's desire to erect a building that would require minimal maintenance, the final product was an enduring one. It must have been Dad's ancestral genes that made him build for posterity. After all, the Parthenon was still standing in spite of the bombings and attacks made upon it over the centuries. To him, every home and building he undertook was to be a symbol of pride of workmanship and endurance. He left nothing to chance. He was foremost an intuitive engineer.

When the roof rafters were completed, the pine bough was nailed to the peak. This signified a time for celebration. All the workers were treated to a party. Even our neighbors came over to cheer. It was a happy day for all of us!

10. Completing Our Dream Home and Family

When the roof was completed, it was time to concentrate our efforts on the interior of the house. The skeleton of the house was completed. We needed to consider rough plumbing, electrical wiring, firring strips, which were nailed to the cinder blocks every sixteen inches, and sundry other installations before the gypsum boards could be installed. The gypsum boards were nailed to the firring strips, and we helped whenever we could.

Time was of the essence, and our home had to be finished. The real estate agent was threatening us with eviction if we didn't vacate soon. In addition, autumn was already upon us and one could not rely on clement weather on Long Island. On Saturdays and Sundays, we would be attired in our overalls and do whatever we could in the allotted time. The crew were terrific. They realized the predicament we were in, and Thetis and I made it a point not to interfere with their work. I was often criticized for being overly zealous in what I was doing. Where a few nails would suffice, I hammered a few extra as a precautionary measure. Thetis and I were complimented for our meticulousness and precision of workmanship.

It was time for us to consider site-planning for our particular typography. We recognized we had many basic problems, and our next step was to use judgment as to their resolution. Site physiography dictated that we had to grapple with soil, slopes, surface hydrology, drainage, trees and vegetation. Landscaping was of prime importance and a generous back yard was provided, not only for the children and for the sake of a back yard, but to provide for proper drainage. There was an appreciable length of slope behind the house, and we were apprehensive of the action of water percolating through the soil during the rainy season.

Soil on Long Island is sandy, which makes for good drainage. What made the drainage problem uncertain was pockets of hard pan (the Long Islanders' term for clay) or compacted layers of soil running through the sand. That being the case, we assumed conservatively that we had better provide for an impervious soil. The excavation for the foundation of the garage convinced us that we were correct in our assumption. Digging with a pick axe revealed that there was considerable hard pan. Since the garage was adjacent to the house, the back yard was probably interspersed with sandy soil and clay.

Drainage away from the house was provided for by the incorporation of swale. Swale is a term that site planners use to describe the slope of earth away from a building. The grading is higher at the base of the building than some given distance away from the structure. This allows surface water to flow away from the structure by the action of gravity, thus preventing damage to the foundation. There was an additional reason for the swale. In wintertime the ground would freeze to a depth of about sixteen inches. That being the case, provision had to be made for any accumulation of water away from the house. We allowed grading to occur over a distance of some forty to fifty feet.

In providing such an extensive portion of ground, we were confronted with an abrupt discontinuity in the contour of the hill. To cope with this problem, our inventory of logs we had saved when clearing the property came into play. For a distance of about sixty feet, the contour was terraced in four horizontal tiers. Three tiers were planted with Jackson and Perkins' roses. The top row had mock-orange bushes, and in front of the bushes were sweet williams. Thus the slope stability problem was not only solved but an aesthetic wonder was created, thanks to the innovativeness of Thetis. There evolved a beautiful and artistic garden, some sixty feet in length with four tiers. Our functional requirements resulted in an aesthetic accomplishment.

The first winter of our occupancy revealed a fantastic phenomenon. Mother Nature had most gratuitously endowed us with an ice-skating rink. This was an excellent example of serendipity. The ground was frozen from the cold weather. Then we had a snowfall. This was followed by a freezing rain. When we looked out of our back window, we could see the back lawn was covered with ice. It appeared that our inverse-sloped lawn was flooded to a depth of two inches with a layer of snow and ice. Our judgment in providing for swale proved to be correct. It was enough to get out our ice skates and skate on the back lawn. This we never anticipated.

The reason for the inverse slope was to keep the water from seeping through the cellar rear wall. We had accomplished a successful water drainage system, which Mother Nature would freeze for us during the cold, wintry days at no cost to us. What a sport this was! How convenient and what fun for us all! In all the twenty-one-years we were domiciled there, the back wall of the cellar was as dry as a bone. The cellar floor was likewise dry. We had obviously succeeded in our grading of the property. In addition, we were miraculously endowed with a natural ice-skating rink whenever we had a severe winter storm. Nature had bestowed upon us her blessing. This was indeed a cost-effective measure. It not only solved our drainage problem but also gave us many hours of pleasure.

The stark-white, stucco house in a grove of tall green oaks attracted considerable attention. Reporters from newspapers and magazines wanted to do a feature story on the unique architectural features of the design. One of the reporters referred to it as a citadel on the hill. We knew the house was unusual, but we never dreamed it would create so much attention. We spent considerable time requesting that the house not be photographed or featured in any of their papers or publications. We had a young family, and I had a responsible position. Such publicity at this time was inappropriate and inadvisable.

Notwithstanding the above, we could see people from time to time taking photos of the house from the road. We even received letters requesting that if the plans were for sale, people would be willing to reimburse us. These episodes verified the fact that Thetis's role of chemist had been recast as an architect. Her real talent and propensity lay in naval architecture. The house was designed by Thetis with a nautical perspective in mind. This was accentuated with a facsimile of a porthole in the guise of a circular window in the front next to the front door. The house was painted in pure white, and it had no visible roof. From the road it looked like a ship moored to a wharf sans the stacks. It was a prize-winning architecture—unique in the neighborhood. The side and back of the house were planted with forsythias, mock-orange, roses, tulips, daffodils, and crocuses. The front was planted with yews and cedars.

When the house was finally finished and we had settled in our new abode, we had a housewarming party in October 1947. We had succeeded in beating Old Man Winter and were at last freed of the clutches of "Simon Legree," the real estate agent.

We invited my men who worked with me in the aerodynamics department to our house-warming party. A number of the crew came to help us serve. Preparations for the outdoor event included the installation of lights for the evening, firing up the barbecue, loading the large receptacles with chunks of ice, intermingled with soda bottles, beer, and wine.

There were over 125 people—men, women, and children. Our four-hundred foot driveway turned out to be a grand parking lot and a blessing. It was full of parked cars.

The men from my aerodynamics and flight-test department presented us with an electric mandrel and our daughter, Alceste, with a beautiful doll almost as high as she. It was a memorable sight to watch her cuddle and embrace the doll as if it were a living object. What a beautiful memory!

The four-by-eight-foot grill we had built was constructed entirely by us. Its construction is worth recounting. For materials we used moderate-sized field stones that we obtained from a local farmer, discarded steel plates, and angle iron we had purchased from the scrap department at Republic. With these basic materials, we proceeded to lay out the foundation for the superstructure. The walls of the barbecue as well as the chimney were comprised of field stone. The open top portion was then covered with quarter-inch-thick steel plates. This made for a great surface that could accommodate myriads of hot dogs, hamburgers, steaks, etc., all at the same time. All that was needed was a couple of chefs. The finished product with its chimney blended harmoniously with the bucolic environment. Once the barbecue was in operation, most of our guests conglomerated around it. The radiant heat from the barbecue was welcome because of the coolness of the evening. In addition, the aroma of the food enticed our guests.

It was a treat to watch fifty hamburgers and fifty or more hot dogs sizzling on the hot plates that pleasant autumn evening. At various points throughout the back yard—the back yard extended over a thousand feet to the rear—there was no restriction as to what could be done. We located three large galvanized tubs filled to the brim with various soft drinks to moisten one's whistle and drown one's sorrow.

It is interesting to note that when an engineer steeped in the applied sciences marries a chemist who thinks in four decimal places in quantitative experimental chemistry, a unique combination and attraction exists. This uniqueness has kept our marriage harmonious. We think, plan, and look ahead together in every undertaking we embark on. We make it a point to be guided by the philosophy of systems technology to situations that might arise. This bewilders some of our friends and relatives alike. Fortunately, some have been able to comprehend what we are up to and manage to cope with us.

Now that we had a roof of our very own over our heads and no landlord to bother us, it was time to proceed to our next goal. For an optimum family size compatible with the constraints of the necessity of providing for a sibling for Alceste and the financial requirement for their education, the time had come for its implementation. After all, Alceste was not to remain an only child. This would not be fair to her, since she would have no one in her age category to interact with. Our goal was to have two children. We felt the ideal age difference should be three years. This would give the first child a chance to grow and receive its share of attention. In addition, the first child would be better able to understand the advent of another sibling.

Our daughter was excited when she learned that she would have a playmate. We involved her as a partner in all the preparations for the arrival of the newborn. When we bought something for the unborn, she received something as well. She was happy to choose what she thought the baby would like. It's amazing how intuitively perceptive a two-and-a-half-year-old can be when it comes to choices. Alceste was all set to take care of her anticipated sibling.

Fortunately, the world had seen World War II come to an end some three years earlier, and normal peaceful conditions were fairly well established. We did not have to concern ourselves with food and gas rationing. However, Mother still insisted we have Sunday dinner with her. She wanted to make sure her unborn grandchild was properly nourished. Dad enjoyed having his curly-top granddaughter to talk to and show her his flowers in the garden.

Mother need not have been so concerned about the nourishment of her unborn grandchild. On Thetis's visit to the obstetrician, she was shocked to learn she had gained 52 pounds. This was quite an increase on a 110-pound body. Needless to say, the doctor put her on a diet, since the baby was due in August. As she left his office at the end of June, he warned us that he would be sailing on the Bay the Fourth of July. Hence, we should not expect his assistance on such an important holiday. In view of this caveat, it was our hope that the unborn was eavesdropping and would give us its cooperation.

Accordingly, we decided to spend a quiet Fourth of July at home. I was chopping down trees in the back section of our property. Thetis was planting flowers with Alceste's help when suddenly she felt pains. Oh, no! This wasn't what we bargained for. The doctor was out sailing on the sunny Great South Bay. There was no way we could reach him. Thetis got up from the ground and sat down on the nearest lawn chair. I came running over, wondering what had happened. She tried to compose herself and relax. This was not the time to have a baby. Fortunately, the pain subsided after a while. The baby must have shifted to a more comfortable position at her discomfort and alarm.

On July 14th, we were sitting down to dinner when Thetis recognized that the pains were for real. She could not get up from her chair. I called Mother for help. Mother came to take care of Alceste. Dad and I decided that under the circumstances it was best to move Thetis with the chair she was sitting on, lock, stock and barrel. Our trusty old Packard was rolled out of the garage onto the driveway, and after we placed Thetis in the car, away we went.

At the hospital a wheelchair was brought to her and she was rushed to her assigned room. This was not a false alarm—it was for real. The nurses hovered over her, put her in bed, and can you imagine! Asked her to relax—as if she had any control in relaxing when the about-to-be-born was raising a raucous voice and wanted to be released from its watery confinement. She obliged by saying, "Fine, let me have my book, *Explaining the Atom*, from my suitcase. I'll read until the doctor comes." Why she decided to delve into the submicroscopic world when a macro event was about to transpire puzzles me to this very day. Was it because the macro is a result of the initial micro beginning? The day I understand the workings of the human brain and the resultant human behavior, the better I will be equipped to understand some of the odd things we do.

Fifteen minutes later the nurses came dashing in, and off Thetis went to the delivery room. Our holiday baby did not quite make the Fourth of July but settled for Bastille Day. It certainly was a "day of Glory" for us, for now we were blessed with a beautiful baby boy.

Everyone was delighted. There would be another man in the house. The score was now tied—two to two.

Alceste wanted to see her baby brother, but the hospital staff would not permit children to visit the maternity ward in those days. In the meantime, Mother kept her amused. The two of them baked cookies and pies, which I brought to Thetis. When I would come home, Alceste asked if the baby liked the cookies. The baby did, indirectly. Alceste wanted to come to the hospital when it was time for the baby to be transported home. Well, that day arrived. Alceste and Mother waited in the car, while we came out. The nurse gave baby brother to Mother while Thetis gave Alceste a baby doll. She was delighted. This was a gift for her from baby brother.

Alceste wanted to hold the baby. We told her she could when we arrived home. At home Thetis was seated up in bed when Alceste came in. She remembered the promise we made her. "Can I hold the baby now?" She got up on the bed, and we placed the baby in her lap. It was a beautiful and emotional sight. The rest of us were shedding tears through our smiles. She remarked, "It's like my doll, only it moves."

As parents, one thing we always strive for is to show our children we care for both of them equally and they are both our favorites in their characteristic ways. Each one has its own unique personality and beauty. What can be more fulfilling than having a family with each member exchanging love, respect, and care?

11. Living in a Bucolic Environment

Raising a family was one of our fondest dreams. We had been reared in an atmosphere of always excelling in what we undertook, love of knowledge, and to contribute to society in whatever way we could. We were taught to be grateful for what we received and in return for this legacy, to provide in whatever way we could for a better world for the next generation.

With these goals in mind, we set our objectives accordingly for our children. Alceste and Conrad were fortunate that they had their maternal grandparents by their side next door to us. Granddad was a universalist and could adapt to any change that came along. He was a self-taught engineer, developer, book publisher, and jack-of-all-trades, and no task was too sophisticated or menial for him. In the Great Depression of 1929, he had lost his fortune and had to survive by doing various jobs to keep his family intact.

I did forget to mention that during World War I he epitomized the old-fashioned ice-cream parlors where one could get homemade chocolates, ice cream, and other homemade goodies comprised of chocolate and ice cream. These were the days before the advent of TV. On Sundays one of the greatest treats for the family was the trip to the confectionary shop in town. One had many choices to choose from elaborate ice cream desserts, such as banana splits, hot fudge sundaes, creamy chocolate and vanilla sodas. Some of these desserts were so large that two people could share them. It was a special treat for an engaged couple to share a "sweetheart dish" following a walk through the park.

Grandma was a scholar versed in classical Greek, and all of us were indoctrinated to the philosophies of the ancients—Socrates, Plato, Sophocles, Euripides, etc. In addition, she was the guiding light in morals and ethics, not only in their meaning and interpretation, but also in their practice.

Thus Grandma was the apotheosis of virtue, of duty to family and community, and of upright living. With such a background, the children would always adhere to these principles. Under trying circumstances, they would consult with us and say, "But Giagia or Papou admonished us so-and-so. Are we correct in our interpretations of what they told us?"

With this background, the children had excellent teachers covering all aspects of life—the academic, the ideal, the practical and the hard knocks of life, and how to maintain one's disposition, faith, and hope in an hour of desperation. The education one receives at home is of paramount importance, for it sets the cornerstone for all future activities and actions. One realizes and appreciates what it takes to accomplish what one is striving for. The principle of "sweat before achievement" was one of the cardinal rules enunciated by their grandparents. One must always strive for *arete* (excellence) as the ultimate goal.

It was wonderful that Dad and Mother had purchased the adjacent parcel to us from Gould. They built their home there. It made for expediency in more ways than one. This was especially the case when we had to go on trips. Our homes were some two hundred feet apart, and there were no neighbors between us. This meant we could visit each other on foot without resorting to the use of the automobile. It also meant that when things became dull at our home, the children could go to Mother's. Vigilance was no problem, since she could easily see the children coming down the path from her kitchen windows.

Mother was a great philosopher and teacher. She epitomized ideology, morality, and duty as a citizen. You can imagine how delighted she was to philosophize and rationalize with her grandchildren. Dad, on the other hand, was a pragmatist and accomplisher. Even though he did not receive a formal engineering education, he practiced and applied sound physical principles. He was guided by "common sense" and ethics. If something didn't make sense, a red flag went up in his mind. He would check and double-check with other people to obtain more information before making a final decision. He had learned early in life that "haste makes waste." He was not one for increasing the entropy of the universe if he could help it.

When I entered the family, he would frequently ask me for my opinion. On the other hand, he was one for taking calculated risks.

This is how he made several fortunes in his lifetime. I especially admired his one outstanding quality—being a universalist as an entrepreneur. He could undertake and surmount any business adventure he went into—from ice-cream making to the printing business to building to whatever would bring in revenue in time of need. This quality blossomed full force during the Great Depression years. His disposition was such that he maintained his "cool," and in the event he had to start over again, he would readily roll up his sleeves without too much ado and fanfare.

He loved to show our children how to make things. When our son was ready for a haircut, he wanted Dad to cut it. Conrad considered him the *"barbiere di qualita."* As Connie would say, "Papou is my favorite barber. I want him." Dad was elated that his grandson thought so highly of him. Added to Dad's long list of accomplishments, he was now ranked as an illustrious tonsorial artist! Dad would drop everything to accommodate his grandson. The haircutting took place on the patio behind the house when the weather was warm. At a distance we could see Conrad draped in a cloth with Dad hovering over him ever so carefully, taking well-maneuvered snips with his shears. There was a mutual love established as a result. There were times when Dad and Conrad went to the barber together. We shall always be grateful for the wonderful companionship and training our children had acquired from their grandparents. It was this kind of nurture, more than anything else, that have made our children what they are today.

The children always enjoyed going to Dad's office and to his projects. It was exciting to see houses being built and the hustle and bustle of construction. Disputes among workers and spot decisions that had to be made intrigued and fascinated the children. Witnessing this type of activity in their formative years has helped the children in their later years in their professions. They relished going to Dad's office where they could sit behind a big desk and with pencil in hand pretend they were managers. This too, rubbed off on them. They have grown up to be good managers.

Living next door to one another was a marvelous arrangement for both families. Baby-sitting was no problem. At moment's notice, we could rely on the folks. This was especially important for us because I would very frequently have to go on business trips at the drop of a hat. There was always someone to take care of one another's house when one went away. We felled trees together, shoveled snow together, and did sundry other chores together. In case of an emergency, we could count on one another. People wondered how we managed to get along so well. It was easy. There was mutual love and respect. As Mother would always say, it takes the one hand to wash the other.

Holidays were enjoyable and events we always looked forward to. In anticipation of Christmas, we would install lights mounted on a bell structure that we built. With Uncle Gigi's help, the entire assembly was hoisted into place in the cluster of four tall oaks in front of our house. Strings of lights would decorate the trees and bushes in front of the house. After this we would go down to Grandparents' house to help Uncle Gigi and Dad put up the big star on the balcony in front of their house.

On Thanksgiving Day, we could smell the delicious aromas of the turkey being roasted in Grandmother's kitchen from our house. It was a prelude of the goodies to come. At the appropriate time, we would go down to Grandparents' home for the festivities. In the meantime, I would work up an appetite by raking up leaves and trimming dead branches. By the time the turkey was served, I had a voracious appetite. All at the table wondered how I could ask for a third helping.

It was especially awe-inspiring when a pristine blanket of snow covered the land between us, with the attendant peace and tranquillity that accompanies snow. Snow somehow has a dampening effect on the propagation of sound. Tranquillity and peace of mind transcend the environment. But, alas! This ethereal, chimerical feeling comes to an abrupt ending when one picks up the snow shovel and begins shoveling.

From time to time, as we walked down the pathway, we would look behind us to see our footprints in the snow. It was fun trying to correlate the present with the past. Try as hard as we could, we could not predict what was in store for us in the future. At night we would return with flashlights in hand to make sure we did not stray too far from the pathway. In addition, we had to warn the deer, red fox, and squirrels on our property that we were out walking.

The animals would be the only legitimate traffic we could encounter on our way to our home. However, every now and then, we would flash our light off into the distance to see if there were any prowlers lurking about. At times we felt like intruders of the animal kingdom on their God-inherited land. Our guilt-feeling was not too pervasive, since there were several miles of uninhabited wooded area for them to roam behind us. We felt like good environmentalists who had provided ample refuge for them. During heavy snowstorms, we would cast outdoors fruit and bread for them. We knew they responded by the tracks they left behind in the snow, sans the edibles.

Rather than carrying a flashlight with limited capacity when walking down to Grandparents' house, we decided to set up lights between the two houses. To accomplish this task, I visited the scrap department at Republic Aviation and was able to pick up several industrial ceramic lamps about twelve to fourteen inches in diameter. They made excellent reflectors and could accommodate bulbs up to a thousand watts. This set-up made for a deterrent for animals as well as prowlers. Reflectors were mounted on three of the trees in such a way that a maximum of overlapping would result. In addition, we had an electrician make up a string of lights to span some hundred feet. During Christmas time, colored bulbs of various colors were installed in place of the clear bulbs. In this way we could switch on the lights when we had a barbecue or wished to walk down to Grandparents' house.

As a result of our electrical consumption, we became valued customers of Long Island Lighting Company. Our bills doubled and sometimes tripled. Several neighbors wanted to know if we were shareholders of LILCO in view of all the lights. When we assured them that we were and that we had purchased additional shares in view of our recent installations, we took them by surprise and no further questions were asked. We were so convincing in our rebuttals that some of the neighbors told us later that they had invested in LILCO.

It wasn't unusual to walk into a deer at night. They were basically friendly and enjoyed the apples on our dwarf trees we planted in our back yard. They managed to get to most of the apples before we did. They would usually beat us to the draw, since they were not as finicky as we were as to the degree of ripeness. They were content to eat them in the unripened state.

We were surrounded by tall oaks, and it was necessary to remove some of them to landscape the front and back yards. Being in a wooded section with no fire department in our neighborhood, we decided to provide an open space of thirty to forty feet around the perimeter of the house. This necessitated removing more trees, but we felt it was a prudent, precautionary, fire-safety measure. The two-man saw was great for felling trees. However, cutting them into logs for firewood presented a new challenge. The answer was simple. What we needed was a buzz saw, an engine, and a belt system to operate the saw. After inquiring of several people at the plant, we finally found a second-hand cement engine that used an evaporative cooling system. It was a single cylinder putt-putt of ancient design, but it would suffice.

Our first task was to lay the foundations for both the engine and the buzz-saw platform structure. Given the recommended revolutions per minute of the sixteen-inch-saw blade, we had to determine pulley sizes and belt length. This being accomplished, we assembled all components and started our putt-putt.

It was quite a thrill to buzz through a twelve-inch diameter oak log with the greatest of ease. Being in a rural district, one had to be prepared for all types of emergencies. We realized we were living in the path of hurricanes, and during the months of September through November, we were subjected to them. Winds as high as 125 miles per hour were to be expected. External power lines were vulnerable to freezing rains, and power outage during winter was quite common. Accordingly, a supply of firewood was a sine qua non. All equipment in our home was operated by electricity, including the cooking range. This meant no heat, no water, no lights, no cooking, but a complete state of inoperativeness. The problem of providing standby electricity loomed high in our minds.

This was a decision that we faced later on when we were more firmly entrenched in our new home. Living in a rural area has its amenities, but one must also consider what alternatives should be provided in emergency situations, especially when one has to consider a young family. It kept one on one's toes all the time. At least with firewood, we could heat the house and cook in the two fireplaces.

In December of 1948 we were actually stranded in a snow-and-ice storm, which lasted over a week. Our planning was put to the acid test. Fortunately, we had the firewood to keep us warm. With two youngsters, there was only one thing to do: move lock, stock, and barrel into the living room as close to the fireplace as possible to keep warm. The living room had four sofas, two of which were sofa beds. This would accommodate Alceste and us. On the other hand, Conrad was a baby, so we moved his crib into the living room. We lived, slept, and ate in our spacious living room. This mode of living gave us a great deal of anxiety and convinced us that a standby generator was our next priority item.

Food was cooked on sterno stoves. Meals were simple. This was a period of survival, and epicurean dishes were out of the question. We were grateful that we had made basic provisions for such an emergency and to be able to survive under these circumstances. Soups and canned foods were the order of the day. Fortunately, our pantry was well stocked for just such an emergency, so we were able to exist. When the storm would let up, Uncle Gigi's pickup truck would maneuver through the snowdrifts, thereby opening up our driveway. This permitted us to get some bottled water and rations. Finally, on the tenth day, electric power was restored to our area. During the ten days of confinement that we had endured, we were reminded of the hardships and isolation that our Eastern pioneers suffered.

The snow plows finally cleared away the snow from the streets. What delight and jubilation we experienced when we could resort to all the modern conveniences we were accustomed to. We could cook again on our Westinghouse electric range, could hear the water pump replenishing the empty water storage tank, were able to take a shower, hear the furnace blower in operation with its characteristic high-frequency sound, and turn the lights on again. We had transcended from the Dark Ages to living again in the twentieth century. This experience reminded us of all the things we take for granted, not fully appreciating the advances made by science and engineering.

After this experience we realized that since we were to be at the mercy and capriciousness of hurricanes and the inclemency of snowstorms, we would have to resort to investing in a standby generator. Living in an all-electric home was great, but this meant putting all your eggs in one basket. Should the basket overturn, all reliance on eggs was gone. When we would lose our electric supply, we automatically reverted back to the "horse and buggy days," "the good ole days." There were times when even the town could not keep up with the problems the storms wrought up.

A second-hand, war-surplus, stand-by generator was purchased and located in the garage. For ease of movement, we built a platform of two-by-six-inch planks mounted on wheels. Before purchasing the unit, we calculated the minimum amount of energy that would be required of the generator. We made several compromises: the water pump and electric range would not be put on simultaneously, a bare minimum of lights in the house would be operative, the fuel-oil furnace would be operated when all other units were turned off. In short, we would make sure that units would not be run in parallel but sequentially. Under these conditions we compromised on a five-kilowatt output generator. The electric range could not be run on 220 volts since the standby unit was designed for 110 output. This restriction, however, was not too severe. All necessary connections from the generator to the electric panel in the cellar could be made easily when the need arose.

Being in a rural area imposed conditions on living that are foreign to urban life. Local farmers would help clear some of the driveways with their tractors adapted to accommodate a snow plow. People living in the outer fringes of the town learned to survive by helping one another. It was a beautiful camaraderie that brought tears and laughter. And in times of emergency and isolation, we'd always say, "And this, too, shall pass."

One of our favorite hobbies was working with wood. We envisioned a rumpus room in the cellar, furniture that would be custom-tailored to meet our specific requirements, a permanent layout for the ever-expanding Lionel train system we started years ago, and sundry other projects. This meant we would need a table saw, planer, electric drill, vise, sander, etc. With this equipment we set about making furniture. For the living room, we built two six-foot window seats. The cushions were of heavy vinyl so that the children could kneel on them and look out of the rectangular picture window. We actually built two corner units, four end tables, and a long coffee table. This activity kept us home with our children during the weekends and holidays. It was fun for all. The furniture not only had a functional use, but helped fill in the many voids that were prevalent. Being creative and productive is reward in itself, the transformation of an idea into a functional object.

As the children grew older, they were helpful in handing us small tools, nails, brushes, or whatever we needed when we called out for them. It was an apprentice period and a learning experience for them to work synergistically for the benefit of all concerned. An enjoyable time was had by the four of us. At times Grandparents, Uncle Gigi, and even neighbors would stop by to see what our latest project was.

When we were finished with the living room, replete with furniture that met our requirements, we progressed to the library. The library needed a desk. The thought of constructing a desk with drawers, etc., was too complicated for our amateur techniques. The next best thing to do was to find a second-hand desk and restore it to our specifications. Again I made use of the scrap department at the plant. I found a solid oak desk six feet long and three feet wide with seven drawers. The top was in great shape. All it needed was a sheet of quarter-inch plate glass. However, the three sides were scratched deeply. No problem! This could be remedied easily by serrated plywood with the ridges running vertically.

The handles on the drawers of the desk were either missing or half off. We removed the remnants of the handles, sanded the wood carefully, and designed new handles made of steel tubing one-inch in diameter, eight-inches in length, chromium-plated, with translucent plastic inserts at the ends. The handles were a labor of love, very innovative and gave the desk "real class." The final result made us very pleased with ourselves. It was our pride and joy, in addition to being downright practical.

The desk was placed in the library. This section of the house constituted my inner sanctum sanctorum. The library was off limits to the rest of the family. They respected my privacy and did not interfere while I was working. Since the master desk was off limits to the rest of the family, it was only equitable that desks should be assigned to the rest of the executives of the family corporation. Accordingly, Thetis was provided with the walnut desk that I used to have. At her request it was relocated near the kitchen in the all-purpose room. This was a convenient location, since Thetis spent a good deal of her time in the kitchen.

This room was a combination laundry room, sewing room, and sundry room. We installed wall cabinets on one side of the room, which contained cookbooks and other sundry kitchen utensils and equipment that were used occasionally. Any household item that couldn't be assigned to any room of the house was delegated to the all-purpose room, which served most adequately as a catch-all storeroom. We also provided desks for Alceste and Conrad in each of their bedrooms. Now, everyone was happy and content.

As we admired the library with its renovated "swanky" desk, I exclaimed, "Now all we need is a drafting table." Before you could blink an eye, a sturdy eight-foot drafting table was in place in front of the nine-foot picture window. The light from the window was just perfect when the sun shone. What a way to contemplate and schematize one's thoughts and then look through the picture window for divine inspiration. It was great relaxation to look at the oak trees in the distance.

We had one up on Ulysses. Homer, in the *Odyssey*, states that Ulysses stopped off at Dodona to receive divine advice as to how he might best return to his native land of Ithaca, since he had been absent for such a long period of time. The oak trees in nearby Dodona were reputed to give oracles by the sonorous sounds emitted by the vibratory motions of the leaves. Just imagine! All we had to do was to watch our oak trees in the front portion of our grounds for our divination. The story of Ulysses inspired us to name our property the "Tomaroaks." Mount Tomarus is the mountain near Dodona.

It wasn't long thereafter that my older six-foot drafting table ended up in our son's bedroom. This infusion of desks and drafting tables caused some of our engineering friends to say, "You just can't get away from your office." Or, "Do you plan to start your own firm at home? What gives? If so, keep us in mind."

When Alceste was born, I had decided that we should have a train encircling the Christmas tree. This would be something for not only our daughter to enjoy but for all of us. Just imagine! The lighted tree with a whistling, smoke-emitting, choo-choo train running around it. This action on my part was a manifestation of my boyhood frustrations coming to the forefront. As a boy, I had wanted a toy train, a Lionel, but Father ordained otherwise. Even when I had saved enough money to buy one for myself, Father emphatically said, "No." In his opinion it was a waste of money that could better be spent on books of learning. Even though my father was basically a generous man, he had assimilated into the New England environment and had become proselytized into the Connecticut Yankee way of economizing. Money was to be spent wisely and prudently. Pleasure-seeking activities at the expense of one's education were taboo.

Well, before long, there was an additional locomotive with its corresponding set of cars. We progressed from the steam locomotive to the diesel. The fun would begin on December first when both Lionel sets of trains would be unwrapped from their packings. The trains were laid out in the living room and the adjacent library. In so doing, the children and I were encroaching upon Mother's lenience and patience by permitting us to lay out the track in her neatly arranged rooms. The tracks and switches were set out carefully around the living room between the sofas and chairs, under the coffee table, around the end tables, into the library, around the massive desk, and in between the legs of the drafting table. There I was with the children, running trains and switching the locomotives from the living room into the library. It was a beautiful family picture to behold. This went on even after the Christmas tree was removed from the living room.

To Thetis it appeared that there must have been a jungle of track no matter where she looked. One had to tiptoe ever so carefully to avoid coming in contact with track. We had to warn our guests to tread cautiously as they walked into the living room. After a while they got into the swing of things. The train set-up was a great way to transport peanuts and crackers on the flat cars to the guests sitting at various points in the room. They enjoyed the thrill of selecting their choices as the cars went by. It was akin to snatching a ring as one approached the outstretched arm housing the rings on the merry-go-round.

When February would come around, Thetis would start her negotiations with the triumvirate—she now had an association of three that comprised a coalition. This necessitated great diplomacy on her part. She would start asking ever so tactfully and politically permission to put the trains back into their boxes, so that they could rest until next Christmas. When the children would hear her request, she was a "persona non grata." This situation was a typical case of granting a person an inch to be followed by a request for an extension to a mile. She would give in for a few weeks. Then, by the Immortal Gods, on February 28th, Thetis would literally put her small foot down and say, "That does it! No more until next Christmas. What's fair is fair. I compromised by extending the deadline by two weeks. Now it's your turn to compromise."

Ever so gently we would start packing the trains to store them away for next Christmas. The atmosphere was one of sadness akin to a funeral dirge. Thetis felt downright terrible. She was a spoilsport. Her reputation for being kind and understanding was in jeopardy. What to do to resolve this situation? What to do to arrive at an overall, compromising decision? After all, the children by this time recognized us for making prudent decisions.

A provocative thought entered our minds. We had a tremendous cellar that wasn't being utilized to its fullest extent. Then emerged a bright idea. Eureka! Why not a playroom in the basement? In this manner we could always enjoy the thrill of operating the trains all year around.

Now the triumvirate changed membership. Thetis was now on the side of the children. They had to convince me that they would all help in the construction. With the circular saw in place, and the required ancillary equipment at hand, the playroom eventually became a labor of love. Thetis's reputation, above all, would now be restored.

This was a project we had to undertake on our own. Dad and Uncle Gigi couldn't be counted on since they were knee-deep in their own work. To hire outside help would be too costly. The decision as to how to proceed was obvious—on our own with the assistance of the newly formed triumvirate.

We set aside 60 percent of the cellar area for the playroom. The walls were lined with horizontally placed tongue-and-groove knotty pine siding. Fortunately, the wood was not very hard and nailing into the firring strips was not a problem. The siding was given a limed finish to brighten the room. The huge brick fireplace with heatilator at the other end of the play room would provide heat.

It was quite a job for both of us to work on our knees as we laid the vinyl tiles on the floor. It was a slow process, since we had to lay each tile separately. Special care had to be exercised to make sure that each tile lined up exactly. Had we allowed small misalignments to occur in the beginning of our layout, we would have been in serious error by the time we reached the end. Each misalignment would compound the error to a point where we would have been appreciably off our finishing point. This was a precarious undertaking, as we soon found out as we proceeded. After a while of this fastidious work, it felt as if we had laid thousands of tiles. At this point in time, we all felt the playroom was overly ambitious. However, after it was all finished, we were glad we didn't change our original plans. We were all very proud of the work we had accomplished. Nonetheless, we needed approval of the quality of work we had done. When Dad came in to check on our progress, he gave us his stamp of approval. He was so impressed by what we had done that he offered us a standing job if we ever needed it.

Now that we had a playroom, with one corner devoted to the trains, we still had a problem of filling in the remaining void. We had stored away in one corner of the basement our old-dining room set, which looked forlorn and discarded. After several flashes of ESP between Thetis and me, a bright idea came to fruition. Why not transform the buffet and server into a bar? Our first step was to attach the buffet and server with appropriate lumber. The outside and sides were covered with the same knotty pine that was used on the basement walls. This made for continuity and a harmonious blending with the surroundings. We now had a twelve-foot bar.

The top was lined with a light pine-colored formica. Storage space was automatically provided for by the compartments that we had inherited in the buffet. A cornice was incorporated around the formica to allow our bartender for the evening to safely slide the glasses down to where the guests were located. The front of the buffet and server now served reverse roles. They were now at the back of the bar. This was handy because these cabinets could be used to store wine and liquor. The drawers contained towels and miscellaneous bar equipment. Finally, to finish off our chef d'oeuvre, we incorporated a rail running peripherally around the base of the bar about a foot off the floor. Our guests could now relax in comfort by resting their feet on the rail as they imbibed. The bar-rail was fabricated from leftover two-inch galvanized pipe painted in gold color.

We still had ample space for additional furniture. For recreation and exercise, we decided upon an eight-by-eight-foot Ping Pong table that was made of two four-by-eight-foot compressed wood panels mounted on wrought-iron legs placed side by side. Even though these dimensions were greater in width than the standard tournament table, we wanted to be able to rearrange the tables so as to have a dining table of sixteen-by-eight-feet for parties. This set-up was in line with our desire to have multifunctional furniture coupled with flexibility and innovativeness. This also provided for those Ping Pong players who would be challenged on a sixteen-by-four-foot table.

Whenever we had guests, we would announce that there were options open to them as to where we could dine. An inspection of the playroom with all its spaciousness, non-formality, a unique bar with bar stools, and a huge table thoroughly convinced our guests there was but one place to assemble. The bar set-up next to the sixteen-by-four-foot table made for an ideal and propinquant set-up.

A platform structure was erected for the Lionel trains. Three sections of four-by-eight-foot plywood, half an inch thick, were arranged to form an "L"-shaped table, mounted on two-by-four-foot legs. This arrangement was approved by all. Should we tire of this configuration, we could easily add to or set up other arrangements. Everyone was delighted with the flexibility of the layout. To provide for rapid rearrangements, we resorted to clamps to tie the various sections together, rather than resorting to nails or screws. We spent many a happy and joyous hour arranging various combinations of track, switches, tunnels, bridges, and elevated structures. The various arrangements made for versatility, imagination, and innovativeness, not only for the children, but for us as well.

As time went by, we acquired four locomotives, two coal burners, one diesel, and the Santa Fe. What a relief! There was plenty of room for expansion if need be without imposing constraints upon Thetis. The train layout was now a permanent fixture in our home. There was no need to pack and unpack the trains each Christmas season. In addition, the family could run the trains whenever they wished, subject to constraints upon the children. As parents we took care not to allow the children to become addicted to the trains or the TV. We made it clear to the children that overindulgence in whatever undertakings one engages in was not to their advantage and could easily be to their disadvantage. We recognized, however, that it was great relaxation for all of us if one recognized mediocrity.

Christmas and Easter were happy times. Invariably there was snow on the ground to enhance the beauty of our rural area. The children would ask us to drive them through the residential areas and towns to see the beautiful Christmas lights and decorations at night. The multivariate colored lights made for kaleidoscopic patterns in the snow and eerie formations of patterns through icicles. There was tremendous neighborly pride and competition to have the most beautiful Christmas display. It was a challenge that grew keener with each passing year.

One Christmas Conrad received the green wagon he wanted. It became his favorite toy. This gave him the opportunity to help Grandma and Mother. He became a self-appointed messenger, making his appointed rounds between the two houses when the occasion would arise. There were so many things he could do with it. He would run errands between our home and his grandparents. He was fond of collecting insects, bugs, caterpillars, red carpet ants, and other specimens in jars and transporting them in his green wagon. The collection of specimens was quite a hobby for him. He would have Grandmother and Thetis save glass jars for him. He insisted that we clean the jars well. These specimens needed a sterile environment. Then he would take the metal tops of the jars and punch holes in them in our workshop in the cellar. "Why?" we asked. He was dumbfounded and flabbergasted when we first asked the question. "Bugs need air to survive, just like we do," was his reply. We were now convinced he had the correct scientific approach in his method.

One day Thetis heard Conrad screaming for help. As she ran out of the house, she wondered what had happened to him. There he was, standing by a huge oak tree with an open jar posed up against the tree. "Hurry, hurry," he cried. "Are you hurt?" she answered. "No, I want to save this bug." "Do you really need it?" Thetis asked, staring at an entomological marvel. It was a colorful insect some two inches long and a half-inch in diameter with wings. Frankly, she could have dispensed with it.

"Please hurry. I dropped the cover. It's next to the tree. I want to close the jar," Conrad responded, somewhat frustrated and annoyed with her delay in reacting. Well, they finally managed to capture the critter in the jar. It took Thetis a while to regain her composure. Nevertheless, it was really interesting to watch Conrad collect his specimens with such zeal and enthusiasm to create the proper environment for their survival in vitro with soil, leaves, twigs, flowers, and water, depending upon where the specimen was found. He instinctively recognized the importance of preserving their local environmental surroundings. This behavior on Conrad's part was a harbinger of his passion for learning and love for research. We began to think we had a Charles Darwin in our midst.

Actually we weren't too far off in our prognostication of Conrad's future profession. His love for this type of research led him to neuroanatomy and surgery. We kept him supplied with jars and hoped he would not get stung while on his hunting expeditions with his green wagon.

Currently, every day we go into our garage, we are reminded of Conrad's green wagon. Our garage houses Conrad's green Vega, the first car he bought on his own. This is the car he drives when he comes to visit us. Even though it is old, it is kept in tip-top condition, a beautiful reminder of that green wagon that carried his jars of specimens. With the passage of time, Conrad transferred from foot-power to horse-power.

Our daughter, Alceste, also enjoyed the trains. It was fun to watch the family gathered around the train table. However, Alceste always showed promise of being a good dancer. When she had started to walk, her steps had a distinctive rhythm. As parents we recognized this capability and realized that we should plan to develop this inclination in the future. A few years before she went to kindergarden, we enrolled her in a ballet school.

This increased Thetis's motherly duties. There were tutus and costumes to sew. For a while she became a stage mother. Grandmother was concerned that we were creating a ballerina. We assured Grandmother that was not our goal. Alceste needed to release her energy in her own creative way. It would also develop poise and grace in her body movements. In addition, dancing came naturally to her.

To this very day, those who have danced with her comment on her well-coordinated dancing steps with her partner. Grandmother should not have been concerned; she herself was a good folk dancer. In fact, both grandmothers were terrific social dancers. Alceste had other interests as well—writing, the clarinet, histrionics, managerial proclivity. All these characteristics were fostered first at home, then in high school, and finally college. Each rung in the ladder of experience led to the next higher rung.

Not only did we enjoy and cherish the companionship of our parents next door but the creatures of Nature as well. Nature provided us with companions that we enjoyed feeding and providing whatever shelter we could during inclement weather. We had deer, chipmunks, squirrels, a red fox, rabbits, and birds. Wildflowers were plentiful—violets, lady slippers, daisies, buttercups, bachelor buttons, oak and pine trees, dogwood trees, mountain laurel, blueberry bushes, and garden snakes on our property. All these were an integral part of our property and scattered throughout the many acres. This was Nature's way of extending her amiability and graciousness to us. To us it portrayed sheer beauty, tranquillity, and peace of mind. With such a background, one cannot help but become an environmentalist.

We came to live harmoniously and symbiotically with the environment and creatures of Nature. In due time, deer would come to within such a close range that we could toss them bread and food. We befriended and aided the birds the same way. We had sparrows, bluejays, warblers, scarlet tanagers, red-winged blackbirds, and towhees on our back porch, waiting for their share of bird seed and bread. We had developed such a rapport that when they did not find anything on the porch, they would make it known to us by their chirping and warbling that we were being negligent in our duties and responsibilities to the creatures of nature. Even when we would open the back door to toss them food, they became so accustomed to us that they did not fly away but stood firm in their demands. When the children were sick in bed, one particular towhee would perch on their bedroom window waiting to be hand-fed. This was our crowning experience with Nature.

One of our precious little rabbits loved petunias. He would not only eat our petunias but Grandmother's as well. The squirrels were ingenious rascals and would manage to find the crocus bulbs we planted. If the squirrels didn't find the bulbs, the moles would take up the slack. They were all considerate, however, since they left a few for us to enjoy when in full bloom. Consequently, we had to plant extra bulbs for our pleasure. Competition was quite keen between the animal kingdom and us. Even though we were annoyed at times, it was great fun. We fully appreciated the role Nature assigned to them to preserve order and balance among the various creatures.

This, then, was our memorable and indelible experience with the bucolic environment we enjoyed and cherished so much.

12. The Education of Our Children

Our area was formerly a wooded section interspersed with several farms and residential homes on large parcels of ground. It was basically a rural community, which was just beginning to grow when we first moved into the area. Residential plots had to be at least one acre. This attracted the professional class who desired to live away from New York City, yet be close enough to commute to work within ninety minutes. The opening of the Long Island Expressway accelerated the change in demographics. More and more developments appeared on the scene. Farmlands were absorbed by developers and subdivided into acre plots for residential purposes.

In addition, firms like Republic Aviation Corporation and Grumman Aircraft, etc., were expanding and hiring personnel. Consequently, our school district felt the impact of these professionals. As a result, the school district became one of the better ones on Long Island. The parents were very interested in the education their children were receiving. PTA meetings and parent visiting days were busy ones.

The teachers were encouraged by the interest shown by the parents and their cooperation in raising the standards of education. Accordingly, the students received a good education and in addition, had many opportunities to participate in extracurricular activities, such as science fairs, music, dramatics, and sports.

Our daughter played the clarinet and participated in the science fairs. Science projects required perseverance, determination, and hard work. The students were free to select a suitable topic of some originality and carry the project through to completion. They had to present a summary of their findings, the techniques used, analysis and conclusions. A report had to be written, which developed writing skills and critical thinking as well as innovativeness. In addition, they had to explain their project to the judges and visitors who attended the fairs. To evaluate the project, the judges would ask questions to determine how well the presenter knew his subject. This was akin to defending one's doctoral dissertation. It was an excellent way to develop self-confidence in being able to answer spot questions under pressure. Questions were asked as to the value of the experiment, why such an experiment was conducted, and its possible applications.

As it turned out, those who entered the fair were the top-ranking students of their respective classes. The competition and presentations were of very high caliber. Thetis and I were very much impressed by the quality and complexity of the subjects selected. The students selected challenging and up-to-date topics in the areas of computer science, biochemistry, the DNA and RNA molecular structures, mathematics, modern physics, the Krebs cycle in biochemistry, etc.

Alceste was successful in attaining first prizes, which delighted her grandparents as well as us. We shall never forget the year when both Alceste and Conrad had exhibits. Alceste's prize-winning project involved the stability of soap films. She illustrated her demonstration by dipping a circular wire in a soap solution, and as she withdrew the wire, a film was formed, having as its boundaries the circular wire.

She then introduced a second circular wire of smaller diameter into the outstretched film of the first wire. As she withdrew the smaller ring from the first, a surface of revolution was formed. The surface would remain intact until a critical length was reached when the film would break. This illustrated that instability was associated with how far the film could be stretched. By using different soap films, she could vary the critical length. It would appear that the elastic properties of the film varied, depending upon the different soaps used.

She then made a cubical structure, and within this structure, she centered a smaller cubical structure. The entire assembly was immersed in the soap solution, and she found many, many more configurations. From this she experimented with many different three-dimensional forms, such as tetrahedrons, and other polyhedrons. All these experiments were conducted in the laundry room of our home under quiescent conditions. When the weather was fine, she also worked outdoors. By working outside she had an additional variable to contend with, the wind.

The question that arose in her mind was, how stable was the film in the wind that was formed across the perimeters of the wires? On certain days when the wind was a mere trickle, the film would quiver but remain intact. On days of appreciable winds, the film would rupture. Admittedly, this was a qualitative approach, but she was curious about the wind and what it would do to the film. As long as the wind caused small perturbations, the film remained intact. However, when the wind was of sufficient intensity, the film between the two wires would rupture. This would imply that beyond a certain threshold value of the magnitude of the perturbation, instability would occur.

When Alceste told me of her results, I became interested in her explanation of what she observed. This could have far-reaching results. In every case when the film ruptured, it was not possible to return to its original configuration. The process was irreversible.

At this point, I should like to inject some of my thoughts on the experiences encountered on the P-47. Flow instabilities occurred on the aircraft during compressibility dives when the air flow over the wing became transonic. Alceste observed that at a certain point in the elongation of the film, the film ruptured and pulled apart, to be reformed into the areas of the two circular wires. This reformation occurred suddenly. If any such similar change were to occur in a compressible flow, as when deflecting an aileron, the effects might be a sudden loss of control with little possibility of regaining control, just as there was no possibility of reforming the original shape of the soap film.

Conrad's project was entitled "Formation of Tsunamis and Their Effects." This was his third science project, the first one being "The Development of Flight," for which he was awarded the blue ribbon. This was quite a feat, considering that he was in competition with the winners from most other schools in Suffolk County, Long Island, New York. His second project was "Experimental Tectonics." For the second year in a row, he received a regional award for his project. This award was made as a result of his presentation before the Future Scientists of America.

In order to study the characteristics and effects of tsunamis in the laboratory, Conrad had to build a tank with proper dimensions to insure that the phenomenon was approximately reproduced in the small-scale experimental model. He needed space to build his model.

The ideal place was the basement workshop. This was one time when we had to lend a helping hand and to encourage him to proceed.

Tsunamis can be caused in several ways. A sudden landslide under the ocean will result in a wave. Underwater earthquakes and volcanic eruptions can also create them. Man can create tsunamis by exploding nuclear bombs at the surface of the sea. All these causes illustrated that Conrad was dealing with impulsive forces, forces that occur suddenly. The tsunami is a series of huge waves. A tsunami can attain a velocity of five hundred miles per hour; hence its great destructive power when coupled with the high density of water.

A tank was constructed with a length of five feet, width three inches and height twelve inches. The back, sides, and bottom of the tank were made from wood boards. The front section was part wood and glass for observation of the wave propagation and its characteristics. At one end of the tank, a caulking gun was installed at the bottom. At the other end of the tank, various shorelines could be simulated by two-by-four inch wood blocks, cut at angles of 15, 30, 45, and 60 degrees. A twelve-inch plastic scale was mounted on the glass in front of the shore line so that the heights of the waves could be measured.

The caulking gun simulated the impulsive force of the tidal wave caused by an undersea volcanic eruption quite well. When the plunger of the gun was pulled down, the water was sucked down into the barrel of the gun, simulating the shoreline as it actually happens in nature, free of water. The plunger was pushed up quickly, simulating the sudden eruption of a volcano. The water rushed in toward the shoreline with a series of waves. The waves traveling back and forth were very realistic. The method of simulating an undersea earthquake was accomplished by using a paddle to suddenly displace the water in the tank. Here again, the water is drawn away from the shoreline and then returns with huge waves, breaking on the shoreline.

When the day of the fair arrived, Thetis managed to get both exhibits in the trunk of the car and off they went. Arriving at the school, there were many trips back and forth from the car to carry all the necessary charts, screens, equipment, beakers, etc.

Once the exhibits were set up, the students visited and looked over what their classmates were showing. At the appointed hour, the judges came around to talk to the student exhibitors. The judges included engineers, teachers, chemists, physicists, medical doctors, and professionals from other disciplines. We thoroughly enjoyed listening to the judges asking poignant, appropriate questions, and the corresponding answers of the students.

In the afternoon the winners were announced in the auditorium. The announcements were so arranged that the winners from the junior high school came first. Then followed the winners from the senior high school. Thetis's parents were with us in the audience. When they announced the first prize from the junior high school, Conrad's name was called. Grandparents and we were delighted and proud of his achievement. We were especially gratified to know that our children demonstrated the principle of "sweat before achievement." It has been said that talent consists mainly of hard work. Our children had learned this, and to this very day, they produce and contribute commensurate with their natural gifts. In this respect, we had achieved our goal as parents.

Announcements were finally made for the winners among the seniors. Grandmother was especially concerned. This was Alceste's senior year in high school. What if she did not get a prize? As good fortune will have it, she did get the first prize in her category. She also received the top prize of the fair in the form of a scholarship. Grandmother relaxed and was proud of her grandchildren. As a mother, Thetis was exhausted and relieved.

For the first time, a sister and brother had won gold medals at the Seventh Annual Suffolk County Science Teachers Congress. Alceste won the gold medal for her science project, "The Role of Surface Tension in Life Processes." Conrad, who was a freshman, won his gold medal for his work on "The Formation of Tsunamis and Their Effects."

Alceste was judged the top student scientist on Long Island when her paper along with those of other winners of science congresses were judged by the Council of Long Island Technical Societies. She received the Council Grand Award and a scholarship at the CLITS Exposition of Technology dinner. Her project was on exhibit at the CLITS exposition held in Nassau Community College.

The training and experience the children received while in high school have been of inestimable help in their future careers. Both received doctoral degrees from the University of California, Berkeley. Conrad, who received his degree in neuroanatomy, was anxious to perform microsurgery and accordingly, he obtained his M.D. degree from the George Washington University in 1984.

Both have pursued their desires to contribute to their professions. Alceste has specialized in budgetary problems associated with educational institutions and organizational societies. Her dissertation was "The Identification and Utilization of Objectifiable Elements Requisite for Budgetary Decision-Making in Student Affairs."

Conrad has written several papers with Dr. Marion Diamond of the University of California, Berkeley, on the cerebral cortex. After graduation from Berkeley, he performed research with Dr. Klaus Bensch of Stanford University. It was there that Conrad decided to obtain his M.D. degree.

Conrad's research entailed microsurgery on the brain of fetal mice. This constituted a real challenge and love for surgery. Conrad has the patience and perseverance for such microscopic surgery. The human brain was exactly what he wanted to probe into.

Following his graduation from the medical school of George Washington University, he served his residency at the Barrow Neurological Institute of Saint Joseph's Hospital in Phoenix, Arizona. During his residency, Conrad decided to specialize in epilepsy, which is a dysfunction of the brain. This interest led him to a fellowship at Yale Medical College. Conrad is a prolific writer of his medical researches and has received awards for his contributions. His early desire as a child to become a doctor has come to fruition. He is now a neurosurgeon and assistant professor.

Alceste is a partner with KPMG (Kleinveld Peat Marwick Goerdeller). Her activities center around current budgetary issues and changes facing post-secondary education and social organizations. This entails interactions with a wide variety of constituent groups, e.g., legislators, citizen groups, business leaders who have their own requirements and concerns regarding post-secondary education. It is interesting to note that Alceste has adapted the techniques of systems technology to the analysis of educational problems. This illustrates the universality of the method.

Alceste has demonstrated to us the necessity of taking a qualitative approach to real-world problems. The problems are so complex and contextual that there is little hope for a quantitative analysis. What is of prime importance in her opinion is the ability to select subjectively the key components of the system that will lead to an approximate answer. A sensitivity analysis needs to be made to determine whether the key components arbitrarily selected are in truth key components. This can be determined if material changes in the component result in significant changes in the result. If not, other components can be considered. This process entails one of trial and error.

We enjoy listening to Alceste and Conrad explain their research in their respective fields. It is truly a revelation to hear their approaches to the analysis of a problem. This is especially true when it comes to the intricacies and operation of the brain. Advances being made in computer technology are patterned after the human brain. For example, we have AI (artificial intelligence), which has as its aim the capability of the computer to make decisions like the human brain. The brain apparently has the ability to accommodate information in parallel as well as in series. This can materially shorten the time it takes for the computer to produce an output. The networks of the brain are so arranged that multiple manipulations and transfer of information can take place simultaneously.

It is interesting to note that John von Neumann was preparing a paper entitled "The Computer and the Brain." He was one of the greatest applied and theoretical mathematicians of the twentieth century and one of the pioneers in the development of the electronic computer. His apparent objective was to simulate the intricate mechanisms of the human brain to the computer. In the 1950s, the brain was known to accept information in parallel rather than in series, as the original electronic computer was designed.

Von Neumann also recognized that the nervous system operated in two modes, the digital and analog. The transmitted nervous pulse can alternate from the digital to the analog mode. He was in search of how the brain was organized in terms of a network and the interactions of stimulation. His ultimate goal was to simulate the brain as much as possible. He recognized the field of neuroanatomy could contribute materially to computer technology if only we could unfathom the brain's inner workings and processes.

Unfortunately, he developed cancer as a result of his participation in the development and testing of the A-bomb. He died before his paper could be completed. This paper was to be presented as the Silliman Lecture at Yale University. The university did not cancel the lecture. Instead, his unfinished work was presented by the lecture committee as a fitting tribute to him. This decision was a most prudent one, for it stimulated and is stimulating further research in this area.

13. Experiences at Edwards Air Force Base

Muroc Dry Lake Bed—California

As an Eastener, I was unprepared for life on the desert. Republic Aviation sent a group of us out to the Air Force base at Muroc Dry Lake Bed, California, to witness and supervise flight tests that were being conducted on one of our fighters.

When we checked in at the base, the temperature was around 105 degrees. The humidity, unlike that on the East Coast, was quite low, which made the temperature tolerable. Our first task was to check in with the sergeant of the base who was in charge of doling out blankets and other paraphernalia that we would need for the night. We were designated to bed down in one of the hangars at the base.

When we confronted the sergeant, we were promptly informed where we would sleep. Since we were assigned to cots in a hangar, we were told we would need blankets for the evening. This remark was beyond my comprehension. How on earth (bear in mind I was not proselytized as yet into the ways and living modes of the Western deserts) could anyone in his right mind ask whether I would need several blankets (Yes! I used the correct form of blanket in the plural) or not? I rather liked the paternal disposition of the sergeant but I thought he was carrying out his welcome and hospitality too far. After all, it was summer where maximum temperatures could easily exceed 100 degrees Fahrenheit.

For appearances' sake, and recognizing this was my very first day at the base, I thought I would humor the benevolent sergeant and ask for one, and only one, blanket. Again, I was reminded that I would need blankets, not in the singular, but in the plural. By this time my Mediterranean blood was approaching the critical boiling point, and I insisted that one was all I needed! After all, I was a grown boy and had weaned away from my mother by this time and could make my own decision, for better or for worse.

Accordingly, I was assigned one blanket rather reluctantly by the sergeant who had my best self-interests at heart. I was so pigheaded that I couldn't listen to reason and benefit from the experience of the sergeant. Lo and behold! Night came around as sure as day precedes night, or is it the other way around?

Well, as night approached, the temperature began to fall rather rapidly and I began to wonder whether the sergeant wasn't right after all. With each passing moment, I became more and more convinced he was right and I was dead-wrong.

By the time bedtime rolled around, I was thoroughly convinced I was dead-wrong. Sheepishly and with great remorse, I asked what the temperature was at around 10:00 P.M. When I was told it was forty-two degrees Fahrenheit, I knew I was in trouble. I should mention that we were not in a luxuriously outfitted room, but in one corner of a huge hangar. Needless to say, there was no heat to count on—one additional problem that compounded the situation. I thought to myself that, at least, I should have been informed of the temperature range that was to be expected. Eventually I was told that during the summer months, maximums over a hundred degrees Fahrenheit are common during the days and fifteen to thirty degrees during the nights. The average rainfall annually is less than five inches. These statistics are typical of deserts. Be that as it may, I prepared my cot by placing the bedsheet in place, pillow case, and alas! one blanket—a thin one, at that.

When things go haywire, it is an immutable law of Nature that they will really go sour. From the moment I undressed, I was in a cryogenic state. I literally shivered and had difficulty controlling my actions and reactions. Fortunately, I had my raincoat with me. With the blanket and raincoat, I was able to survive through the night.

The next morning I approached the sergeant with the vestiges of my tail between my legs and apologized profusely for my stubbornness and disrespect I had exhibited in not accepting two or three blankets, as he had recommended the night before. I must say he was the most compassionate and understanding person I met during my stay at Muroc. Maybe it was because he realized I was from the East Coast where temperatures remain fairly constant throughout a twenty-four-hour period.

I was excited to be at Edwards Air Force Base for no other reason than to be where Chuck Yeager was conducting tests on the XS-1 to penetrate the mystical, psychological, sonic barrier. This research airplane was under the aegis of the Army Air Force. The navy, in turn, was not to be outdone. It produced the D-558-1 research airplane for flight in the transonic range. Its mission was similar to the air force. NACA corroborated the activities of the air force and the navy. Not only would service pilots fly the aircraft, but NACA pilots as well. NACA would install the necessary instrumentation under their supervision. This synergistic effort with the Army Air Force and navy resulted in a series of flights that finally penetrated the sonic barrier. This event was of tremendous importance, since it opened up the age of supersonic flight.

The P-84 Thunderjet was finally scheduled to fly, not only from a mechanical point of view, but now also the required number of dignitaries from the plant had arrived. In flight-testing one learns very quickly that when everything appears to be ready, that ain't necessarily so! Mechanical devices have a last-minute change of heart and require adjustments and fixing. It's a wonder sometimes how a military airplane with all its complications can be expected to fly when you want it to at moment's notice.

This raises a very important point during an emergency alert under wartime conditions. What is the probability of readiness of the airplane when needed now, not an hour from now or even a few minutes from now. If the airplane is plagued with necrosis of repair, tantamount to its sitting on the ground 90 percent of the time, the aircraft as a military weapon is practically of no use. I sometimes wonder about some of our truly sophisticated modern vehicles and their ability to perform when needed. The more subsystems we cram into the airplane, the more likelihood it has of malfunctioning.

There is a magnificent saying of Sir William Rowan Hamilton, the great Irish philosopher and mathematical physicist, who said, "The greater the extension, the lesser the intention." He made this remark when he announced his discovery of the quaternions— similar to the vector analysis of today, which deals with three components instead of four. Hamilton incorporated the scalar component in addition to the vector components in his quaternionic theory. He was told by his colleagues that he had essentially reinvented the wheel. Grassmann, a German mathematician, had arrived at an ndimensional analysis of the problem a few years prior. Hamilton's theory was a simplified version of Grassmann's theory.

Staying at Muroc was very interesting and an eye-opener. It was interesting in that there were many new airplanes from various manufacturers that were being tested for acceptance by the air force. The crews assigned to these aircraft were jovial and a delight to speak with. This was the case with the experimental pilots who flew these new types. They were ebullient, intelligent, and full of enthusiasm, knowing they were probing and gnawing away at new vistas of knowledge. This prevailing feeling throughout the entire base to me was tantamount to being present at the ancient Academy of Athens where new ideas and thoughts were being expounded, the wisdom of proceeding along certain lines to solve a problem, and the discussions that ensued.

I became nostalgic about Edwards when I read Chuck Yeager's book entitled *Yeager*, especially the chapters entitled "Pancho's Place" and "Flying in the Golden Age." As an air force pilot, Chuck was keenly interested in proving out the end product by demonstration tests in flight. I, as an engineer, was concerned with how our various hypotheses, which we made during the design phase, would turn out in flight. The designers were responsible for meeting the requirements set forth in the RFP.

The designers owe a great deal to the "jocks," as Chuck makes reference to in his autobiography. We at Republic Aviation had our roster of notables: George Burrell. Lowery Brabham, Joe Parker, Frank Sinclair, Carl Bellinger, all pilots of great fortitude. They represented a group of dedicated individuals who were firm believers in pushing the knowledge of aeronautical engineering to greater and greater heights, constantly making contributory suggestions that we designers might incorporate into our future designs. Their motives and actions were altruistic and very practical. I shall always cherish the spirit and camaraderie these men represented. A spirit of synergism existed between pilot and designer that enriched the entire aeronautical field and that led to an accelerative pace of progress. I am convinced that with such cooperative efforts, we have made gargantuan steps forward and will continue to do so in the future.

While I was at Muroc in 1949, reservations were made for me at Pancho's. Most of the gang were bunking in there, and little did I know of Pancho's celebrity and background. She was quite a gal. At first I couldn't believe what I heard emanating from her, inviting us to mingle with her gals at the bar, to forget the pains and anguish of decision-making of the day, to let our hair down and have a hell-of-a good time. I thought we were being cast for a Western movie, gun-toting gals, booze, and the works. She was very descriptive and precise to the point, blazing away a mile a minute, making profuse use of her vast scatological thesaurus of four-letter words. In the event she didn't like someone who ruffled her hair, she was even more demonstrative. I must say it was a most memorable and in-delible experience. I had never experienced anything like it in my entire life.

Underneath this barrage and outburst of bravados, her bark was louder than her bite, unless you had done her wrong! Then, watch out, bud! You would have been lambasted with all the curses of the immortal gods. In spite of her crudeness, she was sincere and forthright. These were my impressions of her when I met her a few times. Those of you who have read Chuck Yeager's book and feel he has exaggerated in describing Pancho, rest assured! 'Tain't so! Believe every word he says.

I was surprised to learn that the Mohave Desert constitutes one-fifth the area of the state of California. On a few occasions when I had an opportunity to investigate the landscape adjacent to the air base, I learned a bit about a desert environment. The air base itself was amazingly flat and the surface hard during the dry season. Compaction of the soil has taken place over many years, and the movement of heavy equipment and aircraft over its surface presented no problem. The soil is so fine that manufacturers of toothpaste will use it in the preparation of their product.

An investigation of the landscape as one approaches the moun-tain ranges surrounding the lake bed revealed many interesting things. Typical plants can be categorized as widely spaced low shrubs, similar to sagebrush, malformed Joshua trees, creosote bushes, mesquite, various species of acacia, and various forms of cacti. The Joshua trees, when in bloom after the rainy season, are spectacular and a sight to behold. The plants are xerophilous and have the capacity, like the camel that has the ability to store water, to survive under severe temperature and extended drought periods.

The sky was a clear, Mediterranean blue. Because of the low

humidity in conjunction with a clear sky, wide temperature ranges occur between day and night. Nights become cold because the heat, which has been stored in the ground during the day, can readily radiate skyward because of the lack of a cloud coverage. The existence of such a cloud coverage would reflect the transmitted heat back to earth, thus resulting in a warmer night than would result with a clear sky.

In the vicinity of the mountain ranges, desert animals of many descriptions appeared. There were rodents of all sizes, snakes, reptiles, and many different species of birds. These animals existed in greater numbers in the mountainous areas because of the more abundant supply of water. I was quite surprised to see the size of rabbits in the Mohave area. On the East Coast, rabbits of large size are called jackrabbits. Technically speaking, they are classified as hares.

As we approached them along the side of the road, it was most amusing to watch them scoot away from us. They would move with great speed and venturing a guess, would jump some twelve to fifteen feet. Their ears were very long, and I could see more ears than head. Nature apparently has endowed them with supersensitive hearing sensors. This enables them to survive in a hostile, predator environment. What was even more spectacular in their hop movements was the occasional high leap in the air. I can only surmise that this constituted a reconnaissance maneuver, to enable the hare to see where the pursuer might be. The hare can be classified as a composite design created by Nature, possessing high speed, reconnaissance capabilities, highly maneuverable, and alacritous.

Much of the existing prevalent esprit de corps in effect at Edwards Air Force Base was due to Col. Albert Boyd, the commandant of the base. He set the pace because he was an experimental test pilot himself. He would very frequently test the various aircraft to arrive at an independent appraisal of their flying qualities and characteristics. Accordingly, the pilots would perform their very best to prove they were on a par with him. In the event they disagreed with him on any flight test result, they were at liberty to tell him.

While at the base, I had the opportunity to talk to him. I remarked that I was impressed with the camaraderie that existed and by what I saw and experienced during my brief stay at the base. During our conversation I gathered inferentially that he was frustrated with Congress, since the budget he submitted to Congress had been cut drastically. With the advent of the penetration of the sonic barrier, he could envision the necessity of expanding the facilities of the base to cope with the problems of supersonic and hypersonic flight. He felt that the base needed improvements and additions to provide for the coming of the new flight age. Much of the existing equipment was antiquated and had to be replaced. These changes were of paramount importance to him. He was fully aware of the research and development that would be required to determine the effectiveness of any design defects that might be inherent in supersonic military and commercial aircraft.

World War II had vividly demonstrated to him how far behind we were after the war. We trailed the Nazis in the introduction of jet aircraft. They had inflicted havoc and great losses on our bomber fleets during the air raids over Germany. We were trailing in missiles and rocketry. There was an urgent need in his mind that preparations had to be made for the coming of supersonic flight, both manned and unmanned. The colonel conveyed his portent and concern of the ascendency of the high-speed age to members of Congress. In spite of his presentations to Congress, they did not act favorably.

I was saddened to hear of his plight and disappointments with Congress. I appreciated his strategic planning approach, but most budget managers are primarily interested in short-term projects and will set up their priorities accordingly. As a result, by the time all short-term projects are accounted for, only very few traces of fiscal morsels are left.

He was upset to think that tight-fisted Congress regarded research and development low man on the totem pole. Try as hard as he could, he could not get Congress to appropriate the necessary funds to fully carry out his plans to renovate the base. Accordingly, he wanted us, those of us in industry, to talk to our superiors back home about the existing conditions. I assured him that liaison between the military and industry was, is, and will be an essential link to provide for an air force that would be the envy of the world.

I assured him that his experience with Congress was a common occurrence. As an example, the people at the Ames Aeronautical Research Center had the same experience of being cut back from what was requested in their budget. Whether or not this was consoling to the colonel, I did not know. It would appear, unfortunately, that when it comes to funding research, whether it be in flight testing, wind tunnels, theoretical, or otherwise, low priorities are assigned. I knew this was the case to a large extent during World War II when most monies were appropriated to the purchase of huge quantities of airplanes. Research in the minds of the money-bag holders is long term, with no apparent return on their investments during their tenure in office.

14. Fourth Anglo-American Aeronautical Conference

Dick Bowman and I were selected to represent Republic Aviation as delegates to the Fourth Anglo-American Conference in 1953. I was delighted that Dick Bowman would be with me. I had first made my acquaintance with him during my school days at the Daniel Guggenheim School of Aeronautics. We worked together at Republic Aviation on the design of many of the Air Force airplanes. Since we were both members of the design team, we corroborated our efforts by helping make decisions as the design progressed. In addition, he had a good sense of humor and was a great story-teller.

The conference was held at University College in London. The conference was sponsored jointly by the Royal Aeronautical Society and the Institute of Aeronautical Sciences (now the AIAA, The American Institute of Aeronautics and Astronautics). I looked forward to going for several reasons. The British were heavily engaged in research in high-speed aerodynamics and had made substantial advances in the field. I was anxious to see the advances made by the Royal Air Force in their jet fighters and bombers. I was aware of the heartaches that Air Commodore Frank Whittle of the RAF underwent in developing and promulgating jet propulsion for aircraft in England. Our professor, Dr. Alexander Klemin, was a graduate of the University of London, and it was our desire to see the college in person. The college is famous for its contributions to learning and education in many fields and over many years.

This type of meeting was ideal for exchange of technical information. We met not only delegates from the United Kingdom but also from many countries in the British Commonwealth and the continent of Europe. All of us found opportunities for renewing friendships formed at earlier conferences and for making new ones. Meetings were regularly scheduled every two years on an alternating basis between the two countries.

When we learned that we would represent Republic Aviation at the Fourth Anglo-American Aeronautical Conference in London in 1953, we were delighted. It would be our first trip to London and Europe. To put it mildly, we were excited. There were many decisions to make.

This was an opportunity to sail the *Queen Mary* and enjoy all her amenities. We had heard so much about her hospitality and cordiality that we were anxious to verify her reputation. (For the record: all our expectations were verified.)

Our children were quite young, and we were concerned to leave them for five weeks. Fortunately, our parents were ready to help, assuming responsibility and pampering our darlings for the duration.

The next decision was the matter of finances. The company would pay for only one passage. After building a much-needed home, our coffers were low. This would mean the trip would diminish our account to even greater depths. Well, we decided to go ahead and proceed with the trip. After all, you're only young once, and why give up such an opportunity?

Preparing for the trip was an adventure in itself. We were given a list of instructions by our host, which included proper attire for all the formal and very elegant events. It started with the basics needed to carry all the paraphernalia needed for the scheduled meetings, social events, and dinners. Luggage included a man's three-suiter, a twenty-four-inch case, a jack-knife bag to hold formal gowns, a twenty-six-inch woman's Pullman, a hat and shoebox hand piece, a train case, and two briefcases. One look at these eight pieces of luggage was a sight indeed! We wondered from time to time how we would manage all these pieces. This is the price one pays for formality! It is no wonder people are gradually veering away from such conventional practices.

Then there were the trips to New York City and Manhasset to buy the appropriate attire. First we purchased a midnight-blue evening jacket for cool evenings and a white one for warmer ones. The clerk in the fashionable men's shop was beside himself with such a handsome order, which also included shirts, ties, cummerbunds, and all the extra items to be properly dressed for the evening. In addition, the dark, striped suit for attending meetings was required. This represented the ultimate in regimentation!

Dressing a woman for gala evenings was even more formidable.

A mink stole was a must, plus all evening gowns were to be very formal and bouffant. At the beginning, all this fuss was fun, but after a while, it became tedious. Every time Thetis tried on a gown, usually I or Mother would stand by and comment on her appearance. One gown that was the "masterpiece" was a pale blue, appropriately low decolletage and a bouffant silk and tulle skirt, which had a circumference of some twelve feet. This was ideal for the gala dinner-dance. When Thetis stood on the pedestal for the seamstress to mark the hem, she created a sensation in the store. This really gave her ego a lift, and all was not in vain. She felt almost "queenly." Fortunately, the dress did receive the proper glances and comments whenever she wore it. Decades later, she gave the dress to a theater group that needed a gown for "Scarlett O'Hara" in their *Gone with the Wind* production.

Saying good-bye to our young family was difficult. We set sail on the majestic *Queen Mary*. There was a lump in our throats as we passed the Statue of Liberty, as it reminded us of the feelings our parents had experienced when they first saw her towering above her pedestal with her outstretched hand bearing the torch of liberty, freedom, opportunity, and a new life of hope and aspiration. Having passed her in all her majestic glory, we were on our way to Le Havre, France.

The *Queen Mary* was a beautiful and majestic ship. Her crew were always there at your beck and call. The food on the *Queen* was exquisite. The couple who shared our table had an endless supply of Piper Heidsiek champagne. Various members of their family had so arranged their daily schedules that each succeeding day one or two bottles would be served by the sommelier of the ship.

After a while we were almost convinced that the Atlantic Ocean was a huge pool of champagne. The champagne was also welcome when we encountered hurricane weather. It made the rock and roll of the ship in phase with the rock and roll produced somatically by the champagne. Dancing during those pitches and rolls of the *Queen* became more daring and difficult. Walking for most of the passengers was only possible by holding on to the ropes along the passageways provided for such emergencies. The acrobats among us had mastered the unique technique of balance. Passengers resorted to playing cards and games during the storms. Many would retire to their staterooms to sedate themselves with tranquilizers.

All was not rough voyage. Fortunately, there were times when watching the porpoises was a delight, and at night we could see lights of other ships in the distance. It was nice to know that we were not alone in this void of expanse and that there were others on this vast Atlantic with us. Our admiration for Columbus and his crew grew materially with each passing day. Had we not seen land after five and a half days, we began to wonder whether the ancients were not correct in their hypothesis of eventually reaching a precipice of doom and destruction. In the case of Columbus, the monotony and anxiety of not knowing when one will see land again can incite hallucinations of despair and doom.

The trip on the *Queen Mary* was most delightful and leisurely. There was a certain majestic atmosphere about the ship that emulated the spirit of the *Queen* herself. Sojourns to the bar, decks, and dining room made for a relaxing day. Changing one's attire for each occasion provided a certain uplift, a rejuvenation or rekindling of the body. For exercise I would take a dip in the pool. The pool was miniscule, and one or two strokes would propel me from one end to the other. On one occasion I found myself in a rather awkward position. The ship had been pitching and rolling rather vigorously as a result of a nearby hurricane, which the captain hadn't quite circumvented. At one moment in my traverse across the pool, I was immersed in water, propelling myself with my hands and feet and the next moment beating myself against the bottom of the pool sans water. The ship had lurched quite violently and as a result the surface of the water in the pool was overflowing at one end with ensuing spillage while the other end was practically uncovered. Fortune would have me at the low end!

After five and a half days at sea, we docked at Le Havre. When we arrived at Le Havre, the train was waiting to take us to Paris. Fortunately, our high school French got us through customs, and we were able to converse with the conductor on the train.

We stayed in Paris from August 31st to September 7th, at the Hotel Plaza-Athenée. The purpose of this visit was to go to the company's Paris office, see French aircraft, and discuss their experiences with high-speed flight.

There was so much to see in Paris. It was truly a beautiful city. Now that we had regained our command of French, it was fun going out shopping. Thetis found the French very helpful wherever she went. Some of the saleswomen in the stores insisted she speak French while they spoke English. It became a quid pro quo, and we were teaching one another our own language. It was a beautiful exchange relationship and experience that she shall always treasure.

The Louvre, with its *Venus de Milo* and other treasures, lived up to its fame. There was so much to see—the Place de la Concorde, the Obelisk from Egypt, the Pantheon, Le Tour d'Eiffel, the Place de la Madelaine, Notre Dame, etc. The boat ride on the Seine was most enjoyable, since we had a commanding view of the environs. The performance of *La Traviata* at the L'Opera was magnificent when sung in French. The voices and acting were superb. Then, of course, we also went to the Folies Bergere one night.

Thetis especially enjoyed her visit with the Bob Kinkeads. Bob was the company's representative in Paris. His wife invited Thetis for lunch, which was most delightful. It was her first taste of turbot, a delicious flatfish of Europe. Actually, the turbot can grow to thirty to forty pounds. It is really a jumbo flounder, with smoother texture than the flounder and more succulent. The Kinkeads had a French couple who shopped and cooked for them. The woman was an excellent cook.

One of Thetis's interesting experiences occurred when she was alone shopping and decided to walk through a residential area to see firsthand how the French lived. The buildings were old and very charming. High-density buildings were predominant, and no driveways could be seen. Thetis was led to believe that the residents resorted to walking to the shops rather than relying on the automobile. After walking for a while, she realized she had covered quite some distance and should return to the hotel in time for our evening dinner reservation. Fortunately, she was able to find a cab.

When she entered the cab, she gave the cabbie the address of the hotel in French, of course. At that point he turned around and looked at her. At first Thetis thought, perhaps, she should get out and walk away from the scene as fast as she could. However, she was so tired and exhausted that she decided to sit tight. His first remark was in French: "You speak French well and you're very polite, so you cannot be an American. Where are you from?"

Thetis was so shocked that she could not respond to that remark. Well, he turned around, put his hand on the steering wheel, and away they went. You can rest assured Thetis watched every road he took to make sure she was not going for just a ride. From then on he began to talk about his career. He was a violinist by night and a cabbie by day. He needed both careers to support himself and his family. He gave quite a discourse on music, famous musicians, and recitals. Needless to say, he was one of the most enlightening cab drivers Thetis ever had.

When they reached the Plaza d'Athenée, she gave him a generous tip, but he would not accept it. She was "très gentile," "very kind." Finally, she insisted that it was for him to buy his wife some flowers and a toy for his son. He was so overwhelmed that he kissed her hand as she stepped out of the cab. The doorman at the hotel was amazed. The passersby were intrigued. Oh well, it seemed as if Thetis was acting on a stage with a huge audience. Totally unreal! But, that's Paris!

It was September 7, 1953 and time to leave Paris for London. We boarded a British European Airways Viscount, Discovery Class aeroplane. It was called the Silver Wing. This was a turbo-propeller airliner with four Rolls Royce Dart propeller/turbines. The propellers were driven by jet engines. The cruising speed was 291 miles per hour for this Vickers-Armstrong Ltd. aeroplane. There were forty-seven passengers and a crew of five. It was a smooth flight. They served us chicken and champagne for lunch. It was British hospitality at its best.

When we arrived in London, you could still feel the excitement lingering on from the coronation of Queen Elizabeth on June 2, 1953. The Dorchester Hotel was to be our home base during our stay in London. The Dorchester was a sedate residential hotel and very proper in every detail that one could possibly ask for. Across the street were the spacious, tree-decked acres of Hyde Park. It was a marvelous place to stroll in and enjoy the people—nannies with their charges, young couples, children feeding the birds, etc. Serenity and tranquillity predominated the entire area. We felt relaxed and were at peace with Nature.

London was in a festive mood. Tourists from all over the world were visiting the city. Souvenirs galore were being sold. Yet, here and there, as one walked the streets of London, one could see vestiges of scars and ravages inflicted by the Nazis on the environs during World War II. Britain had just coronated a young queen, and with her came the hope of peace and the energy of a youthful leader.

People were rejuvenated by this prospect of the future and were looking forward for better things to come.

As Americans, we did not see our mainland marred by the war. The scarred buildings and voids in the city blocks of London were shocking to us. Our sufferings were primarily for human life. These scars magnified our fears and sorrows of the past. What we saw was indeed a revelation of that grim reality again. The engineers in their desire to improve transportation designed the airplane for the betterment of mankind. Little did they originally conceive of its dualistic role in time of hostilities between nations. It was not long after the first flight of the Wright brothers that the military conceived of the airplane as a weapon of war.

There was much to see in London. While I was attending meetings and the air show at Farnborough, Thetis was sight-seeing and shopping. From time to time, we were able to get together to see the changing of the guard at Buckingham Palace, Parliament, the Tower Bridge, Trafalgar Square, and Piccadilly Circus. A statue of Eros with bow in hand stood in Piccadilly Circus. This was one of London's busiest centers and appeared to be the focal point for celebrations and rejoicing. There was a Woolworth store there where we were able to buy sundry items and even imbibe in a cool Coca-Cola drink to satisfy our thirst.

We were unable to get into Westminster Abbey because they were still busy removing scaffolding and decorations from the coronation. However, we did get into Saint Paul's cathedral, which was in some ways even more beautiful than Notre Dame of Paris. It was distressing from time to time to see the ravages of war. Where buildings once stood were gaping holes, partially bombed buildings that needed reconstruction. It was encouraging to see that in some areas there was a rebirth of building activity. The process of restoration would be long and tedious.

During our peripatetics throughout London, we pondered over the change that occurred when *vergeltung* (retaliation) took the place of Schiller's *Ode to Joy, "Alle menschen werden bruder, wo dein sanfter flugel weilt"* (All mankind shall become brothers, where thine soft wings fly). Beethoven's pleadings, *"O freunde, nicht diese tone"* (O friends, not these [repulsive] utterances) went unheeded. These feelings were set to music in Beethoven's immortal Ninth Symphony. Handel, Haydn, and Mozart likewise set to music their humanitarian beliefs in their works. The poets and musicians were doing their part to bring about a unified world that could exist in a peaceful, harmonious way. It was a long-range outlook into the future when mankind would experience mutual understanding and respect through the implementation of peace and reason rather than war.

London was indeed a very cosmopolitan city. One could hear many languages spoken. It was often our experience while standing at a corner or waiting to cross the street to have someone come up to us and ask for directions in some foreign language. At this point one wished he could converse fluently in several languages to help. We tried English and French. Sometimes the inquirers understood, and they departed happily in the pointed direction. The use of hands became "handy" when giving directions and for indicating numbers less than or equal to the number of fingers on both hands. It was fun. After all, we were endowed with hands. Why not make use of them as a last recourse?

We had become so accustomed to speaking and listening to French in Paris for a week that it was almost like learning to speak another language at times in England. The Queen's English was not always like the American English we knew. *Ascenseur* in French was easy to remember; the English word "lift" was a little more difficult to remember. After all, one did get a "lift" from Glenlivet or Chivas Scotch. Why use "lift" to be raised mechanically from floor to floor when one could be raised spiritually by scotch?

Engineers from the days of Archimedes strove for the fulfillment of their desire to contrive mechanical objects and machinery that would result in the alleviation of human toil and drudgery. Their ultimate object is to contribute in such a way that all of humanity can enjoy and prosper in a peaceful world. When Archimedes was complimented on the applications of his mathematics, science, and geometry to weapons of destruction in the attack on Syracuse by the Roman general Marcellus, his reply was that he abhorred the use of his scientific works to the destruction of man. In making his decision, he had to consider the defense of his city and the safety of his people versus the destruction of the enemy.

Ironically, in view of the foregoing, we were in London to attend lectures on new advances in aircraft and to see an air show of modern, advanced vehicles. These included both commercial and military aircraft. Our thoughts were that unless we could achieve mutual respect and understanding of the various cultures of other nations, our ideal Archimedean principles would be in vain. It is interesting to note that Einstein was faced with this very same dilemma when he was asked by his fellow physicists to sign a letter to President Roosevelt, urging him to proceed with the development of the A-bomb. He reluctantly agreed to do so because he knew other nations were nearing the perfection of the bomb. To sit idly by under these circumstances could mean destruction to his country. Unfortunately, the scientist under such compelling reasons is caught in a snare of mental bewilderment. It is very difficult to sit idly by and allow blatant aggressiveness and injustice go unheeded.

A reception was held prior to the inauguration of the meetings. We were welcomed by Sir William Farren, a Fellow of the prestigious Royal Society of London, and a Fellow of the Royal Aeronautical Society.

Presentation of the papers began the following day, September 15, 1953. Papers were presented on some of the more important structural problems in high-performance aircraft and some of the methods and materials currently available to the aircraft designer for their solution. Pod mountings of jet engines, as exemplified by Boeing aircraft, were discussed. Pod mountings permit isolation of the power plants from the airplane and permit division of the power plants into a sufficient number of elements so that failure of one power plant does not reduce the probability of continued flight. The data presented by George Schairer of Boeing Aircraft was a prelude of what was to be incorporated in the first series of the Boeing commercial jets. The Boeing 707's were put into service in 1959.

Our lectures at University College were interspersed with visits to several factories producing transports and bombers for the Royal Air Force. The Vickers Viscount was the world's first propeller-turbine airliner. This was indeed quite an advance for the British designers. Several were ordered for British European Airways, Air France, and others. The Valiant, Britain's four-jet bomber, was ordered for the RAF. This aircraft had several novel features about it that made it an outstanding performer. The engines were buried in the root section of the wing, two engines per side of the fuselage. Aerodynamically, this engine arrangement was ideal, but it would undoubtedly present problems when repairs to the engines would be required.

University College is replete with many famous names in the fields of the arts, sciences, and medicine. Of special interest to the scientist and engineer are Vignoles, a professor of engineering, who invented the flat-bottomed rail used throughout the world; Karl Pearson, known for his research in applied mathematics; Coker and Filon, who pioneered the study of photoelasticity; Thomas Gardner, famous in the field of colloidal chemistry; Hugh Williamson, a chemist of great reputation; Sanderson, an eminent physiologist; Sir Willam Ramsey, the famous chemist; Flinders Petrie, the archaeologist and Egyptologist. The foregoing names are by no means exhaustive, for many famous lawyers, doctors, and teachers received their training at the school. During the "blitz" of World War II, the library lost seventy thousand books. A good deal of damage was incurred during the war, but there was evidence all around us that rebuilding and rehabilitation were in progress.

The following two days were devoted to lectures pertaining to the control of flight, the aerodynamics of compressor-blade vibration, advances in boundary layer and circulation control, and the introduction of the Comet into service. As a result of the first year of operation, experience had shown, that in the future, operators must define their requirements more precisely to avoid misunderstandings and ambiguities. It was suggested that a close partnership with the designers and manufacturers be established if the utmost in efficiency and an amelioration in maintenance problems be obtained.

There were many lectures given by distinguished scientists and engineers. The trip to the Bristol airplane factory was one of the highlights of this symposium. To get to Bristol, the delegates rode in a special reserved car on the train. Breakfast and dinner were served on the train. In production at the factory, there were helicopters, fighters, and jet transports. The delegates had the opportunity to fly in the Britannica jet transport. There were four jet engines, which drove propellers sixteen feet in diameter. The plane cruised at 390 miles per hour at twenty-five thousand feet.

The delegates were given several demonstrations of sonic booms. The pilots would point their aircraft in the direction in which we were standing, so that the shock waves generated on the fuselage and wing would strike the ground in the vicinity where we were assembled. This was accomplished by pulling out of the steep dive at the appropriate moment. Depending on the aircraft flown and atmospheric conditions, one could hear a single boom and on other occasions two booms, the second following the first in rapid succession. These booms, incidentally, are representative of the creation of a new drag component, known as wave drag. This pressure wave propagates energy away from the aircraft and is nonrecoverable. This additional component of drag contributes materially to the tremendous amount of power required in supersonic flight. This pressure wave is analogous to the bow wave of a ship. The waves that we see in the water represent energy being carried away from the ship, never to return back to it in the form of recoverable energy input.

Women guests were not invited to go to Bristol. Thetis, therefore, set out alone to shop for our families, secretaries, and friends. In view of the coronation festivities, there were many beautiful gifts to purchase. For our daughter she found many beautiful dolls to choose from. For our son there were so many toy soldiers, guards, and a model of the coronation coach with its attendant horses that Thetis had difficulty in making a decision. To this very day, Alceste and Conrad still have these beautiful, treasured items. Thus, shopping at Liberty and Harrods was indeed an adventure. She could not resist buying her father a derby.

Father always wore a derby, so you can imagine how delighted he was to receive one directly from London. Father was a very handsome man, who was often mistaken for a movie star. He did not appreciate the compliment of people on the streets trying to guess who he was. He wore the derby with pride and great dignity for years.

While shopping for gloves, Thetis passed through the fabric section. There she spotted a breathtaking, beautiful pale ivory, silk lamé, embroidered with gold thread. This was material for a wedding gown. At the time, she wondered what use it might be as a gift and decided against purchasing it. Thetis was halfway out of the store when her subconscious told her that she should reconsider the item. Accordingly, she returned to the counter. She simply could not resist purchasing it. After all, we had a daughter. Even though she was just eight at that time, Thetis bought it with her in mind. For years Thetis carefully stored the lamé until the happy day arrived. The designer who fabricated our daughter's wedding gown was just as amazed as Thetis was at the beauty of the fabric and how well the material had lasted all these years. Our daughter was every inch a queen on her wedding day. As a mother, Thetis was happy that her dream had come true.

There were many places to visit, rides on trains and sailing on the Thames. These sojourns provided us an opportunity to mingle with the people and better understand their habits, customs, and mode of living. Greenwich was fascinating, with its Royal Observatory, the twenty-four hour magnetic clock, and copies of standard measures. Tourists were taking snapshots of one another standing astride the Greenwich Meridian.

A day later we drove to Stratford-on-Avon. On our way we stopped at Oxford University. As we walked on the campus of Corpus Christi, we could sense the spirit of Richard Foxe, the founder of the college who had been elected chancellor of the University of Cambridge in the year 1500. Several portraits and other relics were on display. Desiderius Erasmus, the classicist and patron of the new learning of the Renaissance, had taught at Oxford. In the dining room of one of the colleges, there were portraits of former deans and professors. The atmosphere was purely academic and scholarly. Oxford is noted primarily for its classical teachings, scholars, and humanists.

Stratford-on-Avon was the Shakespeare country we had read about in school. We had to see everything we could within our allotted time. There was the cottage of Anne Hathaway, Shakespeare's wife, and the home where Shakespeare was born. The Shakespearean hotel was full of Elizabethan charm. Our delicious lunch consisted of roast beef and Yorkshire pudding. In addition to all this Elizabethan charm, there was a Woolworth store, which appeared out of place in this hamlet.

Time was running short. We then went to the Castle of Warwick. We saw the castle from the outside. It did not appear to be as large as Windsor Castle. The gardens were beautiful and the landscape a luscious green, interspersed with trees and variegated vegetation. Our allotted time had come to an end, and we then drove back to London.

There was much packing to be done. The next day we would leave the Waterloo Station in London for Southhampton at 9:34 A.M. This was a two-hour train ride to Southhampton where we would board the ship *United States*. It was September 22, 1953, and our arrival date in New York would be September 28th.

The SS *United States* had made her maiden voyage from New York to Europe on July 3, 1952. Thus the ship was just a year old when we embarked. At that time the SS *United States* was the largest and most luxurious ship ever built in our country. It was also the world's fastest and most modern liner. It was 990 feet long, 101.5 feet in beam, with a gross tonnage of 53,300. This tonnage was substantially less than the *Queen Mary*, which was close to 100,000 tons. This differential in tonnage resulted from the usage of aluminum throughout the Unites States. This meant less displacement and higher attainable speed. The ship with its sleek lines was a sight to behold. It felt wonderful to be sailing again and breathe in the fresh salt air.

When crossing the Atlantic on both trips, we encountered the wrath of Poseidon and Aeolius. During the month of September, Poseidon and his partner are in cahoots with each other and love to frolic by creating tropical storms and hurricanes to remind us mortals that they are still around. The *United States* encountered a full-blown hurricane. The waves were some fifty feet in height and broke over the sports deck (highest portion of the ship). Once the ship began its pitching motion, it would go through three complete cycles, each cycle increasing in amplitude. On the third cycle, the bow of the ship would plunge abruptly with all the fury and wrath that Poseidon and Aeolus could muster together. Thetis well remembers to this very day my turning to her and saying, "This maneuver is going to prove once and for all whether the stress analysts performed their job correctly." What an appropriate time to tell her that! What reassurance and consolation!

This pitching motion occurred several times, and we were amazed that on each pitching-motion maneuver, three complete cycles were executed, with an accompanying sensation of a free-falling motion of the bow after the third oscillation. No sooner would the ship quiet down for a while than we would be subjected to the same maneuver. We knew when the stern was out of the water by the sudden whining of the exposed propeller(s).

The weak did not inherit the ship under these circumstances. Only the strong managed to hold on to the ropes and railings to get to the dining room. The rest retreated to their staterooms. Finally, the fury subsided when the immortal gods went on their way to frolic

122

elsewhere, and the passengers resumed their usual activities. Most of the more experienced travelers claimed this was the worst storm they had ever encountered. From then on the trip was pleasant, and we enjoyed a calm ocean.

The day before we arrived in New York, we called our family on the ship-to-shore telephone. Our request was that both Father and Uncle Gigi should each come with their own car. The reason: our gifts and purchases occupied a good section of the ship's hold.

The most magnificent sight on our approach to the harbor of New York was, once again, the majestic and stately Statue of Liberty. Tears welled in the eyes of all who watched this towering, awe-inspiring sight. It was a moment of supreme joy. We could appreciate what our grandparents tried to tell us when they saw that "wonder" and what it meant to them. We decided then and there that it was time for our children to better understand the meaning of hope, liberty, and aspiration by taking them to see the "Venerable Lady." In the spring we took the ferry to introduce our children to the Statue of Liberty. Young as they were, they appreciated that this was where their maternal great-grandparents and grandparents arrived.

It was a bright sunny day when we docked in the harbor of New York City. We were out on deck to spot our folks, but, unfortunately, there was too much congestion. Therefore, we proceeded to disembark. We were able to claim our luggage without too much difficulty. Uncle Gigi and Dad appeared in time to give us a hand with our luggage. We were happy to be back on home soil. Alceste and Conrad had come with Mother and Dad. The children hugged us tightly. Everyone rejoiced at being together again. After the emotional impact had subsided, we proceeded to load our baggage onto the cars.

As we were loading our baggage and boxes in both cars, Uncle Gigi remarked, "It looks as if you bought out all of London and Paris." We ourselves did not realize how much we purchased. Everything we had bought in Paris and London had been sent to the ship's hold. Gigi was so right now that everything had been brought together. The children were also amazed to see so many boxes and realized there must be some goodies in store for them as well. Finally, we were on our way home.

When we arrived home, excitement reigned in anticipation of what surprises might be in store for all. Mother suggested we relax a

123

bit and join them for dinner later. This was a most welcome suggestion, since we were quite tired.

When the hour arrived, the children and we walked down to our parents' home. There were hors d'oeuvres and cocktails all set up for us. Spanning the long archway between the living and dining room was a large banner. It read, "WELLCOME HOME." Mother told us that Alceste was the one who conceived the banner. Mother also told us in private that the two L's in wellcome were intentional on the part of Alceste. She reasoned that we had "come" home "well"—hence, the logical spelling to portray her thoughts was "WELLCOME." The logic of children at times makes more sense than the conventionally accepted modes of expression. Mother had a great appreciation for the wisdom of her eight-year-old grandchild. The children loved their grandmother for fostering freedom of thought and allowing them to express their individual thoughts without interruptions from her.

It was an evening of joviality and happiness. Everyone had stories to tell of what had happened while we were away. Alceste recounted her experiences in school during the five weeks we were away. The folks in turn brought us up to date as to what had transpired in our community. Everyone was most anxious to hear about our experiences abroad. Even though we wrote detailed letters and sent many cards from places we had visited, they wanted to hear from us in person. Eventually, the evening came to a close. It was time to take the children home and go to bed. The presents and surprises would follow in the days to come when the boxes would be opened.

It was like Christmas in September, with all those large boxes waiting to be opened. Not knowing ourselves how the clerks had packed our purchases, we were not quite sure what we would find. We, too, were surprised as we proceeded from box to box. Fortunately, the first box contained the toys we had purchased in London. There was an Ann Boleyn doll for Alceste. Toy soldiers and the coronation coach came next for Conrad. This made the children happy and content. They jumped for joy and hugged us.

As we continued to unpack, the gifts for our parents and friends appeared. There was the black derby for Grandfather, English handbags for the grandmothers, a Scottish cap for Uncle Gigi, silver souvenirs of the coronation, perfumes, bottles of scotch from London, and liqueurs from Paris. Since this was our first trip abroad, we wanted to make sure we did not forget anyone.

Dad was delighted with his derby, and we must say he looked debonair. He wore it religiously all the time and would not part with it. Uncle Gigi knew how to impart to the Scottish cap the proper tilt. After all, he did have a Scottish ancestor who provided the intuitive feel for the proper wearing of the cap. It really showed. He was very proud to wear it and looked as if he had just arrived from the Scottish Highlands.

15. Modernization of the NYU College of Engineering

In 1955 the College of Engineering at NYU celebrated its one-hundredth anniversary. The occasion was highlighted by an award of citations to distinguished alumni. I was one of those so honored. What impressed me most at the convocation was the remark made by Dean Thorndike Saville that the engineer's job is never finished. He must always be on the alert to be prepared for the changes that will occur. He must adapt himself to the needs of a viable and growing society.

This remark was prophetic. This was in line with the legacy that Dr. Alexander Klemin had established when he founded the first Daniel Guggenheim School of Aeronautics in the country. His spirit and ideals for engaging in research for the advancement of aeronautics still permeated the grounds of the college of engineering known as the Palisades.

In 1964 the *Quadrangle*, a publication of the School of Engineering and Science at New York University, devoted the issue to the sixtieth anniversary of the Wright brothers' flight. In it were articles by Dean John Ragazzini, Prof. Frederick Teichmann, Prof. Lee Arnold, generals Marvin Demler and Holtoner. I was also asked to write an article pertaining to the future trends of engineering. All articles illustrated the progress being made and the inevitable change occurring in engineering, the need to change to more fundamental approaches in the analysis of problems via a holistic point of view. It was no longer sufficient to analyze a given problem by considering only engineering inputs. Social, economic, political, budgetary, transportation, pollution, etc., components had to be considered.

The College of Engineering recognized the need for a change in its entire educational structure if it were to remain in a competitive educational environment. The space age had arrived, and many new disciplines had to be incorporated in the curriculum. The new era would usher in interdisciplinarity and extensionalism of concepts and scientific applications beyond belief and imagination.

John Ragazzini was appointed dean of the School of Engineering and Science in 1958. Dr. Lee Arnold was appointed director of the Daniel Guggenheim School of Aeronautics and Astronautics and Toni Ferri director of the Aerospace Laboratories and Astor Professor of Aerospace Sciences, whose responsibility it was to promulgate space science and construct and operate the supersonic and hypersonic tunnels.

In 1967 the Vincent Astor Foundation had granted half a million dollars for a chair in aerospace science to be established at the School of Engineering and Science. Dr. Antonio Ferri was appointed to the Astor chair. Ferri was noted for his work in the development of the first jet airplane in Italy. The Italian Caproni-Campini aircraft, incorporating jet propulsion, had been flown from Milano to Rome in 1940. This flight was made one year after Germany made the first flight of a jet-powered aircraft in a Heinkel He. Britain followed one year later in 1941 with the Gloster/Whittle E28/39. In the field of jet propulsion, the Europeans were well ahead of the U.S.A.

Toni was the first scientist to actually obtain a supersonic flow field in the tunnel and to measure the characteristics of wings for flight through the sound barrier. Burning of a fuel in a supersonic stream was first conceived by Ferri. This concept is known as the SCRAMJET, supersonic combustion ram jet. In 1938 he received the Premio dell'Accademia d'Italia for science, one of Italy's most prestigious awards.

In his announcement of Dr. Ferri's appointment to the Astor chair, Pres. James M. Hester of NYU said, "Man's effort to explore space requires imaginative engineer-scientists with the technical ability to implement their concepts. The Astor chair is gratifying support of New York University's efforts to help meet the need for such leaders by providing outstanding educational programs in space science."

Mrs. Vincent Astor related not only her late husband's interests in space science but also those of his father, John Jacob Astor. She said, "John Jacob Astor wrote a book that was published in 1894. It was a picture of a voyage into the future—capsule, launching pad—the things we are so familiar with today. Vincent Astor, his son, was deeply interested in engineering and became one of the first of the country's fliers."

All three men worked as a team with Toni Ferri as vice-presidents of General Applied Science Laboratories. They all had extensive experience in industry and were well acquainted with the future research and developmental requirements and needs of industrial organizations and government agencies. The trio represented a broad spectrum of engineering. John's expertise was electronics, research and development, sampled data-control systems, and he was a consulting editor for McGraw-Hill Book Company for their publications on control system theory. Lee represented structural dynamics and development, applied mathematics and physics, and the theory of vibrations and random signals. He felt it was high time to foster the concept of engineering science and the indoctrination of research development.

Toni represented aeronautics and astronautics in its fullest glory. He believed in advancing transportation to ever increasing heights. Hypersonic flight and space travel were the means to accomplish this in the future. He was an educator and an engineer par excellence. His ebullience and enthusiasm were awe-inspiring. As far as I am aware, he was the first in the world to obtain supersonic data while head of the supersonic wind tunnel in Guidonia, Italy, in 1937–1940.

When World War II erupted, the Nazis were aware of the work he was doing and made every attempt to confiscate all the experimental work he had conducted in his supersonic tunnel. Toni was alerted to the intentions of the Nazis, and he became all the more determined to make certain his data would not fall in their hands. Accordingly, he became head of the Partisan brigade group Spartaco in 1943–4 with the OSS, Office of Strategic Services. Upon arriving in this country, he joined NACA, Langley Field, Virginia, and was engaged in research transonic testing techniques, supersonic aerodynamics, and gas dynamics. The latter designation is now called hypersonic aerodynamics.

With a trio such as this, the School of Engineering and Science at New York University was well on its way to meet the requirements and changes necessitated by the advent of high-speed flight. It was recognized by Dean Ragazzini that engineering was changing to the scientific approach. By this he meant that the future engineer had to resort to the formulation of problems by starting from fundamental principles derived from basic physics. He introduced three categories of programs of study, which he identified as " Professional," "Engineering Science," and "Science."

To paraphrase Dean Ragazzini, the first category is related to the recognized needs of society and is directly concerned with fulfilling those needs by applying current scientific knowledge to their solution. By far, these professional needs are the greatest as measured by the number of engineers required. Programs were introduced to educate the future professional engineer.

Dean Ragazzini introduced the second category, "Engineering Science," because he recognized the uncertainties that exist in the analysis of problems in the real world. The real world is not the ideal deterministic structure that we suppose it to be, but rather probabilistic and statistical in character. This being the case, the future engineer must be trained accordingly. There also exists a need for the broadly trained engineering scientist who is educated to commit himself to graduate work as an undergraduate and whose objectives are those of being prepared to contribute to the most advanced aspects of engineering development.

Dean Ragazzini characterized the third category, "Science," by stating that the close relationship and mutual support of science, mathematics, and engineering are undeniable, and recognition of this fact has led our school to offer programs of study in the pure sciences. This kinship is mutually sustaining, and the inclusion of this end of the spectrum is essential.

Ragazzini concluded by saying that flight is a symbol of our progress in engineering. The future is limitless; it is unpredictable; but it is a challenge to the young engineer, which will ensure a fulfillment hard to achieve in many other endeavors.

In 1958 a program of expansion was inaugurated by its new director, Dr. Lee Arnold. In line with the objectives laid down by Dean Ragazzini, Dr. Arnold introduced many changes to meet the needs of the current and future developments. It was recognized that "the adoption of a new curriculum stressing the deeper understanding of the fundamental sciences while reducing specialization on the undergraduate level" was in order. The new curriculum was developed to provide the graduate with the background necessary to develop in whatever directions were mandated by progress. In my experience and the experiences of others, those whose training was along the lines dictated by science are most able to readjust themselves to meet the rapidly changing problems of technology.

Toni Ferri was responsible for the construction of several high-speed facilities. These included a supersonic tunnel capable of Mach numbers as high as six and shock tubes for research in the field of hypersonic flow and shock phenomena. The construction of equipment for the study of rarified gases was being planned for the near future.

General Demler covered the aspects of the "State-of-the-Art in Free World Science and Technology." One of his main thrusts was the necessity of cooperation between the military, educational institutions, and industry. Many other cooperative efforts were established such as NATO and AGARD (NATO Advisory Group for Aeronautical Research and Development).

General Holtoner discussed his experiences in the "Century Series" aircraft. He pointed out the limitations that are inherent when one exceeds design limitations. When such limits occur, one must proceed along new designs " . . . which involve all the myriads of evolutions and revolutions that were experienced and resolved in the Century Series" type aircraft.

In my article on "Interdisciplinarity in Engineering," I illustrated the philosophy and design procedures of the Wright brothers. In consonance with the times, the Wright brothers as designers were aware that many disciplines had to be reckoned with concurrently, aerodynamics, structures, power plant, control and safety.

One needed first to conceive in his own mind a concept that hopefully will fulfill a given requirement. Once an idea is conceived, as with the Wright brothers, feasibility studies and experimentation follow to substantiate the concept. Their experimental studies were ingeniously and meticulously conceived and executed in accordance with a well-organized set of procedures. These experiments are described in detail in two volumes, *The Papers of Wilbur and Orville Wright*. Volume I covers the period 1899–1905 and volume II the period 1906–1948. Their program is reminiscent of the space programs that have been carried out in the past. Data on unmanned vehicles was first acquired before sending man aloft as a safety precautionary.

After careful analysis of the data from aerodynamic, structural, and control considerations, the Wright brothers first made glider flights, beginning in 1899. After several such flights, they made the decision to install a power plant with two propellers, and they made their first powered flight on December 17, 1903.

As an aeronautical engineer, I was trained in the early years of 1930 in three major areas, aerodynamics, engineering mechanics and structures, and power plant. Aerodynamics and structures were by far the most important subjects. As I look back at this background of some six decades ago, I am reminded of the tremendous changes that have occurred and the pearls of wisdom that Dr. Klemin had imparted to us. He inculcated in his students the scenario of an ever-changing environment and the constant vigilance required to keep one's head above the rising tide of progress. One could, more or less, keep pace with the overall supervision of a design and know what was going on in detail.

With the constant increase in complexity of design and the era of space flight, one must possess the flexibility of a bumblebee in pursuit of nectar when flying from one source to another. There is no limitation as to the disciplines involved in analysis. As time goes on, new disciplines or combinations of disciplines, with all the possible combinatorics, will surface and become mandatory for the solution of problems.

The example given in the Quadrangle relates to the field of biology. In the area of biology, one must be acquainted with electronics, control-system analysis, nuclear physics, chemistry, hydrodynamics, electromagnetics, instrumention, computer science, etc.

If one considers the functioning of a biological cell and its stability, hydrodynamics plays a very important part. As one trained primarily in the field of aerodynamics and structures, I should like to illustrate some of the thoughts that have occurred to me in the biological reactions of the cell. The cell is made up of several bodies immersed in fluids of varying densities contained within a membrane. The cell is affected by a number of physical entities, such as pressure, temperature, chemical composition, electrical and magnetic constitution, movements across membranes, and diffusive properties, just to mention a few of the variables.

In aerodynamics one is concerned with the flow of air over obstacles, such as a wing, fuselage, empennage, canopy, etc. The flow is determined in terms of local pressure, velocity, temperature, and density. In addition to these items, the stability of the flow is of vital concern. At this point we should define what is meant by stability of flow. If an impulse of pressure or temperature is applied to the flow field in the vicinity of the body, the flow is perturbed. As a result, the steady-state pressure or temperature will manifest local fluctuations over the average or mean value. If these fluctuations result in flow breakdown over the wing. fuselage, etc., the flow becomes detached, thereby seriously altering the flow field.

The stability of the cell is truly one of the wonders of nature. Much has to be done in this area and imagination and intuitiveness are prime prerequisites. Our concepts of control-system synthesis and stability fall far short of explaining the amazing stability of the cell. The stability of a living cell is different from the usual sense of stability for inanimate objects, such as solids, liquids, etc., in that the cell is apparently very well organized in its functional behavior and has the ability of drawing orderliness from its immediate environment. It would appear that the component parts making up the cell interact with each other in such a way that each component lends a helping hand to a contiguous component in the event of need.

Conventional thermodynamics postulated by its founders pertained to a physical system isolated from all external affects. Energy required to drive the system, such as a steam engine, the internal-combustion engine, turbojet engine, all require temperatures materially higher than ambient. The higher we make the temperature, the more efficient the engine becomes. The first law of thermodynamics stipulates that energy is conserved. Energy can neither be created nor destroyed; to paraphrase this statement, the total energy is conserved, but the portion of energy that can be effectively utilized in producing work is diminished due to losses that occur due to addition or abstraction of energy, inherent frictional effects, and conduction of heat in the system.

The effect of these latter three energy losses is considered quantitatively in the second law of thermodynamics. This law stipulates that in any process, the degree of unavailable energy in the form of lost energy is determined by a quantity known as entropy. For irreversible processes the entropy is greater than zero and the higher the value, less energy is available for doing work. As the value approaches zero, the system becomes more reversible, thereby resulting in the production of more work. All practical heat cycles in operation are irreversible.

We know the living system is an open system, being influenced by many outside sources. Yet it is stable. The body processes are homoiothermic, that is, the maintenance of a relatively uniform body temperature. For example, from what source do the muscles derive their energy? To answer this question, the physicists have introduced the concept of negative entropy to describe the possible source of external energy. The entity "negentropy" has been introduced as a mystical pool of energy from which the muscles of the body can function. If this is the case, a reversibility process must be in force. How then, can one reconcile the apparent coexistence of irreversibility with reversibility? Ilya Prigogine, the Belgian chemist, has enunciated that an irreversible process can be maintained if a structure can be found that corresponds to a minimum of entropy increase.

The cell has flexibility and adaptability built into it such that it has the capacity (within limits) of learning how to react properly under extenuating conditions and thus has mechanisms that enable it to survive under varying ecological and environmental conditions. Some of the space flights have demonstrated this. Russian cosmonauts have been in orbit for a period of some two months in a zero-gravity field. No ill effects have been reported, as far as I know. We have sent our astronauts to the moon on several occasions with no apparent ill effects.

This concept of self-adjustments and the ability to restitute, within limits, some damaged part or parts of the cell make stability of the biological cell different from the stability as postulated by the physicist. Stability also depends, for a given volume and shape, upon the constitution of the cell. The internal constitution of the cell is very important in determining the overall deformation of the cell, which in turn defines the stability of the cell. The problem of biological stability may be ultimately tied up with cell division. This continual process of cell reproduction apparently produces a stable situation, thereby permitting man to go on for many years. Cancer apparently does not permit accurate reproduction of cells, thereby leading to instability of the organism, instability in the sense that disorder or randomness prevails.

In view of the foregoing, many new theories of the cell must be formulated to explain some of the aforementioned phenomena. The present laws of physics are probabilistic in nature and as a result explain the natural tendency of mechanisms to lapse into disorder. Biological processes taking place in large molecules, such as DNA and RNA, circumvent the tendency to disorder. What is truly amazing is the process by which a small but highly organized group of atoms is capable of producing such well-behaved and ordered events and processes within the cell. Or is it so astounding that such processes exist when millions of years of evolution and experimentation on the part of Nature have gone into their creation?

Such a situation is unprecedented anywhere else except in living matter. The physicist and chemist deal with inanimate matter, and the techniques employed have been based on mean or average values. Every now and then, however, a certain number of particles can penetrate through a potential barrier, which on the average is neglected.

The cell is an assembly of many different phases (solid, liquid, other?) composed of several different molecular, interacting components subject to a multivariate number of forces (electric, magnetic, etc.). The number of combinations that can be extracted from such an assembly is staggering, to say the least. When the conditions of stability, redundancy, ability to extract order out of the assembly, and many other considerations are taken into account, the possible number of feasible combinations reduces materially.

The foregoing example of the cell is but one of several to elucidate the many applications of all branches of science to a specific problem. Problems associated with unmanned and manned space flight are replete with such examples. Furthermore, it illustrates the need for formulating problems in their holistic structure. These examples also illustrate the need for being flexible and scientifically prepared in order to keep abreast of the rapidly accumulating knowledge taking place today and particularly in the future.

The biological cell can be characterized as an area that can eminently qualify as bio-engineering—it is comprised of the basic disciplines of chemistry, physics, interdisciplinarity, systems technology, information theory, and network theory.

In view of the previous example on the biological cell, the aeronautical engineer of today is confronted with many different disciplines. This is especially the case when analyzing space flight. The Daniel Guggenheim School of Aeronautics needed a complete revision in the courses it was offering to students. Accordingly, the

Daniel Guggenheim School would, in the future, be called the College of Engineering and Science of New York University at University Heights. This change in course was well-directed under the aegis of Dean Ragazzinni to meet the demands of the future, not only in engineering per se, but in areas of transportation, biology, planning, and sundry other problems relating to society.

New York University was founded in 1831 as the University of the City of New York. The College of Engineering was founded in 1855. When the campus became congested, the University Heights Campus was founded in 1893.

The restructuring of the College of Engineering was no sooner accomplished and set into implementation when financial crises loomed on the horizon in the 1960s and early 1970s. The NYU School of Engineering and Science was no sooner reorganized in the 1960s by Dean Ragazzini when President Hester recognized that the school was in financial straits. This was primarily the result of lack of interest on the part of students in pursuing an engineering profession at that time.

This was most unfortunate, since societal problems during the same time period were cropping up at an accelerative pace. Dean Ragazzini was fully prepared to meet this challenge by restructuring the entire school curriculum to deal with the impending problems arising in transportation, traffic, management procedures and policies, space, etc., that needed solutions.

Budgetary considerations finally forced the university trustees to conclude that a retrenchment was necessary if the university were to survive. As part of the retrenchment, the sale of the University Heights campus was part of the package. This occurred in 1973.

The NYU campus in the Bronx was not the only school facing financial difficulties. The Polytechnic Institute of Brooklyn faced similar problems. To solve the dilemma, the state of New York proposed a merger of the two schools, to be known as the Polytechnic Institute of New York. Accordingly, on October 10, 1973, Dr. George Bugliarello was selected its first president. I was greatly impressed by the selection of Dr. Bugliarello, since he also recognized, like Dean Ragazzini, the dependence of society on the role of the engineer-scientist for mitigation of its problems.

The motto of the Polytechnic Institute of New York is most appropriate in that it expresses most adequately the required action that is needed to cope with our engineering, societal, economic, political, educational, managerial, and educational problems: *Actorum Memores simul affectamus Agenda*. A free translation would be: Realizing appropriate action is required (to meet the changes that are inevitable), we at once strive for mitigations that must be inaugurated/addressed.

What was once the school that was the pioneer and leader in aeronautical engineering closed its doors at University Heights. All its graduates have felt the agony of its passing into history. Some of us are consoled by the fact that we have a grandchild that sprang out of the Nassau Division of NYU (now Hofstra University). Through my initiation and efforts, we helped establish the Long Island Campus of Polytechnic Institute of Brooklyn.

I should like to dedicate this chapter to all those engineers who attended the Daniel Guggenheim School of Aeronautics of NYU at University Heights and who have become involuntarily collegiate orphans when the college was disbanded.

16. Republic Creates Thunder across the Sky

Bob Johnson, World War II ace, with twenty-eight victories credited to him and author of *Thunderbolt,* conceived of the idea of a reunion of pilots who had flown her during the war. This was in 1961, twenty years after the first flight on May 6, 1941. After discussing this idea with Ken Ellington, director of Public Relations, Republic Aviation Corporation, invitations were sent out. An air show would be put on for the invitees at Farmingdale, Long Island, New York.

The P-47 Thunderbolt was affectionately called the "Jug" by the pilots. As part of the ceremonial occasion, a Jug was assembled and put in running order for flight demonstrations. Nostalgia swept over the group when the maneuvers being performed reminded them of their encounters over Europe. The good "ole faithful Jug" was uttered by many of the former pilots. The airplane, like a faithful Saint Bernard dog with its small cask of cognac dangling from its neck, coming to the rescue of its master when danger is imminent in the Swiss Alps, was revered and regarded as a godsend when it was battered and mutilated by enemy flak and gunfire. Like a cat, the Jug had nine lives—for which the pilots who flew her shall never, never forget. Many pilots have told me personally at the St. Louis reunion that they owed their lives to the "good ole Jug," not once, but in some cases twice.

After the nostalgic demonstrations in Farmingdale, the group met at the old Commodore Hotel "for more cocktails and a fabulous dinner." It was at this reception that Bob Johnson introduced Levon Aghazarian (Aggie), to the group. He had flown Spitfires and Hurricanes before flying Jugs in Burma. During the festivities that followed, Levon turned to Bob Johnson and suggested that reunions should be held regularly on an annual basis. The idea couldn't have been suggested at a better time. The group was in a *"gaudeamus igitur"* mood, and the idea was approved by acclamation. Thus was the founding of the Thunderbolt P-47 Pilots Association.

To establish a charter for the association, a group of pilots assembled in the New York area to elect a president, vice-president, a secretary, and a treasurer. Aggie was chosen president, Bob Johnson vice-president, Bob Alexander secretary, and Sid Flax treaurer. A charter was drawn up, specifying the goals and objectives of the association. Article II of the charter stated: The purpose of this association shall be to provide a common ground and focal point for members to perpetuate the memories of the P-47 flying days, to socialize and get together as often as possible, and to do anything else necessary to carry out these purposes.

The first reunion under the new charter was held on May 1963 at the Commodore Hotel in New York. The roll call was thirteen hundred strong! The response was overwhelming. Many pilots shed tears that evening for more reasons than one. On an even keel with revival of camaraderie was the good fortune to be alive, thanks to the Jug, to be able to attend.

It wasn't long afterward when the members of the association realized that they had forgotten those pilots who had ferried the P-47's overseas. The question asked was: what about the WASPS—the women Air Force pilots—who flew the P-47's from the factory to their final destinations? Certainly they should be members of the group. It did not take much convincing to accept the ladies into the group. Knowing of their commandant, Col. Jacqueline Cochran, there was no question about it. Who in his right mind would want to challenge her? So be it!

Now that the WASPS were accounted for, what about all the people from the designers of the aircraft to the mechanics who assembled the airplane in the factory and those who tested the final product on the assembly line to make sure it was properly debugged and operating in perfect order?

Rest assured! Something was done. The P-47 Alumni Association of "Jug Lovers" was established in 1981. This involved those people who were engaged in any way with the creation, development, manufacture, assembly, and testing of the Jug. These people represented forgotten entities and had played an important role in the production of the overall, physical product. Even though this group did not participate in aerial combat, they nevertheless devoted many countless hours and painstaking effort in making the Jug one of the most formidable fighters in World War II. The factory worked on a twenty-four-hour schedule, engineering on a twelve- to fourteen-hour daily basis, flight testing as long as there was sunlight. The mechanics assigned to the flight-test aircraft worked throughout the night to make sure the Jug was ready for flight at daybreak. These men were all dedicated and cooperative individuals. They were proud and honored to join such an alumni association.

People such as Larry ("Butch") Micalizzi and Harry Walther worked on both the first and last P-47 built. Frank Tchinnis, a flight mechanic, always made sure that the aircraft was ready and purring for flight the very next morning at the first sight of dawn. To do so meant many sleepless nights and forty-eight-hour days. These men, I am proud to say, personified dedication, commitment, and love of fellow man and country. Nothing on earth would deter them from what had to be done—yes! Family chores, children, parents, loved ones, all took second priority when it came to the Jug. Those of us who were involved with the development of the Jug were grateful for the understanding and patience of our wives and families.

In later years our adult children appreciated the impact of the P-47 on their lives. We would like to recount an anecdote that occurred while we were walking in San Francisco. We were celebrating our daughter's birthday at the Mark Hopkins Hotel in San Francisco. As we walked through the lobby of the hotel, we heard several voices call out "Gus, Gus." We surmised the page boy of the hotel was calling for another person named Gus. Before we realized that the summons was intended for me, a man approached us and said, "Please join us in the ballroom." What a surprise!

It was a reunion of the P-47 Thunderbolt Pilots Association. They had so many stories to tell us about their survivals after combat. Even though the aircraft sustained appreciable damage due to gunfire and flak, they were able to return safely to ground. The pilots came to realize with each successive mission that, inherent in the design of the Jug, they could count on its ability to endure damage to the structure and return safely to base. These remarks were very gratifying to me personally, since during the design of the plane, I was very frequently criticized for specifying aerodynamic loads that were too conservative. Try as hard as these critics could to convince me to reduce the magnitude of the loadings, I would not compromise.

It was a wonderful and rewarding day for us and our children. A beautiful lesson in the belated reward of a job well done, the memory of which will live forever.

During the war some 16,000 Jugs were built at the plants located in Farmingdale, Long Island, New York, and Evansville, Ohio. The overall statistics were quite impressive. The P-47's flew 546,000 combat sorties in World War II. It contributed to the destruction of almost 12,000 planes, 86,000 railroad cars, 9,000 locomotives, and 6,000 armored vehicles and tanks. It had earned seven Army/Navy "E's" for excellence in doing the job. There were 4.6 victories for each Jug lost in the air. In the first five months of 1945, the Jug flew an average of 1,677 missions and dropped 541 tons of bombs a day.

As chief of aerodynamics and flight test during World War II, I was aided by many colleagues in the department. In analyzing the aircraft performance characteristics, I had the assistance of Frank Mulholland, Jerry Pavelka, Richard Lu, and others. It was men like these whose dedication and teamwork that made the Jug what it was. It was not the effort of one or two men, but the dedicated and unstinting cooperation of many.

The Jug has been relegated to the museums and history. Progress has decreed it to be so. All of us who were associated with the Jug in whatever capacity shall always have fond memories of what can be accomplished when we constantly strive for perfection. Yes! I say perfection because at every step of the way, we did everything in our power and capability to improve the performance characteristics of the airplane. Various model designations were established from A to N to incorporate various design changes. A laminar flow wing was installed in an attempt to improve top speed.

When difficulties arose in controlling the Jug in high-speed dives (0.82-0.84M) various devices were being tested to mitigate the tuck-under tendency of the aircraft. As results would come in from the battle front, we would strive to ameliorate the situation. No stone was left unturned. With time and experimentation, it was realized we had reached a limit in performance characteristics in the design of aircraft we were dealing with. To ascend Nature's next rung in the ladder of progress, we had to devise new concepts and somehow extend our knowledge into unknown regions.

The advent of the jet engine as a power plant was a godsend. A comparison of high speeds for the P-47 and F-84 Thunderjet will emphatically illustrate the point. The F-84 had a straight, leading-edge wing but a thinner airfoil section than the P-47. The top speed of the production P-47 was 465 miles per hour, M = 0.70. The top speed of the F-84 was 560 miles per hour, M = 0.84. This represented a quantum jump in speed and was obtained overnight. It was truly amazing! Those of us who made the calculations couldn't believe the results at first. We were certain we had committed an error somewhere. After many independent checks, we were reconciled to the fact that our prediction was correct. No matter how hard we tried to increase the speed of the P-47, the ultimate we could attain was barely over 500 miles per hour. We had literally run into a speed barrier. This occurred on the P-47J.

There was no doubt that high-speed flight had changed the complexion of aeronautical engineering design as we had known it in the past. No longer could we naively assume that the air was incompressible. We were fortunate that we could abide by this assumption from the time of the early pioneers to the early forties. There now existed glaring gaps between what had been considered basic knowledge and the lessons learned in penetrating the sonic barrier. Our combat aircraft during World War II vividly illustrated the problems that were encountered in high-speed flight.

After several modifications were made of the straight wing F-84 (Thunderjet), the swept wing version was built. This version was dubbed the F-84F, Thunderstreak. The top speed of the F was in excess of 600 miles per hour, M = 0.90. The RF-84F Thunderflash was the reconnaissance version. This model was employed by the Allies of NATO. Republic was creating "Thunder" across the sky.

The first flight of the F-84F Thunderstreak was made at Edwards Air Force Base, Muroc, California, and took place on June 3, 1950. The airplane completed its Phase I tests in just twenty-nine days, making a total of nineteen flights in that brief period. This is strong testimonial to the rapidity with which an established design can be tested for its new features. The sequence of design changes followed methodically one step at a time. This enabled us to determine the effects of a single change upon the performance of the plane rather than a conglomerate change.

The next step in the evolution of high-speed aircraft at Republic was the F-105, Thunderchief. This plane was truly supersonic with a high speed of twice the speed of sound. This design incorporated the

Coke bottle concept. This was conceived by Richard Whitcomb of the Langley Memorial Aeronautical Laboratory, Virginia. The objective was to accommodate the resultant flow of air over the entire airplane as though the air particles were flowing over an equivalent, slender body without the appendages of the fuselage, such as the wing, horizontal and vertical tail surfaces, and any other appendages.

The area rule or "Coke-bottle" effect was applied to the F-105 to reduce the drag in the transonic range. This effect can be more vividly described by citing a few morphological analogs. The shapeliness of the fuselage in plan form was frequently referred to as the Marilyn Monroe shape, as Verdi, the operatic composer, would describe the outward form as "Celeste Aida, forma divina!" the heavenly crown of shapeliness. Because of the intricate network of expansion and compression waves resulting from the various parts of the airplane—fuselage, wing, inlets, tail surfaces, and other appendages—it was necessary to consider not each part of the airplane separately, but in toto, holistically.

Each component of the airplane would produce its characteristic pressure wave and, depending upon the design of the configuration, reinforcement or cancellation of these waves could result. It was primarily for this reason that the entire airplane had to be considered rather than component-wise. The area rule was an ingenious method of providing a convenient qualitative way of arranging the component parts of the vehicle in such a manner as to minimize transonic drag. Minimizing drag would, in all probability, ensure a more stable flow, thereby alleviating the severity of buffeting during the transition from subsonic to supersonic speeds.

The goal is to obtain an equivalent fuselage having the least amount of resistance. The procedure is one of trial and error. For the transonic case, cross-sectional cuts are taken perpendicular to the fuselage and its areas determined. This qualitative procedure presents a plot of the areas and should be devoid of any bumps in the plotted curve. Several configurations must be tried to determine the curve exhibiting the least amount of abrupt curvature.

It will be found that as one progresses from the nose of the fuselage rearward, a bump will occur when the cross-sectional areas of the wing is included. The abruptness in curvature of the plot can be minimized by the incorporation of wing leading-edge sweep. In addition, it may be possible to reverse the curvature of the fuselage

142

to account for the area taken up by the wing; hence the etymology of the phrase "Coke-bottle effect." The fuselage itself will usually look like a Coke bottle in plan form.

The reverse curvature of the fuselage in the neighborhood of the wing may be related also to the fact that at supersonic speeds, the column of air flowing over the wing (the stream tube) wants to expand. This is in contradistinction to the subsonic case where the stream tube contracts as Mach number 1 is approached.

The transonic area rule has been extended to the supersonic regime by Bob Jones of the Ames Aeronautical Laboratory. Instead of taking cuts perpendicular to the free-stream direction, one takes areas along Mach cones. The theory applies strictly for a given Mach number. A generalization has been made by Barrett Baldwin and Robert Dickey of Ames that applies to the transonic and supersonic regimes. The result will yield a minimization of the drag over a region of transonic and supersonic Mach numbers by a technique known as the moment of area rule.

At supersonic speeds, the entire aircraft is immersed in a network of pressure waves of varying intensities. Care must be exercised that coalescence of shock waves does not occur. Changes in flow direction must be accompanied by gradual changes in curvature of the surface. Junctures must be carefully studied to permit expansion of flows where necessary. These concerns are but a few of the myriad of others that must be considered.

With very high leading-edge sweep, an additional phenomenon occurs at the leading edge of the wing. At moderate angles of attack, a leading-edge vortex appears that can alter the nature of flow over the wing. This does not occur on straight wings. As the angle of attack is increased, the vortex grows in intensity and instead of leaving the wing at the wing tip, will peel off at some distance before the tip. The form of the vortex is a detached bulbous air mass slightly aft of the leading edge and above the wing. This can induce premature flow separation over a substantial portion of the wing. This phenomenon may necessitate the use of auxiliary devices on the wing to modify the intensity of the vortex at high speeds. Leading-edge flaps may be such a device, or modifications in the nose of the airfoil section. It would appear that the air molecules object to encountering a sharp leading edge and form their own leading edge by providing a more rounded edge. This is especially the case at

143

appreciable angles of attack.

In this connection, it is interesting to note that an opposite effect occurs in the design of high-speed ships. Marine designers have introduced the "bulbous bow" at the stem of the ship to reduce wave-making at high speeds. Instead of using a knife-edge at the stem of the ship, a form similar to half an electric bulb is incorporated. The curvature of the bulb is greatest at the keel line and diminishes as one approaches the surface of the water. This is an example of where the bulbous bow is of distinct advantage in the design of high-speed passenger ships or naval vessels and a detriment in the case of high-speed aircraft.

In view of some of the problems that have been indicated, it is no wonder that a great deal of time was spent in the supersonic tunnels of the NACA. Various configurations were tested and with the assistance of Richard Whitcomb and Paul Purser of the Langley Memorial Aeronautical Laboratories, a final configuration was determined. The F-105 Thunderchief had a short span, very thin swept-back wing, a long Coke-bottle fuselage, and wing-root air intake ducts, thereby allowing radar equipment to be installed in the needle nose of the plane.

17. The Ultimate Airplane

Remarkable as the manned flights to the moon were, I was troubled by the fact that the very costly rocket power plants were discarded shortly after launch. It was time to seriously consider an alternate design that would be more feasible economically. Rocket boosters were an interim solution and an expedient one since much research had gone into the design of rockets from the time of Frank Goddard. Space exploration would become more intense in the future and would require many more missions. Accordingly, it was necessary to conjure up a design that could use the same power plant over and over again.

Since the space vehicle, if launched from the earth, had to fly in an atmosphere, why shouldn't we utilize a jet engine to the limit of its design capability? I was aware of the research that Toni Ferri was doing with ramjets and his innovative ideas involving burning of fuel at supersonic speeds, which was called the SCRAMJET. The ramjet, with combustion at subsonic speeds, would take over at an altitude and Mach number at a point when the jet engine reached its limit of operation. The subsonic ramjet, in turn, would eventually attain its limit at an altitude and Mach number substantially higher than the conventional jet engine.

This occurs since the design of the ramjet was such that the combustion flame could not be maintained at supersonic Mach numbers. Having reached the limit in the operation of the ramjet, the scramjet would go into operation. The scramjet mode could convey the aircraft to the outer fringes of the atmosphere at which point the vehicle would have attained an orbiting velocity of Mach number 25. The pilot could then enter orbit.

All of the above was conceptual at this point of time. I was not concerned with feasibility but was thoroughly convinced this was one approach in the preservation of the power plant(s). Complications and many questions about cost, etc., would undoubtedly arise.

My immediate concern was how could I sell the concept to my boss, Sasha Kartveli?

In 1959 my concept of the ultimate airplane was discussed with Sasha. I knew he was predominantly interested in developing advanced conventional aircraft designs. This design would permit us to enter space as well. The idea was tantalizing. Space research per se was not enthusiastically relished by Sasha. This design had vestiges of conventional design while flying in an atmosphere and would capture the interest of Sasha. My greatest selling point, however, was concentrated on the fact that the military would benefit the most by such a design.

This vehicle could take off from conventional airfields, fly to any altitude, and eventually orbit the earth. The vehicle could remain in orbit, encircling the earth several times, thereby extending the duration of flight. Detection of the vehicle by the enemy would be difficult since the orbital path could be changed at will by the pilot. Reconnaissance capability would be greatly enhanced and could be used as a means of detecting oncoming enemy missiles.

Several sessions were held with Sasha in his office and in his den at home. Finally, after much wrangling and convincing, he put his stamp of approval on the idea. At that time we had Antonio Ferri as our consultant. He was one of the world's leading experts in supersonic and hypersonic aerodynamics. In view of his experience in the fields of inlets, ramjet and scramjets, and exhaust nozzles, I convinced Sasha that Toni would be the ideal consultant for assisting us in the design of the ultimate airplane.

Toni worked with us unremittingly and exuberantly. He was convinced this concept was of great military value and would greatly interest the air force. He also assigned several of his top scientists from his laboratory on Long Island, notably Paul Libby and Louis Nucci, to this project.

Now that we had the concept, the next step was to work out the details. One of the main considerations was the propulsion system. Fortunately, Toni worked closely with von Karman through AGARD. Von Karman had originally met Toni in Guidonia, Italy. Toni had been in charge of the supersonic tunnel for six years, from 1937 to 1943.

Theodore von Karman colloborated with Toni on combustion and propulsion systems and their associated design problems. Von

Karman had developed the fundamentals of burning fuel in an open stream of air. He recognized the problem as being one involving simultaneously, aerodynamics, thermodynamics, and chemical kinetics, which he dubbed "aerothermochemistry."

We were very fortunate to have had Toni Ferri and von Karman advise us on the merits of the ramjet and scramjet engines, which were eventually incorporated into the design of the plane. As the discussions progressed, it became increasingly apparent to me that a more appropriate classification of the ultimate plane should incorporate not only the concept of flight in an atmosphere but space as well. To meld these two ideas together, the term aerospace was adopted.

Consultations with von Karman shed light on some of the problems we would be confronted with and gave us impetus to carry on with the aerospace plane. He was basically an optimist and a philosopher, eager to extend the frontiers of knowledge by working on a project such as the aerospace plane. He recognized the overwhelming odds facing us, but he encouraged us to carry on the research necessary to prove the feasibility of the concept. He liked the idea of corroborating with the military in order to gain their support in such a garguantuan undertaking. If nothing came of the project per se, we would be laying the groundwork for future research and development.

Theodore Von Karman was not only a scientist but a humorist as well. He could equilibrate his ponderous scientific thoughts with anecdotes as well. He would tell us of the many occasions he would encounter when people would refer to his heavy accent and wondered why it was so. His remark would be: "That is so because I speak mit *em-pha-sis!*" Just before lunch hour, he would be served a Manhattan with "two cherries." He would sip on his drink, being ever so careful not to touch the cherries until the very end of the drink. He would then gobble them up with great satisfaction and utter delight of a young boy.

At a party given by Toni Ferri at his home, von Karman was the center of attraction. His stories were of interest partly because of his intriguing accent and what he would relate about his scientific friends and family background. His father had been in charge of education in Hungary and had set up an outstanding school system. The educational system was set up in a way that the cultural aspects were not overlooked. As proof of the broad cultural education he received, he would turn to me and quote passages from Homer in the original to test my ability to recognize where it was from—the *Iliad* or the *Odyssey*.

As an aerodynamicist he had high regard for the research conducted by Dmitri Joukowski, a professor at the Imperial University of Moscow. He, along with Kutta, discovered the law relating the lift of a body with the circulation around it. What was of more interest to von Karman was the mathematical research performed by his student, S.A. Chaplygin, who was assigned the task of investigating the behavior of gas jets at supersonic speeds. This monumental work was performed in 1904 and was apparently the first attempt in an analysis of supersonic flow. What fascinated von Karman was the introduction of a special technique introduced by Chaplygin, known as the "Hodograph" method in modern phraseology.

This technique is used quite extensively in the analysis of supersonic jet streams. The resulting equation obtained was nonlinear. This entailed complications in its solution since very little was and is still known about the solutions of such equations. By proper transformation of the variables, Chaplygin was able to linearize the equation. This procedure approximated the results with sufficient accuracy to produce useful results. In von Karman's evaluation of the technique, this constituted a milestone in the progress of supersonic aerodynamics. Because of the language barrier, this work was not known until the Russian was translated in 1944 by Maurice H. Slud.

Von Karman's appraisals of Nobel Laureates were very interesting and informative—men like Albert Einstein, Max Born, Niels Bohr, and Edward Teller. These men, he felt, should not have shown their disdain and unwillingness to work with the military, but rather than forcing their ideas and decisions onto the military, to present their scientific results on a purely academic basis. He was very proud of the fact that he was related to Franz Liszt, the Hungarian composer.

Sasha Kartveli called me into his office one day and said he had a problem. I naturally braced myself for what the assignment might be. He informed me that he was inviting von Karman to his home for cocktails and dinner. I was relieved to know that the seriousness of the anticipated problem was not more severe and asked what he was troubled about. "Gus, would you know where in hell I can get the genuine Hungarian slivovitz? I can arrange to get the Beluga caviar, but where could I get the slivovitz (a dry colorless plum brandy—a specialty of Hungary)?" The real problem was that Sasha needed it for the following day—time was of the essence.

I immediately called Toni Ferri to inquire if he knew where we might get the slivovitz. This was one time when he was unable to help us. He was curious enough to ask what we wanted with such an exotic liquor. I responded by saying that it was for an exotic person, a special Hungarian. Having heard the word Hungarian, his immediate reply was, "You don't mean von Karman?" When I responded in the affirmative, he laughed and said, "When in Rome, do as the Romans do! Serve red wine!"

After many attempts to get the genuine Hungarian slivovitz, we finally found a bottle made in one of the Balkan countries. The highlight of the evening occurred when von Karman was served slivovitz. He was pleasantly surprised and wanted to know where it was purchased. When told, he said he would have to get a bottle for himself. Upon hearing this, Sasha felt like the perfect host in pleasing his distinguished guest. Sasha had hit the jackpot! Or was it that the honored guest was very polite to his host?

The aerospace vehicle design was based on utilizing an advanced turbojet power plant for takeoff and landing, with an acceleration capability to Mach 3.5. For the remainder of the mission, ramjet engines would be used. The vehicle could then accelerate from Mach 3.5 to approximately 8, by several ramjet engines functioning in subsonic mode of combustion. From Mach 8 to Mach 25, the same ramjet engines were used and operated in a supersonic mode of combustion. Liquid hydrogen would be used as fuel for all the power plants.

The vehicle incorporated a conical body with a lifting wing and a three-dimensional inlet. This inlet was common to all engines and was distributed in an arc of 180 degrees. The exhaust nozzle was also common to all engines and distributed uniformly in the same manner.

Several configurations were studied, which included single-stage and two-stage vehicles. The results of the analyses indicated that a two-stage vehicle could be designed to be about 10 percent lighter than a single-stage vehicle; however, its complexity and cost would be much greater. The configuration finally selected consisted of five ramjets and five turbojet engines.

The vehicle consisted of a lifting body shaped in the form of a large delta wing, with control surfaces attached to its trailing edge. The under surface of the front portion of the wing was used as an open-type air inlet for compressing the air and supplying it to the combustion chambers of the ramjet engines. The turbojet engines were located in the body above the ramjets and were supplied with air by an embranchment from the main air inlet. The portion of the vehicle behind the combustion chamber was formed in the shape of expansion nozzles for the ramjet engines. The vehicle had a horizontal projected area of 8500 square feet and was 219 feet long and 38 feet high. Most of the interior was to be occupied by liquid hydrogen fuel.

On August 3rd, 1960, Sasha Kartveli and I presented a paper entitled "Design Concepts and Technical Feasibility Studies of an Aerospace Plane" before the Institute of Aeronautical Sciences in San Diego, California. The paper was not published at the time because of its security classification.

The overall purpose of the orbital vehicle was manifold. It could take off from the ground in a conventional manner in approximately 6,000 feet, using turbojet power. Then it would proceed to climb to an altitude of 200,000 feet in an accelerating motion, to a speed of Mach 25. From this vantage point, the pilot could maneuver the vehicle aerodynamically in the outer fringes of the rarified atmosphere to an altitude of 300,000 feet. The pilot could then proceed, if desired, to orbit the earth several times for a certain length of time. During this time he could deliver a substantial useful load, earthbound or space-bound. After his mission was completed, he could proceed to effect a normal landing. In addition, he could accomplish other military or commercial terrestrial missions between two points on earth at high speeds and high altitudes.

Toni Ferri had admirable qualities that were inspiring to me. He was truly "A labor-loving and truth-loving man." Concept is one thing, but ideas and implementation are totally different and far between. The arrangement of power plant and inlets originated from him. The selection of subsonic and supersonic ramjet combustion engines was Toni's recommendation to us. He adopted the design philosophy that if we were to control weight, we had to incorporate multifunctional uses of a given portion of the vehicle. This is illustrated by the external use of the bottom portion of the vehicle, from the nose of the vehicle to the entrance of the engines, as the inlet. Not only would the bottom portion of the vehicle serve as an inlet, but with a combination of expansion and compression waves would at the same time produce the required pressure to the combustion chambers. In short, the vehicle was so arranged that aerodynamics and propulsion became functionally integrative.

When I queried Toni how we could actually design for such an extensive range of speeds that required so many different parameters, his reply was: "By the time this vehicle will be built, we will hopefully have the required computers and monitors to automatically take care of the multifaceted requirements." This was over thirty years ago. With the introduction of the Cray supercomputer and the work going on today with super-supercomputers, Toni's prophetic remark is coming to pass.

There is one drawback to conceptualizing too far in advance. One must exhibit determination and doggedness in the pursuit of the concept and exercise a great deal of patience in its eventual realization and implementation. Imagine my joy when the concept was reincarnated when President Reagan, in his 1986 State of the Union Address, stated, "We are going forward with research on a new Orient Express that could by the end of the next decade, take off from Dulles Airport, accelerate up to twenty-five times the speed of sound, attaining low earth orbit, or flying to Tokyo within two hours."

It is especially gratifying to me personally that, in retrospect, I worked with such far-sighted men as Seversky, Kartveli, and Ferri, and that present research is in the most talented and capable hands the U.S.A. has to offer. Administratively, the entire project hinges on synergism between industry, the university, and NASA. I am delighted to see that NASA has adopted the legacy of NACA and is working cooperatively with industry and other institutions.

It is also encouraging to note that a conference was held at Grand Forks, North Dakota, on September 20–23, 1988, on a global cooperative and participative scale. The conference was entitled "First International Conference on Hypersonic Flight in the 21st Century." This conference was sponsored by the University of North Dakota, Center for Aerospace Sciences, in cooperation with NASA, the ESA (European Space Agency), the NAL/STRG (National

Aerospace Laboratory/Space Technology Research Group of Japan), IEEE/AESS (Institute of Electrical and Electronics Engineers/ Aerospace and Electronic Systems Society), AIAA (American Institute of Aeronautics and Astronautics), and the AAS (American Astronautical Society).

Feasibility studies have now entered on an international scale at various companies worldwide, research institutions, and worldwide space agencies. This is most gratifying, for the aerospace plane merits and requires the cooperation of the entire aeronautical and aerospace community throughout the world.

The advent of supercomputers gives one a great deal of hope in controlling and optimizing flows to provide for maximum thermodynamic efficiency on the aerospace plane. This development has many ramifications and applications to structures, stability, control, etc. One stands in amazement when it is realized that the processing rate of almost 2.4 billion calculations per second has been attained. Again, NASA has made great strides in theoretical and numerical techniques, by men like Robert Jones, Howard Lomax, and Max Heaslet of the Ames Aeronautical Laboratory at Moffett Field, California.

In view of the foregoing, it is feasible to perform on the computer complex flow problems. Computational aerodynamics is the term now used to perform such calculations. This technique enables researchers to visualize flows on the screen in a manner similar to computer graphics. The mathematical equations defining the flow are fed into the computer, which produces corresponding flow fields graphically. The designer can modify the design to ameliorate flow conditions where it is observed flow breakdown occurs. Advances are constantly being made to investigate more complex configurations by improvements in algorithms, grid generation, more rapid convergence methods in arriving at the final answer, microprocessors, introduction of neural and parallel computing architectures. The latter item is being considered in order to increase the range of utilization of the computer to a broader group of problems.

There are limitations to what can be accomplished on the computer. Determination of drag and the associated problem of the transition from laminar flow to turbulent flow remains to be resolved. Turbulence is a stochastic phenomenon and as a result, statistical methods must be employed. The mathematical formulation of this problem has always been a stumbling block in the past. Viscous forces constitute a "sticky" problem in aerodynamics, and with many new interactions that have been introduced, the problem has become more complicated. Empiricism must be relied upon to fill the gap between theory and observation.

The aerospace plane is becoming more feasible with the advent of new structural materials that can withstand high temperatures, advances in computational fluid-dynamics technology, advances in computer science, propellants and combustion, innovations in flight controls whereby mechanical systems would be replaced by digital electronic controls, new vistas in computational chemical physics, to mention but a few of the areas where intensive research is going on. All these activities will provide a solid technological base for the eventual realization of the aerospace plane.

It is indeed gratifying that a good percentage of the heavy technological artillery of this country and now the world has been focused on this design. This is so reminiscent of other projects of a similar nature that required the talents and disciplines of many different professions, such as the atomic project of World War II, the man-orbiting projects, the lunar project, the utilization and focusing of outstanding physicists, astronomers, industrialists, etc., on the war effort during World War II, all of which have proven highly effective and successful.

It is historically interesting to note that NACA had been pursuing high-speed flight since the 1950s with the X-15 research plane. The goal was to acquire data for manned hypersonic flight. The Dyna-Soar boost glider was used to obtain data in the hypersonic speed range. The vehicle was rocket-boosted to the outer fringes of space and then allowed to glide long distances by aerodynamic means. The air force and Ames Research Center, under the aegis of Harvey Allen and Al Eggers, and their associates, Alvin Seiff, Clarence Syvertson and Stanford Neice, worked synergistically on this project. Much of this research was prompted by the type of warhead that should be used on the ballistic missile.

Flight tests continued into the 60s, focusing on hypersonic air-breathing propulsion systems. Work since then has concentrated on lifting body designs and configurations and the Space Shuttle. My conversations with Al Eggers and Harvey Allen of the Ames Aeronautical Laboratories in the late 50s instilled in me an appreciation and introduction to some of the myriad of problems associated with hypersonic flight. Their pioneering and research efforts shall remain one of the monumental contributions to aerospace.

It was recognized at the outset that the propulsion system and structural design were the critical areas of this vehicle and would require a considerable amount of research and development, both theoretically and experimentally. The propulsion problems were divided into three major flow regions: inlet, combustion, and exhaust nozzle. In the design of the propulsion system, we recognized that the problem of decelerating the air from hypersonic speed to some lower value of Mach number in the supersonic range should be conducted in a way that the air static temperature at the entrance of the combustor would be between 2000 and 3000 degrees Rankine. This temperature was chosen so that auto-ignition with high reaction rates would result. This would minimize the length of the combustion region and make possible the development of an inlet having a high-pressure recovery characteristic.

With contraction of the stream tube area in going from flight Mach 25 to burner Mach 9, the resultant burner area is a small percentage of the frontal area of the inlet. For example, for the particular configuration considered, the coaxial stream tube has an area of 780 square feet, while the area of the burner is about 50 square feet. For this reason, a hypersonic ramjet engine requires a large size inlet, a relatively small burner, and a large nozzle. As pointed out by Ferri, it would appear impractical to consider the ramjet engine as a separate element of the vehicle configuration. With the long underlength of the body, the required contraction of the stream tube became feasible.

To substantiate some of the theoretical inlet-flow calculations and pressure recoveries at the entrance section of the combustor, exploratory tests were run at the von Karman Gas Dynamics Facility of the Arnold Engineering Development Center, Tullahoma, Tennessee. These tests were run at Mach 18. Preliminary analysis of these test data indicated that pressure recoveries of the magnitude calculated could be achieved.

Since the vehicle was designed primarily for the hypersonic flow range, additional problems in the transonic and subsonic range had to be considered. Among these was the problem of transonic drag rise and low-speed characteristics. The vehicle must have acceptable flying qualities in all regions of speed, including the takeoff and landing phases of operation. Several compromised configurations were studied and analyzed, together with related problems of stability.

The results of preliminary tests and calculations made in 1959–1960 indicated that an orbiting vehicle utilizing ramjet supersonic combustion was highly promising. The results also showed that such a vehicle could perform interesting and far-reaching military and scientific missions. The power plant and vehicle should be considered as an integrative unit and should undergo parallel development. The results attained at the time were very encouraging and merited further continuation of work. We were further encouraged by the test results obtained on the Dyna-Soar project. Much experimentation had been conducted since the mid-fifties. Conversations with Harvey Allen and Al Eggers resulted in some of the problem areas and the need for further research, both theoretical and experimental.

In summary, the primary design consideration of the aerospace plane was dictated by the principle of multifunctionality of as many component parts of the vehicle acting integratively. Unlike the conventional airplane design, which had a fuselage per se, a wing per se, tail surfaces per se, and other appendages per se, the aerospace plane would integrate all these separate components into an integral group. One could not clearly delineate a fuselage per se, a wing, inlets to the power plant, etc. This concept was adopted to conserve volume, weight, and to consolidate into one unit as many different functions as possible.

This was accomplished in many different ways throughout our studies. The lower surface of the vehicle was utilized as an inlet to the combustor. In addition, the lower surface was so designed as to result in a pressure rise by means of a series of compression waves. The conventional fuselage now became synonymous with the wing. In effect, the wing-fuselage became a single unit, an overall aerodynamic lifting surface. The power plant and vehicle were so designed as to be considered an integral part and should undergo parallel development. However, it was realized that the design was primarily focused on the hypersonic end of flight. Consideration had to be given to the lower-speed range to make sure that the characteristics of takeoff, landing, and transonic drag rise were satisfactory. These considerations could seriously affect the outcome of the design.

For my part, the project has been kept in mothballs long enough. Long live the rejuvenator, whoever he, she, or they are, for having resurrected the aerospace plane!

18. Pursuing the Concept of Supersonic Combustion—Scramjet

At the time we were working on the aerospace plane, Toni Ferri asked me if I would want to attend the Fourth AGARD meeting to be held in Milano, Italy, from April 4 to 8, 1960, on combustion and propulsion. I responded with a resounding "Yes." This conference could shed some light on the type of power plant(s) that could be considered for the plane, and I would have the opportunity of being brought up to date on the state of progress in the ramjet and scramjet areas. My knowledge of chemical kinetics was sorely lacking, and I looked forward with great enthusiasm in attending the conference. In addition, Thetis and I are opera lovers and the thought of going to Milano, the home of La Scala, made us all the more anxious to go.

AGARD, an acronym for NATO Advisory Group for Aeronautical Research and Development, was founded by von Karman. He had apparently acquired the teachings, philosophy, and educational concepts of his father to foster and encourage knowledge whenever and wherever he could. He was sowing seeds of technology in the hope that mankind one day might reap the benefits of the harvest. The goal of the group was to bring together scientific talent from all the NATO countries into one body to work synergistically and to foster free exchange of ideas.

Our trip to Milano, Italy, was a most memorable one. Thanks to George Schairer of Boeing Company, we flew for the first time on a jet-propelled aircraft. Our previous experiences were all with piston-propeller aircraft. They were noisy, full of vibrations, and limited as to cruise altitude. Almost invariably, one or two engines would poop out. This was especially the case toward the demise of the piston-propeller transports. In an attempt to increase the cruise speed, the engine manufacturers were compelled by the airlines to increase their output horsepower. One means of accomplishing this was to increase the exhaust back pressure; thereby forcing the engine to operate under more stringent conditions. As a result, the exhaust valves would burn out because of excessive temperatures, which eventually caused the engine to malfunction.

The Boeing 707 was a godsend in air travel. Here we were cruising at an altitude of thirty-nine thousand feet at a cruise speed of 540–560 miles per hour. Our flight time from New York to Orly Field, Paris, was an unbelievable six and three-quarter hours. What a transition from the piston aircraft, which took at least twice as long.

En route on the 707, we were reminded of the *Metamorphoses* of Ovidius, the Roman poet. During the clear night at an altitude of thirty-nine thousand feet, we could almost reach out and touch the stars. It was this imaginative feeling that reminded us of the passage in one of his books: "Who would ever believe that man would ever take possession of the aerial highways?" How apropos! Here was Ovidius in the last years of the B.C. era, forecasting events for posterity. Uncanny!

The aircraft, relatively speaking, was vibrationless and the flight smooth. The pilot could select those altitudes that were free of turbulent air, resulting in smooth flying. The contrast between the piston and jet engine aircraft was overwhelming. The swept-back wing design and jet engines made for one of the engineering marvels of all time.

From Orly we flew to Rome, *urbs aeterna.* There we visited many familiar sites—the Colosseum, the Roman Forum, Saints Peter and Paul cathedrals and several museums.

Architectural details and economic considerations in the construction of the buildings of the Greeks and Romans were of interest. The Greeks used solid marble throughout their columns and other structural members. In the Colosseum, mortar and bricks were used as the primary structure, with a facing of thin slabs of marble. The marble is all gone now, and what remains is the base structure of mortar, stone, and brick. It was a lot easier to remove and cart away thin slabs of marble than it was to cart off several tons of solid marble. There is very little left of the Roman Forum as a result. What vandals can do away with, they will!

We were told by our guide that in 1954 they presumably found the burial place of Julius Caesar in the center of the Forum. From Rome we flew Alitalia Airlines to Milano.

We were so impressed by the city of Milano that a few words are in order. The cuisine was unique, a composite of French, Swiss, and Italian in the right amount of proportions. Only the Milanese can succeed in determining the right amounts of each culinary ingredient. The food stores were a sight to see and marvel at. There was a certain ebullience about the people in their daily activities that made one stop and participate in their pleasure and joy of living.

Milanese would bring their personal jugs to purchase olive oil. The storekeeper would pump out the requested type of oil, extra virgin, etc., from large barrels of oil into the buyer's container. Their delis featured open sandwiches and hors d'oeuvres that were intricate works of culinary art, second only to Michaelangelo. Metaphorically speaking, the sandwiches were superior to the paintings of the Italian masters in that they had an additional quality—they were edible and delicious!

The Galleria itself was a magnificent structure that housed many different kinds of shops. The Romans improved upon the agora by allowing for inclement weather. As a result, a closed structure covered with glass was erected, to permit sunlight to enter the interior. It provided solar heating, and one felt comfortable and protected in such a setting. The architectural design had many fine unique features—typical of Italian art and sculpture.

Shopping in the Galleria was fabulous. There were beautiful silks, exquisite velvets, handsome ties, excellent cutlery, fine leather bags and wallets, and numerous other articles. The chic Milanese demanded and got the best. Milano, in 1960, was the major silk producer in Europe.

One of our favorite *ristoranti* in the Galleria was Savini. There we relished the *risotto alla Milanese* and *ossobuco*. They cooked the filet mignon ever so delicately at one's table. When we asked for roast lamb, the waiter would bring the entire half of a spring lamb to the table so that we could choose the specific portion of our choice. It was succulent and literally melted in one's mouth. There was no need for a knife.

Our trip to the famous La Scala opera house of Milano was noteworthy, not so much because of Puccini's *Turandot* but because of the taxicab driver who drove us to the opera. We told him we were somewhat late for the performance and would appreciate his doing his best to get us there on time. He was more than accommodating, as it turned out. He sped along as fast as he could, cutting across corners by driving over the sidewalks, on sidewalks, frightening pedestrians half out of their wits when he would come within inches of them, slamming on his brakes when he came to a traffic light that was in the purview of a policeman—otherwise he would go across a red light. The taxi ride was more thrilling and breathtaking than a ride on a roller coaster, full of jerks, bumps, and g's due to accelerations and decelerations. Notwithstanding the foregoing we were on time at La Scala. After our taxicab ride, we more than welcomed the opera to soothe and relax our nerves.

The lectures on combustion and propulsion were held at the Polytechnic of Milano. The school, as the name implies, was devoted to engineering, science, and architecture.

Aerothermochemistry problems were discussed, covering the inlet, combustion chamber, and exit nozzle. The problems associated with the SCRAMJET were presented. It was pointed out that high chemical-reaction rates were of paramount importance if the combustion chamber were to be of nominal length.

The design of the SCRAMJET combustor involved several factors that were being investigated experimentally. Recourse to theory was very limited, since the burning of a liquid fuel in a moving stream of air takes place under nonequilibrium conditions. The length of the combustor should be such that sufficient time be allowed to complete or nearly complete the combustion process. This should be achieved just before the entrance of the gases to the exhaust nozzle.

After listening to several of the lectures on SCRAMJET, I was convinced the problem was bristling with many factors that were unknown quantities. There was no doubt in my mind that the entire combustion process had to be monitored and controlled by sensors that would transmit information to various controlling devices. For that matter, the entire propulsion system should be automated. To achieve optimization in efficiency, an optimizing controller would be installed. This controller would, in accordance with a program of indices, determine the optimum values. In view of the foregoing, it is of interest to note that a large percentage of the cost of future vehicles will be in electronics because of the necessity of automation.

The rates of chemical reaction are dependent on many factors. Changes in the internal structure of the atom from the outer electrons to the nucleus determine the release of energy as well as viscosity, mass, and energy transport that take place during diffusion. Concentration, pressure, and thermal gradients exist that complicate the analysis. As a result, transfer of molecules from a higher level of concentration, pressure, and temperature to lower levels takes place. The physical boundaries of the combustor complicate the mathematical problem still further. To arrive at an answer to one's specific problem, so-called boundary conditions must also be satisfied.

Listening to several lectures on flame propagation in a gas of turbulent flow, the various processes involved in arriving at a mixture for an efficient combustion, rate of chemical reactions, the delicate chemical balance of extracting the maximum amount of heat from reactants under nonequilibrium, nonisentropic (nonconstant entropy), nonisotropic (non-uniformity of physical properties as one proceeds in different directions at a given point in the mixture), non-this and non-that conditions, etc., made me wonder whether or not we were being practical in proceeding with the SCRAMJET concept. When one attempts to correlate all of the above considerations, one is led to a staggering state of complexity beyond belief. Even with the most sophisticated theories, reliance on the analytical results is lacking. It was conceded by those attending the conference that recourse to experimentation was a sine qua non.

I queried Toni concerning my impressions of the extreme complexities involved in the design of the propulsion system and whether or not we were not biting off more than we could chew. Toni admitted the analytical approach was even beyond his comprehension when wave mechanics was introduced into the analysis. However, with his characteristic faith and vision, he reassured me that the answers to the design of the SCRAMJET would be forthcoming from experimentation. He did concede that theory was of considerable help, in that it indicated the experimental procedure that should be followed. He agreed that in the design concept of the aerospace plane, we had exceeded the limits of knowledge available to us. He assured me that with patience and determination, solutions would be forthcoming. To him the concept was a challenge bristling with many design questions that had to be answered.

It became obvious that the vehicle would require extensive research and cooperation of many agencies, experimental facilities, and governmental endorsement. Above all, we would need the cooperative efforts of the chemical physicists and kineticists.

We realized that the design would require many additional years of research in view of the advanced concept. In addition, we were faced with budgetary constraints. Much to my chagrin and disappointment, the aerospace plane was relegated to the back burner. This was in 1960. At that time the commercial jet transports were coming into being and were considered a panacea in air travel. There was no great need to push the aerospace plane. It lay dormant for some twenty-six years until President Reagan in his 1986 State of the Union Address reincarnated the program.

It is very gratifying to witness the global effort that is going into the program and the synergistic efforts of many interacting disciplines. Interdisciplinarity in this effort has blossomed into full bloom.

19. The Trienvironmental Plane

I have described in some detail the problems and complexities associated with the aerospace plane. This plane still has many hurdles to overcome before it becomes a reality. From a technical point of view, it may prove to be feasible. The final question that has to be resolved is of an economic nature, such as operational costs. In addition, reliability, maintenance, and other costs must be compared to the revenue that would be generated once in operation. Fares undoubtedly would be sky-high, which in turn would limit the utilization of the plane by passengers.

Our rapid technological progress over the past decades has resulted in an aura of sophistication. Progress inevitably sprouts forth ever-increasingly complicated designs deprived of their original simplicity. With the increase in sophistication, the human being is relegating to automation the functions that were normally ascribed to him. The human being will eventually perform the role of an overseer, providing whatever intelligence automation cannot provide.

The intent of this conceptualization of the trienvironmental plane is to illustrate the level of complexity and sophistication the human mind is capable of envisioning. As a logical extension of the aerospace plane, which has the potential of operating in two environments, the earth's atmosphere and space, why not extend the utility of the aerospace plane by making use of the extensive areas of the oceans? From a military point of view, this would be ideal since the plane could select its own berth, take off and land from either land or water, derive its own fuel from either the atmosphere or the oceans, change its orbital flight at will, all of which would make detection of the plane by the enemy very difficult, if not impossible.

The Polaris missile can be launched from a submerged submarine and has the capability of operation in two environments as well. The aerospace plane would take off from land. On the other hand, the Polaris missile is launched from a submersible platform. The natural question arises: Why not combine both concepts?

The earth is covered with water over 70 percent of its surface. Why not design a vehicle that could operate in all three environments? Such a vehicle could be termed the "trienvironmental." Not only could the vehicle make its home in space, but the oceans as well. This additional feature would have great potential for the military, since reliance on the conventional airfield would no longer be needed. The enemy would have no idea where such a vehicle could take off and land.

A brief technical analysis of the trienvironmental vehicle is in order to illustrate the complexities that are involved. At this stage of the game, we are not concerned with the feasibility and economics of the concept. We need to determine what data is available in order to conduct the necessary research to make the concept achievable. A matrix could be set up to determine what would be needed in the way of resources, manpower, money, etc. In such an undertaking, it is recognized that the services, the navy and air force, would be most interested. In such a concept, many additional complications over and beyond the aerospace plane would be introduced. This phantasmagorical approach is permissible when one is considering a conception. Imagination and perception are prerequisite qualities.

In addition to the requirements imposed by the aerospace plane, one must also consider the submersible aspects of the trienvironmental vehicle. This would entail the navy and all the technological know-how one could muster together to determine what data is available and what research would be required to provide the necessary data. One of the goals would be to conceive of a design that would be self-sustaining as far as fuel requirements were concerned. The oceans and atmosphere contain bountiful sources of oxygen and hydrogen.

The trienvironmental concept would entail a number of problems, such as energy requirements in the production of hydrogen/oxygen from the water, emergence from and landing on water, underwater propulsion, guidance and control, power spectral density plots to determine magnitude of random variables that might occur during flight in the various environments, flooding considerations necessary for the vehicle to approach and reach its underwater destination, to name but a few of the items that must be considered.

164

The external shape of the vehicle would be cigar-shaped, with stub wings to provide air and hydrodynamic lift. Hydrostatic and internal pressurization requirements dictate the utilization of symmetrical cross-sections if the overall weight is to be kept at a minimum.

The required energy for propulsion, extracting hydrogen from water, could be provided by a nuclear power plant. The experiences gained on the nuclear submarines would be of inestimable help in the design of the underwater-propulsion system. This is an area where a great deal of research is needed to keep the weight of the propulsion turbine and the boiler-heat exchanger to a minimum. There is no doubt that in the design of the trienvironmental plane, one of the major hurdles that will be encountered is the provision for the propulsive systems required for underwater and atmospheric operations. To increase the utilization factor of the propulsion systems, every attempt must be made to coordinate the two.

Once in forward motion underwater, hydrodynamic lift, coupled with the release of water ballast, would cause the vehicle to come to the surface. On the surface of the water, the propulsion of the vehicle would revert to a nuclear turbojet-powered system. The vehicle would accelerate to sustain itself on hydrofoils that would be extended during the takeoff phase. Speed would then be increased to the point where the vehicle could become airborne. This scheme would, in all probability, result in a loss in available volume and a low-utilization factor. Other schemes, such as the VTOL (vertical takeoff and landing) mode of operation, thrust-vectoring whereby a rotatable ducted propeller fan would be utilized, would once again result in low utilization since the systems would only be used in the landing and takeoff modes.

Since the goal is to achieve multifunctional utilization of any component or group of components, such as fuselage, wing, etc., it would probably be best to deflect the turbo exit gases downward to provide the lift for VTOL. This would necessitate deflectors in the ducts. This should be a relatively simple matter compared to the other schemes mentioned previously.

Every attempt should be made to utilize as efficiently as possible a given portion (component) of the vehicle in all three phases of flight. This would avoid excess weight, size, cost, maintenance, and increase the overall utilization of the vehicle.

I have briefly described some of the problems that one can encounter when we introduce complexities and sophistication in our future designs. With increases in complexity, we are digressing further and further from simplicity, maintainability, and reliability. These three words are the keywords to good design within the realm of budgets and economics. These fundamental tenets cannot and should not be ignored. Should we choose to ignore them, fewer missions will result. Many hours of preparation and subcomponent checks will be required. We eventually find ourselves in a situation similar to a dog chasing its own tail and accomplishing very little.

There is no doubt the aerospace and trienvironmental planes represent formidable engineering challenges. Transforming advanced concepts into reality always takes time, patience, money, and research. The ideological concepts of today will, in all probability, be transformed into reality in the future. The reaction time required for the realization of the end product may take one or two decades or centuries.

The aerospace plane has taught us many lessons. In such a design, we are reaching for the ultimate in sophistication and complexity. The task of designing such a vehicle is so overwhelming that we need to work synergistically on a global scale. This is already recognized by most nations that are in a position to contribute to the effort. This trend is most welcome and encouraging and should be fostered more vigorously in the future. This type of cooperative effort provides the required binding force that will bring all nations and peoples together in a peaceful way.

20. Entry into Space Technology

With the advent of Sputnik, Republic Aviation was faced with the decision of whether it should enter the highly competitive field of space. It was not only competitive, but vastly extensive in scope, bristling with uncharted areas of unknowns, requiring vast sums of money, the ability to finance negative cash flows for a substantial unknown period of time, and all of the uncertainties associated with space activities.

The basic question that had to be answered was: What would be the magnitude of the investment and the minimum length of time required to make an impressionable imprint on the space market—an open-ended quantity?

Before a budget for such an undertaking could be determined, data had to be obtained. We were aware of the research that was being conducted at the NASA in gearing up for their entry into space, the universities with their pursuit of and research in pure science, the air force, and various scientific groups.

Ames Aeronautical Research Laboratories provided us with a great deal of information and advice. Conversations with Al Eggers, Julian Allen, Smitty de France, Russ Robinson, and Bob Jones were especially informative and helpful. At times I felt like an intruder prying into their affairs, but I was assured that space was so extensive that there was no need to feel that we were interfering with their activities. They pointed out that NASA had to reorganize and add to their staff to meet the challenges and responsibilities of the space age. As a matter of fact, I was encouraged to proceed with our activities because one day they might need our help. They admitted that it was very likely they would have to farm out some of their work on a contractual basis. This type of assurance was characteristic of the camaraderie that existed during the days of NACA and especially during World War II.

NASA was lacking in certain types of expertise and personnel.

167

As an example, they had no prior experience nor qualified personnel in life sciences. The sudden dawning of the space era caught everyone by surprise. Reorganization, determination of the most crucial areas of research, lack of qualified personnel in the field of space science, and a myriad of other space-oriented problems, left us all scurrying around to fill in the voids created by our entry into space. We all needed to help each other for the welfare and leadership of our country. This was typical of the congeniality and caring exhibited by NACA. This legacy was adopted by the newly established NASA.

A trip was arranged in the summer of 1958 that would not only encompass visits to various companies and agencies pertaining to space activities but would also dovetail in with our summer vacation. The trip would also afford an opportunity for the children to see various university campuses and provide for a goodwill mission to visit with former associates and friends. We wanted to introduce our children to the various universities throughout the country, since in a few years they would be eligible candidates for admission.

The children were happy to hear that we would all be traveling together by car. This meant we had to prepare for a cross-country trip. Problem number one we encountered was our pre-World War II Packard, which was adequate for short trips, but not for an extensive cross-country trip. The trunk space was limited. With great reluctance we had to part with our trusty old Packard that carried us faithfully through snow and sleet safely, to the hospital on time for childbirths, and transported us on numerous errands while we were building our home. It was a very sad adieu.

We purchased a new 1958 Buick, with a large trunk. This would be perfect for storing the suitcases we needed. Each of us was allotted one suitcase and one small tote. Our plans were to drive eight-to-ten hours per day. This required an ice cooler filled with ice and juices and a picnic basket for food. These were kept in the car for convenience in the event someone became thirsty or hungry along the way. In this way we could adhere to our eight-to-ten-hour driving schedule without the necessity of stopping at a restaurant.

Our new Buick was to be our mobile home during the day and at night we would stay at prearranged motels. Can you imagine the children's delight when these preparations were going on! We laid out our trip on a large map of the United States. I first encircled the cities I had to visit. The route was then drawn to include universities and points of interest, such as national parks. Our route would take us from Long Island to St. Louis, Missouri, then southwest to Los Angeles and San Diego. From San Diego we would head north via San Francisco to Seattle, Washington. Then we would be homeward bound to Chicago, Buffalo, Albany, down the Hudson River Valley, and finally home. Fortunately, the folks lived next door, which made it convenient for them to take care of our home during our absence. In addition, we would call every two days to keep them informed of our progress.

The week before the trip, we had a family conference to discuss the responsibilities of each participant. A list of items to be packed was assigned to each one. This would be an excellent way to teach the children how to pack their suitcases on their own. There was nothing like indoctrinating them into the responsibilities required of them, and we had no intention of spoiling them. The children gladly accepted the responsibility of packing their own suitcases. This was a welcome relief, especially on the part of Thetis. We also arranged to rotate seating positions in the car en route. In this way there was always a copilot up front with the road map in hand to make certain we were proceeding according to plan.

Our Odyssey began on June 29, 1958. The first business stop was Wright-Patterson Field, Dayton, Ohio. We made this our first stop since the air force was our prime contractor. I felt it was advisable to communicate with their key personnel and to inform them of our intentions to enter the space field. They were convinced this was the way to proceed. When asked what the air force considered of prime importance in setting up space laboratories, they emphatically stressed the welfare and comfort of man under the strenuous environment he would be subjected to. Weightlessness, prolonged flight conditions leading to restlessness and boredom, were of primary concern. Bioengineering problems, in general, would be placed high on our research agenda.

In addition, the air force was working in conjunction with NACA on the Dyna-soar project and was vitally interested in hypersonic flight. This research would eventually lead to the developments of the Shuttle design. With the air force's blessing and sanction, we proceeded on our course.

We then proceeded to McDonnell-Douglas, St. Louis, California

Institute of Technology, Edwards Air Force Base, China Lake Basin, Ames Aeronautical Laboratory, University of California, Berkeley, and Boeing Company. There was a consensus of opinion that the problems associated with traveling in space would be fraught with many new uncharted areas. The answer that I wanted to know was: what specific areas should we home in on to establish corresponding laboratories equipped with the most appropriate apparatus and instrumentation? This question was answered by the type of missions we would most likely concentrate on. Would we be concerned with manned or unmanned satellites? Unmanned satellites designed for data collection? Probing the outer planets? If so, this would require new forms of propulsion devices that would operate for long durations of time.

It was pointed out that in space we had to contend with radiation, meteoric dust, energy fields, space trajectories, new types of instrumentation for monitoring and obtaining physical measurements, communication, guidance and control, structural materials, human adaptation to varying gravitational fields, etc. In the case of prolonged manned flight, additional disciplines must be considered, biological, physiological, and psychological effects of outer space. Long durations of flight would impose severe strains on personnel encapsulated in a confined area.

With the foregoing considerations, it became quite obvious all of us at Republic Aviation had a tough decision to make. What we needed were personnel trained in the space sciences and who, in addition, could transform their results into a practical design. Other than astronomers and physicists trained in theoretical celestial mechanics who had no experience in design, it became obvious we were in for a long period of training the kinds of personnel to effectively perform the tasks required of space. The ideal type of personnel would be those trained in the basics of science who could implement their theoretical results into a practical design. An outstanding example of such a person was Enrico Fermi, who not only contributed theoretically to the development of atomic and nuclear theory, but was able to devise a practical energy source for the production of power.

What made it practically impossible to attain personnel was the sudden demand for such people by industry, scientific organizations, NASA, the military services, and universities. Under these condi-

170

tions, salaries skyrocketed and selling the space program to management became ever-increasingly difficult. I had been asked to make several recommendations in the past, but never had I encountered one so replete with uncertainties, high risks, new manpower requirements, facilities requiring vast expenditures of money. The immense combinations of designs and missions possible, to mention but a few items, were mind-boggling.

To meet our manpower requirements, we were faced with many reorganizational changes within engineering. We could draw on our research department and our Guided Missiles Division. This source of personnel was, unfortunately, a drop in the bucket. It would appear that we were biting off more than we could chew. There was one consolation, however. Everyone we had talked to was faced with the same dilemma. The basic question we had to answer was: could we, at Republic, in the long run, afford not to enter the space field, knowing that our primary client was the air force?

It was a matter of biting the bullet and taking the consequences. In retrospect, I greatly admire the courage and fortitude of our president, Mundy Peale, and the board of directors in making the final decision to proceed with the establishment of a space division. They were fully aware of the great risks involved and the competition the corporation had to face.

Traveling by car with my family had many advantages. I did not have to depend upon scheduled flights of airlines and buses. My family took care of the maintenance of the car, made motel reservations, and became my mobile office staff. With the routine matters that required attention out of the way, I was able to pursue my business more conveniently and efficiently. The children had their opportunity to see several universities and campuses, Washington University in St. Louis, California Institute of Technology in Pasadena, UCLA in Los Angeles, UC Berkeley, and Stanford University in Palo Alto.

We visited Adolph Burstein, a former associate of mine in the stress department at Seversky Aircraft, in Los Angeles. He proudly showed us his home, with the back yard harboring several orange and lemon trees. He pointed out all the advantages of living in California, including its clement weather. He did such a great sales job that we were sold on the idea of moving to California. When the time arrived for a change in domicile location, our decision had been cast. Our daughter was the first to come to California when she matriculated at the University of California, Berkeley.

Adolph Burstein was one of the finest engineers I had come to know. During his career he made several contributions to commercial aircraft while at Convair and space probes while at Hughes Aircraft. While at Seversky Aircraft, Farmingdale, New York, he introduced me to grand opera at the Metropolitan Opera in the early thirties. We would go early enough to get a fairly good position in the standing line that formed outside the opera house. In those early days of our careers, we couldn't very well afford seats. We were delighted to have had the opportunity to gain admission into the opera house, especially when Lauritz Melchior, Kirsten Flagstaff, and Melvin Schorr would be featured in the Ring cycle of Richard Wagner.

Wagner left an indelible impression on me. The performances would last four to five hours. Standing up in an immobile position for that duration of time entailed endurance and stamina, especially when it came to *Tristan und Isold*. Performances are endurable if there is motion and action involved during the acts. In Tristan immobility reigns for five hours when they coo to each other in ever amorous tones for hours at a time. Wagner is reminiscent of a bulldog who will not yield its bone when locked firmly between its jaws. He goes on forever and ever saying adieu in the Liebestod. In a standing mode, one wished he would call it quits and end the agony of not only the singers but the audience as well.

This recollection brings to mind an anecdote of Toscanini. During a performance of *Tristan und Isold* being conducted by Bruno Walter, Toscanini, who was in the audience, turned to his friend and whispered, "If the singers were Italian, they would have had two children by now, but since they are Germans, they need to mull over the decision."

While in San Diego, we paid a visit to two former colleagues, Chemessov and Samoilo, two Russian engineers of the Czarist regime. They were the spitting image of Mutt and Jeff of comic-strip fame. Chemessov was six feet in height and Samoilo was under five feet. The two of them would frequently get into a heated argument, and after the issue was compromised, they were back to even keel again. Samoilo was very proud of the pocket watch he wore. It was given to him while in the service of the Czar, serving as his bodyguard.

It was amusing watching Samoilo work at his drafting table.

Because of his height, he would stand on a platform that he had made and exclaim that since Nature had not endowed him with sufficient height to work at the table, he would make up for the deficiency. When he became the least bit flustered, he would exclaim, "Son of a Gun!" We all knew he was in some kind of a predicament and would go to him to try to resolve his dilemma. Almost invariably the source of difficulty lay with the engineer he was working with. Whenever the engineer changed some of the details of the design midstream, Samoilo would utter his familiar remark "Son of a Gun."

There was no doubt that our entry into space technology would entail enormous expenditures of money. Space also had associated with it a certain amount of glamour and fascination. The question that we had to ponder over was: What would the probability be of our securing advanced space weaponry contracts from the air force in the future? Or would we be facing a short period of infatuation with space that would, like an overinflated balloon, burst when man's allurement wears thin? This necessitated strategic planning. Money outlays were to be made in stages; each succeeding stage would depend upon an evaluation of the success of the prior stage. In this manner the calculated risks would be held to a minimum.

The allurement and enchantment of space was vividly depicted in Disneyland. While I was conferring at UCLA, Thetis had taken the children to Disneyland. They had a lot to recount during the entire evening about their impressions of space travel. They insisted that I go with them to Disneyland to see the presentations they saw. Even though this was not on my agenda, I decided to join them. The future of space and space flight was well portrayed. There was an "Astrojet" ride that demonstrated the feeling that one experiences when subjected to a varying gravitational field. This simulated the different accelerations the cosmonauts would experience during launching, accelerating to orbit and weightlessness. In "Tomorrow Land," there was a satellite view of the earth. In addition, a very realistic trip to the moon was shown. The entire space exhibition was very impressive. Walt Disney was indeed a far-sighted individual. These presentations of what the future of space flight could portend were highly educational to children and adults alike. I was glad I had listened to my children. They were delighted that I shared their enthusiasm. They were happy to know that I was involved in making what they saw a reality.

When Sputnik I was launched on October 4, 1957, public sentiment was aroused to such a degree that Congress accelerated our program on the Explorer. The Explorer was the counterpart to the Sputnik. The Russians were aware of our plans to place the Explorer in orbit and accelerated their program on the Sputnik to have the distinction of being the first nation to do so. These two satellites gave the necessary impetus for further space exploration.

As prime contractors for the air force, it was our desire to maintain that position. In arriving at our final decision, we were encouraged by the fact that the Electronics Research Directorate of the air force, Cambridge Research Center, was interested in pure research that would lead to an understanding of space phenomena. Once a foothold was established, feasibility and development would follow. The air force was constantly on the search for novel concepts and designs leading to advanced weaponry. Such weaponry would inevitably lead to space.

Republic Aviation and its board of directors made its decision to enter the space arena. On the one hand, it was recognized that our entry into an area bristling with unknowns, uncertainties, and risks was hazardous. On the other hand, we could not afford to watch the space parade go by without our joining it. We were proud of the designs we had submitted to the air force and wanted to continue contributing our efforts to the future of flight.

Accordingly, fourteen million dollars was appropriated for the establishment of a space center. The new Research and Development Center at Republic Aviation was named after Paul Moore, one of its founders and a member of the board of directors.

It was decided that the Paul Moore Research and Development Center would be comprised of the following laboratories: the Space Environment and Life Sciences, Plasma Propulsion, Wind Tunnel, Instrumentation, and Guidance and Control. The most important pieces of equipment would be the wind tunnels covering the range from subsonic to hypervelocity speeds, vacuum chambers that would simulate outer space environment, guidance and control and instrumentation.

The air force and NASA were particularly interested in manned space flights of a duration of a month or more. It was our belief that man's presence in space would add materially to the success of the mission. Man has the ability, creativity, and versatility to make decisions on the spot, supplemented by data accumulated through instrumentation. To make proper decisions, it is essential that his hostile environment not interfere with his reactions. Accordingly, it was considered imperative to determine what effects his environment would have on his behavior and endurance. Man would encounter a continuous spectrum of environments, for example, in his journey from earth to the moon.

Since man was to play an important part in space flight, isolation studies were conducted in the Space Environment and Life Sciences Laboratory for NASA. Tests were conducted on various subjects inside a space capsule mock-up. Goggled, specially dressed, and fully instrumented, the subjects spent up to forty hours in confinement for the study of reactions. Our study, called "Sensory Deprivation, Pain and Personality Relationships for Space Travel," was headed by Dr. William Helvey. Its goal was to collect physiological and psychological reactions to isolation from customary sounds, sights, and other sensory factors, and relate these findings to measurements of the subject's ability to withstand discomfort. Such findings would aid in setting criteria for human adaptability to confinement and boredom that would be experienced in space flights.

The study was being conducted under a contract from the National Aeronautics and Space Administration. It involved some sixty male adult subjects, volunteers from a local military installation and seminary graduate students. These findings provided a basis for establishing criteria for astronaut selection and information useful in the preparation of training programs for future space crews. Dr. Helvey aptly described the hazards facing space travelers when he said they would encounter a continuous spectrum of environments from the earth to the moon. This entailed psychological problems and the so-called break-off phenomenon. This effect pertains to the feeling of being completely detached from the earth, which brings with it feelings of apprehension and depression. This phenomenon is analogous to the severance of the baby from the umbilical cord.

Already established and in operation was the Scientific Research Group under the directorship of Dr. Theodore Theodorsen. I was appointed assistant director. The group was organized into four main sections: nuclear physics, applied mechanics, electronics, and aerophysics.

The Plasma Propulsion Laboratory was established to develop a space engine that would meet the practical requirements, both in size and weight for space probes. The engine could also be used for control of reconnaissance and communication satellites for military and commercial purposes.

A major activity of the laboratory was centered around the development of the plasma pinch engine originated by Al Kunen. The potential advantages of this engine over other forms of electrical propulsion included its aggregate combination of good efficiency, broad range of exhaust velocity, stop-start capability, high thrust, simplicity, and reliability. This engine could be operated continuously in near and deep space for years, both for propulsion and vehicle guidance and control. Readily available inert gases could be used for fuel. The fuel became ionized after injection into the engine, and the resultant plasma was electromagnetically accelerated and exhausted out of the nozzle at extremely high velocities. It was the high velocity of the exited plasma that resulted in the unique, economical use of fuel.

Exhaust gas velocities of over 100,000 miles per hour and ejected gas temperatures in the order of 200,000 degrees Fahrenheit were measured. Under these conditions, relatively cool wall metal temperatures of 200 to 300 degrees Fahrenheit were maintained. Accordingly, there was no need for auxiliary cooling effects. Practically no erosion of primary engine components was ever encountered. There were no movable parts in the engine. On the basis of these findings in the laboratory, several contracts were obtained.

The Wind Tunnel Laboratory would be used for determining the optimum configuration of a design in compliance with specified requirements of a specific proposal. These tunnels were designed for the development of future aircraft. Data could be obtained in the subsonic to hypervelocity range up to twenty times the speed of sound. A great deal of research was performed in the various supersonic and hypersonic tunnels. They were used extensively to test a number of different configurations of the aerospace plane.

An environment of radiation and vacuum would require a new breed of instruments to make proper measurements. Such measurements would be essential if we were to design the vehicle to protect man against harmful effects in outer space. Measurements were also essential in monitoring and collecting data essential for automation.

Guidance and control would be an essential element in the success of a mission. Predetermined trajectories must be rigidly followed if constraints, such as amount of fuel available, avoidance of extreme radiation zones, reentry into the atmosphere, etc., were to be adhered to.

Various experiments were being conducted in the Space Laboratory to determine various design criteria for the aerospace plane. Research was conducted on high-temperature hydraulics in anticipation of the hydraulic design. Heat-transfer studies were conducted to determine the type of design to efficiently conduct heat from the structure to the liquid hydrogen. The development of sensors to monitor temperatures, pressures, etc., essential for the automation of the propulsion system was in the initial stage of progress in the instrumentation laboratory.

Republic recognized the importance of being able to manufacture high-strength metals necessary for advanced aircraft and space systems that the engineers and scientists were designing. Accordingly, a manufacturing research laboratory was established a few years before the Paul Moore Space Center. The Manufacturing Research and Processes Division was organized to solve problems involved with shaping and machining the newer, high-strength metals, such as titanium. The group worked hand in hand with designers, scientists, engineers, and manufacturing personnel to develop techniques required for production of advanced designs.

With the inauguration of the Paul Moore Space Center in 1959, the die was cast as Republic crossed the Rubicon to encounter head-on the space challenge. Upon landing on the other side of the river, it found itself heavily engaged in space research. We looked forward with great anticipation to being a part of a new pioneering effort on the part of man to explore and understand the wonders of Nature. With the accumulation of such knowledge, our eventual goal was to reap the harvest of products that would enhance our quality of life and increase harmony, compatibility, and peaceful coexistence with Nature.

21. Establishment of Polytechnic Institute of Brooklyn at Republic Aviation

We found it difficult to recruit qualified people for a number of vacant positions in the newly formed space center. This led to the creation and establishment of the Long Island Campus of Polytechnic Institute of Brooklyn.

With the advent of the coming of hypersonic and space flight, we recognized that industry had embarked on an extended course leading to new vistas in engineering science. This required a new body of scientific knowledge. As a result, we were faced with very few options as to what course we, at Republic, might pursue. Even though we hired many qualified personnel, we were still left with a shortage of personnel to staff the Paul Moore Space Center.

Cognizant of the reputation of Poly and its personnel (Toni Ferri, Paul Libbey, a number of outstanding professors, notably Anthony Giordano, Sebastion Nardo, Nathan Marcuvitz, Herman Mark, John Truxal, Martin Bloom), I approached Dr. Ernst Weber, the president, at an informal meeting. I asked whether he would be interested in establishing a graduate campus at Republic, with the proviso that the land be donated to the Institute. His response was an immediate approval of the idea. I agreed I would propose the idea to Sasha Kartveli.

Since we could not fulfill the quota of qualified scientists and engineers, I proposed an educational plan whereby selected members of the present staff could take courses during working hours. A school next to the plant would be expeditious, convenient, and would save time traveling to and from classes. This appealed to Sasha. He in turn discussed this arrangement with Mundy Peale, Republic's president, and obtained approval.

A back-to-school program was established at the Graduate Center of Polytechnic Institute of Brooklyn on Route 110, in Far-mingdale, New York, which allowed candidates to attend classes on company time. More than ten advanced courses were offered in mechanics, electronics, supersonic and hypersonic aerodynamics, guidance and control, microwave theory, polymer chemistry, macro-molecular chemistry, to mention but a few. Republic was spending more than a million dollars annually to train its personnel.

Thus an unusual union of cooperation between industry and university was inaugurated at the Polytechnic in February 1959. Research scientists from twenty-four American companies attended a two-day seminar on the results of academic research in polymer chemistry. Polytechnic was world famous in this area, under the aegis of Herman Mark. Results of research conducted at the univer-sity in high-frequency electronics, microwave systems, control sys-tems, and supersonic aerodynamics were also on the program. Participants of Polytechnic included Dr. Ernst Weber, Dr. Herman Mark, polymer chemistry; Dr. Charles G. Overberger, polymer chemistry and macromolecular syntheses; Dr. Frederick R. Eirich, colloidal and polymer chemistry; Dr. Herbert R. Morawetz, polymer chemistry and macromolecules in solution; Dr. Nathan Marcuvitz, microwaves; Dr. John Truxal for controls system technology; Dr. Antonio Ferri on trends in experimental research and supersonic flight. Included in the program were visits to Toni's Aerodynamics Research Laboratory at Freeport, Long Island.

In addition to the twenty-five acres of land donated by Republic, Mundy Peale presented Dr. Weber checks for fifty thousand dollars on two different occasions. These funds were to be used for further-ing the Institute's program at its new Graduate Center dedicated to aerospace research.

In addition to my activities at the Polytechnic, I was appointed corporate representative to the Massachusetts Institute of Technol-ogy Industrial Liaison Program. I was also responsible for the development of similar working relationships with other comparable institutions of higher learning. It was very gratifying to me that Republic recognized that our country's universities and technical institutes could be a very valuable adjunct to our own technical capabilities in the solution of problems arising in uncharted and untrodden areas of high-speed flight and space. It was my respon-sibility to coordinate R & D efforts of Republic with the various universities, and interchange information on technical matters of mutual interest and concern. I would inform them of Republic's present and foreseeable requirements for scientific and engineering skills. In this way, the universities could introduce courses that would produce the future scientists and engineers to cope with the problems of the day.

Our associations with universities led us to the University of Florida, Gainesville, and to Duke University, one of the universities of the triangle complex, North Carolina. In each case there existed a desire and resolve to work synergistically with industry. It was recognized that with a spirit of quid pro quo, both university and industry would mutually benefit in such a partnership.

On one of our visits to the University Triangle in North Carolina, the governor was most enthusiastic in promoting partnership between industry and university. We can say it was a very effective means of acquiring and exchanging data that might lead to the solution of a particular problem. Given a consortium of such universities, the probability of eventually acquiring the sought-for data would more likely be found than would otherwise be the case.

During the summer months, Republic hired some of the professors to work on specific problems. A camaraderie was thereby established, which further strengthened our relationships and resulted in a pool of talent that could be utilized whenever a specific, knotty problem arose.

This arrangement brought much expertise to Republic Aviation. We were able to arrange for university personnel to visit the company to discuss various and sundry problems. In turn, the university personnel liked the arrangement, since it afforded them the opportunity to work on problems of immediate application rather than in abstract areas.

As problems arose in unchartered areas, there was need for further expansion beyond the tie-in with the universities. As in the case of the aerospace plane, tie-ins would eventually occur, not only with agencies such as NASA, the Department of Defense, etc., various space agencies in the U.S.A., but with various nations of the world. What was once a single-entity operation had now extended its activities to a global consortium of partners. This trend is apparently the result of the ever-increasing complexity of systems, which is beyond the scientific and financial means of any one nation. This trend has already been demonstrated in the case of the USSR and U.S.A. in the work associated with coupling and decoupling of capsules in flight.

This is an encouraging development, for it demonstrates the need for interdependency rather than independency. This is especially the case on a global scale. One nation can assist the other much more effectively, in the long run, by cooperating peacefully rather than by belligerent means. This is exemplified by the remarks made by Julius Caesar, the general, about his political adversary Cicero: "It is far better to have extended the frontiers of the mind than to have extended the boundaries of the empire." Peaceful cooperation among all nations for the betterment of peoples of the world is far superior to the acquisition of spoils from war.

In my discussions with faculty members of the various universities, the question that remained uppermost in my mind was: How can we train scientists and engineers to cope with the inevitable revolutionary changes that have and will continue to occur in the technological and scientific fields? Coupled with this question were the following constraints: specialization was a sine qua non, interdisciplinarity should be emphasized, which would require basic courses in mathematics, chemistry, physics, biology, logic, computer sciences, systems engineering, and the social sciences. As a further constraint, one cannot ignore the impact science and engineering will have in the future on the political, environmental, demographic, and quality of life that are all components of the overall system.

The aerospace plane is an example of the complexity that has resulted as we progress from one design to each succeeding one. This is a portent of what we can expect in space flight. To explore untrodden areas and probe the unknown is the goal of mankind. In this endeavor, however, we must exercise moderation and caution that we don't violate the environment and the more urgent need for projects other than military, scientific, and national prestige among nations. There should always exist a balance between beneficial and undesirable effects. At times we tend to overlook the basics of humanity and common sense in our impetuosity and eagerness to accomplish miraculous and daring feats.

In my aeronautical and aerospace experience, I have come to realize that future events and occurrences will become more and more complex with time. This is not only applicable to engineering but to societal problems as well. Societal problems add many more dimensions of uncertainty, risk, and lack of quantitative knowledge in emotional and psychological effects essential to their objective solution.

In view of the many unknowns involved in space flight, the advent of vehicle designs and production could take time. To determine the various parameters and data required for design necessitated extensive research and laboratory testing. In addition, production orders from the military would not be forthcoming until such time that safety and reliability were established. Furthermore, space environmental effects upon man have to be ascertained.

The Paul Moore Research Laboratory was headed by Sasha Kartveli. Sasha was an impatient man. He wanted to see things accomplished in a relatively short period of time. He had difficulty in accepting change and readjusting to the inevitability of changes brought about by the space era. He would frequently refer to the advent of the mainframe computer as a device that would stifle man's original thinking by becoming addicted to it, thereby relinquishing his cognitive powers and reasoning. Gone were the days and glory ushered in by Cauchy, Lagrange, Laplace, and other illustrious mathematicians. We were transforming ourselves at an alarming rate to the role of a robot. He would frequently refer to these changes by quoting Cicero: "O tempora! O mores!"

The reason I was able to sell Sasha the aerospace plane was that there were vestiges of design familiar to him. Space work was quite foreign to him, and he had difficulty in accepting it.

Seversky Amphibian 3M-WW; Major de Seversky in the foreground.

Composite photograph of aircraft built during the presidency of Major Alexander de Seversky. From left to right: SEV 3M-WW Amphibian; modified BT-8 two-seat basic trainer; P-35 fighter; original BT-8.

Experimental version of the P-35 with retractable landing gear.

P-47s in formation flight. This aircraft was one of the workhorses in western Europe, performing both high- and low-altitude missions.

Presentation of Certificate of Distinction to the author, April 20, 1944, by Fred Marchev (left), president of Republic Aviation. Sasha Kartveli (center) looking on.

Republic's F-84G midair refueling Thunderjet, the first fighter designated to carry the atomic bomb. Note stabilizing fins on external wing tip tanks.

RF-84F high-speed, high-or low-altitude, day or night photo reconnaissance plane, a modification of the F-84F fighter-bomber.

RF-84F showing an assortment of the armament that could be carried on board.

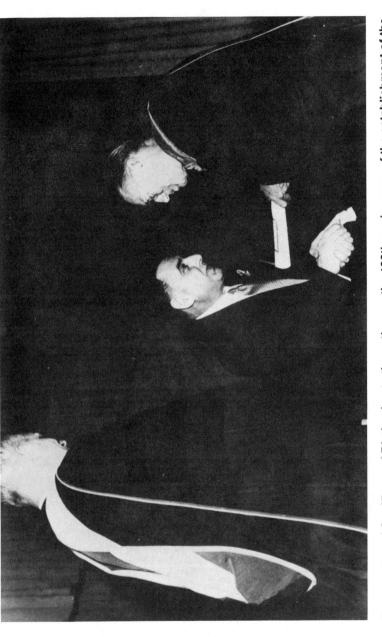

Presentation of Certificate of Distinction to the author on the 100th anniversary of the establishment of the College of Engineering, University Heights, Bronx, New York. Left to right: Henry S. Heald, Chancellor; Mr. Pappas; Dean Thorndike Saville, Dean of the College of Engineering.

Lineup of Republic's P-47 Thunderbolt, XF-91 high-altitude interceptor, and the F-84 Thunderjet.

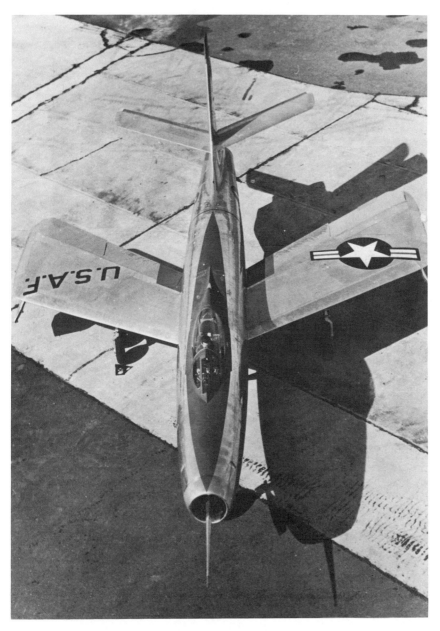

The XF-91, Republic's high-speed, high-altitude interceptor fighter.

The XR-12 U.S. Air Force reconnaissance plane. Top speed 450 MPH. World's fastest four-engine aircraft.

Top view of F-105 illustrating the "Marilyn Monroe" or "Coke bottle" effect.

Republic's F-105 Thunderchief. Mach two supersonic fighter-bomber.

22. Challenges Encountered in Changing Our Life-style

The yearning for a Ph.D. still haunted me. I recalled Dad insisting I return to the university for a doctorate when I had obtained my master's. At that time I was more interested in entering the work force to become a breadwinner. Now that I had spent almost thirty years in industry, I felt it was time to return to academic life. This meant I could take courses that would help me better understand the newer technologies being introduced in space technology. I could also become involved in consulting work.

One of my most interesting consulting contracts involved the investigation of jet noise over the town of Hempstead, Long Island. Flights into Idlewild Airport, now known as Kennedy Airport, would fly over the town. I made many recommendations to mitigate the noise, including extension of runways into the bay to avoid takeoffs over Hempstead. Takeoffs created the highest intensity of noise, since maximum power was employed during this phase of flight. The landing mode was less critical, since power was cut back substantially from maximum.

I suggested that the aircraft fly higher over the town. Height is an important parameter, since noise attenuates inversely as the square of the distance the noise source is from the ground. This technique, however, required a steeper rate of descent once the aircraft approached the landing strip. This entailed an increase in the sinking speed of the aircraft. There would be a limit as to how much an increase in sinking speed would be tolerable on the part of the passengers. Pilots would, of necessity, have to be more precise in making such landings, especially during inclement weather conditions. Several modifications in flight patterns were presented whereby aircraft speed and power could be compromised without seriously affecting the safety of the passengers. Complaints of community residents in the vicinity of the airport eventually led to design of quieter engines by the engine manufacturers.

I attended SUNY (State University of New York) at Stony Brook, Long Island. After some thirty years out of school, refresher courses in modern physics, mathematics and computer science were undertaken. This was a grand opportunity to be a part of the younger generation and participate in their enthusiasm and modus operandi. This constituted a rejuvenation process for me. It was revealing to me the progress that had been made in engineering at the university level since I graduated in 1934 with a master's degree.

Courses such as modern physics given in the undergraduate school were courses taught at the graduate level in the early thirties. Textbooks were much more elaborate as to content and illustrations. They were larger in size and much more expensive. In the past, textbooks cost three to five dollars. In the mid-sixties the prices had risen to fifteen to twenty dollars. In a way this increase was not surprising, since there was considerable increase in content and complexity of material. Engineering was becoming more of an applied science and mathematically more intricate.

Now there were four of us attending school. Thetis was pursuing a master's degree in counseling at Post College, Long Island. Daughter Alceste was attending the University of California, Berkeley. Son Conrad was attending prep school in Lawrenceville, New Jersey. One can imagine how our library at home increased in size with the incorporation of new textbooks, reference books, and two sets of encyclopedias.

While attending classes at SUNY, I received an offer to join Bell Aircraft in Buffalo, New York. This offer constituted a mixed blessing. In one way we were delighted, since college and prep school tuitions were a financial burden. Since we had invested heavily in property and a new home, our cash reserves were low. We had converted most of our war bonds into cash to pay for the children's schooling. Thetis's salary as a secondary-school teacher was inadequate. A second salary would be most welcome and timely. On the other hand, I would have to abandon once again my pursuit of the doctorate.

Accordingly, we had a heart-rending decision to make. It meant leaving the home we had built and loved so much. We had designed the home to fulfill our specific needs. It would be difficult to find another home with a corresponding tranquil and serene environment.

In addition, the children grew up in this home and were quite nostalgic about it. As Conrad aptly said, this was the only home he knew. Having Thetis's folks adjacent to us provided expediency and convenience in so many ways. This feature we would sorely miss, since Thetis and I had to travel quite frequently.

This was our very first home. We had embarked on this project by purchasing land, felling trees, adding amenities by building an outdoor barbecue, a rumpus room in the basement, landscaping, making proper provisions for emergency conditions, etc. How does one leave a home one has enjoyed for twenty years? This was a difficult emotional decision to make.

In the words of Beethoven, we were faced with *"Der Schwer Gefasste Entschluss. Muss es sein? Muss es sein? Es muss sein!"* The ponderous decision was finally made after many discussions pro and con. Our family of four would be split four ways. We soon found out that a fragmented family presented numerous problems. I would report for work at Bell Aircraft in the Advanced Technology Research Department. This meant I would be going alone to Buffalo. Thetis stayed behind in Dix Hills, Huntington, to arrange for the sale of the property. Alceste would be at the University of California, Berkeley, and Conrad would be attending the Lawrenceville school in New Jersey.

Thetis had her hands full purchasing airline tickets whenever it was necessary for us to get together. The girls at the airline ticket counter asked her if she was a travel agent. They were surprised when Thetis told them they were for her family. We developed quite a reputation for being a traveling family.

In a sense we were a divided corporation, with centers in Buffalo and New York. Thetis managed the affairs in New York and I in Buffalo. Activity became very heavy during the final stages of negotiation with the developer regarding the sale of the property. Complications arose when several other buyers began bidding for the house and acreage. Some wanted the acreage alone; others wanted the entire package. As a result of all the combinations presented, it took over a year to complete the sale. Selling property takes time if one is to realize the price he is asking for.

In the meantime, Thetis and I would get together every two weeks to bring one another up to date. We would alternate in our traveling plans between Buffalo and Long Island. To further complicate matters, the State of New York decided to widen the road in front of our house. This meant the taking of four-hundred-foot frontage. At that point we had to obtain the services of an attorney to negotiate the matter with the state. We were primarily concerned with the depth of the taking.

Fortunately, the State spared the house and condemned one-half acre in front of the house. This equated to a taking of fifty-five feet in depth. We were left with forty-five feet frontage. This condemnation proceeding ushered in delays in the sale of the property. We were faced with enough problems in the sale of the property as it was. The condemnation proceedings exacerbated the situation even further. However, we realized the taking was for the general welfare of the people. With patience and several compromises made in our original planning, the property was eventually sold.

When I first arrived in Buffalo, I lived in a room at one of the motels nearby the plant. My living alone in a motel was monotonous and boring. The problem of eating was easily solved. However, being alone without one's family and books was another matter. After working hours the problem of occupying oneself presented a problem. One way of solving this problem was getting to know Buffalo on my own. The highway systems were excellent and provided fast transit. There were museums to visit, various historical sites, and Niagara Falls. Consequently, I started studying the history of Buffalo and its environs. In the meantime, I was in search of an apartment in anticipation of our moving to Buffalo.

Buffalo and its environs have great historical background. The French-Indian wars were fought here as well as the Revolutionary war. The first Europeans to visit the Buffalo area were French trappers and Jesuit missionaries. The area was heavily engaged in military operations up to the close of the Revolutionary war. A great deal of American history occurred here. It was very interesting to me to realize the motivations behind the European nations that wanted to establish a foothold in the area. The insatiable desire to acquire additional real estate practically for the taking and the revenues that could be acquired was a great driving and compelling force. As a result, bitter and bloody struggles between nations were inevitable.

Visits to various forts and stockades used during the wars reminded one of the hardships and perseverance the early settlers had. They were determined to see it through, come hell or high water.

This was emphatically the case when I made the visits during the cold, bitter, blustery months of winter. Sub-zero temperatures in conjunction with high humidity readily made for the formation of icicles in one's nostrils.

Walks through the parks of Buffalo were very enjoyable. In the two years we were domiciled there, in 1966–1968, we learned a great deal about the area. There was pollution of the air and its rivers due to the high diversification of industry. The Peace Bridge, a memorial to the century of the U.S.-Canadian peace, is symbolic of the desire of both nations to live in harmony. The State University of New York at Buffalo was founded in 1946. The staunch supporter of the entire State University system was Nelson Rockefeller, then governor of New York. The area offered unusual opportunities for recreational activities in any season. During the winter the one great sport was ice skating. During the spring and summer, walks through the parks and open landscaped areas were a delight and pleasure for us.

Diversification of industry incurred many problems to the area. During the time we were residents of Buffalo, the area was a leading flour-milling center and a major steel producer. Other important products in the 1960s included rubber, airplanes, chemicals, electric motors, radios, television, hand tools, clothing, automotive parts, and meat.

As a result of the intense industrial activity and the absence of any apparent pollution control measures, the air was polluted to such an extent that one's eyes would water. A walk along the upper part of Niagara River convinced us that the river was highly contaminated with pollutants. I was reminded of the miasmatic texture of the Naugatuck River in Ansonia, Connecticut. A wilderness of countless dead fish could be seen floating along the concrete embankments of the river. It was most disheartening to see so much aquatic life exterminated by pollution.

One of my most memorable experiences occurred one Sunday morning during a stroll around Buffalo. My attention was drawn to an unusual mammoth statue of an Indian on top of a columnar pedestal. This intrigued me no end. Upon further examination I found out that the statue was at the entrance of a huge cemetery. The cemetery under description was the Forest Lawn and the Indian chief's name was Red Jacket, a member of the Seneca tribe and an outstanding orator. The inscription engraved in the stone was impressive, so much so that it sent reverberations up and down my spine each time I read it. He forecast the future of his nation by proclaiming: "I fear for the future of my people because of the white man's greed and avarice."

This was quite evident to Red Jacket, since he could see the squabbles that were going on between the great powers of Europe, namely Britain, France, and the Netherlands, all vying to gain control of this area. The superiority of the European nations in military might would eventually result in the disintegration of the Seneca Indian Nation, with the resultant loss of freedom and dignity and in the end would become subservient to the white man. Acquiring real estate in the new country was a compelling motive of the European countries, since future trading and commerce would bring in additional revenue to these invaders. The Buffalo area was especially a grand prize in view of the Great Lakes and the access they provided to the Atlantic Ocean.

Having read the inscription at the moment, I developed a guilt complex for what had been done in the past. The one consolation that I had was that we, as Americans, are not prone to ignoring such adverse comments but rather want to avoid similar situations in the future. The impression I had was that we were not to ever forget what had happened in Buffalo by inscribing Red Jacket's message in stone for all generations to read.

Red Jacket was an advocate of peace. His eloquence and diplomacy were known not only among the Indian tribes, but by the white settlers as well. Colonel McKenney compared his oratory to that of Cicero. He was instrumental in bringing together the Indian nations from the Niagara frontier to the Winnebago County of the Great Lakes region. This was in response to a peace proposal made by George Washington.

The council of fifty Iroquois chiefs met in Philadelphia in 1792 as guests of Washington and his cabinet. For this accomplishment President Washington presented a huge silver medallion to Chief Red Jacket. The medallion was elliptical in shape, some seven inches long and five inches wide. George Washington was shown on one side of the medallion offering a peace pipe to an Indian chief. In the background was a white man tilling the soil with a team of oxen. The inscription on the reverse side read: E Pluribus Unum.

Red Jacket wore the medallion with great pride and dignity. One of his speeches vividly illustrates his desire for peace: "What is more desirable than that we who live within hearing of each other should unite for the common good? This is my wish. This is the wish of my nation, although I am sorry I cannot say it of every individual in it, for there are differences of opinion among us as there are among the white people."

Upon walking through the cemetery, I encountered a vast expanse of elaborate tombstones. This cemetery reminded me of the Maspeth Cemetery in Queens, Long Island. It, too, is a vast Sargasso Sea of stone as far as the eye can see. It is no wonder that crematoria were introduced to alleviate the problem of space. Inscriptions on the tombstones revealed the vanity of man even in death. I was reminded of the poem "Thanatopsis," written by William Cullen Bryant. The view of death expressed by the majority of inscriptions revealed that man at long last has been relieved of the drudgery and turmoil of the real world and looks forward to a more peaceful and serene hereafter. As a Latin student, I was impressed by the number of inscriptions in Latin. The second time around, I brought my Latin dictionary and syntax with me.

In my walk through the cemetery, I was taken in by the beauty, tranquillity, and serenity of the environment. The day I was there, the sky was of the Mediterranean blue color. Squirrels and chipmunks were numerous and scampering about in the landscape. The green and rolling hills of Forest Lawn made for nesting places for the chipmunks. Their favorite places were under the footings of the tremendous tombstones. As a result, they had the most sacred, palatial homes imaginable. Their nests were air-conditioned in summer, and milder temperatures were ensured during the winter season. This provided for a more or less tolerable temperature throughout the year. Robins were chirping in the trees and were having a feast on the worms they were pulling out of the ground.

One of the most outstanding monuments was the Blocher monument. The life-size statue of the son was shown lying on a marble slab with an angel at his head. Statues were arranged peripherally in a circular edifice enclosed by windows. The circular edifice was topped by a fluted conoidal roof all in white marble. As one made the round around the edifice, one could peer through the glass apertures and see the statues from various points of view. The entire monument was flanked by his parents. This particular arrangement portrayed, at least for me, the desire to be perpetuated forever after we are deceased. This post-thanatotic attitude is reminiscent of the pharaohs of Egypt. This monument illustrated the vanity of man and even in death preyed on passersby for pity and condolence.

Thetis and I enjoyed our automobile excursions along the waterfront of Lake Ontario. There were a number of state parks as far as we could drive in a day. History was recalled at nearly every stop that we made. Recreational facilities abounded along the way, and we would stop and have our sandwiches that we prepared at home. We took advantage of the scenic walkways and enjoyed nature in its natural habitat.

The Niagara River connects lakes Erie and Ontario. The first Great Lakes steamboat, *Walk-in-the-Water,* was built to make use of the extensive waterways available. With the advent of the steamboat, Gov. de Witt Clinton seized upon a proposal, the Erie Canal, to build a water route from Lake Erie, Buffalo, to the Hudson River in New York. Once on the Hudson, access to the Atlantic was readily available. Overcoming great obstacles politically and financially, the governor finally succeeded in making the Erie Canal a reality.

To commemorate the occasion, the governor boarded the *Seneca Chief* canal boat at Buffalo and traveled the length of the Erie Canal to Albany. From there he continued down the Hudson River to New York City. There he emptied two kegs of fresh water from Lake Erie into the salt water of the Atlantic. This demonstrated the accessibility of inland water with the Atlantic Ocean. This established the shipping trade between the Great Lakes region, Canada, and the Eastern United States. Regional states such as Michigan, Ohio, Indiana, and Illinois, prospered under this development.

Gov. de Witt Clinton was a far-sighted business man. He could visualize the impact such a canal would have on the overall economies of the area. The canal would foster development and growth of the area; commercial, freight, and industrial expansion would ensue; and passenger travel via the waterways would become a reality.

Buffalo has always been an important economic and diplomatic link in the relations between the United States and Canada. How the name Buffalo came about is a mystery to this very day, for there are no indigenous buffalo in the area. Accordingly, several attempts were made in the past to change the name, but the populace objected strenuously to any change.

There were several outstanding architecturally designed buildings. The most noted one that we visited was the Albright-Knox Art Gallery. Greater Buffalo International Airport was being extended during our stay in the mid-sixties and is now considered one of the finest international airports in the United States. The Kleinhans Music Hall was a great asset to the city of Buffalo and added to the cultural flavor and aesthetic appreciation of the city by providing a balance between its industrial complex and the arts, science, music, and love for Nature. The myriad of parks, recreational areas, botanical gardens, zoological gardens, and national historic sites enhanced the beauty of the city.

Architectural variety was most prominent in the residential areas. This was particularly the case north of Niagara Square. There the diverse demographic population of Irish, German, Italian, and Polish was most pronounced. Each ethnic group had introduced their particular architectural design. Such a mixture provided for innovation, uniqueness, and variety. We enjoyed visiting this area just to see the variations in design that are possible. There existed a harmonious blending of different designs, which resulted in a congruous, proportionate, and pleasing appearance.

23. Alone in Buffalo, but Not for Long

Mr. William Smith, Chief Scientist, Research Department, Bell Aerosystems, called me one day at home and wanted to know if I wanted "to get back in harness." I inquired what he had in mind. He responded by saying that he was expanding the Advanced Technology Research Department. My assignment would be to investigate conceptual designs. This type of work appealed to me, since I would be able to pursue research on the aerospace plane.

I was aware of the research work Bell had conducted on the X series of experimental aircraft. Major Yeager at the time (1947) had flown the Bell X-1 for the first time at supersonic speed. This flight demonstrated the myth of the "sound barrier." Subsequent to the flight of the X-1, Bell built the series extending from the X-1A to the X-1E. All these aircraft were built to investigate aerodynamic-flight qualities of aircraft in the transonic and supersonic range, and thermal effects. The X-2 was expressly built to further investigate the nature of the problems in the transonic and supersonic range. The X-5 incorporated a variable geometry wing by varying the leading-edge sweep from 20 degrees to 60 degrees. Flight investigations were conducted to determine the feasibility of such an arrangement.

In view of the foregoing, I was aware of Bell's receptiveness to conducting research into the unknown. This would afford me the opportunity to probe into hypersonic flight vehicles. Accordingly, I accepted the position, knowing that I would have to go alone. Thetis would have to remain behind to close the sale of our house in Dix Hills.

When I joined the Advanced Technology Research Department at Bell Aerosystems, my overall task was to investigate conceptual designs worth pursuing. The designs would not necessarily be restricted to aircraft. Applications of aerospace techniques to other forms of transportation could be considered. The basic question that had to be determined was: What does it take to make a concept feasible? I had to start with what was already known and demonstrated in flight. Since funding was most likely to come from the military, my conceptual designs had to demonstrate military potentialities.

In view of my prior experience with the aerospace plane, I envisioned that hypersonic flight would become a reality. My task was to outline those areas in which design data was lacking. This was accomplished by making a matrix tabulation of what was required. From the data available, I could determine what was needed. I consulted with various members of the departments throughout Bell to obtain their suggestions and opinions. As suspected, there were many items that required research. To research these areas would require time, personnel, and experimentation. Our aim was to obtain funding to conduct the necessary research in the area of hypersonic flight. I believed Bell was in an excellent position to obtain funding, since it had conducted pioneering work for the air force and NACA.

I worked closely with the Future Systems Research Department. It was important to communicate with that group, since they would be the one to submit the overall proposal to an agency. The Future Systems Research Department submitted a proposal to the Department of Transportation on the mag-lev (magnetic levitation) system of rail transportation in 1966. This system permitted the rail cars to levitate by means of a magnetic bubble. Propulsion is achieved by linear-induction motors.

The principle involved is best described by taking a conventional induction motor and slicing it open so that the stator and rotor are flattened out. The stator (magnets) are attached to the rail car and arranged linearly. The flattened rotor now becomes the rail. This system was capable of achieving a speed of 400 to 450 miles per hour. Such a system would alleviate much of the existing traffic on our highways. Unfortunately, the mag-lev principle was not accepted in this country. Foreign countries, on the other hand, applied our concept to their rail systems.

Bell was involved in the production of the Air-Cushion Vehicle (ACV)/Hovercraft. Improvements in its efficiency were constantly being investigated. Nozzle design, minimization of pressure losses, and optimization of pressure ratio requirements throughout the duct system were a few of the items being investigated.

Hovering is attained over the surface by means of a peripheral jet of air ejected from the bottom of the vehicle. The action of the jet produces thrust. Lift, in turn, is produced by the reactive forces induced by the thrust. (To every action there is an opposite and equal reaction.) Thrust is obtained by the product of the mass of air ejected per second and the difference in velocities of the entering atmospheric air and exhaust velocity. The greater the difference in velocities, the greater the thrust.

This principle applies to propellers, helicopters, and any other device that utilizes the principle of momentum change per second. Forward motion of the ACV is accomplished by a propeller mounted at the rear of the vehicle. This causes a change in momentum per second in a horizontal direction resulting in a reactive force that propels the vehicle forward.

In the case of a turbojet engine, a greater velocity differential is attained by the combustion of fuel. This adds thermal energy to the air molecules, thereby accelerating them to much greater velocities. To increase the efficiency of the engine, the designer has two recourses he can pursue. The one is to increase the mass of air and/or increase the velocity differential.

At the time I joined Bell Aerosystems, Thetis was unable to join me. As a result, I had to eat out. One day I ventured into an Italian restaurant located near the motel where I was staying. The food and service were better than most of the other restaurants I went to. Anna, one of the waitresses, was a very hospitable and convivial person. Her motherly attitude made me feel at home, and she took great pains to make sure I was properly fed. True to Italian hospitality and tradition! With the passage of time, Anna asked me if I would like to join a select group that dined together in true family style.

I told her I would be most pleased to do so. Accordingly, she relayed my acceptance to the proprietors, Mario and Nicolo. These brothers had inherited the business from their father. Consequently, I was admitted to the inner sanctum sanctorum. The event was called the "Boys' Night" and was strictly stag. The group consisted of prominent businessmen, developers, and loyal customers of the restaurant. Its members were primarily of Italian origin. I felt privileged to have been admitted into the group.

My experiences with the group were unique and unparalleled. I witnessed sincere companionship, hospitality and exchange of knowledge in all fields of endeavor. The discussions pertaining to philosophy, music, politics, and community problems were all informative. In addition, I learned how and what to order in Italian. I have been able to retain this information because of my knowledge of Latin. A good number of the words are derived from the Latin, with most of the Italian endings corresponding to the dative case in Latin.

My experiences with the members of the sanctum sanctorum were memorable. The dinners were usually held once a week. The varieties of cuisine and expressions used to describe the various dishes were a revelation. The spirit, humor, and Italian hospitality and gastronomy left me with an indelible impression reminiscent of the ancient Roman feasts that were celebrated during their festivals.

The discussions we had pertaining to opera, music, and politics were very informative and enlightening. Coupled with this was the outstanding epicureanism displayed at the table. The combination of eating, drinking, and discussions that ensued with accompanying jovialness were unforgettable. In retrospect, I was happy and privileged to be with this group. This was the apotheosis of brotherhood.

Most of the members joined in the many discussions we had pertaining to the works of the original composers of the eighteenth. century. One of the principal Italian composers was Antonio Vivaldi. The discussions centered around what they considered his greatest work, *Le Quattro Stagioni, the Four Seasons.* My fellow comrades pointed out that Vivaldi was a gifted violin virtuoso and probably the greatest in his era. This explained the complexity of the violin part in the *Four Seasons.* There were few violinists at the time who could do justice to the composition. He was a prolific composer and wrote some 450 concertos for practically every instrument in the orchestra. He also delved into opera, sonatas, oratorios, cantatas, and religious music. I was told that Vivaldi exerted great influence on Johann Sebastian Bach, who in turn transcribed several of Vivaldi's concertos.

In addition to Vivaldi, mention was made of Pietro Locatelli, Arcangelo Corelli, Francesco Geminiani, Niccolò Paganini, and several others. I can still remember these composers since they are the most popular on classical radio programs. It was pointed out that these composers were violin virtuosos. Paganini introduced novel, very complicated techniques in violin playing, such as the elaborate use of pizzicato, and an extensive use of harmonics. His style influenced Liszt and Rachmaninoff. Paganini had the kindness to help Berlioz in his hour of financial need.

My fellow companions were very proud of their musical heritage. This was evident when discussions centered around Arturo Toscanini, Giuseppe Verdi, and Giacomo Puccini. The discussion would become quite heated when the operatic merits of Verdi and Puccini were compared. One group thought Puccini surpassed Verdi when it came to passionate melodies. Everyone agreed, however, that both were masters of operatic drama. The arias were of par excellence quality for both composers, especially when it came to emotional and amorous plots. The consensus was that Verdi was the more mature and philosophical of the two operatic composers. This was especially the case in Verdi's later years when he composed *Aida, Otello,* and *Falstaff.* Verdi had come under the influence of Wagner's music and had, as a result, modified his earlier style of writing. Puccini, on the other hand, was devoted to the portrayal of true love in the heroines of his operas. Examples were given in *Tosca, La Boheme, Madama Butterfly,* and *Turandot.*

The boys venerated Verdi more than Puccini. Verdi was a strong advocate for the unification of Italy and for his strong patriotism. This is portrayed in his opera *Nabucco,* where in the Temple of Solomon in Jerusalem, the Israelites bewail their fate. It was pointed out that Verdi was born under French rule and accordingly was a French citizen. When Verdi studied in Milano, Milano was under Austrian rule. These changes in government increased Verdi's frustrations, which were expressed vividly in *Nabucco.*

One anecdote relating to Puccini's marriage is worth recounting. The love scenes in his various operas made his wife suspicious that he might be carrying on with some of the prima donnas. Accordingly, she would prepare her meals with an excessive amount of garlic. Finally, Puccini complimented his wife for a most delectable meal, but he wondered if she was not using too much garlic. She responded by saying that she wanted to make sure that no one would approach him because of his breath. In the event one couldn't resist the temptation, asphyxiation would do the trick. Portrayal of love scenes in operatic dramas was one thing, but carrying on such scenes beyond the stage with his more attractive prima donnas was more than she could bear.

I could go on with more anecdotes about the early Italian composers, their contributions, and the profound influence they had on succeeding composers, such as Beethoven, Berlioz, Wagner, Liszt, etc.

It's time to move on to another trait characteristic of Italian heritage. Variety is the spice of life. We are referring to the culinary and gastronomic aspects of the joys and pleasures manifested in participating in food and imbibing in wine. I never dreamt that there were so many different kinds of Italian dishes. I was aware of the extensive Chinese cuisine, with its innumerable combinations and dishes. I was assured by Mario and Nicolo that many different combinations of dishes exist throughout Italy. One must remember that there are Sicilians, the Romans, Calabrese, Firenzians, Milanese, Veronese, Napolitani, etc. Each district of Italy has its own cuisine and its characteristic use of condiments, olive oil, and sauces.

Besides music, we often discussed the ancients who contributed so much to science and mathematics. Pythagoras and his school were located along the coast of the toe of southern Italy. The people were known as *Italiotes* by the Greeks and *Graeci* by the Romans. Pythagoras was the founder of the Pythagorean system of philosophy, which had its main adherents in Magna Graecia. Magna Graecia was the name given to this area by the Romans.

Archimedes was a Sicilian Greek living in Syracuse, Sicily. Archimedes, the Syracusean, was a mathematician and inventor. It is interesting to note that he desired his inventions to be used only in the advancement of science. He was the son of Pheidias, an astronomer who was related to King Hieron of Syracuse. Some of Archimedes' inventions are still being used to this very day. Examples are the Archimedean screw, which is used, for example, to bore a hole in the ground. As the spiral or screw penetrates the soil, the dirt is conveyed to the surface of the ground by being forced upward along the spiral. Another example is the meat grinder for producing chopped meat. The meat is fed into the hopper where it is forced by the Archimedean spiral through a plate perforated with small holes, which produce the ground meat.

In the siege of Syracuse by the Roman general, Marcellus, Archimedes devised a parabolic mirror, which focused the sun's rays into a parallel beam of high energy. This energy was directed at the Roman fleet, which was anchored in the gulf. This set a number of ships ablaze. He was instrumental in terrifying the Romans. As a result, the siege was protracted for a period of three years.

There were a number of other mechanical contrivances concocted by him that were used against Marcellus' warriors. He applied the principle of levers to a number of contrivances used to thwart the enemy. Some of the applications of his scientific investigations were pulleys, catapults, and sling shots. It is of interest to note that Julius Caesar in his conquest of Gallia (France) and Germania (Germany) employed these same machines of war.

There is an interesting account of Cicero's visit to the tomb of Archimedes. As Quaestor, he visited Sicily to determine for himself the illegal and immoral actions of Verres, then praetor of Sicily. Cicero, in his orations in the Roman Senate against Verres, mentioned that Marcellus was deeply distressed when told that Archimedes had been slain by a Roman soldier. This occurred when a Roman soldier ordered him to stop drawing the geometrical figure in the sand. Archimedes was so absorbed in what he was doing that he paid no attention to the commands of the soldier. Upon further orders from the soldier without response, the soldier became so infuriated that he drew his sword and killed Archimedes.

While in Sicily, Cicero visited the tomb of Archimedes. He had been slain in 212 B.C. When Cicero saw the site in 75 B.C., he found the site in shambles, unkept with bushes and thorns abounding the area. The thing that impressed Cicero was the representation of a sphere inscribed in a cylinder. It was the wish of Archimedes that he be remembered in posterity by what he considered his greatest discovery.

In his geometrical studies involving spheres and cylinders, he arrived at a proposition that stated: Every cylinder whose base is the greatest circle in a sphere and whose height is equal to the diameter of the sphere is 3/2 of the volume of the sphere and its surface together with its bases is 3/2 of the surface of the sphere. This proposition was regarded by him as his most valuable achievement above all the other discoveries he had made. His other discoveries included the laws of buoyancy and flotation (associated with this discovery is the famous "Eureka," I have found it!); the leverage principle ("Give me a place where I can stand and I will move the earth"); his approximation to irrational numbers; the theory of limits leading to the basic principles of integration laid down formally by Leibnitz and Newton centuries later; the quadrature of the parabola, which involved the theory of limits and integration, on floating bodies; and the sand reckoner, which involved a special number system involving very large numbers.

The problem of the sand reckoner led Archimedes to devise a new number system. In correspondence with Gelon, the eldest son of King Hieron, the question arose among mathematicians of the day as to how many grains of sand could be fitted into the then universe as visualized by the astronomer Aristarchos of Samos. Archimedes realized that to solve this problem he would need to devise a new number system capable of expressing extraordinarily large numbers. The existing Greek method of expressing numbers by means of the alphabet was far too limiting in scope to be applicable to such a problem. Not only was the existing number system limiting, but very cumbersome and time-consuming to perform massive numerical calculations. To arrive at an answer to the proposed problem would require several lifetimes if one were to rely on existing conventional numerical techniques.

Accordingly, Archimedes then proceeded to establish a system of so-called orders and periods, by which one arrives at large enough numbers to solve the problem at hand. Starting with the conventionally accepted 10,000, he adopted as his unit the myriad myriads (10,000 x 10,000 = 100,000,000). The system so devised could attain numbers up to 80 quadrillion zeros in our decimal system. This is equivalent to one followed by 80,000 million zeros. For Archimedes this was a sufficiently large numbering system to cope with the problem at hand.

His system is reminiscent of the Arabic decimal numbering system, which we now employ. We employ 10 as a unit. It is remarkable how Archimedes in principle conceived of the concept of units. He used the myriad myriads as his unit, whereas the decimal system employs 10 as the unit. As an example, the number 1125 can be written as 10 cubed + 10 squared + 2 x 10 to the first power + 5 x 10 to the zeroth power.

Gauss, considered to be one of the three greatest mathematicians of the world, along with Newton and Archimedes, lamented the fact that Archimedes missed the boat when he didn't latch onto the decimal system of numeration as we now know it. Gauss's remark was: "To what heights would science now be raised if Archimedes had made that discovery!" Gauss, like Archimedes, found himself faced with intricate calculations involved in arithmetical and astronomical calculations.

Archimedes calculated the number of particles of sand in Aristarchos' model of the universe to be one followed by 63 zeros. This number is called vigintillion in the American numbering system. As one can readily see, the newly devised numbering system was more than adequate for the solution to the Sand Reckoner problem. For those desirous of pursuing the problem in more detail, T. L. Heath's book, *The Works of Archimedes*, is highly recommended.

It is a characteristic trait of mathematicians to propose problems that have never been considered before. The object is to challenge their fellow mathematicians either for a proof to a proposition of theirs that they intuitively feel is correct or to arrive at a solution to a problem. The mathematicians have their intricate way of reaching their rainbow.

This was how I managed to keep myself sane without my family. As Julius Caesar said, "Gaul is divided into three parts." However, my family went a step further! We were divided into four. I was in Buffalo, Thetis on Long Island, Alceste in Boston, and Conrad in California.

We were planning to move to Buffalo in the summer of 1967. At that time school would be over and three graduations would have occurred. Thetis would be receiving her master's degree in counseling from Post College, Long Island University, in January. Alceste would receive her bachelor's degree from the University of California in June. Conrad would be graduating from the Lawrenceville School, New Jersey. This was a banner year for graduations. We were all looking forward to these events with great anticipation and the feeling of pride since mother, daughter, and son had arrived at their next rung on the ladder of educational achievement.

We decided to move, even though the property had not been officially sold. What remained was the signing of the final papers. In moving we were faced with a real dilemma. We had to move from a ten-room house to an apartment. During the twenty odd years we lived in Dix Hills, we had acquired quite a library, ancillary equipment such as a standby generator, a circular saw, drill press, garden tools, furniture, drafting tables, several train sets, etc., which would be of no further use to us.

Books were given to the school libraries, workshop tools and generator were sold, furniture was donated to charities, and two drafting tables were sold. The children had to make some decisions of their own as to what to discard or give away. Over the twenty years, all of us had not eliminated anything either for sentimental reasons or for concern that one day we might have renewed use for them. Much was eliminated in the process of cleaning up, but much still remained. Conrad was especially attached to his Lionel train sets and would not part with them. To this very day, we have eight cartons of trains and track stacked away in cartons measuring 13 by 19 by 11 inches. Thetis and Conrad took the brunt of supervising the moving men on what to pack. Thetis moved our personal items by our car several times. This trip entailed a distance of some five hundred plus miles one way, from our home in Dix Hills to Buffalo.

Thetis and Conrad packed the last remaining personal items, locked the house, and headed west to Buffalo. This was the only home Conrad knew. He was born and reared there. As Thetis drove down the driveway, Conrad turned around for a last look of the house and surroundings he had come to know so intimately and affectionately. The trip took some ten hours of intensive driving. The weather cooperated and the scenery along the way was pleasant and relaxing on the New York State Turnpike.

In the meantime, we kept Alceste, who was at Harvard, informed of our progress. The three of us were happy to be reunited again in our new home in Tonawanda, just north of Buffalo. We no sooner moved to our apartment in June when Conrad had to depart for Whittier College in California. Our living in the Buffalo area turned out to be a pleasant experience for us. The people were very friendly and we often wondered if this was because the winters were so bitterly cold and inclement. Was this a manifestation of commiseration thereby leading to a mutual closeness? Or perhaps was it the beautiful mix of ethnic cultures that bound us together?

Whatever the reason, we welcomed the hospitality, cordiality, and gemutlichkeit of the people. When I took Thetis to Como's for dinner, Anna was delighted to see her. She served Thetis more than the usual amount of food because she felt she was undernourished and needed to put on more weight. This flattered Thetis, who felt she should be on a diet but Anna thought otherwise. When we went shopping, the clerks in the stores were extremely cordial and helpful.

Our experience in the fish market was a revelation. There was a tremendous assortment of ocean, lake, and river fish. We were accustomed to shopping at the docks in Babylon, Long Island, where the fresh catch of the day came in. Here we were able to purchase only ocean fish, such as lobster, flounder, blue fish, cod, whiting, and mackerel.

When we asked for Maine lobster, the fisherman in Buffalo regrettably answered that he didn't have any more left. He suggested that in lieu of the lobster we should try the Danish lobster tails. We were assured that we would prefer them to the Maine lobster. He urged us to try them. These tails were small, but he assured us they were very succulent. He was so right! These became one of our favorite dishes.

The meat shops offered a great selection and variety of meats because of the diverse ethnic cultures. The butcher introduced us to homemade Polish sausage. This was a savory delight, especially in those days when cholesterol and sodium intake were not taken seriously. The liverwurst was as delicious as that in Germantown in New York City. No matter what food shop or market we went to, there was always a marvelous selection of delicacies. Eating at home or in restaurants was always a delightful experience.

Living in Buffalo made it convenient for us to drive to Cambridge, Massachusetts, to visit Alceste at Harvard. We would take the New York State Thruway and the Massachusetts Turnpike to Cambridge. This afforded us an opportunity to see the Harvard football games. On our way home from one of these games, the weather was fine from Boston to the New York State border. As we approached Albany, it started to snow slightly. When we reached Syracuse, the intensity of the snow increased. Just before we reached Rochester, Thetis knew we would be in for trouble. Having taught Earth Science to seniors in high school, she explained why we might experience a snow squall.

The first indication of the impending squall was the sudden drop in air temperature. We were experiencing a cold front. As we approached the Great Lakes region, extremely humid, relatively warm air mixed with the cold air, which produced a full-fledged snow squall. The snow was falling at such a high rate that we could not see where we were going. Thetis became navigator and by instinct guided me to keep us on course by trying to follow what she could see of the side of the road. The squall lasted for more than an hour.

We were making very little headway. We literally prayed all the way home, and by the grace of God, we made it to Tonawanda. Fortunately, the fury of the storm subsided just a few miles from our destination.

These snow squalls are typical of the area. In time we became accustomed to them and took them in our stride by avoiding them whenever possible. The weather in the Buffalo area is very microclimatic. Very often in winter, we would start off for the airport in sunny weather and abruptly encounter a snow squall en route. During this sequence of events, there apparently exists a sharp line of demarcation on one side of which the weather is fair and on the other side inclement. This is typical of the Great Lakes region.

The predominant cold weather of this section of the country was conducive to ice skating. Our Canadian neighbor across the Niagara River also provided excellent skating rinks. During the winter months, a group of us would take lessons on the fundamental techniques of figure-skating. During my boyhood days, I would play ice hockey and accordingly, I used hockey skates. Our figure-skating instructor had us purchase figure skates. Thetis took to the figure skates better than I did, since this was her first time on ice. As a youngster she did roller skating, the techniques of which did not interfere with her learning figure-skating.

The difficulty I had in readjusting to figure skates was in acquiring the ability to shift the center of gravity of my body more toward the rear, to prevent the sawlike teeth at the toe of the figure skates from digging into the ice. In hockey one utilizes the forward portion of the skate for immediate start-offs. The hockey skate does not have teeth at the tip of the skate. I had become so accustomed to the hockey skates that I would trip over when leaning too far forward on the figure skates.

In due time we found figure-skating to be the most challenging. It required more precision and adherence to stricter techniques than hockey skating. It was analogous to comparing a ballerina with the run-of-the-mill type dancer. Figure-skating required graceful body movements and above all, coordination of all parts of the body.

One of our most beautiful reminiscences of Buffalo was the Niagara Falls. The falls exhibited panoramic views, not only during the summer months, but in winter as well. The falls were more breathtakingly beautiful in the winter when snow and ice added additional kaleidoscopic beauty to the landscape. Multicolored floodlights on the Canadian side created an unforgettable kaleidoscopic fantasy of the falls. During the day, we marveled at the rainbows the mists of the falls created. Driving across the Rainbow Bridge from the American side to Niagara Falls, Ontario, provided us with a different view of the falls from the Canadian side.

Our stay in the environs of Buffalo was enjoyable and memorable. We learned much about the history and the hardships that our early settlers endured. We witnessed the progress that was inaugurated in the Great Lakes region and the impact it had in making the United States the great nation that it is today. We admired the courage, the determination, and the pioneering instinct that were vividly displayed in the building of the Erie Canal, the promulgation of culture, the peaceful relations with our Canadian neighbor, and the friendliness and caring of people.

24. Our Move to the West

In the spring of 1968, Alceste informed us that upon completion of her master's degree at Harvard she would be returning to the University of California, Berkeley, for her doctorate. Since Conrad would also be at Berkeley, perhaps we should consolidate forces and move to California. The decision was made, and in June we headed for the West Coast.

It remained for the three of us to join Conrad in California. Conrad was appointed our West Coast representative. Alceste joined us in Tonawanda, and the three of us started off in two automobiles. To relieve the monotony of driving the same car, we would alternate cars. We could appreciate what the settlers had to endure when crossing the great span of our country in their covered wagons. Since this trip was the third time we would be crossing the United States, we decided to keep our sight-seeing to a minimum.

Traveling with two cars and only three drivers complicated the situation. We did not want Alceste to drive alone. As a result, one of us would always accompany her. This meant Thetis or I would be driving alone from time to time. A communications problem had to be resolved. In order to communicate with each other, we established a system of using our directional signals in the event a particular need arose. Stopping under various conditions to gas up, rest, change of route because of detours, and any emergency would be indicated by on-off flashes of the signal light. The person not driving would assume the role of navigator. The route we would take was laid out the night before, with predetermined stops in the event our cars were separated by heavy traffic. This strategy was essential since there were times when we would be traveling on two-lane country roads.

From Buffalo we proceeded to Cleveland, Gary, Des Moines, Omaha, along the North Platte River, to Denver. This portion of the United States constitutes the interior farmlands and Great Plains. Driving during this time became rather monotonous, since there was no variation in scenery. As we approached Denver, the Rockies appeared. Since we were near the Rocky Mountain National Park, we decided to spend some time there to see the Colorado peaks. We took the Trail Ridge Road, one of our nation's highest. For eleven miles this road was above 11,000 feet. There were areas along the road that were above 12,000 feet. At this altitude we could see forty-two higher peaks laden with snow. The Indians called them the Neversummer Mountains. The highest point of the park was Long's Peak, some 14,255 feet.

After our visit to Rocky Mountain National Park, there was no doubt in our mind that it is one of the wonders of the world. The views of the pristine surroundings were breathtaking when one experiences the vastness and enormity of the endless landscape. This area could well be described as a befitting abode of Zeus or of Wotan. This was Nature in her most magnificent and variegated splendor. The existence of so many forms of animal life, plants, and forests made for an unparalleled environment. When we saw this splendor, we were literally in communion with God. Commingling with the creatures of Nature made us feel as though we were an integral part of the ecosystem.

At one of the vista points, Thetis got out of the car Alceste was driving to walk to the car I was driving. The wind was strong and the temperature uncomfortably low. In addition, the atmospheric pressure was substantially below that at sea level, at 12,183 feet. She could barely walk the short distance between the two cars. She felt as if her lungs were about to burst, and she was shivering from the cold. Thetis warned us not to get out of the cars and to proceed slowly down across the Continental Divide. We were fortunate we were able to descend slowly without mishap. All of us felt a sigh of relief when we could start breathing normally again.

Our trip across Colorado on Route 40 was so planned that our next stop would be the Dinosaur National Monument in Utah. The park is located on the border of Colorado and Utah. This area contains a wealth of dinosaur remains. An ingenious structure has been erected against one of the cliffs containing a profuse amount of fossilized skeletal remains. From a balcony in the glass-enclosed structure, we could see the fossil bones and paleontologists working ever so slowly and meticulously brushing off the sand of some of the remains. Our guide informed us that the largest brontosaurus measured almost eighty feet in length. Some of the other remains indicated a wide range of size, the smallest being about the size of a vulture.

Many theories have been expounded regarding the extinction of the dinosaurs. The accumulations of these remains in this particular area still intrigue the paleontologists. Looking down at the exhibit from the balcony was like seeing an open book exposing the history of paleontology. We were witnessing what transpired millions of years ago by journeying backward in time. It was an eerie feeling to be transported back in time. One felt as if one were being metamorphosized.

The drive through Utah was most spectacular. The colored sandstone cliffs along the route ranged in color from deep red to gold for miles on end. We all agreed that we would return to Utah to see the spectacular canyons of this beautiful state after we had made our home in California.

We proceeded to Elko, Carson City, South Lake Tahoe, Sacramento, and finally Concord, just north of Berkeley. This would be where we would join up with Conrad, who was attending the University of California. The reunion was a happy one. We celebrated the event with champagne at dinner that evening. There was so much to say, exchanging information. Now that we were together we had to plan where we should go house-hunting. The consensus was that we should start investigating Palo Alto. Our previous visits to the Bay Area during World War II and 1958 convinced us that this would be a good starting point.

We were fortunate to find an apartment in Palo Alto within a month. The apartment was on the eighth floor, with a panoramic view of the San Francisco Bay and Mount Diablo. We were located between the Berkeley and Stanford Universities. In addition, we were conveniently located with respect to the San Francisco Airport. Conrad was able to come home over the weekends. This was a welcome relief for him, since he was staying at his dorm during the week. Since we only had two bedrooms, we had to improvise and create an additional bedroom for Conrad. There was a dining room off the living room area for which we had no need. Our entertaining could take place in the penthouse directly above us. The penthouse was used exclusively for parties. It was fully equipped with a bar, refrigerator, utensils, tables, chairs, and paraphernalia required for a banquet. There was also a large sitting room, which could easily accommodate a hundred people. This arrangement was ideal.

The dining room was converted into a bedroom by separating the living room from the dining room with high bookcases that came close to the ceiling. Since Conrad had many books of his own, we were able to fit additional bookcases and a desk in this area. In place of a door, we purchased a high folding screen as a substitute. After everything was put in place, the arrangement worked out beautifully and functionally.

Apartment living imposes a severe constraint on space. This was especially the case since we had our books to contend with as well. Fortunately, we had a tremendous foyer area that could be effectively utilized for storage of books. The remaining books were placed in the other bedrooms. We enjoyed apartment living because we could travel whenever we wanted at moment's notice. Our manager was always on hand to watch our apartment and collect our mail.

Since California would now be our new home, my next move was to obtain a professional engineer's license. Accordingly, I prepared for the examination. Since I already had a professional engineer's license from the state of New York, I would only be required to take a two-hour examination. I appreciated this reciprocity that existed between New York and California. I received my professional engineer's license in mechanical engineering from California in June 1969.

With the attainment of my engineer's license a fait accompli, I could officially practice engineering on my own in the state of California. This was important to me. I have always felt that the life, health, and safety of the public should be protected by the licensing of engineers. I looked forward to attaining a working relationship with the many industries in the Bay Area.

25. Tau Beta Pi—San Francisco Alumnus Chapter

Thetis and I have made it a practice to maintain our membership current in our professional societies whenever we move to a new locale. Now that we attained our professional engineer's license, we concentrated on notifying the American Chemical Society, the American Institute of Aeronautics and Aerospace, and Tau Beta Pi of our new address.

Since very few people outside the engineering profession are acquainted with the aims and goals of the Tau Beta Pi Association, we would like to say a few words about it. It is the national honorary engineering society, equivalent to Phi Beta Kappa. Its aim is to "mark in a fitting manner those who have conferred honor upon their Alma Mater by distinguished scholarship and exemplary character as students in engineering, or by their attainments as alumni in the field of engineering, and to foster a spirit of liberal culture in engineering colleges."

After settling in Palo Alto, it was not long after when we realized that there was considerable justification for the formation of a Tau Beta Pi alumnus chapter in the Peninsula Area. There were many scattered electronics companies, such as Varian Associates, Ampex, and a myriad of other technological companies, General Electric, Lockheed Missiles and Space, Fairchild R & D, Hewlett Packard, Ford Aerospace, FMC Corporation, to name but a few. These organizations represented a pool of diversified talent. Such a group could readily deal with the doctrine of interdisiplinarity as it related to the solution of societal problems.

The decade of the 70s was fraught with cutbacks in the defense industry, financial crunches in the economy, with the resultant impact on industry, and unrest in the universities. The engineering and scientific potential existed among the diverse industries scattered throughout the Bay Area for effecting mitigation of these problems.

An alumnus chapter of Tau Beta Pi could also provide the mechanism for transfer of information among the various branches of the profession. In addition, interaction among engineers in academe and industry could be fostered, leading to a better understanding of the problems of both. Counseling for the students could be inaugurated, which could provide better opportunities for them in industry.

The establishment of an alumni chapter could benefit the community by encouraging full utilization of the capabilities of engineers in the mitigation of civic problems. Furthermore, the general public could be made aware of the potentials of modern technology. The public in turn could voice their opinions and suggestions to the organization.

There were also benefits for the individual alumnus member. Members could meet other members in the area, thereby leading to an exchange of ideas, which could provide an opportunity for rendering service. Programs could be established that could provide continuing educational opportunities and inform members of employment opportunities.

Based on the interest of Tau Bates in the Peninsula Area, a petition was presented to the Executive Council of Tau Beta Pi, requesting an alumnus chapter charter. With the cooperation of the secretary-treasurer, Robert H. Nagel, twelve hundred mailings went out to the Peninsula Area Bent subscribers.

The response was most encouraging. We received about 20 percent of the mailings we sent out. Accordingly, we set up an organizational meeting in the centroidally located area of Mountain View. Organizers included Dr. John R. Manning, assistant professor of mechanical engineering at Stanford University, Dr. William Eads, Hewlett-Packard Corporation, and Dr. E. Dale Martin, of the Ames Research Center.

It was interesting to note that letters sent to potential Tau Bate members replied by saying that too many engineers and laymen alike viewed the technologist's role as ended with the generation of alternatives presented in a tidy report to be filed and too often forgotten by the decision-makers of society. This was viewed by members of Tau Beta Pi as totally unacceptable. This approach was rejected as invalid in an era when technical and social issues were no longer separable; members expressed their desire to develop and exercise their expertise and to implement their ideas. These were indeed encouraging remarks! We were not alone in our concern for the safety, health, and general welfare of our communities.

February 23, 1971 was the day when the San Francisco Peninsula Alumni Chapter of Tau Beta Pi was chartered. Bob Nagel of the National Association presented the charter. He in turn was accompanied by other national association officers, Vice-President Mancil Milligan and Assistant Secretary-Treasurer Ralph Warmack. At long last we were on the road to implementing one of the goals and objectives to stimulate creative engineering professionals to work on environmental and societal problems. These areas could hopefully be filled by those displaced engineers seeking reemployment. To accomplish this meant reorientation programs on how to apply fundamental concepts to new problems. Many engineers were highly specialized in specific areas and were at a loss as to how to apply their knowledge to new fields. In this way jobs could be generated for the unemployed.

The agenda included election of officers, charter presentation, and discussion of goals of the chapter. All members of Tau Beta Pi, their wives, and guests were invited. Attendance included faculty members of the universities of Stanford, Santa Clara, San Jose State, students from collegiate chapters, industry presidents, council and chamber of commerce representatives.

Discussions that ensued during the meeting were most provocative and informative. Engineers and scientists were rapidly coming to realize that their relationship to society was changing. What was done technologically in the past was open-ended. We did not consider sufficiently the impacts technology had upon the environment and ecology. As a result, technology and science were looked upon as the cause of many problems facing society. A number of critical, emerging problems were discussed including: environmental pollution, depletion of natural resources, urban problems, rapid transit, transportation. It was recognized that as a result of these additional demands, a transition from the more conventional type of engineering problems to new areas had to be accomplished.

Additional components, such as political, psychological, ecological, emotional, demographic, had to be considered in the holistic approach. These components were foreign to the conventionally trained engineer. It was realized that these components would present difficulties in estimating their effects in any analysis, since they could not be evaluated quantitatively. Nevertheless, it was agreed that an evaluation of these additional components should be arrived at by a consensus of opinion of the action groups assigned to the various components.

Accordingly, the Peninsula Alumni Chapter decided to inaugurate action groups that would set up programs to help solve local community problems. Accordingly, groups were established in the following areas: Air Pollution, College and High School Relations, Land Use (formerly coordinated area planning), Unemployment, and Transportation.

The Air Pollution Group, under the chair of Eugene Hill, discussed several possible approaches for the mitigation of pollution. It was decided that to get a foothold on the overall problem, he would first have to obtain enough background information in the general area. With this information, the group could focus in on a feasible and practical objective. Peter Venuto, the president of Citizens Against Air Pollution, Inc. (CAAP), gave an illustrated discussion on air pollution and the activities of his organization.

The College and High School Relations Group suggested that the chapter hold sessions with the collegiate chapters at Stanford, San Jose State, Santa Clara University, and the University of California, Berkeley. The brainstorming sessions would be devoted to improving relationships between the academic and industrial organizations. It was pointed out that future talent was being diverted from science and engineering because of the miasma imposed upon society by the popular belief that technology had gone awry. Accordingly, the chapter could launch various educational programs aimed at the college and high school levels to define what the aims and goals of the engineering profession should be, particularly in reference to the societal problems of the future. It was also recognized that a definite need existed for some means by which high school and college students could see and visit Bay Area engineers "in action." Bob Markevich and Austin Marx took an active role in this endeavor.

The Land Use Group originally became involved in studying a developmental project prepared by a group of consultants for the city of Palo Alto. Several sessions of the group were held to develop a plan of approach. It was finally resolved that the approach should be first, the determination of compliance with the general plan, any impacts the proposed project might have on the contiguous and surrounding properties, and finally the economic benefit to the city in the short and long terms. Projects that would require an excessive amount of maintenance in the long run were looked upon askance. An equilibration of expenses and revenue to the city was the keyword to the overall evaluation of a project.

The Unemployment Group discussed what action should be taken to help the unemployed Tau Bates. Members were made aware of the AIAA Workshops, the activities of the various Experience Unlimited groups throughout the Bay Area, and what steps might be taken to establish a dynamic group to encourage the development and/or improvement of products and processes.

The Transportation Group concentrated on what steps should be taken for a preliminary study and analysis. Many modes of transportation were discussed, including BART trains, buses, automobiles, bicycles, and several futuristic schemes, including the electric car. Reports of many political and industrial groups concerning Bay Area transportation were perused and the pros and cons discussed in detail. Prof. Roy Lave of Stanford University presented an informative talk on the complementary relationship of transportation and communication. Drivers would be alerted in the event of traffic jams and alternate routes that might be taken to avoid delays.

Under the chairmanship of John Hansen, a suggestion to research minibuses as an economically feasible means of short distance transportation was proposed. We were faced with a paradox. To make such a system practical, the frequency of operation was essential. If a passenger were to miss one bus, he should be able to count on another within a matter of minutes. The question that arose was, would the population density be sufficiently high to merit such an arrangement economically?

A Tau Beta Pi Peninsula Newsletter was established, to notify its members of the progress being made by the five action groups. The wives were encouraged to participate in any group projects, chapter projects, and to suggest any need for new endeavors. Thetis was appointed to coordinate this activity. To help defray expenses, the membership voted to establish Chapter dues of three dollars per year. Dues were waived for those unemployed.

As our chapter grew, it became necessary to introduce three new programs. A membership board was established to find more of the "lost" Tau Bates on the San Francisco Peninsula. A programs committee was formed to obtain speakers and to suggest appropriate programs for future meetings. Finally, a publicity group was formed to inform the media of our actions and decisions and to inform the members of the chapter of its activities.

Speakers were invited to address the various groups. Talks were given by Jack Beckett, vice-chairman of the Metropolitan Transportation Commission on regional public transportation; Al Baker of GTE Sylvania spoke on transportation concerning vehicle location, scheduling, and control using electronics; Robert M. Powell, vice-president of Lockheed, spoke on industry and the environment and the need for a reevaluation of man's ethical, moral, and technological responsibilities.

In subsequent meetings the Air Pollution group concentrated on three major objectives: (1) development of an in-depth understanding of air pollution in the context of its effect on the population's health; (2) selection and definition of a scope of activity that would be within the group's capability for taking effective action; (3) creation of a working relationship with some other larger group active in the field of air pollution, hopefully as technical advisers to that group.

The Student Relations Group participated in various programs with students of the various collegiate chapters to determine the nature of societal problems. Alumni members were anxious to join in empathetic discussion with the students and to contribute their experience to problems of their concern. Stan Deller, collegiate president of San Jose State, undertook the task of setting up a conference entitled "Technology for Society, the Great Misunderstanding" at the school.

This type of conference could be the most beneficial type of activity that the alumnus and student chapters could perform jointly to help revitalize the sagging image of the engineer. The day's activities centered around a panel discussion of technologically and nontechnologically oriented people, covering the gamut of interdisciplinary approaches to cures of social ills. Plans were made for additional conferences of this nature to promote interaction of the engineer and his community in discussions regarding problems of concern to everyone.

As assistant director of Tau Beta Pi alumni activities in California, I was privileged to attend the seventy-fifth anniversary of the founding of California alpha on April 17, 1982. It was a momentous occasion for the Tau Beta Pi members of the University of California, Berkeley. This was the first engineering college in California to join Tau Beta Pi.

The celebration was highlighted by a talk delivered by Dr. Melvin Calvin, MI beta 1931 (Michigan College of Mining and Technology). Dr. Calvin, a nobel laureate in chemistry, discussed his research in photosynthesis on hydrocarbons for use as a fuel. In appreciation he was presented with a special engraved version of the Chapter's seventy-fifth anniversary medallion. Present at the celebration were District 15 Dir. John Pedersen, chapter adviser Andrew R. Neureuther, and several former collegiate presidents.

It is interesting to note that California now has twenty-one collegiate chapters. Following the entry of Berkeley into Tau Beta Pi were California Institute of Technology, Stanford University, the University of Southern California, the University of California, LA, Santa Clara University, San Jose State, etc.

It was, and still is, my fervent desire and hope that Tau Bates throughout the United States will supplement their activities and become more involved with the myriad of societal problems confronting the nation. There is a vast pool of talent available, and leaders in their chosen fields of engineering can materially help in alleviating and mitigating many of the problems confronting the populace. We need to become more involved with the social implications of technology.

I hope that the goals, objectives, and experiences as outlined heretofore will be emulated and pursued by all alumnus chapters throughout the nation. The collegiate chapters—there are over two hundred of them throughout the nation—are composed of members who are committed and dedicated young people, eager to better the environment encompassing them. Upon graduation they look forward to joining the ranks of their fellow alumni members who have contributed to the scientific community as well as to our society.

Society has much to gain if Tau Bates carry the Olympic torch and light the way that will lead to the amelioration of social and economic problems confronting mankind, not only locally, nationally, but on a global scale.

26. The Unemployed Professionals

The Vietnam War in the sixties, the ensuing stagflation, the Cambodian situation in the seventies, student unrest in the universities that led to a reevaluation of our social, moral and economic values all contributed to uncertainty in our economy. Cutbacks in the defense industry and space activities, tightening of credit led to unemployment in almost all industries. In our immediate area of Palo Alto, Lockheed Aircraft Corporation was especially affected. Unfortunately, we found ourselves immersed in the recession of the seventies. We were faced with the paradox of the failure of application of old ideas to predict the real trend of events. In the economic sector, we were faced with stagflation, a phenomenon that could not have been predicted using established economic theories. Change was the predominant order of the day.

To assist unemployed members of the scientific and engineering profession in obtaining employment, the Workshops for Professional Employment concept was inaugurated. The workshops originated in Los Angeles in March 1970 by the AIAA, based on the experiences of Forty-Plus and Thursday 13. It was funded by the Department of Labor, DOL, and NASA for presentation in thirty-six cities. The sum of money was approximately $134,000, and the contract was to expire on August 31, 1971. The workshop contract with the DOL was extended through December 1971.

The Northern California coordination was being provided through AIAA, WEMA (Western Electric Manufacturers Association), IEEE (Institute of Electrical and Electronic engineers), and NCTPC (Northern California Technical Personnel Committee). Counselors were volunteers who received training in presenting the workshop sessions.

WEMA's principal role was one of supplying clerical help for making reservations for attendees. When a sufficient number of applicants had been reached, WEMA notified them as to location, date, and time of the workshops. Lockheed printed and provided the manual entitled "Job Hunting: Seven Steps to Success." It covered self-analysis, market research, sales promotion, and negotiations. The IEEE was the custodian of the "Job Catalog," which listed job opportunities. Unemployed members were notified of the service and were encouraged to use it.

The NCTPC provided the workshops with the required number of counselors. A counselor training program was arranged by Lockheed in the fall of 1970. The training sessions were recorded and were used extensively by many groups and counselors. Wherever possible, two counselors served each group, the one supplementing the other. Counselors for each session were selected according to their abilities and experience. Approximately twenty-five counselors were on our staff since the inception of the workshops.

The makeup of the workshop was composed of a group representing thirty local companies, professional engineering societies, and a trade organization. Our basic approach was to invite and coordinate the efforts of all splintered groups of unemployed engineers who were mushrooming all about in the Bay Area. It was recognized at the outset that to help the engineer and scientist effectively, a united and coordinated front and effort were mandatory. This approach would eliminate a great deal of duplicative effort, both participatory and financial.

As an Associate Fellow of AIAA, I was appointed to serve as chairman of the workshops. My first assignment was to recruit counselors to carry out the program. Volunteers from the various companies and professional societies were interviewed. Those who were selected were briefed in the techniques of counseling. Among those selected was my wife, Thetis. As a chemist who had taught chemistry, physics, and science in high school, she was well versed in the fundamentals of science. In addition, she had a master's degree in counseling. The two of us became involved in assisting the unemployed. All those involved in the program were volunteers. Their reward would be the gratitude from those in need. In counseling the unemployed, encouragement and motivation were stressed throughout the lecturing process. These people were desperate. Mortgage payments and family expenses ran high. When people are unemployed, financial problems compound with time.

Thetis and I personally visited several unemployment groups

throughout the Bay Area and made several observations. The engineer was essentially an independent worker, wrapped up in his field of specialization, practically oblivious of his social responsibilities. The scientist and engineer did not communicate with his local civic groups, the planning commission, the council within his community, with the result that the general public was unfamiliar with the potentials and benefits of modern technology. There was very little interaction among different types of engineers in industry. This resulted because of various classifications of security placed on defense contracts with the government and military and the proprietary restrictions placed by the companies on their projects.

As a result, there was a lack of interdisciplinary tie-in with the different branches of the profession. With the outbreak of student unrest, a reevaluation of societal values, contracting difficulties with the Pentagon as a result of the technically unrealistic and financially infeasible concepts concocted by the "whiz kids" of former Defense Secretary Robert S. McNamara left many technical people cynical and critical of government action and sincerity. Many did not want to be associated with defense work. Many engineers felt they were signaled out as culprits in their endeavors for the government. They were stigmatized for the work they did by their own fellow citizens.

These comments on the government were quite contrary to the ones I was accustomed to, especially during World War II. We reminded our audiences of the rapport and cooperativeness that existed between the scientists, engineers, and the government in the early forties. The government, hard-pressed for hardware, solicited the engineer-industrial complex for assistance and guidance. On many other occasions the reverse happened. The engineer-scientist showed the need and importance of various concepts and systems to governmental officials.

Admittedly, these events came about because of the war effort, but there was something we could learn from past experience. Innovative ideas could lead to new jobs. This latter concept has resulted in many entrepreneurial establishments throughout the Bay Area. Thetis and I pointed out the risks associated with starting any new economic venture. On the other hand, the rewards as an innovator could be great. It was suggested that one way to proceed in the entrepreneurial business would be to form a group of different types of engineers, thereby assuring not only interdisciplinarity but also in introducing a product that could be brought to the market.

The structure of the workshop consisted of at least three sessions. The most difficult session was the first, because of its broad material coverage. Finances and budgets, job self-analysis, market research, and marketing strategy were some of the areas covered. The total number of sessions for each series of the workshops was three to four. The second and third sessions covered resumé writing and interviewing techniques. Experiments were conducted with the introduction of a panel-type meeting in which four or five panelists were assembled, each an expert in the above areas. This concept was introduced after the third session and was favorably received.

In view of the forementioned problems of the seventies, several actions to ameliorate the unemployment problem were undertaken. We inaugurated strategy meetings composed of several groups to formulate what the engineers earnestly believed could be done to alleviate the unemployment problem on a professional level. We set out to establish guidelines and goals that were meaningful and beneficial to the nation.

It was proposed that an assembly of civic and political group leaders, social workers, service associations, school and university people, ministerial people be established to discuss the overall impact unemployment created. Every attempt was made to publicize the workshops. Announcements were sent to a number of professional engineering societies, such as the IEEE, ASME, ASCE, ACS, the Santa Clara Council of Engineers, CSPE, etc., to alert unemployed engineers and scientists by appropriate announcements in their respective newsletters, publications, etc. A publicity coordinator was appointed and announcements were sent out to about 30 radio stations. I was interviewed on our local TV station to present and explain our programs for the unemployed. Ads appeared periodically in the local newspapers. The media were very helpful in assisting and publicizing our efforts.

In addition, we were coordinating our efforts with other local AIAA sections. Announcements were distributed to community bulletin boards, HRD offices, engineering societies, grocery stores, churches, libraries, employment lobbies, firms planning to lay off anyone or who had been laid off. Every means was taken to notify people of our activity and what we had to offer in the way of assistance.

At the invitation of Congressman Gubser, a presentation was made, entitled "New Vistas for the Scientist and Engineer." The object of the presentation was to establish the need for an amalgamation of all engineering activities and the need for a rapport between the engineer-scientist and the politician, particularly in the solution of societal problems.

A trip was made to Sacramento at the invitation of Assemblyman Vasconcellos to discuss the general unemployment situation. While there, we had the opportunity to discuss the activities of the AIAA workshops. Conferences were also held with Senators George Mascone and Peter Behr. A report entitled "Statistical Data Workshops," covering the types of engineers and scientists affected by unemployment, was given to them. The contents of the report were discussed, and a good rapport was established.

When I discussed the many applications systems engineering could shed on the solution of societal problems, including political ones, George Mascone became very interested. He was anxious to be kept informed of future progress and asked for suggestions as to what we could offer to mitigate the unemployment situation. This laid the groundwork for future discussions and contact with Sacramento. Copies of the report were also sent to our area congressmen and legislators in Washington and Sacramento, respectively.

To further our endeavors to assist the unemployed, we submitted a proposal entitled "Creativity Needed to Generate Jobs" to several newspapers throughout the Peninsula area. Its purpose was to illustrate the need for instilling incentive in the creative unemployed professional. It was asserted that our nation and state cannot afford the creative professionals to be frustrated, thereby leading to a lack of productive ideas. Furthermore, the majority of unemployed are dependent upon the creative professional. He is the one who supplies the basic ideas and concepts so essential to the development of a system.

Wives of the attendees were invited to attend the workshop sessions as well. Coping with the economic and emotional problems at home was an important part of the problems facing the unemployed. Exploring career choices and employment possibilities for women became part of the training program. On the average, 5 to 7 percent of the wives attended the sessions. Since various churches, adult schools, and community groups had organized similar workshops for women, we decided our sessions were duplicative. Thereafter, the wives were invited to attend the general panel discussions with their husbands. Approximately 20 percent of those attending were women.

Our activities were requested by the collegiate community. We were asked to counsel the graduating seniors at San Francisco State College. Two counselors were used for this session, which lasted approximately three hours. This seminar was received favorably by the students. Accordingly, announcements were sent to other universities in the area notifying them of our student counseling sessions.

Several areas were covered in the workshops with an open and free exchange of ideas and opinions among the attendees. The Socratic approach was employed. Foremost in the minds of the attendees was the changing market circumstances and how to adapt oneself to these new situations. These changes were not new to the older engineers, who had been subjected to a nomadic existence. This was especially true for the aeronautical engineers. I well remember the comments made by Dr. Alexander Klemin, who admonished us as students to be prepared for changes in the aircraft industry. He indicated that the wise engineer would travel to where the contracts were being funded.

Our discussions with the attendees led to several conclusions. The majority of unemployed were dependent upon the supervisorial professional who supplied the basic ideas and concepts for a given system. Lacking such a source, the majority will remain stagnant until such time as information is forthcoming from the supervisor as to what to develop and eventually reduce to hardware. This situation is a manifestation of overspecialization in a very restricted field. This applied especially to chemists and aerospace personnel. Despite the higher education and ability to think through and solve complicated specific problems, many were not resourceful and needed guidance.

A paradox existed, since their higher specialized education had prevented them from viewing a problem holistically, a manifestation of the inadequacy of our higher educational system, which has been geared to specialization. Many needed additional courses. The survey indicated that 30 percent of the attendees did not bother to update their knowledge. In today's world that is committing hari-kari. An additional 30 percent of the attendees took miscellaneous courses.

The question was asked of the unemployed attendees: Are you acquainted with the concept of the systems approach to the formulation and analysis of problems? The answer from the unemployed was one of consternation and bewilderment. What on earth was the systems approach? Since this concept was not familiar, we resorted to the desire of scientists to unify all branches of science. As examples we pointed out the unified field theory of Einstein and the concept of interdisciplinarity.

It was not too surprising for us to hear that the forementioned concepts were not familiar to the unemployed. After all, they were specialists in a specific area. As a further example, we illustrated the unified workings of Nature through her basic doctrines of ecology and the environment. The lack of such understanding was precisely the nature of their predicament. Had they the training and understanding of the holistic approach, they could have found jobs in other areas more easily.

The attendees who were unemployed with less than a bachelor's degree or a bachelor's degree numbered 45 percent. Those with a Ph.D. numbered 4 percent. It would appear that those possessing the Ph.D. degree were the most valued by industry. Accordingly, they were in the minority to be released. The groups hardest hit were the EE's, ME'S, and business administration personnel. Attendees belonging to no professional engineering societies numbered 29 percent. A total of 9 percent were members of IEEE, and 35 percent were members of miscellaneous societies. What was surprising was only 9 percent were members of the AIAA, the society most related to aerospace activities.

It was necessary to evaluate the attendees' economic and emotional state of affairs. There was the necessity of maintaining morale and to consider his family's welfare and existence. This meant involving the spouse. The counselors had to determine the strength, fears, and weaknesses of the attendee. In many cases this necessitated a possible change in the nature of the type of work that he was familiar with. This change posed a real problem to the unemployed. Changing one's field of endeavor to another constituted a major hurdle. To adapt and prepare oneself to qualify in the new fields of endeavor meant hard work and challenge.

The counselors instructed them on how to prepare resumés and letters to employers. They were shown how to plan and conduct a well-organized job search. In addition, means of finding employer information were available. The counselors also explained how the attendees could adapt their already acquired skills to new job situations.

A questionnaire was sent to all participants of the workshops, inquiring as to their success in attaining a job as a result of attending the sessions. Of the four hundred who attended the workshops, 30 percent responded. In addition to the replies of the questionnaire and from the few letters and the many phone calls we received, it appeared that many have benefited directly or indirectly. Many expressed sincere thanks for what they learned and many acquired self-confidence and poise, especially as a result of the interviewing session.

In response to the question: What kind of position would you like, 35 percent stated they wanted out of the aerospace industry, 26 percent were content with the same position, 22 percent indicated entry into the environmental sciences, and 17 percent had no particular wishes.

We were gratified that 93 percent of the attendees responded yes to the question: Are you willing to take courses to qualify for a position outside of your present category, providing there is a job requirement?

With regard to the question: Do you think the workshop will help in your job-hunting efforts, the response was an overwhelming 92 percent yes. The cross sectional representation of people associated with professional societies was of interest. A total of 19 percent were members of the IEEE, 9 percent AIAA, 5 percent ASME, 3 percent ASQC, 35 percent miscellaneous, and 29 percent belonging to no professional groups.

Distribution of types of professionals as affected by unemployment was of interest: 51 percent engineers of all types, 17 percent management, 15 percent military, 10 percent sales, 6 percent teaching.

The distribution of college degrees ran as follows: 27 percent bachelor's degree, 22 percent bachelor's + degree, 15 percent master's degree, 12 percent master's + degree, 2 percent doctorate, 2 percent doctorate + degree, 18 percent less than a bachelor's degree.

The categories by university degrees hardest hit were: EE 29 percent, ME 21 percent, Business Administration 12 percent, Industrial Engineering 6 percent, Physics 6 percent, Aeronautical Engineering 5 percent, Chemistry 4 percent, Miscellaneous 17 percent.

It is becoming more and more apparent that what is required to keep abreast of the ever-increasing changes in trends is a broad background in engineering science and bioengineering. More emphasis should be given to fundamental subjects, such as mathematics, physics, chemistry, social science, economics, systems analysis, and management. With this educational background, one would be better equipped to tackle new fields of endeavor when they arise. In our workshop sessions, it was apparent that the unemployed were bewildered as to what steps to take when a demand arose for pollution control, toxic-waste disposal, transportation engineering, critical shortage of affordable housing, etc.

This type of education is more appropriate to meet the changing trends of the future. This can be illustrated by what I experienced during World War II. At Republic Aviation, we needed additional aerodynamicists to meet the demands of the air force schedules. Our first recourse was to the trained aeronautical engineer. None were to be had because of the great demand imposed upon them by the war. Cognizant of the ability and training received by the mathematical physicists and mathematicians, I hired a number of them, much to the dismay and chagrin of my supervisor.

In a period of some three months, these personnel were able to familiarize themselves, first of all, with the semantics associated with aeronautics, second with the aeronautical literature, to a point where they were making suggestions and contributions to high-speed aerodynamics. After all, they promptly informed me that high-speed flows could be treated by equations already developed at least a century ago under three basic classifications, the elliptic (subsonic regime), the parabolic (transonic regime), and the hyperbolic (the supersonic regime).

Now that we have given an account of the unemployment problem in the aircraft industry in the 70s, we are faced with similar problems in the 90s. It appears that similar events occur periodically. In the 70s the commercial airlines were confronted with the introduction of several new wide-bodied aircraft, the Boeing 747, the McDonnell/Douglas DC-10, and the Lockheed Tristar 110. Simultaneously with the development of the supersonic transport (SST), the Concorde, by the French and British, Boeing was building two prototypes of the SST, only one of which would be flown. The second prototype would be a different version of the first prototype.

Many design questions were still unanswered in the first version, and it was considered prudent to have a backup to the first design. As I recall, very little was known about the transonic range of flight. It is known that stable aerodynamic flows exist in the subsonic and supersonic ranges. To achieve supersonic flight, the plane had to cross the transonic flow region. This region exhibits unsteady flows, with possible buffeting of the aircraft. Theoretical investigations provided inconclusive results, and very little experimental data was available at the time.

In addition to a number of questionable design considerations, there were other questions that were raised by different groups. The question of whether the SST should be built was determined largely by the environmentalists in this country. The SST would cruise at an altitude of seventy-five thousand feet. This altitude was selected at the time because maximum cruise speed could be attained at that altitude. Serious concern was expressed on the effects of the emission of nitrogen oxide in the depletion of the ozone layer. Calculations made at the time indicated a reduction of the ozone layer in the neighborhood of 20 percent. This was indeed alarming. A depletion in the ozone layer would permit more hazardous radiation from the sun to enter our environment. This being the case, passengers would, accordingly, be subjected to harmful radiation. The problems of noise on takeoff and sonic booms were of concern.

Other factors entered into the wisdom of proceeding with the building of the SST. Payload would be sacrificed at the expense of carrying huge amounts of fuel to feed the gargantuan appetite of the avaricious jet engines. This consideration led to an economic analysis, which predicted that the profit-and-loss statement for the SST would be seriously affected. Such an aircraft would only become profitable if the fares were to be enormously increased. This meant fewer passengers could afford to fly the SST, thereby aggravating the problem of whether the increase in speed was warranted. This prediction, coupled with the low existing revenues of the airlines, made the decision to proceed with the SST all the more doubtful and highly controversial.

These principal factors led to the demise of the SST in the early 70s. The Senate, after due deliberation, voted not to appropriate any further funds to the project. A valiant counterattack was made by the companies engaged in the development of the SST, but to no avail. Those against the SST had more convincing arguments than those in favor of it.

Like the 70s, the 90s will be crucial decision-making years for the airlines. Many of the aircraft that are in service now have been flying for over ten years. In this period of time, the aircraft have been subjected to sporadic vibrations due to the turbulent nature of the atmosphere. Due to pressure, thermal, and wind gradients prevalent in the atmospheric environment, the atmosphere is in a turbulent and undulant state, thereby subjecting the aircraft to sporadic vibrations. Predictions based on theoretical considerations are not reliable. Recourse must, therefore, be made to measurements of the basic parameters in flight.

The trend for commercial aircraft is bigger in size and faster. With increase in speed, the aircraft will be subjected to more intense jolts from the longer wavelengths of the turbulence spectrum. Turbulence is an elusive quantity, since it can not be formulated in precise terms. Its analysis involves four-dimensional space. The characteristics of turbulence vary as a function of altitude; turbulent wave lengths can vary from sixty feet to sixty thousand feet. Turbulent motions are determined using average values of the parameters, resulting in an approximation. This necessitates the use of random/stochastic processes.

In view of these vibrations, the question arises: How many such vibrations can the wing structure endure before it will develop cracks due to fatigue of the metal? The irregular up-and-down motions of the wing can be likened to the failure of a metal that we bend by hand in a similar way by up-and-down motions. The wings on the wide-bodied aircraft have been designed to be flexible. Flexibility of the wing structure is desirable, since aerodynamic loads are alleviated when the wing flexes due to gusts. On the other hand, the increase in flexibility incurs more vibrations. The spate of accidents in recent years has led to considerations of safety. Since the aircraft have been flying for many years, the probability of fatigue can be high. Such considerations have been raised by the safety personnel and have suggested that these aircraft be overhauled and examined at crucial structural points throughout the wing, tail surfaces, and fuselage.

In view of the aging problem of the current series of aircraft, the airlines are at the crossroads of what to purchase in the near future. Serious review by the airlines is in progress as to which course of action to take. The replacement of current aircraft appears imminent. The question that comes to mind is: What shall be the cruising speed of the next generation of commercial aircraft? It is generally conceded that the Concorde has not been successful financially. Is it more economical to cruise at 0.92-0.95, the speed of sound, or at speeds of 2-5M?

Reincarnation of the SST in this country is now under way. NASA is currently investigating the development of a new SST. Firms in France and Britain are conducting studies of their own as to which type to develop. The lure of flying at supersonic speeds has rekindled interest in view of the future trade with the Pacific Rim countries. The distances involved are great, and the time element becomes crucial.

Should this country decide to proceed with the SST, it will not be before the end of this century when they will become operational commercially. As in the 70s, present cuts in defense are forcing companies to shrink in size and personnel. This will undoubtedly have an impact on the study of the SST, thus delaying its progress. In view of the negative reception the SST received in the 70s, companies working on the project are proceeding with caution. As a result, NASA at the present time is concentrating its efforts on the impacts the SST will have on the environment, sonic booms, and noise emitted by the engines over populated areas.

NASA has taken the approach it has because it does not want a repeat of the entanglements it encountered with the environmentalists in the 70s. It is also aware of the remarks made by David Doniger, senior attorney at the Natural Resources Defense Council. He is quoted as saying "This project (the SST) is a guaranteed loser just looking for trouble. It's pouring money down the rat hole." At the present time, the aeronautical industry is not only at the crossroads of change but of all the alternate roads to follow, it is difficult to find the one that is the most likely to be the best compromise.

The unemployed professional was a manifestation of changing conditions in the economy. To anticipate changes it is necessary to analyze what constitutes change. How does one foresee changes that occur in our economy and employment? In a later chapter, we shall discuss the fundamental notions of progress and opportunity, which are the virtual driving forces that result in inexorable and unrelenting change.

Today's engineer is no longer an independent worker wrapped up in his field of specialization. He is more aware of his social responsibility and has become more active in governmental issues. Community involvement affords us the opportunity to repay some of the benefits we received from society and various organizations. These benefits were acquired while we were establishing ourselves in our respective professions. We recognize the monetary benefits and values we received as students during our school years in the form of subsidization. A portion of our university course payments were subsidized by others, advice and counseling was received by us in regard to our future careers through our teachers, our charitable organizations as well as our professional societies were on hand in time of need and emergency.

Accordingly, the time has come for us to reciprocate and contribute our services to society. In this way we can relate our experiences and guidance to the younger generation and to those who need counseling. How to cope with changing times, uncertainties, mind-boggling problems are a few of the areas we could help in outlining procedures to be followed for their ultimate solution.

We hope that through such services the upcoming generation will find a better place and environment to live in than what we acquired in our generation.

27. Our Association with the Commonwealth Club

We were attracted to the Commonwealth Club of California by the various types of activities it had to offer. It afforded us the opportunity of coming in contact with the entire spectrum of professionals. The membership consists of people from all fields of endeavor. This was appealing to us, since the analysis of societal problems required such a mix of professionals. Members represented international relations, sciences, administration, economics, financial, arts, ecology, the environmental, the legal profession, education, diplomacy, business, government, etc. What an ideal setup for the holistic approach to an analysis of civic problems!

Speakers encompass the entire gamut of fields ranging from the president of the United States, governors, business executives, entrepreneurial managers, to many other experts and decision-makers. Several study groups dealing with specific problems confronting local government, state, and the nation were in operation. These groups operated on an ad-hoc basis, and new groups were readily established to investigate new problems. Flexibility and the willingness on the part of the program committee to tackle new problems without undue delay were especially appealing to us.

Since the club offered foreign-language conversation groups, we attended several of these groups. This was a good way for us to continue our study of languages. The study of languages has long been a hobby of ours. In studying French, Latin, and German in school, we became cognizant of the common thread interwoven in these languages. As a result we became interested in etymology and cognates. The club afforded us the opportunity to study Japanese and Russian. In addition to these languages, French, Spanish, and Italian were offered. Since we were planning to embark on several tours, we found it convenient to study these languages. We learned that one way to a foreigner's heart is to make a humble attempt to say a few words of greeting and concern for their well-being in their language.

The study tours arranged by the club also attracted our attention. This provided us with the opportunity to visit Europe and various parts of the globe. Imagine our delight when we received notice of a trip being planned to visit the USSR and Eastern Europe. Here was our opportunity to brush up on our Russian, Polish, and Hungarian. Fortunately we had studied some Russian previously on the East Coast. We felt we could get along somehow in Russian, with the aid of a dictionary. Our problem was the Polish and Hungarian. We had no prior knowledge of these languages. Polish, we knew, was related to the Slavic language and a knowledge of Russian would help. Hungarian was the real obstacle. Since the Club did not give these languages, recourse was made to tapes.

Prior to our leaving for Europe, we were invited by the Russian consulate in San Francisco for a briefing. They were helpful in telling us what we might anticipate and the restrictions we should be aware of. We were surprised that they served us Cokes rather than vodka. It would appear that we would have to wait for vodka until we arrived in Moscow. One could sense an air of caution in their manner. The briefing was short, and we were glad to be on our way.

On June 15, 1975, we boarded our TWA flight for London. The flight time of thirteen hours included a stopover in London. The next day we departed for Warsaw, Poland. We were impressed by the way in which the Varsovians were resurrecting their city, totally devastated by the Nazis during World War II. We admired their indominable spirit and courage. They lived up to the motto of the city: "Contemnit procellas," the city does not fear the storm. This was not surprising since in the history of Poland, Warsaw had been destroyed completely three times.

When we were there, the Varsovians were beginning to live again. Yet on every street, there were grim reminders of the massacres and persecutions that took place during the Nazi occupation. These sites were marked with memorials citing the number who died. Fresh flowers were always present on these memorials. This was a grim reminder of the horror and brutality of war. It was a chilling sight to behold.

The cordiality of the Varsovite touched us deeply. With dictionary in hand, Thetis and I attempted to translate what was quoted on the various memorials. Our apparent interest in deciphering the

Polish attracted many passersby. When an individual realized we could not speak Polish, he summoned someone who knew English. The translator gave us the information we wanted on the plaque. The date and the number massacred were recorded.

We were invited to the American embassy for a briefing. They were helpful in informing us of points of interest in Warsaw and in answering our questions. We were on our own to shop and dine where we desired. This was a great opportunity for us to feel the spirit of Copernicus, Frederick Chopin, Marie Sklodowska-Curie, and Ignacy Paderewski. The Poles were especially proud of the fact that their mathematicians prior to the outbreak of World War II were leading the rest of the world in abstract mathematics.

We toured the city, but the highlight of our stay was the new opera house. The Grand Opera House (*Teatr Wielki*) was originally opened in 1833. In 1944 it was completely destroyed, and finally in 1965, it was reopened with modern technical equipment. The interior of the silver-colored dome was especially beautiful. It portrayed the paths of the planets about the sun according to Copernicus. The opera we heard was *Tosca*, sung in Italian by Polish singers. The singers outdid the bona fide Italian singers in their emotional and histrionic presentation. It was the most stirring performance of the opera we had ever seen or heard. The singers were apparently moved by the clandestine motives of the prefect of police, Scarpia, reminiscent of the actions of the Nazis in Warsaw. The audience wept profusely. It was all we could do to keep a dry eye. To the Varsonites, *Tosca* represented the fate of Warsaw.

We stayed at the Hotel Forum, an affiliate of the Intercontinental Hotels. It was opened in Warsaw in January 1974. The food in Warsaw was delectable. The *kaczka* was duck roasted with apple. We also enjoyed their goulash, ham, and pastries. The chocolate tortes were especially delicious. The waiters were helpful and anxious to please us. Some of them could speak English and would help us with Polish. We always had our Polish dictionary with us and made constant reference to it. The waiters would look over our shoulders in their curiosity to find the English equivalent of the Polish word under consideration. We had established a quid pro quo, which was most pleasant.

In summary, Poland left an indelible impression upon us. Hitler may have done his best to crush the spirit of the Poles, but they rose above the systematic Nazi destruction of their city with an unbelievable vigor, determination, and fortitude. Their philosophy, hope, and belief were inspirational to us. With great resoluteness, they rebuilt their city from the ground up, so extensive was the bombing of the city. What the bombers did not destroy, the ground troops made sure that whatever remained was completely and totally demolished.

The next destination of our sojourn was Moscow. When we boarded the Aeroflot plane, we were shocked to see the seating arrangement. Passengers were literally packed in like sardines, and the aisle was so narrow that one had to walk sideways. This was no way to encourage air travel. We felt compassion for our fellow travelers who were taller than we. Thetis and I found our knees touching the backs of the seats ahead of us. Thetis's height is five-two and mine is five-five. Those in excess of this either had to force their knees in the back of the seats or, having run out of space, had to dangle their knees in the aisle or in the lap of the adjacent passenger. Anyone in the center seat was squeezed in like the filling of a sandwich. The compression depended upon the height and size of the adjacent passengers. Those who were tall and stocky begged to be seated in the aisle seats.

Much to our chagrin, we were seated in the center because of our small stature. We felt sorry for the hefty flight attendants when they walked down the aisle with passengers' legs and feet protruding in the aisle. Serving our snack was quite a maneuver for them. To compound the problem, a cart was not utilized because of the narrowness of the aisle. Fortunately, the flight was of short duration and all of us were counting the minutes when we would be landing. This experience left us with the impression that the quality of life in the Soviet Union does not compare with the quality of life in the United States. Such amenities as comfort and leisure for the hoi polloi are of secondary importance.

Disembarking from the plane was quite a chore. Our feet were numb and our backs ached. We could just about walk down the platform of steps to the terminal. We had to pick up our luggage and carry it to the next point. From there we were herded to the customs officials. We noticed the people in front of us were undergoing quite an interrogation and examination of their luggage. At this point we became apprehensive. We had made it a point not to bring a camera or film with us. However, we had several Polish, Russian, and Hungarian dictionaries and guide books in our totes.

The buxom customs official asked us to open our tote. In the meantime she asked what we were carrying in the tote. We told her we were carrying dictionaries. She then asked why. We told her we had studied Russian in school and found the language challenging. Again she was intrigued by our reply. We answered by saying that our names on our passports were exactly the same in Russian as they were in Byzantine Greek. In studying the language, we had found that 60 percent of the letters were of Greek origin.

She picked up one of our dictionaries in our tote that was actually printed in Russia. She asked where we had bought it. We told her that there was a Soviet bookstore in San Francisco that sold all kinds of Russian books at reasonable prices. We told her we had not only purchased Russian dictionaries, but books on Russian literature, technical books, and poetry, all at a very reasonable price, at a price that was cheaper than what we would have to pay in our country.

At that point she told us to close our tote and then stamped our passports. We had apparently inflated her ego and patriotic emotions by our complimentary remarks. We were even more pleasantly surprised when she did not bother to check the rest of our luggage. At this point, Thetis and I were totally convinced that we were on a good footing in the Soviet Union.

When we were officially cleared with customs, the group proceeded to the Rossiya Hotel in Moscow. It was the highest and largest hotel in Moscow, occupying an entire block with over three thousand rooms. In addition it was conveniently located, just two blocks southeast of the Kremlin. There was a TV in our room and two single, narrow beds. The beds did not have mattress springs. As a result, there was no cushioning effect, and we felt as though we were sleeping on a concrete floor. When we diplomatically registered our complaint to management, we were assured that mattress springs were not good for one's back.

There were no washcloths in the bathroom. The towels were unlike anything we had ever seen. They were apparently cut from table cloth. The bath towel was about eighteen inches wide and four feet in length. It was heavily starched linen and had very little absorptive qualities. In effect it functioned as a displacer of water rather than as a drying agent. Consequently, it took us an inordinate amount of time to dry up, since we had to rely on the process of evaporation. Had we known we would have brought terry towels as well as bath tissue from home.

Our itinerary was arranged by INTOURIST, the official Soviet Tourist Agency. Visits were arranged to the art gallery, Agricultural and Industrial Exhibition, the Kremlin, and the Pushkin Museum.

The Kremlin was extremely impressive. It enclosed sixty-four acres and the brick wall around it had nineteen towers and five gates. The word *Kremlin* is from the Tartar language, meaning citadel. Since the Italians were noted for their construction of fortification walls dating back to the Romans, Ivan the Great had imported Italian architects to build the walls surrounding the Kremlin. The Tartars were constantly attacking the city, and a protective wall was imperative to ward the enemy off. Within its walls were Lenin's tomb, the Cathedral of St. Basil, the Cathedral of the Annunciation, the sixteenth-century bell tower of Ivan the Great, the Kremlin Palace of Congresses, and numerous other buildings. On one wall we could see several plaques of deceased famous Soviet leaders.

When our group toured the Kremlin, we had planned to visit Lenin's tomb. We were amazed to find a long line of people waiting to be admitted. Our guide told us it would be a wait of several hours. Accordingly, we decided to visit St. Basil's Cathedral. The cathedral was planned as a memorial to eight saints. Each chapel is covered with an onion-shaped dome, and the eight chapels are so arranged that they form a compact interrelated group. The church represents the Orthodox triumph over the Tartar invaders.

The structure had not been maintained for a number of years, and repairs were in progress. Artists were restoring the icons and the Russian Byzantine inscriptions on the walls with gold leaf. It was a painstaking effort, and progress was slow. The neglected and unused votive lamps were in sore need of repairs.

We then walked over to the Bell Tower, which had twenty-two large bells and over thirty smaller chimes. Next to the tower stands the Kremlin's largest bell, called the "Czar Kolokol." This huge bell was 22 feet high, 19 feet across and weighed 197 tons. During the installation, the bell fell from its scaffolding. The chip that broke off weighed 11 1/2 tons. Ironically, the bell was never rung.

To ward off Tartar attacks on the city, a huge cannon was built that could hurl two-ton missiles. We were informed the cannon never fired a shot. The two huge wheels were very elaborate and ornate. The cannon was mounted on an ornamented carriage which in turn was attached to the two massive wheels.

There were many personal items of former czars on display in the Armory Museum. When we saw the boots that Peter the Great wore, we were convinced he was of tremendous stature. The size of the boots was either a 15 or 17, with two-to-three-inch heels. Czar Peter stood seven feet in his stocking feet, and with his boots on, he was a towering giant. The vestments of former patriarchs and archbishops were beautifully brocaded with gold. Many garments were studded with pearls and gems.

We have ridden the elevated trains in New York for years and marveled at the engineering feats that were accomplished when the service was extended to include the subway system. Our Intourist guide took us to the Moscow Metro. She warned us that the escalators were geared to move very fast and we should be very careful in getting on and off. She was so right! We had to get on and off at a jogger's pace. A slight hesitation on anyone's part would result in a receding shock wave, with a pile-up of bodies. The rapidity at which the escalator moved required the agility of a gazelle to get on and off it.

The walls and ceiling of the stations were covered with mosaics, depicting various historic scenes. Chandeliers hung from the vaulted ceiling. Each station had different scenes and chandeliers. The station was spotlessly clean and no graffiti was to be seen. Our guide told us that work on the subway had begun in 1932 under the supervision of a British engineer. The Moskovites were very proud of their Metro.

Our tour of the city covered many interesting monuments and historic sites. The most impressive monument was an obelisk dedicated to the Russian pioneer in rocket and space science, Konstantin Tsiolkovsky. On top of the obelisk is a space ship portraying launch into space. He was the counterpart of our Robert Goddard and preceded him by some twenty-five years. Tsiolkovsky was an advocate of liquid propellants, a position held today by many rocket experts.

We were well entertained. One evening we saw the performance of the circus. It was beautiful to witness the coordination between the riders and their horses. Their movements were precise and exhibited agility beyond belief. The trained bears and the clowns brought such laughter that tears came to our eyes. It was understandable why the Russians are so fond of the circus.

The next evening we saw the Moiseyev Folk Dance Ensemble. This world-famous dance group performed various dances in native costumes representative of different parts of the Soviet Union. It was a colorful presentation. The petite movements of their feet created an undulating motion as they danced effortlessly across the stage.

Since we had enjoyed the previous evening of entertainment, we decided to see a presentation of the ballet *Giselle*. The music for the ballet was composed by Adolphe Adam. This ballet is one of the most famous for its dramatic characterization. Unfortunately, it was not one of the better performances we had seen. It appeared that the orchestra and the dancers were out of phase. During the intermission, we went up to the cocktail lounge of the theater. There we enjoyed a cold glass of vodka and caviar. This raised our spirits somewhat and hoped the rest of the performance would improve. However, this did not occur, and we decided to leave the theater. It appeared to us that since it was summer, the principal Bolshoi Ballet Group was not making the presentation that evening.

As we left the theater by ourselves, we proceeded down the walk to return to our hotel. We were stopped by the military police. He asked for our passports and inquired where we were going. We replied that we were returning to our hotel by the entrance we came in. He asked why we were leaving before the performance had ended. Thetis replied she had a vicious headache and was not feeling well. Rather than downplay the performance, she felt this was a polite and diplomatic answer. He would not let us return by the short route we had taken to enter the Kremlin but made us take the circuitous route outside the Kremlin wall. Fortunately, even though we were watched carefully, we were not stopped along the route by any other military policeman. We breathed a sigh of relief when we finally reached the Hotel Rossiya.

It was a warm night, and we were very thirsty. We decided to go to the snack bar in the hotel. We sat on the stools at the counter. As we were looking at the menu, we saw brown spots moving on the counter. At first we attributed this phenomenon to our eyes. However, a second glance convinced us those brown spots were roaches. Accordingly, we lost our appetite for the pastries and decided to order a bottle of soda. Presumably the contents of this bottle had not been invaded by roaches.

In preparation for our trip to Leningrad, our group was ordered to have their luggage in the hall by 4:00 A.M. Our flight to Leningrad was to depart at 6:00 A.M. The flight took a little over an hour.

Leningrad was an impressive city, founded by Peter the Great. He created a city from the swamp lands on the delta of the Neva River. The swamp lands were drained, thereby creating 101 islands. A network of some 200 miles of canals interlaced the city, and 35 arched bridges spanned the waterways. There was a total of some 600 bridges over the Neva River. Leningrad is called the Venice of the North. The site for this city gave Peter the Great a door to Western Europe on the Baltic Sea.

Our first tour of the city took us to the Hermitage. The Hermitage was enormous, with its three hundred rooms that were filled with several million exhibits and paintings. On exhibition were arts from ancient Greece, Rome, China, India, Italy, France, and Spain. It had the largest collection of ancient Greek marble that we had ever seen. There was a whole room of original works by DaVinci, Raphael, Michelangelo, and other Italian masters. One of the most beautiful rooms was the Malachite Hall, which was dazzling in its green and gold splendor. The Hermitage Museum was part of the Winter Palace of Peter the Great.

Peter the Great named the city St. Petersburg. Later the name changed to Petrograd and then to Leningrad. The city is close to the North Pole, being situated at 60 degrees north latitude and 30 degrees east longitude. While we were there, we experienced daylight during the night. We were fortunate to be in Leningrad during the latter part of June when the sun's rays penetrate the area. The French call the "*nuit blanche*" the sleepless night. The Russians call them the "*Belye Nochi*," the white nights. The golden domes of the cathedrals were resplendent in the glow of the white night. The brightness did prevent us from sleeping when we first retired. At midnight it was so bright that it was difficult to fall asleep. Eventually fatigue overcame us, and we were able to go to bed.

We went on board the cruiser *Aurora*, which was anchored outside the city in the Gulf of Finland. This ship was a grim reminder of the insurrection against the government in July 1917. Sailors from the naval base of Kronshtadt joined hands with workers and soldiers to demonstrate their anger against the bureaucratic tyranny and brutality that existed for centuries under the czars. This was the beginning of the Bolshevik Revolution. It wasn't long after the demonstration at Kronshtadt that Lenin and Trotsky landed at this port to assume their roles in the formation of a new government.

The visit to Dostoevski's flat revealed many reasons for the insurrection that began in 1917. The serfs were maltreated and practically served as slaves. Most of Dostoevski's literary efforts were devoted to the poor folk, illustrating the tragic aspect of life. He abhored the treatment the serfs were subjected to by government officials. His works in the latter part of the nineteenth century laid the foundations for the insurrection in 1917.

One of his greatest works is the "The Humiliated and Downtrodden Ones." It is a story of the uneducated serf who was regarded as a slave and flogged by the property owners when something was not to the liking of his master. So great was Dostoevski's religious feeling about the Russian serf that he characterized him as the symbol and apotheosis of all goodness, humility, and kindness in man. So vehement and forceful were the writings of Dostoevski on behalf of the peasant that he found himself in trouble with the government. He was considered a violent militant reactionary of the 1870s and a leader of revolutionary activities in St. Petersburg. He was, accordingly, sentenced to Siberia and served a prison term for a number of years.

From the contents of the bookcases throughout his apartment, we were able to form our own impression of the man. He kept abreast of many fields of knowledge and had books pertaining to the classics, medicine, and engineering. In addition to books in Russian, he had works by Schiller, Goethe, Victor Hugo, and Shakespeare. We were told by our guide that he studied medicine in Moscow and had entered the army engineering college in St. Petersburg. There were a few texts on mathematics, which indicated he had studied engineering. So great was his urge for writing that he abandoned these pursuits.

On the last day in Leningrad, we visited the Cathedral of St. Isaac. St. Isaac's iconostasion was similar to the one we saw in the Annunciation Cathedral in Moscow. It spanned the entire width of the church, with tier upon tier of paintings of religious figures rising to a great height above the floor. The iconostasion is a partition separating the nave from the sanctuary. On it was portrayed Jesus Christ, the Virgin Mary, the twelve apostles, and many other religious figures. It is interesting to note that the Russian church played a great role in preserving Christianity. The emperor Constantine, fearing the loss of St. Peter's in Rome, constructed the Agia Sophia in Constantinople as the second site of the Roman church. When the Turks seized the Agia Sophia, Moscow automatically became the seat of Eastern Christianity.

The greatest impression we acquired of Russia was the pioneering efforts of Peter the Great. He was a man of great vision and recognized the need for change. Moscow to him was set in its ideas and was content with the status quo. When Peter took over his reign of Russia, he realized Russia was behind times. Change, in his mind, was of paramount importance if Russia were to keep abreast of other nations in Europe. He was a dichotomous figure. He exhibited many dual roles in life. He was humble yet an aristocrat to the core.

His plans for building St. Petersburg were strategically and economically sound. He would acquire an access to the Atlantic via the Baltic and North seas and could keep an eye on the West. The site, however, was marshy and required ingenuity to convert the land into a building site. This obstacle did not prevent Peter from going ahead with his plans. With the help of the serfs, he accomplished his goal. All this was to the betterment of Russia.

On the other hand, his czarist ambitions got the better of him. He spent huge sums of money building the summer and winter palaces. This was keeping up with the Joneses. All this was for the royal family and aristocracy at the expense of the poor and needy. This fostered and bred discontent among the serfs.

Another example of his dualistic role in life was exhibited when at the time of building the summer palace, he had a small hut built for himself. He would spend most of his time in this modest abode.

There is a parallel between Gorbachev and Peter the Great that is worth noting. In view of the changes taking place today in Russia under the leadership of Gorbachev, a quote from the *Encyclopedia Britannica* is appropriate:

> Russia at the beginning of Peter's reign was backward by comparison with Western Europe. This backwardness inhibited foreign policy and even put Russia's national independence in danger. Peter's

aim therefore was to overtake the developed countries of Western Europe as soon as possible, in order both to promote the national economy and to ensure victory in his wars for access to the seas. Breaking the resistance of the boyars, or members of the ancient landed aristocracy, and of the clergy and severely punishing all other opposition to his projects, he started out on a series of reforms affecting, in the course of 25 years, every field of the national life—administration, industry, commerce, technology and culture.

If one substitutes Gorbachev for Peter and the Politburo and presidium for the boyars, the foregoing quote resembles what Gorbachev is going through in the way of a much-needed reform. To accomplish his goals, Peter abolished the order of boyars.

I well remember asking our guide what she thought of Peter the Great. She responded by saying that he was a great leader and helped establish Russia as a major power. That being the case, why was the name of the city of Petersburg changed to Leningrad? Clearly, in view of the facts, this change was not warranted. She thought for a while and silence ensued thereafter. She was apparently unable to give a logical answer.

We departed Leningrad via Malev flight 121 for Budapest. While there we stayed at the Hotel Gellert. We made a full day tour of Old Buda and New Pest. While in Russia we lost weight. There were times when we lost our appetites when food was served us. At breakfast we were served eggs sunny side up with black spots on the yoke. The chicken was served with skin intact. The base of the shaft and barbs of feathers were still in place. It was tough and non-appealing in appearance. The chicken must have been the size of a turkey.

We were able to regain the weight we lost in Russia when we were in Budapest. The contrast in food and service was like comparing night with day. We had a large menu to choose from and whatever we chose, poultry, meat, or fish, was done to perfection and to our liking. For breakfast we had all sorts of cold cuts, hot dishes, sausages, fruit, juices. For luncheon we had an even greater assortment of dishes. There was beef Wellington, and a variety of other preparations.

We would almost inevitably choose the fogash, fish freshly caught from Lake Balaton. Fogash is a pike-perch. We no sooner tried the fogash for the first time when we were convinced that it was one of the finest fish we had ever tasted. It reminded us somewhat of the turbot we had in Paris in that it was white and flaky. There was a sweetness associated with it, which harmonized perfectly with the white wine we were having. We were informed by our waiter that the fogash we were having came from Lake Balaton. He gave us a glowing description of the Balaton fogash. When we told him we had never tasted anything like fogash, he assured us we were correct. Even though there are other types of fogash, the one from Lake Balaton is indeed in a class all its own. We tried other fishes listed on the menu, but none of them compared with the Balaton fogash.

The pastries were a treat and delight. Their honey-cake, multi-layered chocolate cake, and the cheese *gnocchis* were delectable. Time did not permit us to try their many other pastries.

There was no doubt that the Hungarians, like the Poles, extended to us their most cordial hospitality and amicability. Unlike the Moskovites they were ebullient, full of vigor and gaiety. They were most anxious to hear what was going on outside of Eastern Europe. The Hungarians' spiritedness pervaded the atmosphere and made us feel intoxicated with their joie de vivre.

On one of our bus tours of the city, the guide used carefully selected words in addressing us on board. We sensed he was being cautious in the event he was being taped while speaking through the microphone. When we got off the bus and were alone with the guide, he was a different person. He voiced his unfettered opinion of the Soviet bureaucracy and inefficiency. He was convinced that the Soviet system lacked economic and political know-how and would eventually collapse. He pointed with great pride and satisfaction to the progress being made in Hungary in spite of the Soviet dominance. People in general expressed their political and social feelings more openly here than in the other Eastern countries.

We decided to walk from the hotel to the business section of Pest, the newer section of the town. To do so we had to cross the Danube. When we arrived at the end of the bridge-crossing, we looked back at the hotel and its environs and noticed that the Buda side was hillier than Pest. Pest, the more modern portion of the city, is built on relatively flat land. Activity on this side of the city was more pronounced than on the Buda side.

In our walk about the town, we came upon a vast marketplace—what we would call a farmer's market. One could purchase vegetables, meat, poultry, fruit, fish, and miscellaneous sundry food items. We were most intrigued by the way people were buying fish. We could see myriads of fish swimming in a huge tank. The fish vendor was attired with a rubber apron covering his chest and extending to his ankles. He wore a short-sleeve shirt and carried a huge net.

The need for his paraphernelia became evident when a customer approached him. The customer and vendor focused their eyes intently upon the fish in the tank. It was reminiscent of one watching a specific horse at the races. At the appropriate moment, pandamonium ensued. The customer had focused his attention on a particular fish that met with his fancy.

The vendor now came into action. With net in hand, the problem now was to catch that particular fish. On occasion the vendor could net the fish in a resonable length of time. There were times, however, when the elusive fish would cause consternation on the part of the vendor. Try as hard as he could to persuade the determined customer that some other fish might be more readily caught, the customer would not compromise. On one occasion the vendor took as long as ten minutes to net a particular fish. From the conversation that went on, tempers must have flared up.

It was amazing to us that with all the fish and the squirming that ensued in the chase how the vendor and customer could keep their eyes focused on a particular fish. Had we been selected judges to proclaim that the specific fish that was originally spotted was the one that was finally netted, we would have been in trouble. With experience, patience, and perseverance, one may acquire the technique required to achieve the end result.

Our walk through the market convinced us that Budapest was thriving economically more than anywhere else in the Eastern bloc. Food was displayed in great quantities, controls were apparently less stringent, and judging from the bags people were carrying, they had enough money to buy their essential staples at least. The fact that so much produce was on display led us to believe that the Hungarians were still quasi-independent farmers, unlike their counterparts in Russia, where private land ownership was nonexistent. This scene was a welcome sight after what we had seen in Moscow and Leningrad. A comparison of what we witnessed convinced us that the forecast made by our guide was probably true.

The vitality exhibited in the market is a clear manifestation of the success of their economic progress, the indomitable spirit of the Hungarians, and their strong belief and insistence on and tenacity in their human rights. The latter belief is not surprising, since it was they who accomplished the first Human Rights Charter on the European continent. The Hungarian takes great pride in being descendants of fierce warriors who settled and founded Hungary. All these innate characteristics make for a freedom loving, independent, creative, and above all a fun-loving, amiable person.

Our group was invited to attend a lecture on the methods and techniques used in their educational system. There were two items that were stressed during the lecture. Grade-school children and university students were indoctrinated into industry and agriculture during the summer months while they were still in school. In this way the student better understands and appreciates the applications of the theory he is being taught in school. This stimulates the student in his studies, since he can see the practical value of theory.

Emphasis was placed on fundamentals in science, mathematics, history, and languages. Their aim in educating the student was to have a well-rounded education. In this way the student would be better equipped to acclimate himself to changing conditions taking place in the world. Their educational system strongly emphasized the awareness of the existent competitive force. This explained the emergence of so many outstanding scientists, writers, musicians, and professional people from their educational system. Men like Theodore von Karman, John von Neumann, Edward Teller, Leo Szilard, Wigner, Szentgyorgyi, George Polya, and many other professionals were graduates of the Hungarian educational system. Many of these men came to the United States and are known for their contributions.

There was one common element prevalent in all three countries. This was their bookstores, with an abundance of books in all fields, in many languages, and at very reasonable prices. These countries apparently subsidize the publication of books and encourage their purchase. There were always many people browsing through the bookstores. It was interesting to note that many of the books were translations of the American into their respective languages. We also found many of their authors translated into English, French, and German.

One book, in particular, that aroused our interest was a book edited by K. Lissak of the University Medical School Pecs, Hungary, entitled *Hormones and Brain Function*. This book contained the proceedings of the Congress of the International Society of Psychoneuroendocrinology held in Budapest in July 1971. This was one of the books our son needed for one of the papers he was writing. We had difficulty in obtaining this book for him and had to send away for it. Imagine our surprise when we saw it at half-price in the Budapest bookstore. The hard-cover book was printed on glossy paper and professionally bound.

Following our short but enjoyable stay in Budapest, we departed for Paris via Malev 550. This permitted us a full day in Paris. We were shocked at the prices we now had to pay for our meals at the Hotel Grand. They were considerably higher than our last trip. The following morning we were en route to San Francisco via New York. It was great to be back home in the United States. Our appreciation for our country had grown even more so after our experiences in Eastern Europe. After witnessing the many varied forms of economic, political, administrative, and legislative formations in the Eastern bloc, we were all the more convinced our Founding Fathers brought forth a form of government we can all be proud of.

28. Odyssey to the Olympic Sites with Our Children

We were not only involved in our professional societies but in our alumni associations as well. When we came to the West Coast, we became interested in the University of California, Berkeley. Since the children were graduates of the university, it was natural for Thetis and me to attend the various alumni functions. At one of the alumni meetings of the College of Engineering, I casually mentioned I felt like an orphan with no alma mater to turn to. The Daniel Guggenheim School of Aeronautics from which I graduated was no longer in existence. This struck a sympathetic note from the dean, who said, "Consider yourself adopted by Cal." We have enjoyed the meetings with the professors, alumni, and students. We met Chancellor Albert Bowker, Vice-Chancellor Michael Heyman, Toni Oppenheim, Provost George Maslach, Gene Trefethen, Richard Otter, Richard Hafner, and many others.

As a Tau Beta Pi member, I became involved with the chapter at Berkeley. We attended several of their meetings. Thetis became a member of the board of the University of California, Berkeley Foundation. At one of these meetings we met Prof. Steve Miller who was director of the archaeological excavations of the ancient Pan-Hellenic sanctuary at Nemea, Greece. This project provided the students a unique learning experience and field work for their studies in archaeology. We were delighted to learn that Professor Miller was planning a trip to Nemea for the alumni. Our children were especially enthusiastic, since this afforded them the opportunity to see Europe for the first time.

Chronologically, Nemea is considered the fourth Olympic site, since it was officially constructed in 573 B.C. Olympia was the first, 776 B.C., Corinth, 586 B.C., and Delphi, 582 B.C.. The Olympic games, from their very beginning in 776 B.C., have registered awe, honor, and camaraderie. No other assemblage, and in a sense a limited duration of brotherhood, lasted for nearly twelve hundred years. When Theodosius I, a Roman emperor, declared an end to the games in A.D. 393, the 293rd Olympiad had been registered.

The Olympiads had aroused so much interest and enthusiasm in the past that revival was inevitable. Scholars all over the world read accounts of past Olympiads and were convinced that resurrection of the games would be highly desirable. It was Baron Pierre de Coubertin who succeeded in reviving the games in 1896, which were held in urban Athens. In 1968 we celebrated the twenty-fourth modern Olympiad. The spirit of the games is best explained by the word "athlete." This word is derived from *athlos*, which means a contest for a prize. The athlete then is one who contends for the prize.

The prize itself was a wild olive wreath or a laurel wreath, depending upon the location of the games. Originally, the prize was solely for the honor attached to it, with no materialistic rewards. Idealistic as this may sound today, athletes benefited tremendously when they returned home by monies that had been collected by the local residents, influential positions in politics, the army, etc.

The indomitable spirit of the Olympic games is beautifully accounted for by Herodotus, the historian of the Persian wars against Greece. At Thermopylae pass, where the Greeks had taken their stand to ward off the Persian invasion:

> There came now a few deserters from Arcadia to join the Persians—poor men who had nothing to live on, and were in want of employment. The Persians brought them into the King's presence, and there inquired of them, by a man who acted as their spokesman, "What are the Greeks doing?" The Arcadians answered: "They are holding the Olympic games, seeing the athletic sports and the chariot races." "And what," said the man, "is the prize for which they contend?" "An olive-wreath," returned the others, "which is given to the man who wins." On hearing this, Tritantaechmes, the son of Artabanus, uttered a speech which was in truth most noble, but which caused him to be taxed with cowardice by King Xerxes. Hearing the men say that the prize was not for money but a wreath of olive, he could not forbear from exclaiming before them all: "Good Heavens! Mardonius, what manner of men are these against whom thou hast brought us to fight?—men who contend with one another, not for money, but for honor!"

In view of the XXIV Olympiad held in Seoul in 1988, we decided to record what we observed when we visited Nemea in 1976 and the indelible impressions that have left an everlasting imprint upon our memories.

We left San Francisco International Airport via United Airlines for Seattle on May 2, 1976. At Seattle we boarded a Scandinavian Airliner and flew the polar route. The aurora borealis was spectacular. The bursts of multicolored light emitted by the trapped accelerating and decelerating electrons traveling from pole to pole in the earth's magnetic field was a spectacular wonder.

We arrived at the Kastrup Airport in Copenhagen. The following day we left for Rome and arrived at the Fuomincino Airport in Rome. There we visited the Vatican and St. Peter's Cathedral. What a thrill it was to stand in the cathedral and read the inscriptions around the base of the dome in Latin and Greek. All of us felt a great reverence and awe when we were told Saint Peter, who had been crucified and hung upside down, was entombed in the crypt below.

We also visited ancient Rome and in particular, the Coliseum. We saw the individual dens in which the lions and other beasts were kept. Looking out into the arena, we could vividly imagine the gladiators fighting the beasts. A section of the Coliseum was marked off, indicating where the emperor and his entourage of officials sat. Before the gruelling and bloody games would start, it was protocol for the gladiators to stand before the emperor and declare: "*Ave, Caesar, morituri te salutant!*" (We who are about to die salute you). With that salutatory remark, the games would begin.

From Rome we proceeded by train to Florence (Firenze). We spent two days there and visited the Medici Chapels, the Academy of Fine Arts, the Baptistery, and the Duomo. Florence is, in our opinion, the real cultural center of all Italy. It was founded by the Etruscans long before Rome. To this very day, quite a vociferous argument can erupt among the Italians as to which city, Rome or Florence, is the real cultural center. In the vicinity of El Duomo is Santa Croce (Saint Cross) where the tombs of Michelangelo, Galileo Galilei, Giacomo Puccini, and other illustrious persons are found. Florence is noted for its red wines, which are among the finest in the world.

From Florence we took the train to Naples. Naples has a particularly unique nostalgia about it. It was the home of Enrico Caruso, and everyone was in a happy, jovial mood. There is a famous saying about Naples and its fabulous view of the bay: "*Vede Napoli, a poi muori*" (See Naples and then you can die.) This saying is in reference to the spectacular view one experiences when one looks over the bay. It was amusing to hear occasionally a Napolitano ad lib by adding to the accepted phrase "*dal puzzo*" (from the stench). Apparently the Napolitani are not too conscientious about the resulting effects of pollution.

From Naples we proceeded by train to Brindisi. The train ride was long and tedious, especially since we had to sit on wooden seats that were hard on the posterior. Every bump that we experienced on the rails was transmitted directly to our rumps without any cushioning effect—we all uttered "Ouch!" on many occasions along the way. Apropos to our ride, the train was called the *El Rapido*.

The word *Brindisi* has two meanings. The most common one is "a toast," apparently a derived word from the German "*Ich bring' dir's*." The other more likely explanation stems from the Roman name *Brundisium*—"Stag's head," derived morphologically from the antler-shaped inner harbor of the area. In ancient times it was a key port for transporting materials and military equipment from Rome across the Adriatic to the island of Corcyra (Corfu) across Greece to Byzantium. This was the overland supply line in existence between Rome and the Near East. The overland route was called the "*Via Egnatia*," which ran across Greece from the Adriatic to Byzantium.

We were still en route to Nemea, the real purpose of our trip. From Brindisi we arrived at Corfu and spent a day there sight-seeing. The name of our ship was the *Egnatia*, the word for a Roman proper name. At Corfu we visited the German Palace, formerly the palace of Elizabeth of Austria, where Kaiser Wilhelm of World War I fame spent most of his summers vacationing. There is a statue of Achilles on the grounds that bears an inscription attributed to the Kaiser: "To the greatest of the Greeks from the greatest of the Germans." An exhibition of human vainglory in the highest!

We then headed for Ioannina, via Igoumenitsa on the Ionian Sea. There is a memorial to the Souli near the area where the ferryboat docked. The Souliotes were reputedly the bravest of the Greek soldiers who fought under the command of Lord Byron. This memorial commemorated the struggle of the Greeks in their attempt to free themselves from the yoke of the Ottoman Empire. Lord Byron, the poet, sympathized with the Greeks and took command of the soldiers. Being the Hellinophile that he was, he gave unselfishly of his money, time, and energy.

From Igoumenitsa we were headed for Ioannina by bus. We were now on the Via Egnatia, once the main artery of the Roman Empire linking Rome via Brindisi, Thessaloniki to Byzantium. Horace, the Roman poet, called the Via Appia in his day the "queen of long-distance roads." En route we saw many roadside shrines in memory of those killed on the highway. Candles were lit in front of an icon enclosed in a cubicle. As we approached Ioannina, we could see the Pindus Mountains looming up before our eyes. The views were panoramic and breathtaking. They were unlike those in the Western part of the United States in that the rock formations were not as colorful.

Ioannina is most famous for its Lake Pambotis and its caverns, which are very colorful and quite extensive. The lake is six miles long, twenty-four square miles in area, and fifteen hundred feet above sea level. The city is at the base of Mount Mitsikeli and rises to an altitude of approximately six thousand feet.

One of the most impressive sights in Ioannina was Saint George Plaza. There was a small shrine to Saint George. The inscription read: "The believer who suffered for Christ was hung on this spot, the new martyred Saint of Ioannina, George." He was hung by the Turks. Saint George is always portrayed in a *foustanella*, unlike all other saints.

A visit to the mosque of Ali Pascha stands as a reminder of the Turkish domination of Ioannina. Inside the walled city still stands an old Turkish bath, with its typical dome structure. We were surprised to see so many of the old Turkish buildings still standing. We surmised that the visitors bureau in Ioannina preserved them as tourist attractions.

We were now headed for Meteora, with its monasteries dating back to the Byzantine era. The etymology of Meteora signifies "raised from off the ground." The word adequately describes these straight-up-and-down cliffs. The only way to get to the top is by mechanical means. As one drives through the area of Meteora, one sees isolated monoliths (pinnacles) 85 to 300 feet high, composed of a conglomerate of gneiss, mica slate, syenite, and greenstone. These massive rock formations resulted from erosion by a prehistoric sea.

On the top of these monoliths are monasteries housing monks.

In many cases the monks are raised to the top by a net. At one time they were fairly populated. The monks told us that they were dwindling in numbers. The monks were very cordial and hospitable. They discussed their mode of living, their devotion to religion and prayer, and were very proud of their wine presses. They loved making their own wine and as one monk described it, "Wine is food for thought and contemplation." As we were leaving the monastery of Saint Stephen, one of the monks gave us postcards depicting the icons of the Virgin Mary and Jesus Christ.

On the lowest rock, we visited the nunnery of Saint Roussani. This was the first monastery to be converted to a convent. From there we continued through the rugged mountain terrain to Kalambaka and to Delphi. On our way we proceeded via the pass of Thermopylae, where King Leonidas of Sparta and a handful of his warriors staged their heroic defense against the horde of Persians. Herodotus, the historian, in his account of the Persian wars, stated that a plaque was placed at the pass, which read: "O passerby, announce to the Lacedaimonians that here we sleep (in death), obedient to those laws (as decreed by our nativeland)."

At long last, we arrived at Delphi! The first of four Olympic sites to be visited, Delphi was built against the rock faces of the Phaedriades (bright, beaming rocks), two masses of rock that encompass the valley. We saw remnants of the Roman *agora* (market place), the treasury building, the remnants of the Temple of Apollo, the amphitheater, and the stadium. The design of the amphitheater, typical of all amphitheaters throughout Greece, is remarkable. If one stands at one of the focal points of the stage, the voice can be heard at the outer perimeter (top row) of the amphitheater. The audience varied from 15,000 to 40–50,000. The Temple of Apollo was located at the sheer faces of the Phaedriades.

The stadium was known especially for its chariot races. The stadium is two hundred yards long and its twelve tiers of seats are still more or less intact. The stadium had a capacity of seven thousand spectators. Three columns of a Roman triumphal arch, through which the contestants entered the stadium, were still standing. The stadium was used during the Pythian games, which were held every four years in September in commemoration of Apollo's victory over Python (serpent slain by Apollo, thence surnamed the Pythian).

After breakfast at the hotel in Delphi, we boarded the *leophoreion* (bearing-people bus) headed for Piraeus via Thebes and Athens. Athens! The city of Socrates, Plato, Xenophon, Thucidides, Pericles, Euripides, Sophicles, and many others too numerous to mention, who made and established what we call Western civilization. What a treat it was to see the Parthenon! Even stripped of its former glory and splendor, it still stands out majestically, like a glistening jewel. The architectural, engineering, and scientific methods that were used in its construction and erection are mind-boggling to this very day.

As an example of scientific application in the construction of the Parthenon, we observed when we stood close to the edifice that the columns on all four sides bulged more in the center than at either ends (bottom and top). The steps leading up to the building incorporated curvature with the center portion being higher than either ends. Yet, when one stands off in the distance, the human eye perceives them to be perfectly straight! How on earth the designers of the Parthenon knew enough of the abnormalities of the human eye to correlate the effect into corresponding variations in the dimensions of the columns and steps, we shall never know. This effect may be explainable by the ophthalmologists and architects of today.

As it miraculously turned out, Pericles was a far-sighted entrepreneur. The investment made at the time has paid off more than anyone can estimate, not only in terms of money, but in the preservation of the ideals, human rights, and democratic principles that he tried to establish. In spite of the opposition of the citizenry (human behavior and characteristics have not changed over the millennia) to such an outrageously expensive project, Pericles went ahead and took the flak of his people. He was determined to erect a structure that would forever remain as a symbol of the democratic principles that were established in Athens.

There is so much to say about Athens that space nor the patience of the reader will permit. There is one item that deserves mention, however. At the *agora*, the north end adjacent to the railroad track, Stella Miller stood on the *lithos* (a block of stone) used as a platform during court trials. According to Stella, who discovered this stone during her archaeological excavations in Athens, Socrates, the accused, pleaded his case from this raised stone. The existing street was some twenty feet above the agora. This difference in height indicated the amount of silt that had accumulated over the millennia. Saint Paul also lectured in the agora. As one stood at the edge of the north wall, it was apparent there was more to the agora that was still unearthed. We could see the base of a column partially protruding from the existing retaining wall.

I wish we could say much more about Athens, but we must move on. Cicero, who studied at the Academy of Athens, referred to the city as his "beloved city."

The *leophoreion* proceeded to Piraeus, the port harbor of Athens. From there we boarded the MTS *Jupiter,* bound for our Mediterranean cruise. Piraeus was a major port in antiquity. Pericles, in the fifth century B.C., proposed construction of the port because the existing port at Faliron was inadequate for Athens' maritime needs. The city and port of Piraeus were laid out by Hippodamus, a geometrician, and were considered a model in planning in classical times.

The ship arrived at colorful Mykonos, with its carefree and artistic atmosphere, early evening. Early the next morning, we approached the volcanic cliffs of Santorini. We passed close to the rim of an active volcano that blew its top and collapsed some thirty-five hundred years ago. Santorini suffers from earthquakes and in 1956 an earthquake destroyed two thousand homes. Santorini is a contraction of "Santa Irene," the patron saint of the Island during the Middle Ages. Thera, the official name, is derived from Thiras, a Dorian from Sparta, who first colonized the island. What appeared to be snow on top of the mountains was actually the city, whose buildings were painted white. White and pale blue are the favorite colors of most villagers wherever we went.

The island of Santorini consists of sheer cliffs, which tower above an archipelago of volcanic cliffs. The whole island forms a crescent that is the remains of the volcanic crater. The caldera is twenty-five miles square of deep water encircled by three islands, Thera, Thirasia, and Aspronisi.

Recently, scientists have speculated that the explosion of the island of Thera inspired the legend of Atlantis. Plato mentioned the event and described the landscape of the lost continent. Archaeologists believe that a violent subterranean volcanic eruption took place. The void that resulted was filled in with water from the sea. Subsequently, *tsunamis* were felt in nearby areas and Crete. The conjecture is that the Minoan civilization was obliterated, due to the ensuing gargantuan flooding. Excavations were going on at the former Minoan city.

The archaeologists now believe that there is some truth to the "Lost Atlantis" of Plato, since many elaborate frescoes have been unearthed beneath extensive layers of pumice. What is most intriguing is that the shards, when pieced together, portray in one case a blue monkey and in another a pair of antelopes. Is the answer to be found with the tectonophysicists for an explanation of the infiltration of African animals into the Minoan area? What an archaeologists' paradise!

Our next stop on our odyssey was Herakleion on the Island of Crete for a view of the Minoan civilization at Knossos. Crete is the largest of the Greek islands. The white mountains have peaks ranging from 7,000 to 8,000 feet and are snow-covered. We visited the Palace of Knossos, which is three miles inland from Herakleion. It was Schliemann's intuition that led him to believe the huge mound hemmed in by the low hills would be the Palace of Knossos. Evans, the English archaeologist, started excavations in 1899.

The palace was built in 1800 b.c. over the ruins of an earlier structure. What fascinated us the most was the Egyptian influence on the design of the palace. The columns of the buildings were short and stubby, with diameter of the column greater on top than bottom, resulting in inverse taper.

The vast complex of the great palace consisted of large courts, sacred ways and altars, royal apartments, a great throne room, and numerous reception halls. Many advanced plumbing concepts were incorporated in the system. There were channels for the transportation of water, drainage systems throughout the palace, and disposal of water waste. There were elaborate areas where food, wines, and stock were stored.

A visit to the Herakleion Museum revealed that the Minoans were great lovers of bulls. The first bullfights were held in Crete. The participants took the bull by the horns and somersaulted over the huge beasts—no swords were used. To my knowledge, this is a feat the Spaniards have not performed as yet in their bullfights.

Our next stop was the Island of Rhodes, the largest and most populous island of the Dodecanese. Lindos, one of three cities on Rhodes, has an acropolis on top of a high headland whose flank falls precipitously to the sea. The civilization in Rhodes reached its pinnacle in the fifth century B.C. The harbor of Lindos is where apostle Paul was supposed to have landed in A.D. 51 to preach Christianity.

The great harbor of Rhodos was a part of the Knights' fortification. A castle was built by the Knights of Saint John of Jerusalem in the 1300s. Rhodes is the island of roses. Rhodians sailed from across the Mediterranean to Marseille and reached a river in Provence, France, which was named after them, the Rhone. Rhodes shall be remembered by its numerous windmills that were erected along the fortifications in the harbor.

After leaving Rhodes we docked in Kushadasi (Turkish for "bird island") in Turkey. A short motorcoach ride took us to Ephesus. Ephesus is richly endowed with history, beginning with the first city, which was built in 3000 B.C. The third city was built in the fourth century B.C. by Alexander the Great. Cities in those days were pillaged and razed to the ground by the enemy, a common practice. The new city was built over the rubble of the former city. After two such razings, Alexander decided to play the role of developer. With cheap labor readily available, the problem of rebuilding was no great financial burden.

Whenever there was doubt about who first settled an area, the Greeks had a cure-all for such a dilemma. They would frequently resort to the Amazons, a legendary warlike group of women. Homer, in the *Iliad*, describes them as having settled in Scythia. Phrygia and Lycia in Asia Minor also lay claim to their having settled in these areas. Ephesus was next in line to lay claim that the Amazons were the first inhabitants of the area. The word *Amazon* means "breastless." The "*mazos*" is used in reference to a woman's breast. They were regarded as fierce warriors, at least in Greek mythology. The fable goes that their right breast was removed so as not to interfere with their bowstring when shooting arrows.

There was a spot on the plain strewn with stones. It is said that it could be the site of the tomb of Saint Luke. Excavation of the crypt required the sanction of the Pope in Rome. At the time (May 1976) this permission had not been granted.

The walk led to the lower *agora*, along a descending path laid with marble slabs 160 meters long. It stretched from the Curetiae Street to the Grand Theater. Excavations and restoration were being conducted under the aegis of a German team of archaeologists. On either side of the marble way, there were many columns, remnants of marble buildings, the temple of Hadrianus, Roman baths, and the fountain of Trajan. Many inscriptions in Latin and Greek were chiseled in huge blocks of marble. Much of the history of Ephesus has been preserved in this manner.

The House of the Virgin Mary and the Sacred Water in front of the House of Virgin Mary were of particular interest. It is said that the Virgin Mary spent her last days drinking the water. Even the Muslims visit this place to pray.

There is so much to say about Ephesus that it would take a whole book to adequately describe what we saw. We hope we have kindled your appetite and curiosity sufficiently to read more about Ephesus. The history of Ephesus is similar to a hearing of a symphony. The first hearing is but an introduction. It takes several hearings to fully appreciate it, never reaching the ultimate value of appreciation and understanding.

On our return to the ship, we stopped at Patmos, where Saint John the Divine received the inspiration for the Apocalypse. Patmos is one of the Dodecanese islands. The island is arid and volcanic. This was the scene of Saint John's revelation during his exile in the first century A.D. The church of the Apocalypse was located on Mount Kerketeos.

After landing at Piraeus, we departed from Athens by private coach across the Corinthian Canal to the city of Corinth, our second Olympic site. On our way we stopped at the Isthmus (any narrow passage or connection). The Isthmus divided the Gulf of Corinth from the Gulf of Saronicos. The canal was a magnificent piece of engineering, straight as an arrow. Work was begun by the Emperor Nero in A.D. 67. The ship canal was opened in 1893. It is four miles in length, sixty-nine feet in width, and twenty-six feet in depth. The canal was cut through limestone.

The games held at Corinth were called the Isthmian Games. They were held in the second and fourth year of each Olympiad (a period of four years—a quadrennial). In Corinth, the Temple of Apollo was located on a hill. The temple was built a century before the Parthenon. It was totally destroyed by the Romans in 146 B.C. Julius Caesar rebuilt Corinth in 44 B.C. Corinth is remembered not only as an Olympic game site but also for the Corinthian Epistles of Saint Paul. Corinth had developed a reputation for its loose morals and lewdness and was a prime candidate for moral and religious reform.

From Corinth we proceeded along the Corinthian Gulf via Patras to Olympia, our third site of the Olympian games. The Gulf of Corinth was an inlet of the Ionian Sea, separating Peloponnesus from mainland Greece. It was eighty miles long and between three and twenty miles wide. Olympia at long last! The site of the first Olympic games. The time period of a quadrennial was called an Olympiad. Time was reckoned in Olympiads since accurate accounts of the games were recorded.

Olympia was dedicated to Zeus, the head of the immortal gods. In Wagner's Ring cycle, it would be Walhalla. The Olympic games, instituted as a sort of continuation of religious rituals, made Olympia the center of the Hellenic world. Games were held to remind the Hellenes of their unity and nationalism. Olympia survived for ten centuries up to A.D. 393, the last of the ancient Olympic games.

Upon inspection of the rock that was used for the columns, one could actually see shells and fossils buried in the rock. This would indicate that the rock at one time came from the sea. The sacred grove sheltered the ruins of the buildings where feasts were held during the original games and where an altar held an eternal flame. The flame that is brought to the site of present-day games originated from Olympia.

The *palaestra* was a place for athletic exercise in general. The original meaning of the word was a wrestling school, wherein wrestlers were trained, commonly by public officers. Training would commence ten months prior to the inauguration of the events. The events of the day were comprised of the standing broad jump, foot races of different length, discus throwing, javelin-throwing, wrestling, horse and chariot races, boxing, *pankration*—the almighty— wrestling combined with boxing, and finally the pentathlon, a five-fold event. The only classification imposed on the athletes was by age only—boys, adolescents, and men. Height, weight, and other physical characteristics were not requisites.

The games offered an opportunity for *ekecheiria*, literally a "holding of hands" or a cessation of hostilities for a period of time, the games lasting five days and festivities that followed for an unspecified length of time. The chief judges at the Olympic games were called the *hellanodikai*. The prize at the Olympian games was a

270

wreath of dry wild celery. At Corinth and Nemea, it was again wild celery. At Delphi the wreath was sweet laurel, the plant of Apollo. The wreaths were but a miniscule token of what was to follow in terms of benefits, financial as well as hero worship.

Famous poets would glorify the athletes in praise and eulogies. Others showered great wealth when they returned to their homes. All this sounds familiar to us. Instead of poets we now have TV to glorify our recipients of medals. Commercial enterprises shower money and opportunities upon the medallists. Human nature over the past twenty-five hundred years has not changed in behavioral patterns.

Having visited the ruins of the site of the first Olympic games, we were finally en route to Nemea, the fourth Olympic site so designated chronologically. We proceeded via Tripolis and Argos to Nauplia. Nauplia was the center for tourists visiting Nemea, Mycenae, Tiryns, Argos, and Epidaurus. We had traveled the Peloponnesus from Olympia to Nauplia, in a west-to-east direction.

On our way to Nemea, we visited the amphitheater and the ruins of Epidaurus, home of Aesclepius, father of medicine, and Mycenae with the beehive tombs. Mycenae was the home of King Agamemnon, leader of the Hellenic forces during the Trojan War.

Systematic excavations of Mycenae began in 1840. The most famous of the discoveries were made by Schliemann, the archaeologist of Troy. A cross-sectional cut through the enclosure of Agamemnon's tomb appeared to be parabolical, thereby forming a paraboloid of revolution—hence the name "bee hive," which is the shape of a beehive. Apex of the paraboloid was approximately thirty to forty feet above the ground.

The Lion Gate leads to the six shaft graves excavated by Schliemann. The golden treasures that were unearthed are now in the Archaeological Museum in Athens. The acropolis of Mycenae was entered by this gate. A cyclopean lintel supports a triangular slab. Two lionesses stand on their legs, with their paws resting on a column.

Schliemann was an avid reader of Homer. Before embarking on any of his archaeological expeditions, he would read and reread Homer assiduously for any clues. Homer's description of Mycenae, based on the findings of Schliemann, was accurate, thereby leading one to believe that the accounts described by Homer were not entirely fictional.

Agamemnon's palace stood on a narrow plateau on the top of a hill. Remnants of a wall were still standing. After the destruction of Knossus, Mycenae became the dominant power in the Aegean. Mycenae was burned and destroyed by invading Dorians about 1100 B.C. Mycenae revived during the Hellenistic period, and a new temple was built on the Acropolis, around 300 B.C.

Nemea is the site of the University of California, Berkeley, archaeological excavations. Nemea was derived from *nemos*, "a wood with open glades and meadows for cattle." It was a wooded district between Argos and Corinth. The purpose of the excavations was to uncover the stadium to learn more about the details of the games and the manner in which they were conducted. The Nemean games (*Ta Nemeia*), as they were called, were in honor of Nemean Zeus. The Nemeia were celebrated in the second and fourth years of each Olympiad. The victors were called the Nemeonikae.

The excavations at Nemea were beyond our expectations. The Altar of Zeus was almost fully exposed. Its northern end was missing, since it was disturbed by the farmers' plowing. At the southern end of the altar were several monument bases, which must have supported statues. The day we were there, some coins, tweezers, small implements, and more foundations were unearthed.

The excavations at the stadium (racetrack) and the area of the Temple of Zeus were quite extensive and impressive. While we were at the racetrack, we witnessed more of an amphibian track than a conventional dry track. Early, premature rains had inundated the area. It was quite a sight to see workers in their bare feet with their trousers rolled up to their knees, removing the rain water from the track, bucket by bucket. Every now and then, one of the workers would slip in the clay mud, performing, quite extemporaneously and unexpectedly, a variety of Greek dances, depending upon what was required to restore equilibrium in the upright position. On one occasion the worker would resort to a *sirto*, on another occasion a *hasapiko*, and on other occasions to an unnamed intricate foot movement and body mobility to restore equilibration.

The area had not been completely excavated, but we could see most of the starting line. Steve Miller brought us up to date in 1976. The youngsters of the neighborhood enjoyed lining up for a race. Of particular interest was the fountain house, which fed the water channel running peripherally around the stadium at the foot of the spectators. This water was used as drinking water for the athletes and, I assume, the spectators.

One could barely discern the outline of informal seating that was carved out of the hillside. There were approximately sixty rows with a total capacity of forty thousand. The stadium incorporated thirty starting gates and a turning point. The Nemean project was inspiring to us for several reasons. It was a great sight to see so many of our students from various universities in the United States participate in the zeal for uncovering new knowledge that might shed light on the details and operations of ancient athletics.

From talking to the students, we learned they were exuberant about the similarities that could be found between what was uncovered at Nemea and the other three Olympic sites. It was this type of correlation that was most rewarding and interesting. Steve was the catalyst in this respect, since he had prior experience in archaeological excavations at the other sites. The local residents along with the students exhibited an esprit de corps that was beyond imagination. The resident workers were excited emotionally, knowing that they were uncovering artifacts of their ancestors and the knowledge that what they uncovered could be of value to mankind.

Even though the vaulted tunnel had not been discovered while we were there, we would like to say a few words about it, since it sheds light on history. One of the greatest finds at Nemea was the uncovering of a vaulted tunnel that led from the temple to the stadium. The tunnel was estimated to have been constructed twenty-three hundred years ago. What is of particular interest was the graffiti inscribed on the walls of the tunnel and the fact that the tunnel is a vaulted structure incorporating the keystone principle, which holds and stabilizes the entire structure. Both finds were of historic interest.

The graffiti were of importance in establishing the approximate date of the construction of the tunnel. The Greeks were very meticulous in erecting statues and recording the names of the Olympic victors, along with the designation of the Olympiad. Graffiti, as a rule, defaces and mars the appearance of buildings with the hodgepodge scribblings that are smeared upon them, but in this case, they are archaeological blessings. Richard Parker, a University of California Santa Barbara graduate student, was in charge of the digging of the tunnel. Steve and Richard deciphered a number of inscribed names that could be traced back through the athletic chronicles. In a few instances, they were able to associate the names on the wall of the tunnel with that which was recorded. What a find!

Up until the discovery of the Nemean tunnel, it was believed that the arch structure, with its keystone, was introduced for the first time in architectural design by the Romans. With the latest discovery at Nemea, that is no longer the case. Because of the date of the tunnel, Steve hypothesized that Alexander the Great conveyed the design from Persia when he came to Nemea. Alexander was a great patron of athletics, and he himself was a great athlete capable of performing many of the Olympic events. Someone asked Alexander why it was that he didn't enter the games, since he could easily win the coveted wreath. His reply was: "I shall enter the competition only if all the other contestants are kings."

Excellence (*arete*) in competitive sports was the coveted goal of all athletes who entered the games. Furthermore, the games were a reminder that unity and a common Panhellenic heritage among city-states should be preserved and maintained for the safety and general welfare of all. This was particularly important since for years external forces were a constant threat to their very survival. The manner and spirit in which the athletes executed the events was of prime importance. It was considered an honor to be in the same legendary class as their predecessors, an honor unsurpassed by any materialistic gains.

Ideology is one thing and practicality another. Ideology, if not transformed into action and accomplishment, remains just that—ideology. The end result is rhetoric and epideictic oratory. The ancient Greeks, unfortunately, would not give up their independence as city states. Isocrates, an Athenian citizen, tried to convince the Athenians that the common enemy existed not among the Greek City-States, but to the East. Warring among themselves would only result in the eventual downfall of Greece. Athens, unfortunately, chose the latter rather than give up her prominence and indomitability.

The XXIV Olympiad demonstrated the competitive athletic spirit that prevailed during the games. All nations were under one canopy of friendship, compatibility, and brotherhood. This was especially demonstrated at the close of the ceremonies. All athletes joined hands and sang odes of joy and friendship. All were united in one common bond of knowing, whether victor or not, that they gave of their utmost to attain *arete*. This theme is most aptly expressed in Beethoven's Ninth Symphony. Beethoven cries out to all mankind to work synergistically in order to effect peace, tranquillity, mutual respect, and brotherhood. Expressing one's feelings and beliefs in music is most appropriate, since it represents a universal language that all mankind can readily understand.

The quest for excellence is never-ending—that is the genuine spirit of the Olympian games. Homer expressed it very well when he said: "To forever excel and be above all others." This spirit is indomitable, since it has existed for some 2800 years ever since its beginning in Olympia in 776 B.C. There were times when the spirit slumbered for a while, but revival of that spirit has been rekindled time and time again by all mankind. It is like a smoldering fire that never ceases to extinguish itself, but rekindles periodically into a full blaze, to remind mankind that the ultimate in life is peace, mutual respect, and brotherhood among all nations.

The Olympic games have demonstrated to us the meaning and pursuit of excellence. It is a goal that all of us strive for and never quite reach in our lifetimes. When we think we have reached the ultimate in excellence, its attainment is evanescent, only to be pursued with renewed vigor and hope for its eventual achievement. Business, government, and all managerial institutions would do well to inculcate the same spirit, ideals, and quest for excellence. The concept is far from new—what it takes is the will and persevering determination and commitment to attain it. The rewards can be very great and gratifying.

Now that we have covered the archaeological activities at Nemea, we would like to relate in some of the social activities that had been planned for us by Steve. Steve and Stella were the perfect hosts during our stay at Nemea and especially the *glendi* (barbecue and entertainment) we had one evening at the site. Three lambs had been roasting on spits during the entire afternoon. Grapevine branches were used for the fire to insure proper flavoring of the meat. People took turns rotating the lambs ever so slowly to insure proper uniform roasting. Much innovativeness and improvisation took place when we considered what could be used for tables, chairs, etc.

In the improvisation of a table, the natives assembled planks used in the foundations of the half-completed museum, mounted on discarded box containers. For chairs, cement-covered planks were also used mounted on five-gallon oil drums. We were privileged to be the first to dine on the patio of the half-completed museum sans dinner jackets and the usual pomp and circumstance. On the table were bottles of ouzo, retsina, red and white Nemean wine, copious buckets of feta cut in chunks, which one picked up with his fingers, *choriatiki salata* (salad made of fresh, garden-cut tomatoes over-powering one with their delicious aroma), *kalamatianes* (olives and onion all doused in olive oil and lemon). Since knives and forks were at a premium, most of us ate with our fingers—if Mother could only see us now!

After dinner, all took to the floor to participate in the native dances. The Hellenic cordiality and hospitality touched all of us deeply. Students, natives, and local politicians all contributed to a memorable evening.

Berkelians and students representing sundry universities were proud of what was being accomplished at Nemea. Much was done and much remained to be done. Under the aegis of the Graduate Group of Ancient History and Mediterranean Archaeology at the University of Berkeley, the planning, organization and execution of work at Nemea was exemplary. The museum at Nemea is Berkeley's monument to posterity. It will house not only the present findings, but other relics and findings originally unearthed at Nemea at other museums throughout Greece.

For those desirous of acquiring more detailed information about the excavations and findings at Nemea, we can highly recommend *Nemea—a Guide to the Site and Museum*, edited by Stephen G. Miller and published by the University of California Press in 1990. The book covers the history of the excavations, the museum, the sanctuary of Zeus, and the stadium.

On several occasions the natives at Nemea told us with tears in their eyes and choked-up throats how grateful they were for what Cal was doing, not only for uncovering and bringing forth their ancient civilization and heritage, but also in creating job opportunities.

29. Back to Europe

When we returned from our whirlwind trip to Nemea in 1976, Thetis and I came to the conclusion that we had not seen enough of the northern part of Greece. Our ancestors came from Ioannina, Kastoria, Macedonia, and Thrace. We wanted to explore in more detail the history of Ioannina and Kastoria. In addition, we decided to visit the Greek Islands again. The islands had a great attraction for us. On our first trip to the islands, we were especially impressed by the open-heartedness and hospitality of the islanders. The islands had a mesmeric and soothing trancelike effect upon us, which came from the tranquillity and serenity of nature herself.

We were on our own when we visited Ioannina and Kastoria. We decided that the best way to see the islands would be to book passage on a cruise ship. The ship's itinerary covered not only the islands, but the Black Sea as well. Navigating the Black Sea in a clockwise direction, we visted Bulgaria, Russia, and Turkey. From there our ship proceeded to the Greek Islands of Patmos, Mykonos, Rhodes, and Heraklion.

We departed on September 15, 1977, and arrived in Athens the following day. This gave us an opportunity to return to our favorite restaurant, Floca. The meals were wholesome. The waiters were very cordial and couldn't do enough to please us. In ordering Greek coffee it was necessary to specify the degree of sweetness one desired, e.g., plain, medium, sweet, or very sweet. We enjoyed Floca, not only for the quality and wholesomeness of its meals, but because of the meetings that would go on with the local politicians and businessmen. This type of political seance in conjunction with coffee-sipping is usually held in the *kafeneion*. It was interesting to hear their arguments for and against political candidates, proposed construction plans, and condemnation proceedings. These conversations would go on for hours while sipping their Greek coffee. These conversations went on while we were having our dinner and continued unabated as we left the place.

While having an afternoon snack and coffee on the terrace of Floca's one day, Thetis turned to me and said that the building across the street looked familiar. Unfortunately, I could not verify her impression. We tried in vain to decipher what letters were engraved in the frieze of the building. Our curiosity got the better of us, and I suggested we walk across the street to read the inscription on the building.

Imagine our surprise when we accidentally discovered the home of Sophia and Heinrich Schliemann, the archaeologist who was credited with the excavations that took place in Mycenae, Troy, and Tiryns. The saying "so far and yet so near" was illustrated demonstratively when we saw the inscription on the building "Iliou Melathron," "The Palace of Troy." We immediately recognized the handiwork of Schliemann, since we had read his detailed archaeological accounts of his excavations in Troy. The building we are referring to was Schliemann's mansion. In designing the flat-roofed mansion, Schliemann incorporated several of the architectural features of the palaces he had uncovered. At the time the mansion was built, it was located in the outskirts of the city. With the passage of time, the boundaries of the downtown city engulfed the mansion.

Fortunately, the gate to the mansion was open and we proceeded to enter the building. We knew we were in Schliemann's home when we saw the marble *metope* of Phoebus Apollo and the four horses of the sun hanging in the foyer. Apollo is portrayed riding his chariot. This *metope* was uncovered by Schliemann in the excavation of Troy. Schliemann regarded this find as one of his finest and risked his reputation when he wrestled it from the Turkish government. Schliemann had broken his word when he finally managed to carry off the *metope*.

We were somewhat puzzled after we entered the building when we encountered no one. We thought the home had been converted into a museum and that a guide would be present to welcome us. Instead, the caretaker approached us and wanted to know the nature of our presence. We informed her that we were Americans touring Athens and were surprised to find Schliemann's home. She assured us it was indeed his home and that it was not a museum. Instead the second floor was used as a court house, and the government was

278

contemplating its conversion to a museum.

She added that the building was officially closed, but she allowed us to inspect the first floor only. The second floor would not be accessible to us. We thanked her for the courtesy extended to us and assured her we would be careful not to touch anything. The rooms were beautifully painted, with various scenes depicting different events and heroes from Homer's *Iliad* and *Odyssey*. We were told by the caretaker that the upper floor was originally Schliemann's study.

Schliemann was an avid admirer and student of Homer and attributed his archaeological discoveries to him. Most of his decisions as to where to dig were attributed to Homer. He supplemented his research by reading Pausanias. As a geographer and traveler, Pausanius was so imbued by the contributions, glories, and deeds of the ancient Greeks that were made to art, philosophy, music, the military victories and strategies employed at Platea and Marathon, the Athenian form of government, culture, and customs, that he wanted to record what had transpired for history's sake. Accordingly, he traveled throughout Greece to see the ruins at Olympia, Delphi, Corinth, Nemea, Macedonia, and Epirus. This was in the second century A.D. His writings take up ten volumes, and these works are of inestimable value as a guide to archaeologists. Had it not been for Pausanias, much hypothesizing and guesswork would have been necessary to piece together what had transpired between 400-500 B.C. and A.D. 200.

People would refer to Schliemann's discoveries as fortuitous and how lucky he was in his findings. He retorted by saying that Homer gave him the necessary clues to his discoveries. These clues, however, had to be pieced together like a crossword puzzle. It took, first of all, patience and perseverance to master the Greek of Homer.

Schiemann read and reread passages until he could decipher what Homer was alluding to. In short, it took a lot of meticulous and painstaking research. To a person not acquainted with the real understanding of toil and sweat that goes into research, it appears that when a discovery is made by the person he was "lucky and fortunate to have hit the jackpot." Remarks of this sort irritated Schliemann who promptly assured the person that discovery is not achieved in this manner. He would remind the person that the surface of the earth was so extensive that to dig randomly would be futile.

While in Athens we proceeded to our next point of interest. This was the changing of the guard on Constitution Square. The Evzones, in their white fustanellas, stood guard in front of the Tomb of the Unknown Soldier. Inscribed in marble on the wall we read, "For the whole world is their sepulchre of famous men . . . " part of the speech Pericles delivered commemorating the dead who gave their lives during the civil war fought between the Spartans and the Athenians, the so-called Peloponnesian War.

The fustanella is the modern version of the tunic the ancient Greek and Roman warriors wore. It is made up of many layers of starched cotton or wool. The Scot Highlanders have an equivalent in their kilt. It is not multilayered like the fustanella. Changing of the guard occurred every hour. In the background was the Parliament building, the former royal palace founded by King Otto.

One morning we took the street leading to Lycabettus Hill. The hill is of limestone almost a thousand feet high. On the top is the pristine white church of Saint George. From the top we had a panoramic view of Athens. When we described our memorable hike up Mount Lycabettus to our waiter at Floca's, we were told that we should come back during Eastertime and join the endless procession of people with their lighted candles after the Resurrection services. It was like coming down from heaven with renewed hope and faith.

Our next stop in our itinerary was Ioannina, east of Albania. Our flight took us over Piraeus, the Corinthian canal, the gulf between Delphi and Peleponnesus to Patras, then due north over Agrinion, Arta, Dodona, to Ioannina. The landscape was brown and mountainous. As we approached the mountains of Ioannina, the landscape suddenly became a lush emerald green.

Ioannina in Epirus brought forth many nostalgic memories for both of us. Our parents and grandparents had told us many fascinating stories about places and people in Ioannina which we were anxious to see. My dad was an Evzone in the 1897 Greco-Turkish war in Epirus. The etymology of Evzone is interesting. The literal translation is "well girded." The implication is that the implements carried by the soldier are supported by the belt or girdle. Photographs of Evzones picture them as carrying two or three curved daggers and a small firearm in the girdle.

The Highlanders of Epirus banded together to oust the Turkish occupational forces. They called themselves the Evzones. The organization spread throughout all of Greece and were instrumental in driving out the Turks from Greece. They exhibited great heroism, doggedness, and perseverance. Not only did they demonstrate their valor during the War of Independence but in ensuing wars. To this very day, they represent the ultimate in patriotism and love for country. The greatest honor that a youth can attain is to be assigned to the task of standing guard at the Tomb of the Unknown Soldier.

The story of my dad becoming an Evzone is heart-rending. His family had settled in what was Iconium, Turkey. Dad's father was well-established in the tobacco business and was well-to-do. As a boy Dad had everything he could desire, and even his very own horse. During one of the Turkish massacres of Christians, his parents were killed. Dad and his sister were rescued and taken to Komotini, Thrace. At this point in time, he became an Evzone. His sister married and settled in Marseille, France.

My dad and Thetis's parents had several discourses about their adventures in Ioannina and its environs. Thetis's grandfather and mother had told her so many adventures about the *antartes* (guerrillas) who were constantly harassing the occupational forces of the Turks. These *antartes* would sneak into Ioannina under the cover of darkness for food and supplies. There was many a time when the Turkish military police would invade the homes of the residents of Ioannina in search of the *antartes*. There were many close calls, but fortunately none were caught in Grandfather's house.

During one of these searches, Thetis's grandfather was struck in the face by the butt of a rifle by one of the Turkish police. As a result he lost some of his teeth, but the *antartes* who was in hiding was able to escape to the mountains. Grandfather and Grandmother were raised on the principles of democracy and freedom. Centuries of Turkish domination of their forefathers had worn their patience thin. They yearned for liberty and freedom. They knew the United States could offer these principles in the democratic form of government. Accordingly, they emigrated to this country.

Thetis had a reason to see Lake Pamvotis. She felt the spiritual need to personally see the lake and its island. The island in the lake has five small monasteries, which were built from the thirteenth to the seventeenth centuries. Saint Pantelimonos, most merciful, is the monastery where her great-grand-uncle, John, was studying to become a bishop. One day when he and some of his fellow novitiates were studying by the lake, he heard cries for help. He saw one of his friends struggling to keep above water. Even though John could not swim, he made the valiant attempt to save his friend. Unfortunately, Uncle John misjudged the depth of the water and he disappeared into the lake. His friend was rescued, but Uncle John was never found.

The lake is fed by a number of underground streams producing cross-currents, which result in a non-stagnant lake bottom. Channels exist underground that drain the lake. This makes for a complicated network of sources and sinks. As a result, recovery was difficult since the existence of cross-currents precluded finding anything in any particular location.

Lake Pamvotis (all nourishing) is six miles long, twenty-four square miles in area, and is at an elevation of fifteen hundred feet. The lake abounds in fish, eels, frogs, crayfish, trout, and yellow fish. At one of the restaurants on the island, fresh-caught fish could be ordered at a moment's notice. When one was ordering fish at the restaurant, the waiter was summoned to the huge dodecahedral-shaped conical fish tank. With net in hand, the waiter caught the fish we wanted. This procedure reminded us of the fish tank in Pest, Hungary. The fish was served with *Zitsa*, a sweet pink champagne. Zitsa is a town just north of Ioannina. We did not venture to try the fried eel. Our waiter told us we were missing a treat. He informed us that the French considered the eel a real delicacy and accordingly were importing eel and frogs' legs from the lake.

We had taken the ferry, *Despina*, to the island in the lake. En route we could see Mitsikeli Mountain of the Pindus mountain chain towering over the lake at an elevation of some six thousand feet. It was now time to return to the city.

In the tour of the city, we visited the fort. The walls of this fort were built by the Normans in the eleventh century and now enclose the old city. The square outside the fort was named after Saint George. There was a modest shrine, containing an icon of Saint George in Evzone costume. He was executed by the Turks for his religious beliefs on January 17, 1838. He is the only saint in the Greek Orthodox church to be portrayed in Evzone costume, fez and *Tsarouchia*, the unique soft shoe having a pompom on its upturned toe.

To find out more about the town we would take to the streets and sight-see for ourselves. The stores in the old quarter were predominantly featuring embroidery, gold and silver ornaments, and jewelry. Meats in the butcher shops were hung in the open where everyone could see what was available for the day. As we passed one of the homes, we saw an old lady who was standing at her front door. We greeted her and relayed our good wishes to her. True to her Greek hospitality, she invited us into her home to have coffee with her.

We inquired where we might find the Plaza Kormeki. Thetis's mother had mentioned that Kormeki was her great-great-grandfather who fought against the Turks in the nineteenth century. Those were the days when Lord Byron led the Greek forces against the Turks. The name *Kormeki* is of interest, since it is the Greek spelling of a Scottish name. Kormeki was saved from execution by the Turks upon the intervention of Queen Victoria.

Our hostess told us that the name was familiar to her. It was her belief that the Kormeki Plaza was near the old fort in the vicinity of the shrine of Saint George. She had vivid memories of the Nazi occupation of Ioannina. She remembered the execution of many Greeks who had harbored the Jews. The residents were horrified at the atrocities committed by the Nazis. It was reminiscent of the Turkish occupation. It is a wonder the peoples of Greece, and for that matter many other European countries that had been caught in the crossfire of invasion, have survived so well. When we mentioned that the people of Ioannina bore great misfortunes, grief, and hardship, she agreed. She replied that it was hope, faith, and love among the oppressed that kept them from buckling under the extreme tyranny of the Nazis. The belief in these three keystone qualities enabled them to survive.

There was a considerable amount of building construction going on. The Nazis had extracted their toll of destruction throughout the city. At one of the construction sites, we stopped to see what was being erected. As we were evaluating the project, we were surprised to hear someone addressing us in English. He offered to help us in whatever way he could.

We thanked him and told him we were visitors inquisitive about the city of Ioaninna. We were interested in the city, since our ancestors originated from the area. Thereupon, he welcomed us with open arms and invited us to join him in his office. He told us more about himself. He was born in Konitsa, a town just north of Ioannina near the Albanian border. He had just returned from Australia where he spent the past eight years in the construction business. He was anxious to build in Ioannina and was in the process of erecting a complex of commercial buildings, condominiums and retail stores. He exhibited great pride in what he was doing, and his ultimate goal was to contribute to the restoration of the city.

He also told us that the city was building a university complex, which would have a medical college in addition to the other liberal arts and engineering colleges. He was extremely enthusiastic about the university because it in turn would create a demand for more housing and commercial needs, thereby enhancing the overall economy of the city.

Since we were in Ioannina, we decided to visit Dodona. This area is fourteen miles southwest of Ioannina. The ancient oracle with the worship of the Goddess Earth and Holy Oak dates back to 2000 B.C. This area was the sanctuary of Zeus in Epirus. King Pyrrhus, of "Pyrrhic victory" fame, built the amphitheater with a capacity of twenty thousand in the third century B.C. It was one of the largest ancient theaters of Greece. No temple was built at Dodona until the fifth century B.C. Prior to this time, the ceremonies apparently took place in the open under the oak trees. The Greeks believed in the divination offered by the rustling of the leaves in the wind. What we found most intriguing was the fact that the interpretations of the sounds emitted by the leaves were given not by priests but by priestesses. This constituted an inconsistency in our minds, since women were not generally permitted to participate in governmental affairs and athletic contests.

The diameter of the theater is 443 feet. The stage was of a semicircular form, surrounded by columns on the outside. One structural aspect was of interest. During the reign of King Pyrrhus, the west and east ends of the hollow were formed by towerlike supporting structures to take the thrusting loads caused by peripheral forces. The stone stage ended with two ends of quadrangularlike structures, which surrounded and enclosed the proscenium, the forward part of the stage ahead of the curtain. It was built with a natural hollow in the western end of the mountain ranges, south by east in the direction of the major axis of the hollow. The length of the stadium was 820 feet.

This was one of the few ancient stadiums that had stone seats for the spectators. The spectator from the top of the theater had a picturesque view of the hollow and in addition, the two highest peaks of Mount Tomarus. The theater has been restored, and performances of ancient dramas are given during the summer.

Now that the East was more or less secure from future invasions by the Persians, Pyrrhus looked to the threat from the West, namely, Rome. His exploits were so costly in terms of men, finances, and extending himself so thin that he failed in his overall goal of accomplishing security against the Romans. When one cannot sustain his temporary successes financially and managerially, the whole structure gradually crumbles. Alexander the Great, who preceded Pyrrhus, also left an empire that was vast and extensive. After Alexander's death, it crumbled, due to the lack of his leadership. The insidious quarreling that ensued among the various district managing generals also contributed to the eventual collapse of the conquests. Alexander did not live long enough to witness the collapse of his empire.

Our next destination in our tour of northern Greece was Kastoria. We took the bus route from Ioannina to Kastoria, passing through Zitsa and Kalpaki. Konitsa is a colorful little village close to the Albanian border. Kalpaki has a memorial honoring the soldiers who thwarted the advance of the Italian and Nazi troops in Greece during the years 1940–1941. On October 28, 1940, the Italians forced Greece into the war by invading the country from Albania. Gen. Alexandros Papagos drove the invaders back and occupied one quarter of Albania. The "OXI," no, was the Greek commandant's reply to the Italian invaders. In April 1941, the Nazis attacked Greece via Albania, Bulgaria, and Yugoslavia.

The occupation of Greece lasted until October 1944. To conquer the Greeks, the Nazis employed twenty-seven field divisions, seven panzer divisions, plus air power. This military exploit by the Nazis was a result of Mussolini's failure to occupy Greece. The Nazi intervention in Greece caused a serious time delay in the military operations of the Nazis. This time delay could have resulted in the Nazis having to grapple with more than anticipated inclement winter weather in Russia.

While in Kastoria we stayed at the Hotel Xenia du Lac. Kastoria is a city and *nomos* (department) of Greek Macedonia. The town stands on a promontory reaching out from the western shore of Lake Kastoria, 2060 feet above sea level. Kastoria, like Ioannina, is noted for its lake. The lake is eleven square miles in area and is located in a deep hollow surrounded by limestone mountains. It receives its affluents from the north and west and is drained on the south by a tributary of the Aliakmon. The lake is called Oretias in honor of the town's reputed founder, Orestes, son of Agamemnon. Kastoria is identified with the ancient town of Celetrum, captured by the Romans during the Macedonian campaign. As we roamed around the lake, fishermen were cleaning their nets while the swans were sleeping during the heat of the day.

In the seventeenth and eighteenth centuries, Kastoria derived prosperity from its extensive trade in furs. The animals are not trapped in the area of Kastoria, but the pelts are brought in from various parts of Europe. The furriers are noted for their skillful piecing together of scraps of fur left over from cutting. Furs from different animals can be purchased by the yard in a manner similar to any woven textile. The fur industry is a four-hundred-year-old industry. As a teenager, I well remember my mother telling us about the fur industry in Kastoria and how her parents and grandparents had derived their living from it. The town, like Ioannina, is also an agricultural trade center with fisheries on the lake.

We had to cut short our visit to northern Greece to board the ship, the *Royal Viking Sky*, which was docked in Piraeus. We flew from Kastoria to Athens via Olympic Airways. We regretted the cancellation of our trip to Komotini, Thrace. Since we had a day to spend in Athens, we decided to take a bus tour of Attica and see the ancient temples at Sounion, the southern headland of Attica, southeast of Athens.

We boarded a Chat Tour bus in Athens and proceeded along the Saronic Gulf, reminiscent of the Big Sur in California. On the way we passed Mount Hymettus, which was as brown as the hills in California in September. The sea was very blue and the reflection of sunlight from the waves was scintillating, which made for a bizarre kaleidoscopic pattern before our eyes. As we proceeded along the waterfront, we could see many rocky caves and islands. From the extreme tip of the Piraeus promontory, a coastal road runs parallel to the ancient long walls of Themistocles and winds round the headland of Kastella above the harbor of Microlimano.

The Temple of Poseidon on Cape Sounion was erected at the time of Pericles. The cape is the most famous of Greek headlands.

Fifteen Doric columns remain standing, and the temple crowns the cliff rising perpendicularly from the sea. The temple, with its gleaming whiteness, stands out like a beacon to ships approaching the Saronikos Gulf. The all-encompassing view of sea and conglomeration of islands was one of the most spectacular we have ever witnessed at sunset. We felt as though we were with the gods at Mount Olympus. Looking out toward the sea, one could phantasize the Persian fleet on its way to engage battle with the naval forces of Themistocles at Salamis.

On one of the slender columns, Lord Byron presumably carved his ubiquitous signature. In the nineteenth century, young Englishmen considered it fashionable to carve their name on Greek antiquities. The Temple of Poseidon originally had thirty-four marble columns. Nine have remained standing, and six were re-erected. Byron was inspired by the beauty and splendor of Sounion to write in *Don Juan*:

Place me on Sunium's marbled steep,
Where nothing, save the waves and I,
May hear our mutual murmurs sweep;
There, swan-like, let me sing and die:
A land of slaves shall ne'er be mine—
Dash down yon cup of Samian wine!

—Canto III LXXXVI 16

In this passage Byron also expressed his love for freedom from restraint and as one who believed and acted according to his impulses.

As we drove back to Athens, we had a setting sun and a rising moon. It was a most inspiring view when the sun began to peak through the clouds. With such an environment and historical background, it is no wonder that poets have and are being inspired to write down their innermost thoughts and feelings of what their imaginations have rekindled. It is a portrayal of the phantasmagoria of the poets' inner soul, which was kindled by a procession of sensible and mental images.

We sailed on board the *Royal Viking Sky* from Piraeus at sunset for a cruise of the Black Sea and the Dardanelles. The port and the famous Long Walls of Themistocles were constructed in the fifth century B.C. Three hundred years later, the city was completely destroyed by the Romans. Piraeus did not recover until the establishment of the Greek kingdom in the nineteenth century.

To gain access to the Black Sea, we went through the Strait of Dardanelles, the Hellespont in ancient times, which links the Aegean Sea with the Sea of Marmara. This is a natural channel, like the one the United States built in Panama linking the Atlantic and Pacific oceans. The Corinthian Canal was built by the Romans, linking the Aegean Sea with the Ionian sea. The Corinthian channel permitted Hadrianus a direct water route from Rome to Athens and Asia Minor. The Dardanelles have a long line of history associated with the passage of Xerxes' army by the construction of a series of pontoon bridges. Many wars have been fought over the millennia because of its strategic importance. It permits access to the Mediterranean from the Black Sea and Istanbul.

Our first stop on the Black Sea was Varna, Bulgaria. From 1949–1956, Varna was called Stalin. Since 1956 it reverted to its maiden name. It is a major industrial center and Bulgaria's main seaport on the Black Sea. There is a big shipyard for seagoing vessels up to ten thousand tons and a dry dock for ships up to twenty-five thousand tons. Varna is an important cultural and educational center. Their people are ardent lovers of the opera and the symphony. Many famous opera singers have had their training in Varna.

The city had its origin some twenty-five hundred years ago when the Milesian Greeks founded it in the sixth century B.C. It was during the first Bulgarian kingdom that the city was named Varna. The Romans had left their indelible construction of the baths throughout the city. The baths were a plumber's ultimate in design, which incorporated an elaborate system for heating water and creating steam. The Roman imprint could also be seen in the remaining portions of the Roman aqueducts. The aqueducts to this day are an engineering marvel when one sees the remains of elaborate ducting systems for conveying water.

The bus drive along the waterfront was spectacular. The coast is lined with many beaches. The first one we arrived at was Varna beach. The beach is made up of fine-grained quartz sand. At the proper setting of the sun, the reflection of light from the sand produced a most spectacular resplendent color pattern to the eye. As we proceeded farther up the coast line, we arrived at the resort area known as the Zlatni Pyassutsi, the Golden Sands. This area of two miles and five hundred feet wide was composed of a golden, silky sand. One was tempted to take off one's shoes and stockings and walk barefooted through the sands. It was somewhat reminiscent of the sands on the beaches of Sarasota, Florida. The sand there was almost pure white, but when walking barefooted through the sand, one experiences an eerie, squeaking sound. Neither time nor proper behavior allowed us to make a more quantitative comparison of the two beaches.

While at the Golden Sands resort, we had luncheon at an outdoor restaurant. Menu included a salad of tomatoes, feta and peppers, roast mutton, potatoes, bread, tiropita, grapes, brandy, wine. The meal was very much like the one we experienced in Athens. We were entertained by music and dancers typical of the Balkan states. The men and women were attired in colorful native costumes. The headpieces and jewelry showed Turkish influence. This is not surprising, since the Bulgarians were also overrun by Ottoman Turks and remained under their rule for five centuries.

Our stay in Varna lasted a matter of hours. As a result, we were not able to see their renowned opera house nor attend the symphony concert. We landed at Varna at 8:00 A.M. and departed at 4:00 P.M. the same day. As we pulled out of the harbor, we could see many excursion boats ply up and down the coast from Varna. Based on our very limited stay in Varna, it was interesting for us to note the many similarities in customs, food, and culture of the Bulgarians and Greeks. They were both subjected to Turkish domination over many centuries, which left an indelible imprint on the languages, food, and customs.

Our next stop in our odyssey of the Black Sea was Odessa in the Ukraine. We were aware of the many special attributes of its peoples. During World War II, they made a valiant effort to stem the Nazi onslaught in 1941, but were unsuccessful. Tchaikovsky on several occasions conducted at its opera house. Pushkin immortalized the city in many of his poems. We were able to compare the Russians of the north with those of the south. We found the Ukranians in Odessa much more cordial and hospitable than their counterparts in Leningrad and Moscow.

The city is very old, and its history can be traced back to the late third and second millennia. Odessa is derived from the Greek, to travel/to pass through. The city has always been a prominent seaport, even in ancient times. As a port it provided a means for passage or throughway to ships. Leningrad is regarded as the largest port in the Soviet Union. Odessa follows as a second in size and capacity. It is the largest port on the Black Sea, and its whaling facilities and activities are the world's greatest. We were impressed by the design of the passenger terminal we berthed at. It was a modern structure of concrete and glass, which at a distance resembled a ship docked along the shore.

Upon disembarkation the group proceeded to the Potyomkin staircase of 192 granite steps. This led us to Potyomkinskaya Square, which commemorated the massacre of two thousand Odessans. This incident occurred when the citizens rallied behind the sailors' mutiny of the *Potyomkin* battleship in 1905. The width of the stairs is greater at the base than at the top. This results in deceiving the eye that the two sides of the stairway are parallel when viewed at a distance. This design feature was reminiscent of the design of the ancient Greek columns and stairways.

There was a huge memorial in the form of an obelisk at the end of the walkway dedicated to those who defended Odessa in World War II. It took the Nazis seventy-three days to establish a foothold there. The prolonged defense resulted in a great number of casualities and destruction of property. Much damage incurred during the subsequent occupation and liberation of the city. Its citizens and their progeny have not forgotten those who sacrificed their lives. Odessa has been called the "Hero City." An honor guard of children stood at attention at the memorial. The guard was composed of children whose ancestors lost their lives in the defense of Odessa. It was an inspiring sight to watch the children perform their ritual in honor of their fallen heroes. They were all attired in the same dress and took their assignments very seriously and punctiliously.

In the square where the city hall was located, we observed long lists of names and portraits of citizens who were recognized and honored for their outstanding efforts. This list changed weekly. Many citizens proudly wore their medals, which they received for their services to the city.

Our captain told us that the city attracted more passenger ships than any other Russian port. As a result, a new quay was built to handle the increase in traffic of tourists. Odessa is noted for its health resorts and the tranquil, warm waters of the Black Sea. Because of the heavy flow of passenger traffic, we were warned that arrival in Russia was often a slow process. As Americans, we should not expect the usual rapid and expedient service we were accustomed to.

Accordingly, we exercised great patience during disembarkation. It was amusing (and sometimes frightening) to be on the gangway when too many of us were on it. When this happened, the gangway began to sway laterally and vertically. We often wondered whether we would get to the end intact. This behavior was reminiscent of the sudden urge and drive for airplane passengers to herd together once the plane lands—all in disobedience to the instructions issued by the airline hostess.

The opera and ballet theater was one of the most beautiful structures we had seen in the Soviet Union. Chaliapin and Caruso sang there.

Proceeding counterclockwise around the Black Sea, we arrived at Yalta. The Black Sea area was anciently called "the inhospitable," deriving its name from the savage tribes surrounding it. Homer described its inhabitants as dwelling in a remote realm of mist and gloom. They were a nomadic people dwelling about the Crimea who overran Asia Minor about 635 B.C. Herodotus, the historian called it the *Euxenos*, "kind to strangers."

The name *Yalta* was intriguing to us. We suspect the name was originally derived from the word *Ialos*, glass. The sand surrounding the beach was composed of some kind of clear, transparent stone. Thetis believed the name was derived from the smooth, tranquil surface of the water blending into the sands of the beach. The intermingling of the water and sand is so smooth as to give the appearance of a continuous plane of glass. This is an optical effect, which makes it difficult to discern where the water ends and the sand begins. The origin of names lies in the eyes and imagination of the beholder.

The distance from Odessa to Yalta was 211 nautical miles. The *Royal Viking Sky* docked in Yalta at 8:00 A.M. As we were docking, we could see the summits of the granite mountains that encircled the harbor. Sheer granite cliffs could be seen in the background. It gave the appearance of Yalta being at the stage of a huge amphitheater.

291

Our first stop on our land tour was the gardens and waterfalls of Count Vorontsov's Alupta Palace. Alupta is derived from the Greek, meaning fox.

The name Vorontsov is one of the most illustrious in Russian history. Various members of the familial lineage were diplomats, ambassadors, and army officers serving their czars. Mikhail Vorontsov introduced steamboat service on the Black Sea early in the nineteenth century. For his outstanding services in various military exploits, he was made a field marshall and a prince. This was one of the finest palaces we had seen in our travels. The inner garden court was filled with marble statues and exotic plants. The palace at Alupta was a few miles east of Yalta. It was interesting to note Arabic letters inscribed on the interior of one of the arches. We were informed the quotations were taken from the Koran.

The favorable climatic conditions, like Odessa, have made Yalta a popular resort. There were many sanatoriums and health centers for the elderly and sick.

Lividia, three kilometers outside of Yalta, is best known as the meeting place where Churchill, Roosevelt, and Stalin met to discuss various political issues and cooperation between the Allied countries at the end of World War II. We visited the great hall of white marble of the Lividian Palace where the Yalta Conference between the Allied leaders took place. The enormous white Italian Renaissance palace was the summer residence of Czar Nicholas II. FDR stayed in the palace during the Yalta Conference in February 1945. What impressed us most was a large painting that showed a very thin, unhappy FDR, a sad, skeptical Churchill, and a very complacent, relaxed Stalin.

It was not long after Roosevelt returned from the conference that he passed away, a broken-hearted man. He realized that Stalin's promises had backfired. He ignored the pledges and agreements he made for a new world order. Instead, Stalin established a consortium of Communist nations from Poland to Bulgaria. What the Allies feared most about the Soviet Union finally came to pass.

Our next stop on the Black Sea was Sochi, Georgia, USSR. It is located at the foot of the western part of the Caucasus range. This was the country that Sasha Kartveli and Seversky called their birthplace. They described their country as mountainous, imbued with the spirit of independence and freedom. The terrain provided ideal grounds for sheep-raising, and hunting expeditions were organized for wild boar and bear. Sochi was like Odessa and Yalta—there were many sanatoriums and health resorts for people to recuperate and rest. It is the largest of the Soviet seaside resorts.

We boarded a bus at Sochi and arrived at Dagomya, twenty kilometers outside of Sochi. The area is famous for its tea plantations. This area was the home of Russian tea. We could see acres upon acres of tea-growing plants. We stopped at a mountain cottage where we were served tea. Our tea was prepared in samovars. Small chips of wood and charcoal were placed in a metal cylinder and lighted to keep the water hot. The tea we had had a smoky taste. Tea was served in the open, but we could not enjoy it because of the myriads of wasps that transcended upon us.

Differences in language and culture between the people of the north and south of the Soviet Union became evident to us after we had talked to the natives of Yalta, Odessa, and Sochi. The people in the north were more of Russian extraction whereas those in Yalta and Odessa were Ukrainians. Those in Sochi were Georgians. The people in the south were more cordial and hospitable than their counterparts in the north. In the past whenever I mentioned to my former White Russian NYU classmates that I was employed by two Russians, Seversky and Kartveli, I was corrected. They promptly informed me that my employers were not Russians but Georgians. In fact, Kartveli's name in Georgian was Kartvelivili, the *vili* ending signifying "the son of" Kartveli. Each ethnic group in the Soviet Union is quite distinctive, and each has its own cultural pride.

On our way to Istanbul, the ship's crew entertained us one evening with Norwegian folk dances and songs. The ceremony began with a grand buffet, abounding with all sorts of tidbits and pastries. The staff captain treated us to aquavit and Norwegian beer. All members of the crew took part—cooks, stewardesses, technicians, all donned their native hand-made costumes, which they called *bunads*. Our stewardess, Ingrid, was one of the dancers. It was a real treat to see the different types of dances representative of the various regions of Norway. Not only did the dances exhibit distinct characteristics. but the costumes as well. Instruments such as the *lurs*, long, wooden birch-bark horns, *langeleik*, a string instrument resembling a pedal-steel guitar without the pedal, all contributed to a Norwegian environment.

30. Our Crusade to Istanbul, Ephesus, and the Greek Isles

After three days of cruising the Black Sea, we arrived at Istanbul. The city is situated on the European shore of the Bosporus, Istanbul Bogazi, a strait about nineteen miles long. The ancients called the strait the Bosporus, the Ox-ford. This name originated from Io, who crossed it in the form of a heifer. The strait connects the Black Sea with the Sea of Marmara. Istanbul is encircled by the Golden Horn, the Bosporus, and the Sea of Marmara. The Golden Horn, in Turkish *Halic-canal*, is an inlet of the Sea of Marmara. We encountered several fishermen in their boats as we sailed down the Bosporus to the Sea of Marmara. En route we went under the Europe-to-Asia Bosporus Bridge. This bridge was built to commemorate the fiftieth anniversary of the founding of the Turkish Republic on October 29, 1923.

We became nostalgic as we sailed under the bridge. It reminded us of the Verrazano, the George Washington, and the Golden Gate bridges. All of these bridges are of the catenary suspension type. The Bosporus bridge is the fourth-longest in the world and its cables from the catenary are not vertical as in the American bridges, but in the form of triangles, with the apex of the triangle at the catenary. The length of the bridge is 3,540 feet. The Verrazano-Narrows Bridge is the longest, with a span of 4,260 feet. The Bosporus Bridge links two continents together, Europe and Asia. A bridge linking the two continents would result in closer ties and a bolstering of commerce between the two continents. This was conceived by the Turkish government in partnership with a consortium of European firms.

We were greeted with a beautiful sunny day in Istanbul when we docked at our berth near the Galata Bridge, one of two bridges spanning the Golden Horn. On our full-day excursion, we crossed the Galata Bridge to the Hippodrome. In search of a new location for his seat of government, the Emperor Constantine was attracted to the strategic topography of the area and the seven hills, which, coincidentally, were similar to the topography of Rome. The overwhelming factor was the excellent strategic position of the locale. Each hill has its own landmarks.

Our bus struggled through the winding streets, encountering very heavy traffic. The obelisk at the Hippodrome is made of Aswan granite, 105 feet high and 10 feet square at the base, and was sheathed in gold. It was constructed in the fifteenth century B.C. A spiral column removed from Delphi by the Romans stood opposite the obelisk. This column commemorated the Greek victory over the Persians at Apollo's shrine in Delphi. Constantine the Great brought it to his city, Constantinople. Three serpents' heads located on the top of the column disappeared in the eighteenth century. There was also another obelisk erected in honor of the Emperor Constantine.

Our next point of interest was the Blue Mosque, the mosque of Sultan Ahmed. It is to its mosques that Istanbul owes its distinctive skyline. To enter the mosque, we had to remove our shoes. We were only permitted to stand in the rear portion of the edifice. The floors were covered with red Oriental prayer rugs and were very cold. There were six minarets encircling the mosque. The minarets were beautiful, slender, lofty towers surrounded by many projecting balconies from which the summons to prayer is cried by the muezzin, one who calls Muslims to prayer. In the past, religious men would climb the steps to the top of the minarets five times daily to call the faithful to prayer. This is no longer done. Instead, raucous loudspeakers are mounted on the minarets and recordings call the hours of prayer. We were disappointed when our guide told us that the muezzin was a thing of the past. This touch of modernism is somewhat out of place in the old city.

There is an interesting story behind the number of minarets that were built. Sultan Ahmed had ordered a golden minaret for his mosque. The story goes that the architect pretended he had heard *alti* (six, in Turkish) minarets instead of a gold, *altin,* one. The middle dome is eight feet wider than Agia Sophia. The sultan had to do one better than the Agia Sophia of Constantine. The interior of the mosque is of blue tile and has 260 beautiful stained-glass windows. The vertical supporting columns were massive and fluted. Istanbul has over 500 mosques, and the number of minarets indicates the prominence and grandeur of the mosque.

We then proceeded to Topkapi Saray, the sultans' seraglio. With its gardens it occupied the entire tip of the promontory and was enclosed within a fortified wall. The seraglio is now a museum and the scene of the movie, *Topkapi*, made in 1963, featuring Melina Mercouri and Peter Ustinov. The seraglio houses the sultans' treasure and has collections of manuscripts, exquisite china, armor, textiles, etc. We saw the harem, the famous dagger, exquisite jewels, the 86-carat diamond, jeweled plates, porcelain, etc. The treasures were breathtaking and wondrous to behold. One high candelabra weighed a hundred pounds in gold and contained 6666 diamonds, the number corresponding to the number of words in the Koran.

What we enjoyed the most about the seraglio was reliving the movie, *Topkapi*. As we walked in the courtyard, we could rehear in our minds Melina's sexy laughter. When we proceeded to the treasure room, we observed the glass cabinet in the center of the room. However, the dagger was not in the case. It was in the one against the wall. The emeralds on it were enormous. As we looked up toward the ceiling, we could see the windows from whence the man was lowered to lift the glass cabinet. Nearby we could see the spot from which the escapees dove into the water.

The following morning we visited the crown jewel of Emperor Constantine, the church of Saint Sophia, the Hagia Sophia—Divine Wisdom. We were awed by its splendor, and its massive structure exceeds that of Saint Peter's in Rome. The diameter of the dome is approximately a hundred feet. The dome was inscribed with Arabic characters at the summit. We asked our guide for a translation, but he was unable to provide one. He told us the intertwined characters were not only an example of calligraphy, but would also require a scholar to translate. There were some remaining mosaics left in the original, depicting the Virgin Mary and some of the archbishops. There were no icons and the Iconostasion was missing.

The present Saint Sophia is not the edifice the Emperor Constantine built in A.D. 326. His structure was destroyed by fire in 404. It was rebuilt but destroyed by fire again. Justinianus the Great, Byzantine emperor, built the basilica as we now know it in a period of five years, 532–537. It was consecrated on December 27, A.D. 537. Materials for the basilica came from many different sources. Marble was imported from North Africa and the islands of Marmara. Pillars and ornamental capitals came from Pergamum and Ephesus. Many of the original mosaics are missing. It was significant and miraculous to us that of the few remaining mosaics, the one of Mary holding the Infant Jesus was still intact. This could be seen on the apse of the basilica.

We had been awed by the basilica of Saint Peter's in Rome, but our reaction of being in the Hagia Sophia was one of a spiritual exaltation in excelsis. It was stupendous. In closing our remarks on Istanbul, we would like to recount a story that we heard about the probable origin of the word. People from the suburbs planning to visit the city, when asked where they were going, would reply in Greek, "*Eis Tan Polin*," to the city. In time this expression became Istanbul, the official name of the city.

To get to Izmir on the Aegean Sea, our next stop, we had to transgress the Sea of Marmara. The sea was named the Sea of Marble, because the ancients quarried marble from the islands located in the northwestern part of the sea. It was in the Sea of Marmara that Alexander the Great destroyed a Persian army during his first battle in Asia. As we cruised through the sea, we saw many fishermen. There were many fishing and canning industries located on the islands.

To get to the Aegean from the Sea of Marmara, we had to pass through another strait, known as the Dardanelles, the Hellespont in ancient times. Dardanelles derives its name from the city of Dardanus in the Troad. Mithradates VI and Sulla, the Roman general, signed a treaty in 85 B.C., ending hostilities between countries of Armenia and Rome. The strait extends for a distance of approximately 38 miles, with a width of from 3/4 miles to 4 miles. We passed many famous sites en route through the strait, the most notable being the Troad. It is the region of which ancient Troy was the capital, bordering the Hellespont and the Aegean Sea.

Hissarlik is the modern Turkish name of the presumed site of Troy, the Ilium of Heinrich Schliemann. Nine cities were built on this site from the Stone Age to Roman times. Ilium was presumably the scene of the Trojan War. The entire area is replete with historical interest. The entire western coast of Turkey bordering the Aegean has been the site of various battles fought in the past. In its first thrust into Asia in 190 B.C., Rome defeated Antiochus the Great, king of Syria. Xerxes, marching against Greece, built a bridge of pontoons over the Hellespont.

Izmir (Smyrna) has a very modern waterfront with a population of over one million. The city was quite modern in appearance, since most of it had been rebuilt following the fire of 1922. There were more churches than mosques. This was apparently the case since the city was heavily populated by Greeks. At the time of our visit, the high-rise buildings of seven to eight stories were occupied by American soldiers who were stationed in Turkey representing NATO. Izmir is a great port engaged in both commercial and tourist trade. It is a stepping stone to three archaeological sites, Ephesus, Pergamon, and Sardis. The entire area around Izmir is replete with ruins of ancient civilizations and biblical landmarks.

The ninety-minute drive by bus to Ephesus was hectic. The roads were narrow, and our driver had to contend with tractors, goats, sheep, donkeys, trucks, buses, bikes, etc. There were many accidents along the way. Women were picking cotton in the fields while the men were having coffee at coffee houses, the *kahvehane*. The city dates back to 3000 B.C., according to pottery dating. Alexander the Great assigned the task of rebuilding the city to his general Lysimarchus in 300 B.C.

We walked down the marble slab walk past Hadrianus' Temple on our right, as we had the previous year. Opposite Hadrianus' Temple was the Fountain of Trajan, a Roman emperor. The structure was two-storied and is, in our opinion, one of the most elaborate and ornate architectural designs we saw in Ephesus. As we proceeded we passed several triumphal arches as memorials to past notable events. We then proceeded to the Grand Theater, which was originally built by the Greeks with the incorporation of a circular space for the chorus. The Greeks called this area the "orchestra." Seating accommodated twenty-five thousand spectators. It was built to face the harbor, thereby permitting a panoramic view. Our guide was especially interested in the baths. He showed us a public lavatory with seats lined up as in the movie *No Time for Sergeants*.

At the lower end of the long marble walk, we came up to the Celsus Library, which was next to the *agora* (market place). The Celsus Library was very extensive, with the facade of the building practically intact. The dimensions were about a hundred feet across by a hundred feet in height and it was a two-story building. This was the structure we wondered about last year when the Austrian and German governments were engaged in its restoration. They were still working on it, and the work was actually begun in 1891.

There were a series of steps leading up to the building. On each side of the entrance, there were a total of four full-length statutes recessed in semicircular nooks, two statues on each side. The archaeologists uncovered a sepulchre under the library with a skeleton in it, presumably Celsus'. Unfortunately, we were not permitted to enter the grounds, since the workers were still engaged in reconstruction and excavation.

The Arcadian Avenue began in front of the Grand Theater and extended to the harbor. The sea has recessed over the millennia because of the silt and mud brought down by the rivers. The avenue, which ran in a west-easterly direction, was lined with columns on either side. On the northern side of the avenue were the Harbor Baths, which incorporated a gymnasium. The avenue consisted of many shopping areas and served as a promenade.

Thetis and I were awed by the extent of the ruins at Ephesus. The city is located at the crossroads of eastern Europe and Asia Minor. It would appear that every Roman emperor and notable of the day wanted to be remembered for posterity by erecting a structure or monument in Ephesus. There was much to see, and our guide told us that only a fraction of the ruins had been unearthed.

We boarded our bus at Ephesus and arrived at Kusadasi (Bird Island) where we had luncheon. Kusadasi is a resort town which curves around a crescent bay a few miles south of Ephesus. We were disappointed since we were not served baklava, *kataif,* or Turkish coffee.

After luncheon, our bus wound up a mountain road leading to the "House of the Virgin" on top of Mount Pion. The simple Byzantine chapel is hidden among ancient gray-green olive trees. It is believed Mary spent her last days here after being brought to Ephesus by the Apostle John. St. John continued to live and work in this area, and it is believed that he lies buried on a hill top near Ephesus. We could see St. John's Church at a distance. We were unable to go to the church for lack of time. It was Christ's wish that John look after his mother after the crucifixion.

When we first visited Ephesus in 1976, our guide told us there was a possibility that St. Lucas was buried in a crypt in a field near the ruins. This, he maintained, could not be verified, since the Pope had not given permission to open up the tomb. This time around, our guide told us there was no credence to the story that we heard the prior year. There is no doubt there is much speculation going on about the area, and it is a haven for figmentary imagination on the part of the guides. It can be said, however, that the area abounds in biblical settings.

Ephesus was the last place we visited on Turkish soil. We now had the Greek Isles to visit. Our ship took us to Patmos, which we revisited. The distance by ship between Izmir and Patmos is 134 nautical miles. The brown craggy hills with the sparkling white buildings were quite a contrast to the azure blue of the Aegean. On top of the hill is the village of Chora. The seaport where we anchored is called Skala. We boarded a bus in Skala to arrive at the monastery in Chora.

We climbed eight hundred feet to reach the monastery. Remains of the ancient acropolis on the hill above have weathered both weather and earthquakes. A steep-paved road ran between the port and the fortified monastery of St. John. It was at Patmos that the Apocalypse was disclosed to John. The site of the revelation was claimed to have taken place in an alcove near the harbor. St. John was exiled to Patmos in A.D. 95 by the Emperor Domitian for teaching the new religion in Ephesus. St. John dictated the Book of Revelation to his disciple Prochorus in the cave. Patmos is a place of pilgrimage.

The monastery of St. John was a fabulous place. It was founded in 1088 by St. Christodoulos. It had a fabulous collection of illuminated manuscripts. The icons and Fabergé gifts were donated by various Russsian emperors. The purple parchment containing parts of the Gospel of St. Mark is considered one of the most ancient codices. The letters were in silver and the holy names in gold. We were informed that 33 leaves were in the library of St. John; the Vatican has 6, and the Leningrad Library 182. It was spine-tingling to hear the bells in the tower. The whole courtyard reverberated with sound.

When we arrived at the monastery, the sermon was over, but we were fortunate enough to participate in the Antidoron. This is bread that has been blessed, but not consecrated and distributed in small pieces to those present at Mass. The Antidiron is given out after the liturgy. The parishioners were attending the *Mnemosynon* (in memoriam services). As a general rule, the Mnemosynon is first delivered after forty days of internment of the deceased and signifies that the living will continue to remember the departed. Religious feeling is very intense on Patmos, and it was reflected in the faces of the parishioners. We were told that even the donkeys were imbued with goodness, as was seen in their behavior.

After the services were over, a monk approached us and introduced himself. He wondered who we were and when we told him we were visitors from the United States, he greeted us with open arms. He was most gracious and friendly. He showed us the Shrine of St. Christodoulos. His remains were enclosed in a silver encasement, and his head was visible through the silver grill work. This was a most unusual presentation of a deceased. We were taken to the archives of the monastery where we saw a parchment deed signed by a Byzantine emperor, giving the island of Patmos to Christodoulos and granting him " . . . the right to be its absolute ruler to all eternity."

Saint Christodoulos had begged the Emperor Alexis I to lay a foundation for the monastery on Patmos. Today the church has a beautiful eleventh-century icon of Saint John the Divine, and the monastery contains an impressive library, including a text of Plato.

Upon our return to Skala, we toured the waterfront. Tourist shops and restaurants line the harbor. To get back to our ship, we had to board a launch. Our ship was too large to dock at the port and had to drop anchor in the beautiful blue bay. The architecture of the island was typical of cubistic design. On our way out to the ship, we could see in the distance the white-studded homes embedded in a blue sky and the ultramarine of the Aegean. This setting made for a spectacular and unforgettable view. Our only regret as we were leaving this beautiful, holy island was that we could not visit the Holy Grotto of the Apocalypse. It was here that John heard God's voice telling him, "I am the Alpha and the Omega, the first and the last. What thou seest write in a book and send it unto the seven churches which are in Asia. . . ."

Our ship left Patmos at twelve noon and arrived at Mykonos four hours later. It was a beautiful cruise of some seventy-two miles. Mykonos is called the "Jewel of the Aegean." It is one of the playgrounds of the jet-set. The island is one of a group of islands that form a circle, commonly known as the Cyclades derived from *kyklos*, "circle." The Cyclades pertain to a civilization that existed as early as 3000 B.C.

When we arrived at the island, the winds had caused the sea to swell. The first two launches made the trip to land without difficulty, but on the third launch, passengers had to get in step with the oscillations of the launch. At times one had to perform an Irish jig to get on board. After gathering enough courage, we finally made the fourth launch.

Our first greeter was Irene, the pelican. When we asked about her mate, we were told that Petros was on the other side of the island. Irene was very tame and understood Greek. One of the fishermen was feeding her live bait while at the same time muttering tender words of affection. It was interesting to observe the compatibility between man and bird. The pelican on Mykonos is revered as a talisman of good economic times and a symbol of good fortune. As long as there is a pelican around, Mykonos will prosper. Irene was very friendly and much larger than those in the Bay Area of California.

The island was studded with 365 churches with pastel domes. The residents have no excuse for not attending church, since they are all conveniently located with respect to the neighborhood. The buildings are sparkling white and literally glisten in the sun. As a contrast, the shutters and doors are painted a vivid blue or green. Only churches were allowed delicate pastel shades for their domes. Winding lanes of scarlet hibiscus, pink oleander, and green trees add to the variegated colors of the island. People take great pride in painting their buildings twice a year.

The streets are effectively wide paths studded with many restaurants, *tavernas*, and night clubs. Every third shop was a jewelry store. Handicrafts were varied and beautiful. Sweaters were bulky knits and fashionably designed. Mykon is a shoppers' paradise. The men in the group became interested in the Greek fisherman's cap. Wearing one of these gave one the feeling that he was the skipper of a yacht. The colors of the cap were attractive, and the price was right. Needless to say, the men succumbed to their purchase and wore them proudly like natives as they walked through the town.

We had dinner at a quaint restaurant and were served a typical Greek menu. For an *orektika* (appetizers), we had shrimp on sliced tomato, *dolmatakia* (rice and meat rolled up in a tender grape leaf), *taramosalata* (a dip of salted red roe usually derived from the mullet mixed with olive oil, lemon and bread crumbs) and marinated octopus. This was followed by shrimp, squash, and tomato, coffee and Metaxa brandy. From there we went to a pastry shop where we

302

bought *Yanniatiko* (à la Ioannina preparation) *kadaif* to take back to the ship. This pastry is composed of *kadaif* similar to shredded wheat filled with walnuts and honey and encased in *filo* dough.

We had no sooner arrived at Mykonos when it was time to leave. We took the 10:00 P.M. launch back to the ship and had no difficulty boarding the launch this time, since the winds had subsided considerably. We were now on our way to Rhodes.

The weather en route was beautiful. This time we were able to dock at a pier. Rhodes is the largest island of the Dodecanese, one of an island of twelve. The great harbor is a part of the Knights of St. John fortifications. We found the dock congested. Summer is six months long on the island. As a result, Scandinavians, Germans, and other sun-starved tourists visit the island in droves. The island is expanding rapidly, and to accommodate the increase in tourist trade, the airport was being reconstructed to handle international flights. This is a boom to the economy of Rhodes, but many of the natives were concerned about the future of the island. They were fearful of rising prices and the ensuing loss of solitude and peace of mind they were accustomed to. Greece is in sore need of revenue to foster jobs for their people. As it is, many of its inhabitants migrate to all parts of Europe and the far corners of the earth. This is a dilemma Greece has been faced with from its very beginnings.

We took a taxi to the Old Town and did some sight-seeing and shopping. The town was comprised of narrow streets, medieval inns, walls, gates, battlements, and mosques. In the cobbled Street of the Knights, there were several fountains in the squares. The shops were reminiscent of the days of the Crusades. Many of the buildings had been restored. The Grand Masters' Palace was rebuilt by the Italians as a summer residence for Mussolini during the Italian occupation. The floors were covered with mosaics taken from thirty Byzantine houses on the island of Kos. World War II broke out and Il Duce never visited his summer palace.

The medieval walls were beautifully preserved and made for an effective defense system with bridges, gates, moats, and secret passages. We also saw the mosque of Suleiman built after 1523 when the island was occupied by the Turks. Upon completion of our tour, we returned to the ship for luncheon. After some deliberation, we decided we would visit the towns of Kamiros, Kremasti, Ialysos, and Mount Philerimos.

In the afternoon we took a cab to ancient Kamiros. Archaeologists have uncovered three levels of ancient settlements. Because of the slope of the terrain, the houses were built one above the other on terraces to avoid soil erosion. Retaining walls of oblong porous blocks were built in an east-to-west direction. The main street of Kamiros led to the part where new excavations had begun. Private houses lined both sides of the street.

The entire region of Kamiros was an archaeologist's paradise. The area was still being excavated, and many finds were still being uncovered. The site of the acropolis was located on the plateau of the summit. The stoa, which provided a roofed colonnade for a meeting place and promenade, was erected on the northernmost part of the acropolis. The foundations of the colonnades and rooms of the stoa have been preserved. The stoa was about seven hundred feet long and had two rows of Doric columns. The inner colonnade stood at a distance of twenty feet from the outer one. The view of the bay from the acropolis was spectacular.

The civil engineers of ancient times recognized the importance of storing water for future use, especially in drought areas. A cistern was ingeniously cut into the soft rock of the west section of the plateau. The interior was plastered with a waterproof coat to prevent seepage of water. Two flights of steps at either end led down to the cistern for cleaning purposes. The water in the cistern was conducted to the town in a special conduit. Two openings with stone lids served to regulate the flow of water.

Kremasti (hung up/hanging) was our next point of interest. The city is located twelve kilometers from Rhodes. Our first stop was at the church of the Panagia (The All Holy, the most common epithet of the Virgin Mary). The steps leading to the church were marble. The courtyard was paved with a mozaic of white and colored pebbles. In the resplendent white church, there was an ikon of the Panagia, which is famous for its miracles. We met the priest, who had visited the United States. He told us of his impressions of what he experienced in the States and was discouraged by the conditions he witnessed in some of our cities, such as Chicago.

A road from the bay wound up to Mount Philerimos (fond of solitude). The top of the hill affords an excellent view of Ialysos. The area of Ialysia abounded in ancient monuments, most of which we saw on Mount Philerimos. The stepped path leading to the monastery in Philerimos was flanked with cypress trees and beautiful gardens. The monastery was erected in a delightful setting of greenery, built in the Italian architectural fashion, attempting to revive the knightly style in Rhodes. The ruined foundations of the Temple of Athena Polias were just west of the door of the Church of our Lady of Philerimos. The cult of Athena was replaced by the worship of the Virgin.

The Apostles Iakovos, Paul, Bartholomew, Matthew, and Peter were portrayed in mosaic in the Chapel of Georgios Chostos. Inside the chapel the walls were covered with Gothic paintings. The frescoes depict the Knights of the Order of St. John, with their patron saints. The vault contained scenes from the life of the Virgin and the Passion of Christ.

At sunset we boarded our ship, which was anchored in Mandraki harbor. The passengers were invited that evening to a reception and gala dinner hosted by the captain. We started with caviar and finished with a flaming baked Alaska. This was our opportunity to reciprocate with our hospitality by treating the staff captain to the *kadaif* we had previously brought aboard.

We set sail for Crete, where we would revisit Knossos and Heraklion. The island of Crete is the fifth largest in the Mediterranean Sea. Since we had visited Knossos the previous year, we cut short our visit there. Our aim was to visit the grave site of Nikos Kazantzakis in Heraklion, which we had not been able to see the prior year. Of all the islands we visited in the Mediterranean, Crete had a special fascination and allurement for us. It was the home of El Greco, the statesman Venizelos, and Nikos Kazantzakis, the author of *Zorba the Greek*. While visiting Knossos the prior year, our guide told us we should visit the grave site of Kazantzakis.

Because of its strategic location in the Mediterranean, Crete is at the crossroads of trade and commerce. Over the millennia, various ancient and modern cultures have left their imprint and influence on the population of Crete. As a result, the Greek spoken in Crete is quite distinct from that spoken on the mainland. Our observation of the people of Crete coincides with the description given by Homer in the *Odyssey* some three thousand years ago, XIX,172–179. The following translation by A. T. Murray, published by the Loeb Classical Library, is as follows:

305

There is a land called Crete, in the midst of the wine-dark sea
A fair, rich land, begirt with water, and therein are many men past
counting and ninety cities
They have not all the same speech, but their tongues are mixed
There dwell Achaeans, there great-hearted native Cretans, there
Cyclodians and Dorians of waving plumes and goodly Pelasgians
Among their cities is the great city Knossos where Minos reigned
when nine years old. He that held converse with great Zeus.

Remembering the comments of our guide from our previous visit to Crete, we were curious and intrigued to see his grave site, situated on the belvedere at Akratiri, a Heraklion hilltop. In addition, the movie *Zorba the Greek*, which appeared in 1964, with Anthony Quinn playing the role of Zorba, whetted our curiosity all the more.

Kazantzakis was a prolific writer. His contributions include many novels, some of which were translated into thirty languages. He was nominated for the Nobel Prize in literature several times, but he never achieved the coveted honor.

He was considered a controversial and dichotomous person. As we approached the site, we could see a simple wooden cross marking his grave. Our conception of the wooden cross was symbolic of the wooden cross of Christ. The site, some twenty feet by twenty feet, was covered with stone slabs. Rising above the slabs was a huge stone some four feet by eight feet, centrally located with respect to the slabs. The tombstone had inscribed on it the following in Greek:

I Hope for Nothing
I Fear Nothing
I am Free

This epitaph was written by the Cretan novelist and epitomizes his final thoughts. We were especially curious about his philosophy of life. He wrote a vivid account of his life, ambitions, and struggles in his last novel, *Report to El Greco*. When he died there were no religious services by the church. However, sometime later the church permitted a plain wooden cross made from the limbs of a tree to be placed next to the monument.

Thetis and I were especially at odds with his philosophy of life. In his *Report to El Greco,* he portrayed life as a struggle and passion rather than being a challenge. Most of us consider life a challenge, and to progress is to change existing archaic structures to fit more in line with existing conditions. Kazantzakis strove to attain greater heights and, as he put it, to reach the "summit." He referred to his endeavors and attainments as: "I should like to represent the ascent, together with the red footprints I left as I mounted . . . because the bloody track will be the only trace left by my passage on earth." These remarks appear to be indicative of someone who regarded life as one battle after another.

Now that we had read Kazantzakis' epitaph, we were better able to arrive at our impressions of him. His very use of the words in the epitaph, hope, fear, and being free, meant to us that he was frustrated in his ambitions, achievements, and in the search of his concept of truth. He was fearful of the consequences of his endeavors, struggles, and what people might think of his literary undertakings. Above all, he welcomed death as a relief from all his travails of life.

Before leaving Crete we visted the Cathedral of Minas in Heraklion. The cathedral is a basilica with a dome. The Metropolis had six large icons by Damaskinos, the Cretan School's outstanding representative and teacher of El Greco. There was an enormous gold chandelier with oval-shaped Byzantine icons peripherally arranged around it. Byzantine icons painted by Stylianos Kartakis lined the dome and walls of the Metropolis of St. Minas.

Next to the entrance of the Cathedral of St. Minas was old St. Minas. This chapel housed a collection of Byzantine icons and wood carvings. Byzantine icons in old St. Minas were painted by the brothers George and Zacharias Kastrophylax. All the paintings depicted various scenes from the life of Christ and the Virgin Mary. They were most intricate and beautiful beyond belief. These Byzantine icons were some of the most beautiful we have seen, including those in Russia.

In front of the cathedral was a bust of Ecumenical Patriarch Athenagoras. We well remember his outstanding services to the community when he was archbishop of North and South America, with his archdiocese in New York City. He organized many professional groups and established many new churches throughout the Americas. He was a warm, compassionate man, who was always eager to help those in need. He had a keen sense of humor and a profound understanding of human nature.

In 1931 he founded the National Greek Orthodox Ladies Society, commonly known as the *Philoptochos* (loving/aiding the poor). His *agape* and commitment to all peoples of the world was his basic mission in life. He was instrumental in organizing the Greek community and in the education of parish priests. He founded the Holy Cross Theological School in Pomfret, Connecticut, and St. Basil's Academy in Garrison, New York. When he was elected Ecumenical Patriarchate of Constantinople, President Truman offered the Presidential plane to fly the Patriarch-Elect to his ancient See in Istanbul.

In line with his ecumenical responsibilities, he visited Pope Paul VI in 1963 to hold a summit of Christian leaders in Jerusalem to further the cause of Christian unity. In 1967 he visited the Archbishop of Canterbury in London, the General Secretary of the World Council of Churches in Geneva, and Pope Paul at the Vatican.

One of Thetis' most precious moments occurred at the time when the Archbishop Athenagoras was present at a luncheon of the Philoptochos. He picked up our toddler daughter, Alceste, on his lap. Our daughter was awed and perplexed by this tall, magnificent person with friendly, compassionate eyes and flowing beard. She was perplexed because this person was attired in black garments with a black beard whereas Santa Claus, whose acquaintance she had made on several prior occasions, was attired in red clothes and a glowing white beard.

At this moment of bewilderment and confusion, the archbishop's eyes met our daughter's eyes. He picked up a lump of sugar and gave it to her. Alceste ate it with much satisfaction and appreciation. Seeing this, the Archbishop was much gratified that his action had proven so successful that he offered her a second one.

At this point, Grandmother became quite concerned that Alceste might have gastronomical effects as a result of having too many lumps of sugar. She was in a quandary as to whether she should tell the archbishop that enough was enough or to hope that he would not offer a third piece. Fortunately, the latter came to pass. The dialogue that ensued between the archbishop in his flowing robes and our daughter was spiritually moving.

Our trip to Heraklion awakened many beautiful memories of Archbishop Athenagoras, who later became Patriarch of Constanople. We found the island of Crete an interesting blend of antiquity and modern cultures. This convinced us that Crete is at the crossroads of the Mediterranean.

From Heraklion our ship headed for the port of Piraeus. This was the final leg of our tour of the Black Sea and the Greek Isles. Our ship had sailed a total of 2,723 nautical miles in ten days. We stayed in Athens for a day and witnessed the changing of the Guard in front of the Parliament building.

To us this portion of our trip was a crusade. It enabled us to emerge from our cocoon of habitual customs and philosophy of life to a higher ecumenical environment. God has apparently ordained multivariate beliefs and philosophies among all peoples of the world and to say any one has attained the ultimate would be quixotic and narrow-minded. In striving for the ultimate, man has attempted in the past to select the best features of each and call the resultant outcome his very own creation.

31. Involvement in Community Activities

Our parents were always active in community affairs. They felt that everyone should contribute their effort to the betterment of their community. To them, good citizenship constituted cooperation among one's neighbors. In addition, each generation had the responsibility to take care of and improve upon what was acquired by them. In the rural area where we built our first home, there were needs to consider that beckoned us for action. Inspired by the exemplary conduct set forth by our parents, it was our natural duty and concern for the welfare of our hamlet to volunteer our efforts in the improvements of our area.

When we had helped set the stage for the future of space flight at Republic Aviation by day, our concerns by night were focused on the urgent need of a firehouse in our little hamlet known as Dix Hills, a section of Huntington, Long Island. Our home was located in a wooded area surrounded by tall oaks and pine trees. In addition, the natural landscape was dense with underbrush and leaves. The threat of fire was of real imminent concern, especially during the autumn season, when a thick layer of additional dry oak leaves and pine needles covered the ground. A carelessly tossed cigarette from a passing motorist could ignite the entire area.

We had no firehouse of our own in our community. We relied entirely on outside help, which at times proved to be too late in arriving. Consequently, trees and underground growth would burn to such an extent that very little could be done. When the firemen arrived, about all they could do was to contain the fire by creating fire lanes. To make matters worse, city water was not available in our area.

To prevent the fire from spreading too rapidly, an immediate response to a fire was essential. This matter was discussed at several meetings of the local residents. It was the consensus of the group that a task force be established. Its function would be to investigate the problem and to suggest various alternatives for its solution. It was decided that we needed to gather together data from neighboring firehouses as to how to proceed in setting up an effective firehouse, the type of equipment that would be most effective for our terrain, the training of inexperienced volunteers to become acquainted with fighting fires in our area devoid of a city water system, and lack of access to some of the hilly areas.

There comes "a time to care" in our lives for the safety, health, and general welfare of the community. We should not exist in our society by being totally independent of each other. Those of us who experienced World War II learned what it meant to work synergistically. We learned through cooperation how successful we could become. Goods and services were cut down to a bare minimum. This meant we had to tighten our belts, do without those amenities we had taken for granted in the past, and learn again to care for one another. We had a common foe to contend with, and our goal was to win.

There were several options open to us. We could take our problem to the town council and request their help. After much deliberation, the group decided that would take too long. With tight budgets facing the city and all the political strings that had to be manipulated, we decided against that approach. Another alternative was to canvas the neighborhood for money from the local residents. Each resident would be assessed on a pro-rata basis, according to the number of acres owned and the appraisal of the house. This, too, was abandoned because of the time element involved to accomplish this.

In addition, there would undoubtedly be objections to such a proposal because of the inequities that would result in arriving at a fair and equitable amount each resident would have to pay. There were several farmlands in the area, which were not threatened by fire. The farmers would, in all probability, not go along with the additional tax for a firehouse.

Time was of the essence. If we wanted something accomplished within a reasonable length of time, we simply had to take the bull by the horns. Since we had no funds available for a fire department, the whole neighborhood rose to the occasion to establish a volunteer fire department. We assigned the design and layout of the firehouse to those members of the neighborhood who had some experience in the fundamental requirements of what was needed—no more, no less. Volunteers were appointed who would install the plumbing, lay concrete, carpentry, roofing, and sundry other details. All that remained in the way of expense was the materials that went into the construction—cement blocks, lumber, nails, roofing materials, plumbing, etc. Those of us who knew some of the dealers of construction materials in our area were able to get substantial discounts once we explained our intentions. A few went so far as to donate the materials for our cause.

Money had to be raised to pay for the materials. The group decided on holding various local affairs to raise money. Our most successful approach was the fair we held. The local farmers donated their agricultural products, and many local merchants contributed their wares for the cause. There were those who donated money and those who offered their sweat labor. The fund-raising fair was a tremendous success. The community turned out en masse. Our publicity campaign resulted in a considerable turnout of neighbors from contiguous areas.

The camaraderie that existed was most inspiring and enlightening to us participants. This spirit of cooperation pervaded us to complete our modest firehouse in record time. The structure was so designed and built to house two units of the pumper class. With no street water available at the time, our immediate need was for pumpers. Not only was a second-hand pumper truck purchased from a neighboring firehouse for a nominal sum, but a modest, functional firehouse was built by the local residents. Each resident contributed to the various building materials and labor that went into the construction. One of the most cherished events of our lifetime took place at the time we purchased our pumper. It was a far cry from what we really needed, but it was all we could afford. It was better than nothing at all. We could at least make a beginning of eventually becoming a full-fledged fire department.

The pumper truck chugged along with the little remaining horsepower the engine had. I took it out for a check run and drove it around the neighborhood to show the residents what we had purchased with their money. They were pleased with our efforts and wished us good luck in our operations. Some went so far as to say they would support any future expansion of facilities when the time came. They lauded our approach in proceeding one step at a time, starting at first with the bare essentials.

After the drive through the neighborhood, I drove the pumper up our hilly driveway and proudly exhibited it to Thetis and the children. At the time they were toddlers and when I sounded the siren, they were ever so proud of their daddy. What a moment of ecstasy for all of us! An accomplishment the young and old could be justly proud of. At long last, we had a firehouse and a pumper truck. It was a simple beginning and a hope and inspiration for more in the future.

There were certain requirements we had to comply with. We needed to obtain the blessings of the Town Fathers to function as a volunteer fire department and the procurement of a charter. The volunteers were required to take training and participate in fire drills before they were officially qualified to perform the duties of a fireman. I well remember one remark that comes to mind, whenever the Dix Hills fire department is mentioned, which was made in jest during our training session. Our instructor asked the group, "How should you open a door in the event of a fire?" One volunteer responded by saying, "Spit on the door knob before you touch it so you don't burn your hand."

Our wives, who had supplied us with snacks, lunches, and coffee during the construction phase, organized the Women's Auxiliary. They were also present whenever there was a fire of long duration. The volunteers were given a "shot in the arm" when members of the Women's Auxiliary appeared with snacks, coffee, and first-aid assistance if needed during these fires.

A system of communication was arranged so that the volunteers were alerted in case of a fire. We were fortunate to manage to have someone always on call. Volunteers received battery-operated blue lights for the roofs of their cars so they could maneuver readily through traffic and be escorted by police if necessary. All volunteers received silver badges, identifying them as volunteer members of the fire department. As a founding member of the volunteers, I became a director of the board. The gold director's badge is one of my proudest possessions. To me, it personifies community involvement and a caring for the general welfare of its residents. An achievement arising out of a will to accomplish a certain goal is indeed most gratifying.

What is of significance is the fact that the Town of Huntington recognized our efforts, and it wasn't long afterward that funds were made available by the town for an expansion of what we had started.

We were now fully equipped with new fire engines and equipment. We were now officially a part of the fire district of Dix Hills.

Our involvement with the founding of the Dix Hills fire department serves to illustrate what can be done interdependently by working cooperatively and for a common cause. Over the past thirty to forty years, most of us have become mesmerized by all the epicurean amenities that science and technology have bequeathed us. As a result we have overlooked our ethical responsibilities to society and have drifted too far in the direction of independence. We have been and are constantly violating several fundamental premises of human behavior and social welfare.

Several examples of this behavior can be illustrated. Families years ago were integrated under one roof—parents, grandparents, etc., were all sharing and contributing to the welfare of each other, pitching in their finances, their help, their pearls of wisdom. Over time we have grown independent, and each member of a family requires a separate home, two or three cars in the garage, and amenities of all sorts. Expediency and the *vita dolce* dominate our present actions. Is it any wonder that we have a lack of resources, money, etc?

As a result, we are reaping today the seeds of what we sowed years ago imprudently and without due consideration of the deleterious effects it might produce in the future. The philosophy of proceeding unbridled in our actions with no social or moral constraints has come back to haunt us in terms of budget crunches, the deterioration in the economic environment, crime, housing, to mention but a few of the myriad of problems we are faced with today.

Another modern by-product of indifference and egocentricity is manifest whenever one drives on our freeways. Many people make their own expedient rules with no regard to laws, which, incidentally, are imposed primarily for our own protection and safety. There is no regard practiced for the required car lengths between the car ahead and the one trailing when driving at high speed, abrupt maneuvering in and out of traffic with very little space available to safely brake the car in the event of an emergency, disregard for the other driver, and a mania for cutting off the car we are overtaking. All these mannerisms are manifestations of disrespect for the law and disregard for the conscientious fellow driver.

In view of our former experience with the workshops for the

unemployed professionals, I decided to enter into politics again. I felt that there was a need for a systems technologist in politics. I also felt that it was time for us to get involved again in community affairs. Our training in engineering and science taught us to become problem-solvers. I was convinced that the applications of systems technology could be applied to the problems of community development. I was fully aware of the generality of the systems approach to multifaceted problems.

Decision-making is best accomplished by means of systems technology. I have illustrated how the concept was applied to the design of an aircraft. The very same principle can be applied to any problem requiring a decision. Because of our unprecedented rate of expansion in technology, we are faced with a myriad of societal problems, which require decisions by planning commissions, city councils, board of supervisors, administrators, educators, demographers, politicians of all levels of authority, and others whose responsibility it is to arrive at a prudent decision.

The training and what to expect in aeronautical engineering have enabled me to extend this knowledge to the formulation and solutions of societal problems. Solutions should be interpreted as measures taken to mitigate or ameliorate a given problem. The last statement can also be viewed as a problem in minimizing or maximizing a given situation. Solutions in an absolute sense do not exist, since the decision we are looking for is subject to many constraints. In addition, we are dealing with a dynamic problem, i.e., the results we obtain at a given period of time will inevitably change with the progression of time.

In my schooling at the Daniel Guggenheim School of Aeronautics, the entire class was forewarned to be flexible and scientifically prepared in order to keep abreast of the rapidly accumulating knowledge that was taking place. Aeronautics was a harbinger of changes that would occur in transportation. We were constantly reminded of the inexorable, unrelenting change that would occur. To this very day, I can hear the word CHANGE, CHANGE, CHANGE, over and over again.

This admonition and advice was natural to a budding neophytic profession. The field of aeronautics was in its infancy in the early 1930s. The prognostications made at the time have all come to pass, and then some. We have not only ascended to the rainbow in our dreams and aspirations, but we have gone beyond. No one went so far as to predict supersonic flight in our lifetime, let alone the inauguration of the space age.

I thought I would try my hand out and either prove or disprove my contention that systems technology is germane to strategic planning. As an attendee of the planning commission, council meetings, and board of supervisors, I was convinced that the issues under discussion were not treated holistically. Yet, decisions were made that lacked several component items that might have an important impact on the overall result. Accordingly, I tossed my hat in the ring of contenders for a seat on the Planning Commission of Redwood City. I was aware of the plethora of problems facing the city: traffic flow, circulation, transportation, balancing the budget, optimization of land use, housing, open space, to mention but a few of the many pressing problems. After eleven rounds of balloting, I was appointed.

My experience on the planning commission was most rewarding and interesting. My concept of systems technology and its applications to the agenda issues at hand got me into trouble at times. In making a decision, it was of paramount importance to me that a break-even point exist at least between what the city might expect in the way of revenue through taxes and what had to be expended in the way of infrastructure, services required, maintenance, and any other items requiring expenditure of monies. It was important for me to determine the economic impact a given development might have on the rest of the city over the long term.

Whenever I would get involved in questions of economics as to what the developer had estimated in his forecasts in revenue over various periods of time, I was promptly told by the chairperson that I was out of the jurisdictional authority of planning. This puzzled me no end! How could one make a meaningful decision without consideration of whether a given project would be advantageous to the city or not? The city, after all, should consider whether in the long run the cash flow would be positive. My arguments in this regard came to no avail at the time. The EIR (Environmental Impact Report) contained no such information. In this respect, it appeared to me that the developer was getting off scot-free.

I was convinced that something had to be done about the situation. Fortunately, at the present time, consideration is being given to the incorporation of an economic element to the general plan. The general plan, in juxtaposition with the economic element, will provide not only a holistic approach to decision-making, but will provide a tie-in with the budget. One without the other is analogous to a lame duck. The general plan provides an overall guide and methodology for the city's welfare and economic activity for the future. The economic element must take into account the cost basis as well as the maintenance of infrastructure, roads, the various services such as fire, police, etc. These expenditures must be weighed against the revenues that any project will bring into the city's coffers.

With the incorporation of the economic element into the general plan, we will have achieved, in effect, a check and balance on our expenditures and revenues relating to growth and quality of life. In addition, it permits consideration of feasibility, acceptability, and cost-effectiveness. These latter items, in turn, will attract and keep good-quality businesses and entrepreneurs in the city.

The economic element in conjunction with the other elements of the general plan will afford a continuous evaluation of policies and programs in existence by the implementation of a cost-benefit analysis, cost objectives, and a cost-containment program. In the long run, increasing returns will result because of the savings in costs/expenditures. In addition, it encourages flexibility of goals and objectives leading to the best alternative course of action yielding the best rate of return. This applies especially to those projects that were introduced having a high degree of risk. This is extremely important in view of the accelerative changes that are taking place in all phases of our society, thereby affecting the coffers of the city.

More needs to be said about the definition of flexibility. The word in our case is synonymous with the ability to change. Projects are known to take several years for all the paperwork and required approvals of the myriad of agencies to come through. Delays in approvals cause further setbacks timewise. In some cases, a project can take as long as ten to twelve years by the time the final hurdle is overcome. At the end of such an extensive period of time, it is possible many changes in real estate values could have occurred. What started out to be land suitable for a specific land use at the start of the project can, after an extended period of time, be inappropriate. In the event land values have changed radically, the initial decision to proceed can now be shown to be an imprudent one.

In such a situation, it is necessary to reconsider what the

decision should now be. Is it wise to drop the original plans and proceed along new lines? In the event a market analysis and economic feasibility studies indicate that in the long run a better return on the investment can be had, allowing for the expenses already incurred, then a decision should be made accordingly. This example serves as an illustration of being flexible in decision-making.

Many distortional factors can arise in the formation and implementation of the economic element. Planning can suffer during times when expenditures exceed revenues. To forestall this eventuality, prudent planning and redevelopment should make allowance for future requirements, such as provisions for retail stores; churches; commercial, parks, and recreational areas; incorporation of new roads, etc. All these items require a lead time of five to ten years for approval by the city's various agencies. Land is usually assigned for these purposes so that when the time is appropriate, requisite buildings can be erected and projects can be put in place. When the city is faced with an imbalance in its budget, its main concern is to bring it into balance. Pressure is brought to bear on the revenue side of the equation. Land-use appraisal in terms of its potential revenue is of paramount importance.

Any land that is vacant in times of a budget crunch is looked upon as a luxury item. Rezoning often takes place to produce revenue. Since the city has its back to the wall, interim solutions will take preference over long-term use of the land. Land that would prudently be assigned for future use would be abandoned in preference to producing near-term revenue.

Priorities must be set up to stay within the limits of the goals set in the economic element. Once expenditures have exceeded the budget, remaining projects must be abandoned or put on the back burner.

One of the most challenging assignments I've ever had was the time when the planning commission was asked to update the general plan. The general plan or master plan is a comprehensive plan that most cities abide by to ensure uniformity and consistency in future development, redevelopment, rehabilitation, and quality of life. This is a sine qua non to keep abreast of social, economic, physical, political, technological, and demographic changes.

In addition, it is of paramount importance to recognize and deal with the interactions of each individual component under investigation with the other remaining components. The general plan serves as a guideline, which the city planning staff and developers should follow in the wise use of our land resources, environmental, ecological, and other impacts that will arise in the event of development, redevelopment, housing, transportation, circulation of traffic, health, safety, and the general welfare of the community.

The sum and substance of the general plan should focus primarily on land use and its resulting economic outcome. Judicious use of land leads to an expanding economy. This, in turn, leads to employment growth, thereby resulting in an increase in housing needs and transportation, further development of retail stores, roads, infrastructure, need for civic centers and child care, education, etc.

The general plan would be more appropriately called a strategic plan. This implies planning for at least a five-year period and the willingness to review the plan for any updating required. It must be recognized at the outset that planning is a continual, unending process. It is a dynamic process varying with time, which is replete with change. The process referred to is "the action of continuously going along through each of a succession of developmental stages," leading to the "highest and best use" of the land. This in turn results in maximum return of revenue.

Future planning should consider the impacts of the actions of neighboring cities. A given city can no longer exist as an independent entity. Interactions occur between cities, and allowances must be made for this regional effect. Accordingly, a regional impact element should be considered and rigorously implemented if we are to accomplish practical, meaningful results in regard to solving community problems. Cooperation between city managers and the county is essential for minimizing impacts that now exist. I believe the day has arrived when we must seriously consider global effects if our local industries are to obtain a piece of the "pie."

Planning should achieve coordination of all departments within the city's operation. Duplication of effort should be avoided. Land-use planning should be given top priority, since it determines to a great extent the state of the economy. The general plan should project the future needs of the city in an orderly way. Above all, it is imperative that recognition be given in the preparation of the general plan to provide for accommodating changing conditions.

As an example of the latter comment, the Bay Area in California is going through its fifth year of drought. I believe serious consideration should be given to incorporating an additional element into the general plan, namely, water resources and plans for providing enough water in the future. It is not enough to impose stricter and stricter water-rationing without considering additional means of supplying water.

The quantitative complexity of the relationships among the variables of the general plan and decision-making, the difficulty of simultaneous comparisons of a large number of combinations and their evaluation/assessment, and the effect of dynamic inputs that introduce changes in an already approved program make decision-rendering intractable from a quantitative point of view. This is especially the case since many psychological, emotional, and political factors enter the picture. These factors are "intangible items," which defy quantification and are usually dealt with subjectively.

Decision-making by governmental officials is very frequently hampered because of the actions of external groups. Such groups can be special-interest groups, political organizations, environmentalists, developers, etc. Decision-making via the initiative process is frequently accomplished by self-interests, with no regard to the overall impact on the general welfare of the community, its value to the constituency as a whole, and the long-term effect of revenue versus the cost of implementation.

Prudent decision-making involves the decomposition of many mind-boggling complex and interactive concurrent issues facing the decision body. Balancing the budget is of primary concern to the elected officials. This is becoming more difficult to control in view of the increasing number of initiatives being introduced by external organizations. Under such conditions, the decision-makers lose control of balancing the budget.

When a particular initiative is introduced on the ballot, the legislators lose control of determining the impact such a measure would have on other programs. Many organizations responsible for introducing the initiative represent a small section of society interested only in their specific desires and requirements. As a result, such initiative(s) as presented on the ballot are uncorrelated with the many other programs the legislators are considering. In addition, priorities as established by the governing bodies become of no con-

320

sequence should the initiative(s) pass.

In line with special interest groups is the composition of members of governmental bodies. This is an extremely important consideration, since the decisive vote depends upon the diversity of the thoughts and qualifications of its members. In the event the members of the governmental body are comprised predominantly of one mind and belief, the vote will be cast accordingly. For a more meaningful and prudent outcome in decision-making, the composition of elected/appointed officials should comprise individuals whose interests and experiences are diverse. In this way a holistic approach to decision-making is effectively accomplished.

One of our major objectives as planning commissioners should be the attainment of at least a balance between revenue and utility value in regard to open space requirement, density, traffic, infrastructure, and environmental and ecological quality considerations. In addition, the development of unique qualities and characteristics of the physical environment we have been endowed with should be vigorously and prudently pursued. Evaluation of alternative plans in terms of their effectiveness and cost, questioning the objectives and other assumptions underlying the analysis should be performed. By means of this approximation, we converge toward an optimal solution, which is what we are striving for in the attainment of "highest and best use." In this connection, it is important to keep in mind not to postpone thinking or making changes until such time that a crisis looms on the horizon.

In the general plan, we need to clearly specify the goals and the method of implementation we wish to achieve, the constraints imposed on the plan, the main components and subcomponents that will determine the objectives of the plan, and consideration of alternatives that will maximize the goals and objectives. These objectives and others should guide us in thinking about how to proceed in the implementation of the overall plan.

32. Change—Inexorable and Unrelenting

> There is nothing permanent except change.
> —Heraclitus, 500 B.C.

Change is ubiquitous and omnipresent, locally, statewide, federally, and globally. Change, for the better or worse, arises from many different sources. Man's desire to improve on the mode of transportation, to advance scientifically, to improve economic conditions and the quality of life, the effects of our miasmatic posture, deregulation of banks and airlines, relaxation in morals, legislative financial crunches, the national defense posture, and the federal budget deficit are a few of the items that have brought about change. These existing conditions and insatiable desires and ambitions of man to progress represent driving forces that activate and fuel change. The force just referred to is not a mechanical force, but a virtual force, a force "in effect." This intangible force is equivalent to a hierarchy of conditions that spawn corresponding changes.

We no longer live in a world isolated from other happenings and occurrences that take place outside our national borders. We feel the impacts of the resultant actions of foreign nations upon our economy, production, employment, the evaluation of the dollar abroad, and their everincreasing competitive efforts. The infiltration and takeovers of our industries by foreign capital, desire of nations the world over to change their form of government are examples of gargantuan changes that are taking place at the present time.

Changes, in turn, bring about opportunities that will draw the attention of scientists, environmentalists, entrepreneuralists, legislators, etc., to come on the scene to meet the challenge of mitigating the severity of the problems at hand.

The problem facing the analysts, legislative officials, and others seeking a solution to the effects or changes we are experiencing is the causes that brought about the changes. Cause is the necessary precursor of an effect. To remedy cause is an arduous, thankless, and compromising task. The nature of cause can span a whole spectrum of reasons, some of which involve economics, political expediency, financial considerations, security, our very survival.

The dynamic problem faced by city governments in arriving at a collective decision is how to deal with time-varying physical, social, economic, and political conditions. Each one of these conditions produces variations and fluctuations. These time-varying conditions cause changes to occur in the general plan and budget. As a result, constant updating is required.

What brings about opportunities and the ensuing changes? Some are natural, others are man-made. We recognize man-made changes, since they occur in our life time. Nature, on the other hand, in her infinite wisdom, deals with changes over much longer periods of time. Her processes are evolutionary whereas those of man are accelerative. What is more, man-created processes are occurring at an ever-increasing rate of acceleration.

Wastefulness, pollution, disregard for the environment and ecology have brought about deteriorative changes over the several past decades. All these conditions can be controlled by man. Nature can help in our dilemma, provided man lends a helping hand to her. Wanton disregard of her resources by ignoring the fundamental principles of conservation and appreciation for what we have inherited has led to a deteriorative change. For posterity, this is not the kind of change we should turn over to our children. To prevent this kind of change from happening, we must be prepared to change our ways of thinking by the indoctrination of more conservative measures. This could entail personal sacrifices. Are we prepared to adopt the doctrines of Stoicism and adopt self-control and self-sacrifice, which are indispensable to survival?

We shall cite several examples of changes that are taking place at the present time, man-made changes and those occurring naturally. Profound changes have been brought about by our military posture. The A-bomb and H-bomb have changed the global outlook on life and the measures we need to consider to prevent a holocaust. Ballistic missiles have been introduced to deliver the warheads at an ever-increasing pace. These weapons have introduced fear and uncertainty in the minds of the populace. In order to maintain military superiority over the retaliatory force, more sophisticated and destructive weapons have been produced.

At the present time, much work and money is going into the SDI (Strategic Defense Initiative) as a defense measure against ballistic missiles and eventually manned spacecraft. The SDI, in turn, has triggered off many new developments and changes in the design of computers, high-energy beams, sensors, etc. All this evolvement has been appropriately dubbed the "spiraling effect." Space flight has and is ushering in changes in our economy, the outlook for the future, how to cope with the unknown, the benefits that might accrue to mankind, and a myriad of other problems.

Change in nature is particularly manifest in the sub-microscopic world of elementary particle physics. A cursory study of particle physics reveals that Nature is in a turbulent, dynamic state rather than a quiescent, static state. It would appear that this condition is Nature's way of attaining stability. Fluctuations and oscillations might be interpreted as the mechanism in search of ever-changing temporal (time dependent) points of equilibrium. Particles are constantly being annihilated and created. On this basis, we should not be surprised that we, too, are subjected to environmental forces that induce and bring about change. The difficulty that most of us have is to cope with the rate of change of the acceleration at which these changes are taking place. As pointed out earlier, we are faced with higher orders of time-dependent derivatives than the second.

The universe provides a happy hunting ground for ubiquitous change. Pulsars and quasars are constantly sending messages to astronomers of the turbulent state of events in outer space. Messages are transmitted from outer space by the emission of pulses of radio energy and light with a period of 0.033 sec. Infrared, ultraviolet, X-ray, and gamma-ray energies can be detected. The radiation in the latter two classes are at least a million times more energetic than ordinary light.

Physicists study the creation and annihilation of subatomic particles in the bubble chamber. An ionizing particle will leave its tracks in a specially prepared liquid, thereby permitting its trajectory to be photographed. From such photographs, the properties of the particle can be determined. Nature has its own equivalent bubble chamber in outer space. Annihilation and creation are occurring on a macro scale. Supernovae exhibit violent explosions. When these explosions occur, new stars are created. This is analogous to the annihilation and creation we referred to previously on a micro scale.

Cosmologists are debating the future of the so-called expanding universe. In view of the changes that are taking place in outer space, the question arises how much longer will the expansion take place. One school of thought believes the expansion will cease and requisite forces will come into play that will draw all matter together again.

Experimentation in the field of particle physics is beginning to show limitations as to what can be measured in the micro-world of sub-sub-atomic particles. The deeper we probe into the structure of matter, the more we are confronted with the time available to us to measure the sought-for quantities. There are indications that man is trying to determine the existence and properties of particles that no longer exist in Nature. Is this an instance of man showing his prowess over Nature? Or is it an awareness that there exist limitations?

In view of the time constraint imposed by Nature, we are faced with the problem of not being able to confirm our hypotheses with experiment. Are we to proceed on pure speculation and rely on rationalism sans experimental verification?

Now that we have discussed a few of the changes that can occur by the military, space flight and exploration, cosmology and research in elementary particle physics, we must make an attempt to answer the question: What position should we strive for in world affairs? We have three choices: Maintain world leadership, a status quo situation, or a deterioration in posture in international affairs, leadership, and pioneering ventures.

We are living in a highly competitive environment, not only in our very own community, but the entire globe. Keeping abreast of events, let alone assuming the role of leader, is becoming more and more difficult. This poses a real challenge. Either we surmount the mulitfaceted changes that confront us or be content with what remains in the cookie jar. If we are to maintain our position of world leadership, it is mandatory that we face global competition with the very best resources we can muster and assemble. Half-hearted attempts and rhetorical arguments in providing the required resources will not achieve world leadership. All resources must be diligently maintained, fostered, and nourished at full strength—second to none.

To assume a status quo is to be content with what has been going on in prior years. This approach may be acceptable to those who do not seek leadership. A status quo state allows competition to forge ahead and take the leading role. Eventually, human inertia and a reluctance to any change develops and, like a cancerous growth, a deteriorative situation ensues.

Limitations in what we wish to accomplish in the way of changes arise because of budgetary considerations. It is of paramount importance to abide by the mandatory constraint not to spend more than what we take in as revenues. This was most emphatically brought out during the discussions of the candidates during the presidential campaign of 1988. Both the political parties had valid arguments. Since we need to (or should) live within a given budget, how is the nation to fulfill the needs of the military, SDI, space research and exploration, the Orient Express (Aerospace Plane), etc., on the one hand, and the many hard-pressing societal problems confronting us, *viz.* pollution, management of toxic waste, education, energy requirements, drugs, AIDS, etc., on the other hand? These very questions and many more were the ones vigorously debated and discussed back and forth during the presidential campaign. It would appear that there is only one solution—compromise.

With the compounding effect of changes that inevitably occur with passage of time, we not only have to contend with budgetary constraints, but complexity and sophistication in the development and implementation of future systems. Space research and exploration, for example, will require radical changes and departures from what we know as prologue.

Changes are created by man as a result of the way in which we interact with our environment, resources, human behavior, etc. We see waste in practically every field of endeavor; waste in the natural environment, education, waste of human resources and potential by drugs, government, etc. All these effects can be characterized by stating that we are an entropic society, a society for which there is disregard for conservation, condoning waste and inefficiency, and not caring for the future.

The introduction of a radical change in a given system must be viewed and scrutinized with an unbiased viewpoint and a willingness to weigh all factors, pro and con. Emphasis must be placed squarely on the safety, health, and general welfare of the community in rendering a final decision. Expenditures must be carefully weighed in terms of eventual return of revenue. In addition, consideration must be given to dwindling resources. This is particularly the case with the generation of nuclear power. We all know petroleum oil sources will eventually become a scarce commodity.

In view of our past experiences with nuclear power plants, many people have become reactive rather than proactive to the concept of nuclear power. We halfheartedly recognize that our energy resources are being consumed at an alarming rate. Yet, when it comes to forward-looking individuals and institutions to supplant petroleum energy with other sources of power, great outbursts of anger and resentment are registered. When these very same people are asked regarding alternative sources of energy that can be relied upon, they draw a blank. They are apparently relying on miracles to be accomplished by the physicists and engineers. When the day of realization comes and there are no practical alternatives available, will they be willing to regress to the horse and buggy? Or will their outcries be that they were misled down the primrose path by the politicians, scientists, engineers, and other scapegoats who will come to their minds?

Many changes in our life-styles are taking place at the present time. These changes are due to national and global effects that are destined to influence the outcome of our future. Some of the items that are bound to change our future course of social, economic, political, and moral conditions are the unprecedented influx of foreigners, breakup of family tie, and illicit use of drugs.

There is an increasing tendency in tolerance for permissiveness, relaxation in standards, and a decline in our pioneering efforts. Corporate acquisitions have involved acquiring profits, not through the medium of productivity, but rather by financial manipulations. An increasing number of takeovers of our industries by foreign capital and control of our industries by foreign investors has been through stock manipulations. Global competitiveness has increased and will become more intense with the passage of time. This poses a problem for the future availability of technically qualified personnel to meet demand.

Deregulation has increased the plight of the savings and loan associations. This has had an effect on real estate. In case of the airline safety, considerations were relaxed in view of the slashes in fares. This resulted in less revenues and belt-tightening. Our country is faced with a colossal budget deficit in the trillion of dollars.

We have and will feel the impacts of the forementioned changes unless the tide of compounding events is held in abeyance. We appear to be immersed in a quagmire of indifference, incompetence, and an attitude that if one is not personally affected by a given change, then the problem is of no concern. We have apparently strayed too far away from communal spirit and cooperation. In short, we have become too individually independent.

It would be to our advantage to tackle our problems synergistically and with greater concern than we have in the past. If we allow a given situation to fester too long, precious time is lost, with the result that irreversibility can take hold. Unrelenting competitive global forces, in the meantime, are exerting their powerful effects on our economy, creating consternations and retrenchment for us.

Other nations have adopted and put into practice many of our ideas, with the result they have forged ahead of us. As a nation we are magnanimous to the extent that we foot a major portion of the research and development bill and publish our results for the edification of the rest of the world. Other nations recognize the value of our ideas and proceed to develop them. As an example, I worked on the high-speed magnetic floating rail car some twenty-five years ago. Speeds up to 400 to 500 miles per hour were contemplated. This design did not materialize in this country. Yet we see rail cars of this design in operation in several foreign countries. It is paradoxical that we did not follow through with this concept, since it was the railroads that made possible the rapid expansion of the West and the prosperity of this country.

If we are to maintain leadership we cannot relax in our endeavors that allow competition in the long run to take control. Changes in our modus operandi of conducting business are crucial. Our daughter, Alceste, in collaboration with Brian Gorman, has written an excellent account of the types of changes necessary to bring us back on course in their report, "Organization Design for the Future, Not from the Past." The report deals with problems of higher education, but their recommendations are of a generic nature. In regard to the formal organization chart they maintain that "by definition, the industrial model of organization which most of us follow is more concerned with the alignment of the boxes on the chart than on the space between those boxes. However, it is through the space between the boxes on the organization chart that your institution actually carries out its business; we work through—and around—people as we seek to accomplish our objectives." In short, we need to work as a team composed of all the disciplines required to accomplish a given task. This method permits each specialized individual to recognize and respect the concerns and responsibilities of his co-workers. In this way each member of the team can voice his opinions and challenge the contentions of his fellow workers. This will eventually lead to an overall compromise, thereby resulting in a better market product.

A change that would be in the best interests of all peoples would be to promote amicability and respect for each other on a global scale. The future could then be viewed as the Elysian Fields of promise and aspiration. This goal is what we must strive for. Each generation has undoubtedly come to the same conclusions as we have portrayed. Our conclusions are probably the same as the ancients'. Whatever we prophesy stems to a great extent from what we have inherited from past generations, but have not necessarily been put into practice. We may very well have reinvented the wheel with appropriate modifications in its texture to reflect what we have learned from our most recent experiences.

33. Can We Afford Extensionalism?

We have repeatedly mentioned throughout the text that we are eventually faced with considerations of limitations in whatever we undertake. As prime examples we discussed the sophistication involved in the design of the aerospace plane and the trienvironmental plane. No matter in which direction we proceed, we appear to be approaching a point of diminishing returns, a saturation point in further progress. There appears on the horizon a point of diminishing returns with the onset of deteriorative effects.

Change is usually accompanied with an increase in sophistication as we introduce new concepts into our decision-making process. Sophistication is tantamount to extension of present and existing systems. The degree of extensiveness will depend upon our competition locally and internationally. One has to exercise good business acumen and managerial ability to know how far to proceed in making the requisite changes to stay ahead of the competition on the one hand and the economic feasibility on the other.

The introduction of ever-increasing sophisticated devices, such as the Strategic Defense Initiative and the quest for further research in elementary particle physics, has prompted us to introduce the concept of extensionalism. Extensionalism deals with the increasing complexity of systems by the addition of components to an already existing system. Extensional trends have been demonstrated by the increasing trend in complexity of systems—from the P-47 to the aerospace plane and to space technology. The question naturally arises: Is there a practical limit to extensionalism due to financial constraints? If there is no such limit, are we willing to put up with the inconveniences, security, safety and health considerations, such as traffic, pollution, quality of life, etc.?

The concept of a future without the imposition of constraints on what we do is leading ourselves to be bogged down more and more in a quagmire. As a result, we automatically create an environment of uncertainty.

There is a fundamental law of Nature that pervades all events and eventual outcome of events, the entropy law. One interpretation of this law enunciates that we are progressing in such a direction that there is a degradation of order to disorder. Another interpretation of the same law is that our natural resources are limited and cannot exist forever. Many natural resources presently available are being used up with no replenishment in the future—this situation definitely imposes a limit on what is and will be available. As John Galsworthy has aptly prophesied, "If you do not think about the future, you cannot have one."

I realize I am on tenuous ground in the announcement of the principle of extensionalism. It has been proven time and time again what was considered impossible and infeasible to achieve today was accomplished tomorrow. However, are we not being increasingly confronted with what we can accomplish within our financial capability and the ability to live harmoniously with Nature?

Outcries are being heard from open-space organizations that growth is proceeding at too fast an accelerative pace, too fast for effective and meaningful control. Societal problems, such as waste disposal, traffic congestion resulting in gridlock, have been looming on the horizon to an ever greater degree over the past decades, with no effective mitigation measures in sight.

As long as the population keeps increasing, no long-term mitigative measures are feasible. As an example, let us assume that additional roads can be built to accommodate the traffic needs for the next five years. If the rate of population growth remains zero, no further changes will be necessary, other factors remaining the same. If there is a rate increase, all we have accomplished is to solve the initial problem for a period of five years, effectively an interim solution. We have simply moved to the next rung of the ladder and have established a new data base. We are back to where we were five years ago. This process can go on ad infinitum as long as population growth continues.

New York City and other large cities have gone through this process and have apparently reached a saturation point in population growth. Available land is practically nonexistent. This occurred when the building footprint became equal to the land. As a result, there was only one recourse left open for further expansion, in the third dimension. High-rise buildings abound, and the only recourse left is to build ever higher structures than those now in use. At the present time, design considerations are being discussed to go to 130-150-storied buildings. Such extensional designs only compound the problems of waste disposal, traffic, infrastructure, etc. Metaphorically speaking, the net result is analogous to a dog chasing its own tail. This process has been named by some as "manhattaniza-tion." Each successive advance from one rung to the next rung of the pyramidal ladder of expansion becomes more and more difficult and costly. This results in ultra-high density structures and in the event of a severe earthquake, the loss of many lives. Are not these trends a manifestation of a limiting process being pushed to dogmatic lengths? Or, are these trends to be expected in the name of progress, come hell or high water?

The SDI is an outstanding example of "What Price Exten-sionalism?" Assuming its attainment, we will find ourselves perched on the next rung of the ladder of sophistication, chirping away at success in having accomplished the impossible. Starting from our newly established base of knowledge and capability, we will feel in time that we are in a stagnant mode. Man's unquenchable spirit and the insatiable urge to progress will drive us on to the next rung of the ladder.

Progress is driven by many forces in addition to the aforemen-tioned innate desire to advance. Competition is another force that enters the scene. Whenever we introduce a product that imbalances the demand-supply status quo, competitive forces are set in motion. This applies to commercial as well as military enterprises.

From a military point of view, there are no options available as to how to proceed if the goal is to attain the role of world leadership. To take the position of parity can lead to the danger of our competitor taking the offensive. Existing under such uncertainties is assuming a role of a back-seat driver. This is a condition the military will not tolerate without a fight.

Extensionalism can experience limitations through the imposi-tion of constraints. In the case of modern military aircraft, a myriad of requirements are imposed on its design. I could see this occurring on the F-105, which was designed in the early 1950s to fly at a Mach number of 2. Since then the sophistication and complexities have grown by leaps and bounds. Flying at supersonic speeds imposes many restrictions on what the pilot can perform manually. As a result, automatic electronic devices need be resorted to. Guidance and control equipment must be incorporated on board because of the short time available to the pilot to make a decision.

One of the most important qualities of any military airplane is its capability of being battle-ready when called upon at moment's notice. The experience on the F-105 taught us the more sophisticated subsystems we incorporate in the design, the higher will be the probability that the overall system will not be available when needed at moment's notice. This increase in sophistication has its drawbacks. One must be aware that there is a threshold value beyond which the advantages of sophistication can become negative.

Societal pressure is being exerted by the environmentalists, ecologists, and conservationists. These additional constraints will impose limits as to how far we can proceed if we are to maintain stability and a level of quality of life satisfactory to all.

The defense shield that is being proposed in Star Wars involves decision-making in a matter of seconds from the time all the data information is gathered and assimilated. Assuming the success of the present system, what will be the time frame required of the succeeding counter-measure system? Are we talking of one or two seconds, milliseconds, microseconds, etc.? The eventual result and outcome will be limited by time.

There are indications that the physicists are rapidly approaching a time limit in the field of particle physics. In the search for a unified-field theory, physicists are probing deeper and deeper into the fractionization of elementary particles. They believe the secrets of nature are intimately bound up in the nature and behavior of fundamental particles—how they annihilate and create each other is one of the puzzles of physics. A limit is beginning to loom on the horizon in respect to cost and time allowed by nature to determine experimentally the characteristics and properties of newly created particles.

One might suggest that since man is limited in his ability to perform the requisite tests in the laboratory, recourse should be made in utilizing the universe itself. Albert Einstein used the universe for experimental verification of the results he obtained from his general theory of relativity by explaining for the first time the perihelion of

Mercury and the sun to prove that light beams are bent by strong gravitational fields.

Apparently the elementary particle physicists are denied the option of appealing to nature for help. In reading *Quarks,* by Harald Fritzsch; *A Brief History of Time,* by Stephen W. Hawking; and *Search for a Supertheory,* by Barry Parker, this approach may not be possible. The very particles the physicists are looking for apparently no longer exist in nature.

This is apparently the case since the particles under investigation have such extremely short lives of duration. According to the "big bang" theory, these particles ceased to exist in nature at the very beginning of the birth of the universe. Now that the empiricists are groping for ideas, it may very well be time for the rationalists to step in and work synergistically with the empiricists. The rationalists have argued from the time of Plato and Descartes that judgments are made from our minds after our senses have been energized by inputs from the external world. Here is a grand opportunity for the rationalists to look for divine inspiration. At any rate, the physicists are at the crossroads of which way to proceed.

Space technology is in a similar situation insofar as costs and time are concerned. As far as research is concerned, there are attempts being made to tackle space exploration on an international scale. Consortiums of nations could be assembled to share not only costs but talent and resources. Many international conferences on hypersonic flight have been held during the past two years covering a vast number of critical design areas. Britain, Germany, and Japan are each vying for a piece of the action. Costs are of a similar nature, but the element of time is diametrically opposite. The particle physicist is confronted with time in the micro-micro range whereas the space technologist is faced with a multi macro-macro period of time.

Physicists the world over have realized in the past that they are limited in their innovative ideas and concepts and look toward their fellow workers the world over. This was the case during the development of the atomic theory. Scientists from all parts of the world exchanged their theoretical ideas and experimental results. This was accomplished by meetings and publication of their scientific findings. This global synergistic effort was discontinued during the development of the atomic and hydrogen bomb. At this point, classified restrictions were imposed.

It is encouraging to note that the space technologists are proceeding along the same lines of cooperation as the physicists. There is a bright and encouraging global change taking place because of the limitations imposed upon a given nation in terms of its talent and fiscal resources. This was demonstrated when Britain and France joined forces to develop the Concorde. Projects of a similar nature in the future will be much more sophisticated, thereby requiring international cooperation and teamwork.

On the political side, Presidents Bush and Gorbachev are setting the ground for cooperation on an international scale. This movement is an extension and embellishment of the United Nations Charter, which went into effect after World War II. The superpowers are setting an exemplary example for the rest of the world to follow. Their primary goal is to fortify and reinforce the mandates of the Security Council of the United Nations in the preservation of peace.

Our experience in complexity and sophistication in the aircraft industry led us to the concept of the manned aerospace plane. One of its applications could be reconnaissance to detect the oncoming of enemy ballistic missiles. With a crew on board the aerospace plane, it could maneuver in position for a kill. Because of the many technological and engineering problems associated with its development, the aerospace plane would not become available well into the twenty-first century. As it turned out, the alternative to the manned plane was the SDI. This concept was introduced to perform this task. This unmanned alternative is also fraught with a myriad of technical and engineering problems and costs.

With the advent of the ballistic missiles and their attendant destructive power, especially with the introduction of nuclear warheads, the superpower nations recognized that technology had extended itself to a point of reductio ad absurdum. The U.S. and USSR came to the conclusion that strategic parity had been attained and that nuclear war would not be a prudent option for either. In this connection, Alfred North Whitehead aptly stated: "Our minds are infinite. We are surrounded by possibilities that are infinite, and the purpose of human life is to grasp as much as we can out of that infinitude."

A plethora of missiles was developed by the superpowers. Missiles of all descriptions were developed that could be launched from aircraft, the ground, and the submarine. Missiles were designated as intercontinental, intermediate-range, short-range. Some of the classifications are ICBM (the Intercontinental Ballistic Missile), the SLBM (the Submarine Launched Ballistic Missile) with various types of missiles (the Polaris, the Poseidon, and the Trident), ULMS (Underwater Long-range Ballistic Missile System), the SRBM (Short-Range Ballistic Missile), ALCM (Air-Launched Cruise Missile), ABM (Antiballistic Missile to counteract oncoming missiles), MRBM (Medium-Range Ballistic Missile), IRBM (Intermediate-Range Ballistic Missile, MIRV (Multiple Independently Targeted Reentry Vehicles), MARV (Multiple Reaimable Reentry Vehicle). These are but a few of the missiles developed in the missile arsenal system.

Development of these missiles led the U.S. to the design of MIDAS. This was a system of detection of enemy missile firings. The U.S. has spent billions of dollars in establishing the Ballistic Missile Early Warning System, which constitutes a radar-detection network system. One can readily see the escalation that takes place. When a given system is developed by either the U.S. or the USSR, countermeasures are introduced to reestablish parity. Countermeasures lead to counter-countermeasures ad infinitum. We mention these developments to illustrate the escalation that has taken place over the past few decades. The number of missiles has long surpassed Heinz's 57 varieties.

The effects of "extensionalism" were realized by the superpowers. Gorbachev described the situation as "If we go into outer space, if we start having an arms race in space, what will be the criteria there? There'll be a fever; who will beat whom? What is more, what if one side sees that it's being overtaken? What then?"

The mounting frenzy for one of the superpowers to be first in superiority, to be followed by a check-mating move by the other, prompted the need for talks to limit the unbridled desire for supremacy. This resulted in the establishment of SALT (Strategic Arms Limitation Talks) in 1969. Talks have been going on since to limit the number of missiles and nuclear aircraft being produced. This situation is an exercise in futility, since each side of the superpowers has more that enough to destroy each other many times over.

There is a more hopeful aspect, however, to the previous statement. Now that limitations have been established on how many weapons of destruction each side can produce, the next logical step will be the eventual destruction of all military nuclear devices. In 1986 Gorbachev proposed a program for the total abolition of nuclear weapons. This would be accomplished in three stages, thus permitting the gradual elimination over a period of fifteen years so that by the year 2000, there would be total disarmament.

In December of 1987, President Reagan and Secretary General Gorbachev signed a treaty on the total elimination of Soviet and U.S. intermediate-and shorter-range missiles. This was a historic moment in establishing the beginning of future cutbacks in missiles and their eventual total elimination.

The extent of extensionalism depends upon the degree of progress made in the principal field of application. Military sophistication, for example, depends primarily upon the rate of progress made in applied science. Applied science has progressed by leaps and bounds. Accordingly, developments in military weaponry have been phenomenal, so phenomenal in fact that the U.S. and the former USSR recognize the futility of further extensions in missile buildup.

34. Tribute to the P-47 Pilots

As we look back on our lives, there are always many memorable events we treasure. One of these pleasant events is the annual reunion of the P-47 pilots of World War II. We enjoyed answering the challenging questions that were asked by the pilots. The inquisitiveness and the keen desire of the pilots to understand the causes that produced the effects they experienced in flight were stimulating and invigorating. The more interest shown during our explanations of the phenomena the pilots encountered in flight, the more detailed the explanations became. They exhibited an insatiable desire to understand the fundamental principles of the events they encountered in flight. To this very day, their thirst for understanding remained unabated. They did not tire of what we had to say.

Thetis and I were delighted to attend the twenty-ninth meeting of the P-47 Fighter Pilots Association in Seattle, Washington, in May 1991. Accordingly, we would like to pay tribute to the pilots who flew the Grand Lady—the P-47 Thunderbolt. In our conversations with them, they exhibited their love of country, an indomitable spirit, love and pride for flying the Jug. They expressed their heartiest thanks and are ever so grateful that the Grand Lady brought them back safely.

The Jug could hang in there, even though it was perforated like Swiss cheese due to enemy fire. The consensus of opinion of the pilots was that the aircraft was rugged and could sustain unbelievable pounding by enemy fire. The pilots recounted that neither flak, nor machine-gun fire, nor .20 millimeter artillery, nor rockets, nor cannon fire, nor other sundry hits could bring the Jug to her knees.

In most cases the pilots were able to make a landing under extenuating circumstances and were able to walk away from the plane. Undaunted, they would be ready for the next mission. We quote a few stanzas from the poem "A Pilot's Prayer," by Madge Rutherford Minton, which characterizes beautifully the caliber of people who flew her. The entire poem was published in "Looking Back 1941–1991," fiftieth Anniversary of the First Flight of the Thunderbolt, P-47 Thunderbolt Pilot Association, Ltd.

Our vision was to fly, and we hardly considered that we might fail.

Eager and proud, innocent and confident, we left farm and city, job and school, and slipped earth-bound traces.

Our purpose held, and with Your help we achieved our hearts' desire: to serve as pilots in our country's cause; to fly in defense of freedom, truth and human dignity.

At our most recent reunion attendance in Seattle, Washington, we were welcomed by the pilots and their wives at breakfast, luncheon, and dinner. When I mentioned I was one of the triumvirate in the design of the Jug, they had many questions to ask. The triumvirate I am referring to was Sasha Kartveli, Dick Bowman, and myself. The triumvirate would meet on a daily basis in Sasha's office to discuss the RFP the company received for a plane that would escort medium and heavy bombers. As we progressed in the design, we would make frequent trips to NACA, LMAL. The staff was most cooperative in assisting us with their latest high-speed experimental data regarding airfoil selection, cowl design, and running wind tunnel tests of the P-47 model in several of their tunnels.

Questions ranged from their experiences encountered in compressibility dives, performance and spin characteristics, and the maximum Mach number that could be attained in vertical dives with full power. Many pilots erroneously believed they had attained a Mach number of 1. The pilots were fully aware of the effects they experienced, but were anxious to find out the reasons for the airplane's erratic behavior in dives. I welcomed the opportunity to explain the phenomena that accounted for the effects.

Of all the questions regarding the Jug's flying characteristics, the one most frequently asked was its behavior in compressibilty dives. I introduced three basic flow regimes that nature had imposed when flying in an atmosphere, the subsonic, transonic, and supersonic. If one were to take a unit cross-section of the flow (a stream tube), one would find that the stream tube would shrink in area as the speed is increased. This phenomenon continues until a local Mach number of 1 is reached. The stream tube attains its minimum cross-section at a Mach number 1. In order for the flow to exceed Mach 1, nature decides to reverse its stance and decrees that the stream tube cross-sectional area expand. The greater the speed, the more the expansion of flow. Why the reversal in the behavior of the stream tube?

The answer to this question was a challenging one to answer since I wanted to avoid the use of mathematical parlance. My explanation was that nature decrees a limit to the amount of contraction the stream tube can attain, since it is phasing out of one flow regime and ushering in a new one. As a result, an increase in speed beyond a Mach number 1 cannot proceed along the rules prescribed for subsonic flow. If we are to increase speed beyond Mach 1, the type of flow governing subsonic conditions no longer applies. Nature proclaims that we must enter a new type of flow field governed primarily by wave motion and a different set of rules that must be adhered to. For the air particles to move supersonically, the stream tube must be divergent.

In subsonic flow the air was assumed to be incompressible. This assumption is difficult to accept. However, experimental results verify that the assumption of incompressibility is a reasonable one, provided we do not attain high subsonic Mach numbers. At high subsonic Mach numbers, deviations do occur. The Mach number at which these deviations occur depends upon the design of the configuration. In supersonic flow we can no longer assume the air incompressible. Compressibility becomes the dominant factor in characterizing supersonic flow.

Whenever any object moves through air, disturbances are propagated through the surrounding air medium. Disturbances are created since the body, however thin, displaces the surrounding air molecules in its passage. The velocity of disturbance is propagated at the velocity of sound as a longitudinal wave motion by a series of molecular collisions. The disturbances created by the body are propagated away from it in all directions. In subsonic flow the velocity of sound is greater than the velocity of the moving object. As a result, air molecules ahead of the body are forewarned of the approach of the body and make room for its approach. This being the case, the air suffers very little compression, since there is no direct collision of the body with the staionary air molecules of the atmosphere.

As the speed of the body increases and approaches Mach 1, collisions between the body and ambient air molecules take place more readily. When Mach 1 is attained, the velocity of disturbance cannot forewarn the surrounding air molecules ahead of the body of its impending approach. All the forward propagating disturbances of the body are now prevented from leaving the body and are piled up in a line of demarcation, known as the Mach wave. Accordingly, the air is compressed. This wave is situated at the nose of the body, which divides the flow field into two parts. All activity in the flow field about the body is then confined to a region behind the Mach wave. Disturbances behind the Mach wave at Mach 1, however, can propagate away from the body.

As the speed increases beyond Mach 1, the disturbances are further restricted since the Mach wave, which was perpendicular to the air stream at Mach 1, is now bent towards the rear at an acute angle to the airstream. The greater the speed, the lesser the acute angle becomes until at sufficiently high supersonic speeds, it approaches the contour of the body. The flow about the body is now confined to a region above and below the body bounded by the Mach waves originating at the nose of the body. Again the flow is divided into two regions, that outside the Mach wave region and that inside it. We now have a situation where the wave disturbances, which at subsonic speeds are propagated away from the body, are confined to the Mach area region. Activity in this area is primarily governed by wave motion. This detailed explanation was more palatable to the pilots in the characterization of supersonic flow.

Compressibility dive effects on the Jug occurred at free stream Mach numbers between 0.85 and 0.90. Local Mach numbers over the wing attained values in the proximity of 1 and beyond. The forward portion of the wing surface was subjected to supersonic flow and the aft portion to subsonic flow, due to the formation of a shock wave over the wing. The wave constitutes a line of discontinuity in flow conditions as the air particles pass through it. This mixture of concurrent contracting and expanding flows can only lead to confusion and instability of flow.

The pilots said that they initially felt vibrations as they increased their dive speed and duration of the dive. At this point they would encounter buffeting and shaking of the airplane. As the dive speed increased further, the intensity of the shaking was correspondingly increased. Prolongation of the dive permits a buildup of pressure drag, thereby resulting in greater intensity of shaking. Should the time be prolonged sufficiently, disintegration of the plane could result. This could occur when the build-up of aerodynamic loads would exceed the structural capability of the plane.

Many pilots were justifiably alarmed when they first encountered this phenomenon. They were alarmed since the buffeting they reported would occur under a 1g condition. They had encountered buffeting of the plane under a 4 to 5g pull-out time and time again. This effect they could understand, since the wing would be operating near the lifting capacity of the wing. At that point, flow separation occurs. In a dive they were nowhere near the stalling point of the wing.

With the foregoing explanation, the pilots were reconciled to the fact that nature was indeed in a quandary with itself in the transonic region. With the onset of the formation of intense shock waves, flow separation would inevitably occur. Separation of flow occurs since the supersonic flow ahead of the shock wave suddenly finds itself subsonic behind the normal shock. The thickness of the shock is quite small, with the result that the flow cannot adjust itself smoothly. With such a rapid transition in flow conditions, the effect is almost explosive in character.

The fighter pilots had great confidence in the Jug. They came to know the Jug could be put into the most strenuous military attack and evasive maneuvers and hold together under all imaginable conditions. This made them more aggressive in combat, which accounted for their fantastic performance in combat and the damage they inflicted upon the enemy during ground-strafing operations.

The pilots loved the Jug for its capability of out-diving any other plane. This was a great military maneuver to focus on the enemy from the rear. However, when in a full-fledged compressibility dive, the pilots encountered several frightening experiences. They knew they had become overzealous in pursuit of the enemy because the plane would go into a tantrum of buffeting and severe shaking, tuck under, loss of trim, ineffective control surfaces, reversal of control, high-stick forces in trying to pull out of the dive. I explained that some of the adverse effects could possibly be associated not only with compressibility but with aeroelasticity. The structure, when subjected to high pressures, will distort in bending and twisting of the wing, fuselage, and tail surfaces. Under such conditions, reversal of controls can be explained. If one side of the outer span of the wing twists due to aerodynamic loading, a roll would be induced.

It is interesting to note that the Wright brothers achieved roll control by twisting the outer span of the wing. This is a case where roll is achieved, not by the motion of the stick laterally, which provides change in camber of the wing, but a reverse effect. A similar example was explained to the pilots when the fuselage bends as a result of the application of elevator in pulling out of a dive. The resulting down load on the horizontal tail increases the degree of bending of the fuselage, which could result in an increase in angle of attack at the tail. In the event the increase in angle of attack overpowers the effect of an up elevator, a reversal in control can result. Instead of pulling out of the dive, the plane would be subject to further tuck under.

Once the pilots had a better understanding of the characteristics of intense shock waves and the radical change in flow conditions behind the shock, they could readily understand why they encountered problems involving loss of trim and control effectiveness. Trim changes could also be affected by aeroelastic effects of the wing and fuselage structure. Trim changes are acceptable if there is sufficient time for the pilot to make the necessary adjustments. Many pilots told us that it was the sudden onset of trim changes that was of concern.

The question "What was the attainable Mach number in a compressibility dive with the application of full power and full nose-down condition?" was answered by reviewing a few principles in mechanics. For a body to be in equilibrium, the forces and moments about all three axes of the body have to equilibrate to zero. The increase in drag of the Jug, which occurred during the compressibility dive, exceeded the combined propeller thrust and the pull of gravity in a vertical dive. This constitutes an imbalance of force, thereby giving the illusion that the plane encountered a barrier. If the sum of forces had been equal to the drag, the plane might have attained a greater speed in a dive. We made this conditional statement, since the compressibility drag rise on the Jug was precipitous.

All the additional energy that would hopefully be transformed into the attainment of more speed would be dissipated in the form of pressure drag. The waves that were generated over the wing,

343

fuselage, and empennage would carry the energy away from the plane to surrounding space, never to be recovered. The Mach number attained by the Jug in high-speed dives was limited by its drag. As altitude was lost, a corresponding decrease in Mach number occurred and probably never exceeeded 0.90. At altitudes of ten to twelve thousand feet, the pilot could pull out more readily than at higher altitudes.

The pilots soon became aware of the different symptoms that compressibility would exhibit. A tuck-under of the plane would occur when the pilot was in a full-fledged compressibility dive. In some instances, one of the pilots told us that in order to pull out of the dive, full throttle was applied. To us, that constituted an amazing feat, with altitude being lost at an even more accelerative pace in a vertical-dive attitude. In view of these conditions, the application of full power was a courageous maneuver! The control stick would literally bounce around randomly. Simultaneous inputs from the erratic flow over the ailerons and elevator would be transmitted to the control column in an erratic manner. When the dive was prolonged, jerkiness of the control column became more severe.

To alleviate the excessive stick force required to pull out of the dive, bob weights were installed in the control system. With an increase in g's during the pull-out, the bob weights would act in a direction as to alleviate the stick force.

The pilots had great praise for the Pratt and Whitney R-2800 engine that was installed in the plane. In many instances, one or two cylinders were blown away by flak, and upon landing, the pilot reported a slight engine roughness. The advantage of having eighteen cylinders in operation not only provided more horsepower and smoother operation, but a loss of one or two cylinders would not be too noticeable.

We assured the pilots that we moved heaven and earth to produce a superior military fighter. Our aim and aspirations were to reach the rainbow in our design efforts. In ever-increasing progressive steps, we came nearer and nearer the rainbow as we constantly improved the performance of the Jug as a result of experiences gained in combat. We finally traversed the entire arc of the rainbow and, like the concentric bands of color from red to violet of the bow, produced the series of planes from A to N. In so doing, we attained the ultimate in performance Our Grand Lady had to offer.

Epilogue

In a short span of time, man has achieved what the ancient civilizations dreamed of. They observed the flight of birds and yearned to fly like them. This yearning has been fulfilled by the aeronautical engineer. We have not only reached the rainbow, but have ventured beyond into outer space.

Our intention in selecting the title *To the Rainbow and Beyond* was to illustrate why we should strive for higher goals. This was personified by our Founding Fathers and the immigrants of the late nineteenth century and early 1900s. The Founding Fathers of our country envisioned the Thirteen Colonies becoming a united country. Their goal was to create a government that one day would be the envy of the world for its democratic principles. Their dream was fulfilled. There was little hope for the immigrants to reach the rainbow in their homeland. They could envision the rainbow across the Atlantic in all its resplendent colors. Their strong desire for freedom and the opportunities available beckoned them to this country. Their aspirations were not only for themselves, but for their children as well.

To maintain the brilliance of the rainbow, there must exist a replenishment of the water droplets that create the rainbow. An analogy exists between the water droplets and the energy we put into our efforts. Our efforts must be well aligned to produce meaningful results. Rainbows are observed when the proper alignment of the sun, the water droplets, and the observer are arranged in a definite pattern. In order to experience the wonders of the rainbow in our personal lives, we must put in a proportionate amount of sweat and toil. The rainbow vanishes quickly if the water droplets disappear or clouds shield the sun. The rainbow reminds us that we cannot diminish our efforts. To persevere is to succeed in one's efforts. Like the rainbow, we must replenish our zeal and desire to maintain our excellence in our private lives.

Our lives have been a series of events in space-time. We were educated in physics, chemistry, and mathematics. These areas constitute inanimate components in our biotic system. To supplement the missing humanistic components, we traveled in this country and Europe. Traveling extended our outlook on life. It was one of the finest ways of achieving an additional education beyond the schoolroom. A broad education is essential for survival in these changing times.

Space exploration has taken man beyond the rainbow. Our astronauts have accomplished landings on the moon. From there they could see the planet Earth. To them the earth appeared like a minuscule sphere in the vastness of space. The hostile environment convinced us how precious the earth is to us. If we are to preserve the resources of the earth, we must be more caring and diligent in our actions.

Now that we have observed the fiftieth anniversary of the first flight of the P-47 Thunderbolt, we look forward to the first flight of the aerospace plane. Hopefully, this advancement will bind all nations in a more united and peaceful world.